MW00770203

PLOWSHARES INTO SWORDS

PLOWSHARES INTO SWORDS

*Weaponized Knowledge, Liberal Order,
and the League of Nations*

DAVID EKBLADH

The University of Chicago Press
Chicago and London

Publication of this book has been aided by a grant from
the Meijer Foundation Fund.

The University of Chicago Press, Chicago 60637
The University of Chicago Press, Ltd., London
© 2022 by The University of Chicago
All rights reserved. No part of this book may be used or repro-
duced in any manner whatsoever without written permission,
except in the case of brief quotations in critical articles and re-
views. For more information, contact the University of Chicago
Press, 1427 E. 60th St., Chicago, IL 60637.
Published 2022
Printed in the United States of America

31 30 29 28 27 26 25 24 23 22   1 2 3 4 5

ISBN-13: 978-0-226-82049-1 (cloth)
ISBN-13: 978-0-226-82050-7 (e-book)
DOI: https://doi.org/10.7208/chicago/9780226820507.001.0001

Library of Congress Cataloging-in-Publication Data

Names: Ekbladh, David, 1972– author.
Title: Plowshares into swords : weaponized knowledge, liberal
order, and the League of Nations / David Ekbladh.
Description: Chicago : University of Chicago Press, 2022. |
Includes bibliographical references and index.
Identifiers: LCCN 2022002128 | ISBN 9780226820491 (cloth) |
ISBN 9780226820507 (ebook)
Subjects: LCSH: League of Nations. | Institute for Advanced
Study (Princeton, N.J.) | Economics—History—20th century.
Classification: LCC HB87 .E43 2022 | DDC 330—dc23
/eng/20220201
LC record available at https://lccn.loc.gov/2022002128

♾ This paper meets the requirements of ANSI/NISO Z39.48-1992
(Permanence of Paper).

For Caton and Lillis

CONTENTS

ABBREVIATIONS

ASKI: Auslands-Sonder-Konto (mark, German currency)
BEW: Board of Economic Warfare
BIS: Bank for International Settlements
CEIP: Carnegie Endowment for International Peace
CFR: Council on Foreign Relation
ECAFE: Economic Commission for Asia and the Far East
ECOSOC: Economic and Social Council
EFC: Economic and Financial Committee
EFS: Economic and Financial Section (later the Economic, Financial, and
    Transit Section)
EIS: Economic Intelligence Service
FAO: Food and Agriculture Organization
FPA: Foreign Policy Association
IAS: Institute for Advanced Study
IBRD: International Bank for Reconstruction and Development
IIIC: International Institute of International Cooperation
ILO: International Labor Office
IMF: International Monetary Fund
IOP: Institute of Politics
IPR: Institute of Pacific Relations
ISC: International Studies Conference
LNA: League of Nations Association
LNHO: League of Nations Health Organization
LSE: London School of Economics
NBER: National Bureau of Economic Research
NGO: Nongovernmental organization
OWI: Office of War Information
RF: Rockefeller Foundation
SDN: Société des Nations
SSRC: Social Science Research Council
UN: United Nations
UNA: United Nations Association

UNESCO: United Nations Educational, Scientific, and Cultural Organization
UNRRA: United Nations Relief and Rehabilitation Administration
WES: *World Economic Survey*
WPF: World Peace Foundation

INTRODUCTION: KNOWLEDGE IN EXILE

Do you know the answers?

PROMOTIONAL MATERIALS,
World Economic Survey, 1935

DUNKIRK OF AN IDEA

On August 21, 1940, visitors enjoying the final days of the New York World's Fair could have glanced into the summer sky and seen an agent of global interconnection at work. Cast in that role was the Pan American Yankee Clipper, which had captured public imagination by demonstrating the potential of the airplane's ability to shrink distance.[1] Its flight that day was actually a transplant operation—moving strategic materials from a fascist-dominated Europe to the United States.

When the aircraft touched down at the Marine Air Terminal (now part of LaGuardia Airport) in Queens, New York, just a few miles from the fair, officials who had conspired for its escape greeted it with enthusiastic relief. Once on the ground, the consignment—the vanguard of a larger shipment that would make its way to the United States by sea via Lisbon—was shuttled past the waiting press. A large car provided by the president of the Institute of Advanced Study (IAS) whisked the cargo away to that refuge in Princeton, New Jersey.[2]

That cargo was knowledge.

The arrival itself was an end to an odyssey of disaster, perfidy, mishap, and hope. This chain of events was later called an ideological "Dunkirk." The journey was another near escape in the general rout of liberal forces in 1940. In a moment of geopolitical upheaval, with the fall of France and the apparent triumph of fascism in continental Europe, a great effort had been made to save something valuable—knowledge.

The Clipper brought key figures and reams of data from the League of Nations' Economic and Financial Section to the United States, where they would stay for the duration of World War II. What had been saved were information and the capability to analyze it, cultivated by the League of Nations over the preceding decade. The rescue demonstrated how the League, once the center of hope for a reformed and peaceful world, had itself had been reduced to a refugee, exiled from events that had long slipped out of its control. Irony was hard to avoid, considering that the League found asylum in a country that had officially turned its back on it two decades before. Unfolding disaster in Europe that threatened the League's very existence had inspired a sudden shift. The League would live on in the United States.

Why? The United States had never officially been a member of the League. What was it that motivated important American institutions and individuals to invest in the support and rescue of one segment of an organization that had never been uniformly popular or politically palatable? The answer was exemplified by the material that disembarked from the Clipper.

This is a story about how information and the knowledge it fosters were used by the United States and others as a crucial currency in world affairs. To govern and defend a modern global order, the United States sought to build a steady stream of information about economics, politics, and other aspects of human experience.

It is striking how many institutions and individuals leaned on the League for information and, equally important, contributed to the processing of the very raw material they had gathered from Geneva. The story behind the Clipper's flight is critical for understanding a larger story regarding liberal order. The League mattered because it was part of a larger group of advocates, a liberal international society that included the United States.

This perspective cuts against the conventional narrative of a set of Wilsonians who looked to the League as a sort of Holy Grail, as a means to achieve a global condominium through adjudication and collective security. The debate over whether the League's political mission could have succeeded were the United States to have joined it has gone on in circles since the League's founding. Speculation on what US membership in the League would have meant has occluded the significance of the United States' cooperation with the League in the pursuit of data and construction of knowledge.

What remains interesting, and largely unexplored, is not that those Americans who cooperated with the League's project of information gathering and analysis were entirely divorced from the political question of collective security embodied by the League. Rather, it is that the interest of those Americans in the organization and its activities was not a narrow expression of hope for the League itself but a consequence of larger concerns about the modern world.

This international viewpoint was hardly particular to Americans, as it meshed with the views and interests of others across the globe. That the League itself was international goes without saying, but the scope of that internationalism was decidedly limited. Nevertheless, it did host, entertain, and circulate viewpoints emerging from other countries and territories, particularly smaller ones. These were part of the value of the body; it connected streams of thought that otherwise would have less opportunity to mix. Politically estranged from the League yet seeking to influence aspects of international dialogues, the United States found itself imbibing concepts and information from an assortment of international tributaries that fed a main stream in Geneva.

The unofficial participation of the United States in the life of the League points to a more international origin of many concepts that supported and still guide US global activity today. American internationalism was, well, international. It relied on external inputs it took from transnational discussions and debates. It also led to something larger, beyond the League—the creation and maintenance of liberal international life. Many in the United States, and elsewhere, turned to the organizations in Geneva and the community that grew up around them because they offered a mechanism to assist in larger endeavors to build an international community. The League was a means to an end, not the end in itself.

At the same time, the United States was a crucial contributor to the League even as it employed the organization's resources for its own ends. Recent research has revealed the role played by American foundations in shaping the League and its various organs.[3] Examining the intersection of economics and policy is a fruitful way to see these mutualistic relationships in a larger context. Measurement and analysis, seen by US officials as instrumental to solving economic and policy questions, suffused discussions of international policy as a means for internationalist liberals to offer options for achieving a stable global economy. The use of statistics and analysis to craft policy was relevant to larger debates beyond the League in the United States and international society, showing how quantitative knowledge could frame and sustain discussions and action on larger global concerns.

SOCIETY PARTY

An early twenty-first-century spate of writing on the League has brought the scholarly gaze "back to the League of Nations." Much scrutiny has been devoted to the institution itself. All this attention has rightfully recovered an organization grappling with questions that seem remarkably contemporary to present struggles with issues of interconnection and inequality.

It also illuminates international interplay not yet constrained by the frigid ideological boundaries of the Cold War, a subject that still dominates much scholarship in international history.[4]

At the same time, focus on the institution itself has limits. Undoubtedly, the League was an important part of a liberal international society that was in a state of being and becoming after the Great War.[5] Scholars have done an admirable job rehabilitating the League as a historical actor—warts and all. This scholarship, which often prizes recapturing the structure and actors in the "dark palace" in Geneva, is fruitful.[6] However, to fully understand the impact of the League, it must be placed within larger world relationships and international history. It was only one channel in a river of political and institutional innovation angling to support and sustain an international order. The League was a hub that remained dependent on input from states and, crucially, nonstate actors. In this respect it cannot be separated from the larger universe and imperatives that moved liberal internationalism. Showing that the League was part—an important part, to be sure, but still just a *part*—of an internationalist ecumene is what this book endeavors to do. Here the League provides focus, becoming a lens to examine elements of an extensive internationalist ecosystem. Thus, the book is not explicitly about the organization. It does not revisit the League in its own right but uses it—as many internationalists did—as a means to an end.

Scholarship on the League does not always acknowledge that the internationalism surrounding the organization was itself liberal. The Versailles order from which it sprang was colored by a particular politics, broadly liberal in orientation. This is one reason the League had implacable critics in its own time. There were simple naysayers, to be sure, but many disdained it for ideological reasons. These foes would never accommodate the League as an actor because it represented a way of organizing international life for which they had no patience. Some were nationalists, but opposition could also be found among those who were attentive to the international. This is a reminder that there are varieties of internationalism—anticolonial, religious, communist, socialist, and even fascist (to name just the overtly visible and ideological forms). These internationalisms are often in competition and even derive their strength from having opponents.[7]

Ringed by competitors, liberal internationalists floated on currents of what has been termed a "progressive age." Progressivism was something larger and vaguer—less a coherent movement or ideology than a plural approach to guiding social change.[8] In their desire for meliorist reforms to accommodate existing structures to the modern world, progressives shared much with liberal internationalists. Largely, they sought evolution and not revolution in response to the tumult of the modern world in an era when other movements were offering the latter.

Progressive reformers occupied both ends of the political spectrum (some could also be found at its radical extremes), and they actively sought solutions to the problems of the day. Their search often led to transnational dialogue and fertilization. In the United States self-conscious progressives could see a pluralist "trans-national America" that sprang from a variety of traditions.[9] There were, by the early twentieth century, well-established connections among reformers that cut across national borders and actively informed movements and policy. Progressive figures were found throughout internationalist movements, but that does not mean that the progressively oriented uniformly stood behind internationalist projects, including the League. Even those American progressives focused on world affairs exemplified plurality. They have been seen as split into two broad wings: unilateral and imperialist on one side, and multilateral and international on the other.[10]

Nevertheless, there were shared ideas, institutions, and patterns. Progressives also nurtured an affinity for social science and institutions as means to solve problems. They shared a perception that the rush of modernity was a global phenomenon. Many societies were confronting similar concerns, and taking cues and sharing information across borders was a mechanism to contend with common problems. There was also a growing appreciation of interlinked global concerns that were beyond the reach of one state.[11] Causes from peace to human trafficking that found expression in Geneva were well-articulated progressive interests. As with internationalists, some progressives were supporters of empire, segregation, and other invidious policies, even as others struggled to foster universalist ideas. However, commitment to a pattern of reform among numerous (but hardly all) influential figures around liberal international society has ensured that they are rightly remembered as progressive figures.[12] This is not to equate the two but to underscore that the lines between liberal internationalism and progressivism at the time were often indistinct, proof of how later categories may not always fit a past as lived.

Both progressivism and international liberalism reflect larger shifts in concepts of liberalism that were themselves products of historical and global changes. "Liberal" can be a confounding term saddled with a variety of meanings that have evolved over time. Liberals sought to forge societies, as well as an international commons, orbiting around markets, the primacy of the individual, and the centrality of rights and law. They also had a generalized commitment to plural democratic politics, even if it accommodated, only sometimes uneasily, with a willingness to accept segregated populations and dispossessed colonial subjects. Pressures of the time were remaking the ideology. A revised liberalism was itself a product of the modern world as thinkers, activists, scholars, and policymakers of a particular ilk grappled with it to create a system to govern new orders of human affairs on a global plain.[13]

To further confound ideological distinctions, there were competing traditions within the liberal pale. It is very true that liberals, then and now, could agree on no single picture of what constituted the "good life."[14] Arguments of how to respond to the perils and potential of modern life cut across the swath of internationalist liberals. There were vocal figures who argued, even in the Depression, for laissez-faire, which would become a basis for a later neoliberal tradition. This tendency could be set against many liberal internationalist positions that saw a place for an activist state and international cooperation to guide reform. The relation of these figures to a constellation of reform that surrounded the New Deal does show the rise of a liberalism that was influenced by progressive tendencies toward meliorating the impact of modernity through an activist state while leaving open space for the individual and civil society.

Liberal reformers standing politically on the left as well as the moderate right saw information as integral to their efforts. This was an urge shared with international peers that underlines the transnational nature of reform efforts and reminds us that ideological discussions were not airy debates but themselves part of the contest that was world affairs in the period. These figures were deeply concerned by competing systems that submerged populations under the state and did so in an openly authoritarian manner. They saw this as a profound historical shift and a clear and present danger, and it forced them to more clearly advocate for their positions and fostered willingness to adopt more confrontation stances.

The liberal international society that sustained a liberal order was a society in several senses of the word. For the scholars who established the concept, it corresponded to an international order that had membership requirements and a slate of norms. Although that order was a galaxy comprising a variety of bodies, it was states that exerted the strongest gravitational pull to keep the larger system revolving.[15] Other scholars have extended this understanding by investigating how nonstate elements came to terms with what many termed "globalization" or the dramatic changes during moments of geopolitical flux.[16]

This study sees liberal international society as linked to both. International society, in its liberal version, was an ecosystem of states, but it still required the inputs of a variety of organisms of society existing within and beyond states to sustain it. In this respect it reflected the liberal view that there were spheres of activity bearing on social, political, and economic life outside the direct control of the state. This was true in many constituent parts of liberal international society, particularly the United States. Its contributions to the care and maintenance of international society flowed not solely through the government but often through organizations of what would later be labeled "civil society." Yet these domestic groups should be clearly seen as part of an extended landscape where they held real power to shape relationships and capacities across international society. Part of their power and influence was generated by a transnational network of liberal activists, scholars, and policymakers. Collectively, liberal international society was sustained by governments, bureaucracies, and ministries, as well as by universities, foundations, civic organizations, advocacy groups, other nongovernmental organizations, and committed individuals.[17]

Liberal international society was also a form of high society, in the sense that it could be largely an elite endeavor (it even had its own politico-social events of the season). Meetings, clubs, associations, universities, as well as other institutions were critical to sustaining it. This clubbiness meant that membership was exclusive in several senses. There was public outreach and engagement—many saw "world public opinion" as a real force to be engaged and sculpted. However, most of those invested in the informational side of things were hardly the hoi polloi. To be sure, not all members emerged from the highest echelons of society, although participants were regularly sorted through a variety of institutions that marked their merit or distinction. Nevertheless, this society had a bias toward elites, imposed gendered constraints, and often toed a color line.[18]

These relationships expose the crucial, if limited, role that a variety of individuals could have in creating the ties that pull order together. Yet for many involved with the League, it was more than a mere clubhouse to foster connections. It was a means to a larger end: governance of complex questions besetting the modern world.[19] In this context, "governance" does not necessarily mean the government. Rather, it references a generalized ability, both institutionally and conceptually, to contend with and control forces that were seen as affecting human affairs. Such capacities could be constructed outside the realm of the state. Civil society could foster these mechanisms of control as well as supranational organizations. Regardless, many saw such capabilities as integral to modern, global interchange. Much has been written about the conceptualization of world order but less about how the whole complicated business was, and is, sustained. One of the fundamentals of maintaining order is a diverse tool kit to promote governance. In the case of liberal internationalism—particularly in the twentieth century—this tool kit demanded information.

IMPOSING ORDER

Many things are needed for a world order to work, and among these are the varieties of sinew required to hold everything together. Liberal internationalism placed great weight on interconnection across time and space. In the critical years of the Depression, there was an increasingly urgent view that the slump was a worldwide reality. What was needed were instruments to gauge this global change to help hold the whole system together. Here, the League and other bodies that supported it provided crucial tools, especially in the realm of economics.

Of course, the League was being guided toward this end by constituencies within a broader international society that desired that it construct equipment for governance. Taken as a unit, the United States was a partner to this effort. This was no simple partnership; it was also a matter of national interest. A critical commodity that moved this interest was information and knowledge. For modern global life, a steady stream of information about economics, health, and other aspects of human experience was as indispensable then as it is now.

Data are a means by which we, as individuals, understand the complicated and diverse world around us. It is a truism to say that the earth is a very large place. To comprehend the extent of human interaction across and around it defies an individual's capacities. No one can grasp it as a whole through personal experience. When discussing the vast topic of the global economy, for example, no single person sees every bushel of fruit being exported from Australia, every shipping container arriving in the Americas, or every drop of oil leaving Azerbaijan. To enable us to comprehend the global patterns that move policy and opinion, such things have to be understood as aggregates. We must substitute metaphors and statistics that provide larger impressions to project a figurative image of the massive, hard-to-comprehend interactions and forces coursing around us. Capital flows, balance of payments, trade deficits, currency valuation—these are the quantities that allow us to apprehend the state of business in particular countries, to evaluate government policy, and in some cases to suggest whether the outcomes of initiatives and even reigning political and ideological systems are just.

International life has come to depend on the ability to collect and compare information. Legions of businesspeople, academics, policymakers, commentators, and regular citizens base daily decisions on such information. The availability of information has grown so common that we hardly notice how the daily news briefs we see online or hear over the airwaves recite a litany of numbers to show us the health of the global economy or the state of trade policy. Major magazines still devote pages to a collection of economic indicators as a benchmark for how states and, by extension, the global economy are performing. Countries vying for global power are judged on the reliability of the data they transmit. In the early twenty-first century, the question of whether the economic statistics of the People's Republic of China can be trusted is a regular and telling critique of the country's suitability to take a commanding role in international politics.[20]

This study uses "information" as a broad rubric. It is equated with data, meaning verifiable facts that can be a means to reasoning and understanding. Within the purview of this study, most often the term "information" refers to statistics compiled or generated by a variety of groups for various ends. In its broadest sense, it encapsulates the range of efforts to gather facts on global topics that were valued by policymakers and activists looking both to comprehend and to shape global relationships.

However, it is critical to understand the point at which data meet analysis. This is where a raw material is shaped into something much more influential. How organizations, from the international down to the local, process statistics and other information and serve it up hints at their own positions, biases, and agendas. Aggregates of the flow of this or that commodity are facts, but concepts like national income or gross domestic product are analyses. Where information becomes deployable, it takes on the power conferred by analysis. It becomes knowledge.

Knowledge betrays the link between information and power. Being able to survey, collect, analyze, transmit, and, most of all, employ information is decisive. It is why governments, institutions, and movements prize it: to control information and its analysis is a means to power in international affairs.

The knowledge provided by information has always had a relation with power. However, the wide range of statistics and other information that girdles the world and makes human interaction more legible is only a recent addition to the armory. Mid-twentieth-century thinkers forged a link between power and knowledge that went beyond that proverbial nugget of long lineage found in numerous traditions that knowledge is power.[21] In critical respects they were riding the wake of an earlier period, when there was a particular sensitivity to the emergence, generation, and dissemination of information and the capabilities it provides for influence and control at many levels of human interaction.

The interwar years fostered their own set of debates about the use of information in modern society. These arguments were connected to other long-standing issues of how to create and control information. The Great War had underlined the importance of wielding information not only for military and strategic purposes but also for propagandist purposes. This was particularly relevant at the end of the war regarding the deeply strategic issue of who got to plan the peace and whose ideas were used to implement it.[22] Such imperatives were undoubtedly related to long-standing efforts of empires and states to cultivate and control an "information order" that not only provided a picture of events on the ground but also allowed for authority and power to be applied in the right places.[23]

Fears about propaganda that flourished after the war segued into larger concerns over how mass societies could be manipulated as much as governed via the control of information. These anxieties crossed borders and disciplines and preoccupied a number of key thinkers. An example was the Canadian political economist Harold Innis. At the time he fretted over the poor quality of information hobbling the response to the Depression, as well as the disruptive power of a rush of new technologies. He was particularly attentive to mass media, so it is not surprising that he became a sage voice on the impact and control of communications. Questions about not only the messages that were being broadcast but also who controlled the transmitter would frame contemporary discussions and much that came afterward. These debates were intimately connected to questions about how societies consumed information as a variety of countries, as well as a befuddled liberalism, adjusted to a breakneck modern world. The gravity of these questions ensured that they were integrated into the thought of leading figures who were attempting to sort out the best ways to achieve and guarantee a "good society."[24]

The pedestrian gathering and dissemination of statistics and economic analysis might seem tangential to such weighty issues, let alone to decisive questions of world politics and order. But the confluence of politics and policy are actually where their significance emerges. Such activity internationally was aimed at a problem that reached well beyond a single state or even empire. The goal was to make the globe legible. Indeed, that scope is what made these sorts of activities attractive, even necessary, to a community of internationalists. It is no accident that information gathering took on greater relevance, even became an imperative, during a global depression. In a period of crisis the ability to diagnose and respond to pressing world issues was understood by a variety of elites and segments of the public as essential.

It was this quality that made raw and processed numbers—a seemingly banal commodity—compellingly strategic to many eyes. Data and statistical methods gave policymakers and experts tools to apprehend and act on pressing questions, as well as the legitimacy to implement policies. In fact, a close look at some of these figures, too often ignored or misfiled under the evasive rubric of "technocrat," reveals that they were very much committed to political and ideological paths. This does not simplistically or irredeemably invalidate their work as politically motivated; rather, it shows that these efforts were working toward an end. For all the rootedness of their efforts and the imperfect pictures their data and analysis provided, information nevertheless had the ability to reflect certain realities.

While the Depression years were an inflection point, internationalism—particularly liberal internationalism—and certain types of data collection arose together. If liberal internationalism was to govern the world, the world had to be known.

Of course, the gathering of information was not purely the province of the internationally minded. It has long been an integral component of state building (and remains so). Historians have traced how national statistics were instrumental to the growth, power, and legitimacy of states.[25] This regime of data was also crucial to the establishment and function of liberal international relations. It was bound up in the general rise of statistical thinking in social and intellectual spheres of life.[26] But information of the type that is critical to the functioning of international society does not just appear. It must be created.

Such creative capacity has not always been present. But the potential of information to make international life in all its varieties not only legible but also controllable was one reason Americans with various agendas invested in the League. Among other internationalists, Americans saw the need for information and analysis to understand and guide the world they wanted. The League, particularly on economic questions, appeared to fill a critical niche, providing data and analysis at a scale and scope that had never before been possible. While the organization's efforts were far from perfect, the League provided gauges to understand global interactions that in turn facilitated policies to shape those interactions. This capability became all the more useful as the world order cracked up.

Instrumental views rooted in the primacy of economic concerns have a longer intellectual pedigree and have been flowing through policy and its implementation for some time. Regimes of understanding and control that made appeals to economic knowledge were not always focused on things that might generically be considered indicative of what is termed "the economy." Social and political questions often were bound together, coded as economic and themselves falling under the urge to quantify. This often had profound implications for the nation-state.[27] But the drive to quantify was also part and parcel of understanding and governing forces at the international and increasingly the global level in the mid-twentieth century.

NOT DEAD YET

"The League is dead, long live the United Nations" was the cry at the final session of the League of Nations in April 1946. Although the international body had been declared dead before, this time it would not rise again.

It couldn't. Its critical organs had been harvested for an emergent world order and transplanted into a successor. The League's dismal record in maintaining the peace through the collective security it promised has long been the focal point of scholarship. It is reflected in the stories told about the League and in its frequent portrayal in narratives of international history as a sad, even tragicomic organization that could not keep order even when the threats were clear. This view is obviously colored by hindsight.

Heir to Versailles, the League was integral to the world order that followed, which many have since defined as fragile and fundamentally flawed. This history is not wrong. The peace that the League and its supporters strove for was not kept, but the blame for this failure extends well beyond the institution. Nevertheless, the League failed in its mission to provide collective security, as many contemporaries were painfully aware. Because of this failure, the history of the institution is often retold as a sort of cautionary tale. But this is only one part of the story. Global affairs then and now are never solely a parable about the prevention or cause of armed conflict.[28]

A decisive reason for the institution's failure was that major powers, particularly Japan and Germany, withdrew. But their withdrawal has been overshadowed by a historical emphasis on how the emerging global heavyweight, the United States, never joined. A decision that "broke the heart of the world" was built on irreconcilable opposition and President Woodrow Wilson's inability, born of miscalculations, arrogance, and illness, to recruit the American public and elites to the mission he saw as so clear. This interpretation became a reliable trope, used during World War II and beyond to remind the United States of the value of international commitments and organizations.[29]

The failures of the League and the order it was to sustain have cast doubts not only on the institution itself but also on the wisdom of its legions of supporters. Why, then, did so many sophisticated people who had seen war and peacemaking firsthand invest in an organization whose flaws were so readily apparent? Quite influential and experienced individuals and institutions continued to look to the League, even in a qualified manner, well after its ability to influence international politics had evaporated. Even more important, they still gave it time and money.

Continued faith in the League motivated many in the United States who devoted much to the organization and other endeavors orbiting it. There is a tendency among historians of the United States to see the League as a settled historical question by the time the Senate squelched Wilson's dream. However, the question of US membership in the Geneva club remained a political live wire throughout the interwar period, with numerous groups agitating for and against it. Liberal internationalists were drawn into the fray by the pursuit of collective security, but another concern remained a major motivator: the governance of the modern globe.

GOOD GOVERNANCE?

Historians have recently come to appreciate the issue, but present discussions of concerns around governance would hardly surprise figures from the past. Attention to governance opens up broad internationalist vistas.

Internationalism is commonly defined as a policy, attitude, or belief that favors cooperation among nations. But internationalism also serves as a conscious way for those with national identities to identify the interests of their nation with forces at work on the world scene. Not all internationalism is positive, cooperative, or even constructive. Indeed, many liberal internationalists in the period were dyed in the invidious racism of the time. They quite willingly, even eagerly, saw modern empire, built on ethnic or racial dominance and exclusion, as a vessel of opportunity and collaboration—at least for certain peoples. At the same time there were liberals and progressives who viewed imperialism as a destabilizing, even dangerous force. However, that was often because it was often seen to bring conflict to advanced states, and not because it denied rights to colonized peoples. Even as some injustices were confronted, many internationalists accepted, or at least did not challenge, many dim global realities that contradicted assumptions about the rights of the individual. As in many broad movements, there were noticeable contradictions.[30]

One view shared by the majority of internationalists was that they lived in an increasingly complex world. Transnational forces—disease, economics, migration, trade, communication—cut across borders at a compounding rate. The challenge was to create an international system to deal with the forces that arose from the remorseless engine of modern industrial society and its dramatic accelerating velocity of interdependence and interaction. It was necessary to build the institutions, conventions, norms, and ideas that could govern and control these forces. The League was but one hub. It is here that we can see these questions being engaged and use the League as a lens to focus attention on larger efforts to understand and govern modern life.

Work pioneered by the League was perpetuated in numerous forms and continues to define the global. Historians have only begun to explore this deeper history. They have been drawn toward it by the League's work in transnational subjects: public health, pollution control, human trafficking, transportation, world statistics, international economics, and other issues that remain current today. The failure of the League to keep the peace has obscured its remarkable technical accomplishments, which defined internationalism and global life in the modern world.

It is through these technical achievements that interactions around the League become a means to interrogate an internationalism that reached far beyond a troubled organization. The League could fully function on many planes of activity only with the inputs of international society. To examine the influence and interest of US actors is to see how the League was part of something larger than itself.

Here the oft-told tale of the failure of the US government to join the

League needs to be revised. There was not simply a rearguard of internationalists showing their faith by reflexively "keeping the covenant."[31]
A shopworn Wilsonian lament has obscured the forward-looking contributions of American civil society (and even parts of the government) to
the construction and operation of an emergent international society in a
critical period. These groups contributed to the League's efforts because
they saw it as an expression of the pressing need to govern forces that were
beyond the reach of a single nation-state.

American internationalists of many stripes saw the potential, even the
imperative, for cooperation as the League evolved a set of tools to contend with the modern world. This is not simply another nail in the coffin
of the moribund idea that the United States was "isolationist." It is also a
signal that the United States—as what historians have come to call, rather
grandly, an "epistemic community"—was a much more active participant
in international society than is often acknowledged. Even if the US government and political figures were often halting in their engagement with
the internationalist hub, significant segments of its activity were undertaken in conjunction with, and in important respects were dependent on,
American inputs. That engagement helped refine Americans' own understanding of the complicated modern world to which they increasingly saw
themselves as bound.

While the League was dominated by the British and French politically,
the cooperation of American nonstate organizations and individuals with
its technical bureaus was, over time, decisive. Indeed, it is impossible to
even consider great swaths of the League's technical work without acknowledging the vast array of American support. Such a review also challenges the assumption that many ideas that the United States employed
to address global concerns and even buttress its waxing hegemony were
purely "American." Assumptions about the world economy, economic development, living standards, and even liberal order itself were hybrids,
bred in transnational interactions and dialogues in which the United States
was an important parent but not the only one.

Indeed, placing this relationship at the center requires at the same time
acknowledging the profound role played by other actors and imperatives
at Geneva. The argument here should not be taken as a statement that the
League and its agencies were thoroughly dominated by Americans (they
weren't) or that the story of collaboration is simply a US one (it wasn't).
Nor is it to say that the League, Geneva, and international society were the
sum of those dialogues and relationships influencing Americans. Focusing
on the variety of US actors that contributed and benefited from endeavors
in Geneva and beyond illuminates an important aspect of a larger tale.

This study aims to reveal that liberal internationalists, particularly

American adherents, were motivated by a particular set of imperatives. It should not be read as a denial of the contributions or agendas of the host of others that aided and surrounded the League and its various component parts. Neither is it simply a study about the League alone; nor is it meant to be a monographic examination of some of its technical bureaus.³²

Rather, it uses a hub of a liberal international society as a lens to focus on its operation of a larger pale of liberal internationalism and the evolution of vital ideas within it. It also shows the significant role the United States played in this development and how this, in turn, fostered changes in US outlooks and even government policy. The League was, obviously, an international organization, albeit one in which many groups were excluded from full membership. Nevertheless, the domestic constituencies of a swath of nations were engaged in and had influence over the course of the League's life.

Indeed, this variety was part of the attraction for American collaborators. The League and its thicket of commissions, conferences, and bureaus brought together voices on critical issues. It put Americans in contact with figures and ideas they might not have otherwise directly engaged. An important part of this story is how the international society that the League helped to facilitate offered many alternative viewpoints that were attractive to the United States. This is particularly true of concepts emerging from smaller polities. Actors from smaller countries were able to transmit ideas and views into a discussion in a manner that either was not easy or simply was not possible before the conventions of interwar international society. These international colloquies are a reminder that exchange occurs not only at the commanding heights of great power interaction and is in fact a more mixed and complicated process than is often appreciated.

American involvement with the League hardly represented a universal commitment by US society; neither the League nor the ideas it represented were uniformly embraced. However, there was a significant and influential section of people who invested in the organization as part of a larger commitment to liberal order. It is yet another reminder that the conduct of US foreign affairs went far beyond the official realm. The Geneva connection is just one element of a much larger and more diverse culture in what is rightly called a "transnational nation."³³

The League's work was linked to and enhanced earlier and existing efforts to bind together the international community. It was not alone in its efforts to measure and analyze those elements that made the modern world a single functioning system. It was part of a longer urge to comprehend the global forces let loose by industrialization that went back at least to the nineteenth century. Technical work done by the League was heir to the ambitions of the international postal union, the International Statistical

Institute, and the International Red Cross. What is more, the League would become an indispensable hub and collaborator for many committed to the cultivation of knowledge or motivated by general humanitarianism.[34]

But the urge to measure and analyze was not confined to these international environs. States and their polities became invested in these concerns as well. Government departments, research bureaus, universities, and advocacy and voluntary groups committed to such issues began to appear.

Foundational concepts that would become part and parcel of American views of a world in crisis and essential to the policy solutions that were to solve the crisis were worked out, in part, on this international plane. There was a feedback loop: as Americans drew from this internationalist community, they paid into it. Vital elements of the United States' response to global issues—indeed, even vital parts of its understanding of what constituted these issues—were established through interaction with the international.

The role of internationalist networks is therefore important. Figures from other national backgrounds brought forward ideas that Americans found compelling and, as the decade wore on, strategically useful. This is another reason the League is a useful lens. Its role as a clearinghouse of liberal ideas helped expose US figures and institutions to concepts that were percolating abroad. It is also a reminder that the United States was not always the sole or prime mover in the international society it was and is enmeshed. Very often it was Americans who were being moved by ideas flowing from counterparts in international society. While the historical focus has been on institutions, not just the League itself but also its American philanthropic patrons, there was an even wider range to the impact of this international society.

THE THING

Just how this internationalist exchange operated reminds us that the categories and methods that populate historical analysis are not always the way that actors in the past experienced events. Technical and technocratic appeals were themselves politically and ideologically charged. Cultural representations were diplomatic efforts. The efforts of civil society and international organizations could eventually move the diplomacy of states— and states might employ nonstate activism to mask their own agendas.

There is a human dimension as well. Prominent figures invested in these institutions because of their beliefs and experiences. Few discussed here reached the commanding heights of high political office, yet many sat at a nexus where influence resided and ideas about order were implemented. Because they could command information on what were billed as technical aspects of world interaction, they did have sway with the powerful. It is a reminder that "international order," a sometimes abstract, airy term, is built and maintained by human agents who have various motives for doing so.

While there were many sites of cooperation, an especially important locus was economics. Emphasis on issues concerning international trade, finance, and manufacturing appeared quite logical to those concerned with international affairs. These issues surrounded all the actors of the period, and their importance was driven home by the prolonged crisis of the Great Depression.

The Depression focused the attention of many on the deep impacts that the economic realm could have in polities and societies across the globe. National boundaries were not respected by economic contagions. The internal impact of these forces—changes to economic policies and, more worryingly, governments and motivating ideologies—were a reason to be concerned about the capacity of international governance to contend with transnational forces. It is why many in the United States and elsewhere asked new questions of existing institutions and pushed hard for those bodies to generate the knowledge that would give them the power to control global processes.

Here the League's technical resources were invaluable. Its internationally focused bureaus could offer unparalleled information and analysis to understand the scope of the crisis. While the United States was divorced from the formal diplomatic goings-on in Geneva, it had direct access to much of the technical work done under League auspices. This did not qualify as official US government interaction but was accomplished through the initiative of what we now call civil society.

American universities, advocacy groups, and foundations cultivated resources at the League that they then turned to their own uses. Internationally minded progressives, sometimes unimpressed with the political machinery, nevertheless saw the League—and particularly its technically minded Secretariat—as a sort of "world university" or "super-university," just the thing to generate the information and analysis needed to govern the modern world. Thus, it was worthy of investment.

Much funding for perhaps the most influential technical organ in the League, its Economic and Financial Section (EFS), was supplied by the Rockefeller Foundation. Influential American academics and officials collaborated with international colleagues through a variety of inquiries on economic and financial affairs under the aegis of the League. A large number of influential American economists, including some who would be instrumental to post–World War II planning, worked closely with League research projects. A set of international figures who would also be drawn into US wartime efforts built their reputations through such League programs.

This international band contributed to the construction of an expanding portfolio of globally compiled and handily comparable statistics on trade and finance (taken for granted today but a remarkable innovation in the interwar period). As much as the raw data itself, the analysis of it that the League also pioneered offered a view of the Great Depression as a global experience. Beyond collaboration with League bureaus, a cross section of American scholars and policy entrepreneurs populated forums like the International Studies Conference, where their ideas blended with peers in international society on questions of political economy. Americans can hardly take total sole credit for the evolution of these League capacities, as other governments, organizations, and individuals made valuable contributions. Nevertheless, it is impossible to understand their place on the world stage without acknowledging these links.

The League's research and analysis also became an important part of the pressing conversation about how to govern a liberal world order, and thus valuable to many Americans invested in that discussion. In this context, the technical relationship that the United States had built with the League became increasingly important as the interwar liberal order fell apart in the crisis years of the 1930s. As the League sought to reform, retool, and reposition itself as a center of technical know-how and analysis, various constituencies within the United States encouraged this. This was less for the sake of a pure Wilsonian vision than a frank view of modern global interconnection.

The one constant of the US government was the inconsistency in its attitude toward the League. While Presidents Hoover and Roosevelt openly and regularly praised its technical activities, the repudiation of Wilson and the League in the 1920 presidential election determined that neither would risk political capital pursuing formal US membership. Thus, they invested not in the League itself but in the particular organs and ideas that could still serve an American vision of liberalism that increasingly defined its own interests in global terms. The fruits of this cultivation became more and more important as world order fell to pieces in the 1930s. This all coincided with attempts to marshal the League's capacities to provide the conceptual frameworks to deal with nagging problems. Geneva offered insights into models of rural development, the place of raw materials in the international economy, and efforts to generally improve people's lives under the newly popularized catchphrase "standard of living." Outlines of what would become the constellation of international development concepts can be seen in some of these discussions and efforts. It was not simply the economic bureaus or the international intellectual exchange supported by the League that projected these ideas into world debates. Varieties of scholars, activists, and institutions in various countries made these efforts possible and ensured that they had traction. These endeavors overlapped with broader seasons of reform brought by the Depression.

Many agendas to which the League contributed were part of these international debates—but, crucially, only a part.

When the themes of interdependence and interconnection that motivated internationalists are given necessary consideration, the critical role of the United States, through its civil society, leaps into view. We then see that the internationalist ecumene was at once broader and more agile, fragile, and resilient than often portrayed.

As the League tried to justify its existence in the late 1930s, it turned to the United States, where a cadre of internationalists and parts of the US government looked fondly on the League's technical work but not necessarily its political efforts. Rather, they valued its inputs because they were means to further the end of creating facilities for a liberal order. Perhaps the proof that the League was part of something bigger is that in its last, desperate years, it accommodated itself to the task of facilitating the operation of liberal order rather than attempting to lure supporters to the grander visions of collective security that attended its birth.

These supporters drew on the information that Geneva pioneered. More and more, these capacities were seen as a way to buttress a liberal order against increasingly aggressive challengers. As attempts to integrate fascist states within a liberal regime failed, members of international society learned to see the facilities in Geneva as an arsenal for global war.

Internal reforms at the League pushed technical work to the fore in discussions of the organization's future. In an effort to convince the American public of the League's value as a force for global integration (and hopefully earn further US government support), the League built its one and only pavilion at an international exhibition—the 1939 New York World's Fair.

There the League constructed exhibits emphasizing its technical work. Political activities were consciously downplayed. The shift in emphasis reveals the League's recognition of itself as one part of a liberal international ecosystem and a means to make the modern world function better in a troubled time. This now-forgotten appeal also demonstrated the hopes and fears of liberal internationalists in the period. Attention to the pavilion opens our eyes to the League's desperate plea for relevance. It situated itself as a valuable purveyor of information in the service of global governance but within a liberal international society. As much as it was an appeal for American support, the pavilion was an articulation in hard, visual form for general audiences of liberal internationalist principles. It helped justify those beliefs at a moment when they were in retreat.

The League's attempts to court the US public ran in parallel with attempts to bring the US government into a reformed League. This was neither a Geneva effort nor solely a vision pursued by starry-eyed Wilsonians. Internationally minded figures who had real influence, including FDR himself, sought and encouraged the institution's technical turn. The courting of the United States was also supported by various figures from other countries who, for their own personal and national interests, wanted that power fully vested as a member of a revised League of Nations.

Tracing this tale exposes the importance of information to the functioning of international affairs. It also allows us to see the continuity of these ideas. The United States not only promoted and sustained the means to produce knowledge capable of governing international issues; it also was central to the integration of these issues into the liberal order during and after World War II. Indeed, a major reason for the preservation of particular League capacities by the United States was so they could be employed to wage war and contend with its aftermath—while denying them to real and potential enemies.

This might seem to be the end of the story, but the role of exiles as well as a roving band of experts—all of whom had burnished credentials in Geneva in the Allied war effort—only further reveals the importance of information in a world in crisis. Influential Americans did not need to be educated on the value of these bureaus, because a large number of them had intimate knowledge of their activities. When France collapsed in June 1940, a representative cross section of international society scrambled to transplant the remaining viable organs from a dying League to prevent them from being grafted onto the New Order in a fascist Europe. Private citizens and exiles rallied nongovernmental organizations to offer refuge as well as to provide cover for the Roosevelt administration as it pulled powerful strings. The operation was not a smooth one, but in a summer of catastrophe this evacuation was a success. History delights in irony, and this was apparent when the League's Economic and Financial Section was successfully implanted in Wilson's onetime home in New Jersey. Already well known to those grappling with the question of how a postwar economic system would be organized, the EFS was a strategic resource. Indeed, the relocation to Princeton emphasizes how the League was itself a component in a flexible, adaptable international society.

Along with the exiles, the phalanx of influential alumni who had honed their internationalist were quickly drawn into the universe of postwar planning taking shape in the United States. Their efforts were sometimes grand, as when those who had worked with the League helped craft the first parts of a new United Nations. More importantly, they contributed to the fabric of constructive acts that eventually helped stitch together the institutions and relationships that were to be instrumental to the revised liberal world order—sought by many but tailored to suit the interests of the United States.

Tracing the fate of displaced Leaguers exposes that basic elements of initiatives and institutions that have been portrayed as rigidly American in conception were actually heavily influenced by international sources and individuals. Particularly important were views fostered by figures from smaller states who had depended on the outlets of international society, especially in prominent forums such as the League, to validate and extend their views. Debates started in the interwar period would frame much dialogue anticipating the postwar period. Influential discussions would flare around the newly defined field of international development. It was embraced and projected by a selection of figures who had utilized Geneva connections to legitimate their views and establish themselves in a wartime United States. The generation of information to be spun into knowledge was essential to all of these efforts. Here continuities can be seen that time and other emphases in histories of the era have obscured.

These rump institutions and exiled individuals would play an important role as the UN alliance conceptualized the world that was to come. The concepts to be used would be drawn from an international dialogue. The EFS would continue to offer its research and analysis to a US and Allied war effort that desperately needed its insights. A set of alumni burrowed into US networks and began building the sort of international governance structures that many had already accepted as the sine qua non for global stability. This was easy for them to do because they had a raft of existing and shared assumptions and analyses to build upon. These led in many directions and fertilized numerous initiatives, including the creation of new institutions for the postwar world. This reminds that the Pax Americana was, in vital respects, its own sort of international institution. Understanding this compels a reconsideration not only of the place of the League but also of some of the basic foundations of the post–World War II order. Many ideas that would sustain US hegemony were never exclusively American. Rather, they emerged from and were sustained by liberal international society.

Even as it provided grist for the planning mill, over the course of its exile the League would increasingly find itself reduced to the very commodities in which it had trafficked: information and analysis. To be sure, questionable aspects of the League's existence stalked discussions of the "new international organization" that the United Nations alliance sought to build. But a widening stratum of this discourse became the explanation for how an international body would function and how it would fulfill the critical function of providing technical services to the international community. This was an imperative not of a specific international organization but of a larger international society that had already charted the need for information and knowledge. For all its cooperation with the League, international society proved ruthlessly unsentimental. As the war ended, international society disposed of the body, harvesting organs of value and discarding the rest.

KNOWLEDGE AS POWER

International society endured. It motored on as an intersecting set of dia-logues, organizations, and individuals, even as key actors and institutions came and went. Even if events could bend and break some relationships, the constellation of groups and individuals constituting international soci-ety showed a remarkable durability. As the League was buried, other bod-ies were hatched to take its place, many of which were populated by its veterans. These varied organizations were able to generate the informa-tion and analysis to sustain a variety of ideas about global affairs and then project them into discourse and policy supporting their ends. What made this loose conglomeration of actors, who did not march in lockstep or even share the same national (or imperial) interests, so effective was that it was not dependent on any single center or backer. This is how a network of individuals, ideas and beliefs, funneled through policies and institutions, were able to navigate the hazards of the Depression, a global war, and the Cold War and not merely survive but reconfigure themselves to influence the course of each.

The arrival of the displaced League staff in Princeton in 1940 was also a sign of a shift in the center of gravity of international society. It signaled that Europe was no longer its central hub, and key institutions and rela-tionships had moved to North America. The story of the Depression years is one of growing US appreciation of the value of information and analysis as a way to apprehend the problems of the world. The war would literally plant these abilities in the United States. This reflected growing US influ-ence within international society. The effort to bring components of inter-national society into the United States was part of an American commit-ment to securing liberal global governance according to its vision. What the war changed was that these elements now were no longer external; they had been made formal, constituent parts of a world order sponsored by the United States—an order that the superpower sought to sustain, secure, and spread.

A history of collaboration with the League demonstrated the need for similar internationally focused institutions as well as domestic counter-parts in the United States itself. The war and the liberal postwar order that followed would maintain the sort of technical work pioneered by the League and channel it into governance on liberal principles. Histori-ans have noted that the post–World War II global hegemony of the United States was built on knowledge.[35] We have forgotten that it was built on foundations laid by the League and by the international society it served.

1: THE LEAGUE IS THE THING

INTERNATIONAL SOCIETY'S SUPER-UNIVERSITY

The League is the Thing.

ABRAHAM FLEXNER, 1927

The area of interest covered by the League's research is world wide. . . .
[I]n this respect, what was exceptional before the creation of the League
has become usual. . . . The League is more and more documenting con-
temporary life throughout the world. . . . [I]t is continuously scrutinizing
fresh proposals which offer the hope of stimulating the development of
an international society.

HERBERT FEIS, 1929

The fact that the League has lost political influence seems to have
thrown it back on the one asset left, namely its ability to serve as an
intellectual center. In this case it seems to be reaching the level of
a super-university.

WINFIELD RIEFLER, 1938

For the first time, this small group of economists documented, measured
and interpreted the ways in which the national economics were inter-
dependent. . . . Historians may conclude that its contribution to world
understanding was not the least of the League's achievements.

JOHN BELL CONDLIFFE, 1966

THE SCENT OF DECLINE

The Abyssinia Crisis of 1935–1936 was appreciated at the time and since
as a decisive moment for the League of Nations. The betrayal of the secret
Hoare-Laval Pact, which bypassed collective security for a great powers

compromise that would have carved up Ethiopia, shook confidence in the League throughout the world, both among the public and in elite circles. If the League had any hope of serving as a rallying point for international order, it would not be on the political front.

For many scholars, down to the present, the crisis over Ethiopia serves as the moment to close the book on what might be termed "the political League."[1] As the international body politic sickened in the second half of the 1930s, the odor of political decomposition at the League was noticeable. Conversely, this political decline during an increasingly tense international situation served to highlight the value of the technical work that was increasingly coming to define the organization.

Taking office in 1933, the League's second secretary-general, the conservative French banker Joseph Avenol, accepted that the earlier Manchurian Crisis and the Italo-Ethiopian War had been diplomatic body blows. These crises, as well as the withdrawal of Japan and Germany from the League, made taking a different tack imperative. By transforming itself into a technically oriented body, the League could claim a neutral, apolitical space in world affairs while ensuring its own continued relevance. This was a stark acknowledgment of the League's poverty of influence in international politics.[2] But it was also a canny policy, considering the relevance of the technical activities conducted by the League—especially its economic work—to international life, particularly for a globe that was still struggling with economic depression. The League had attempted to reshape world economic activity through major conferences, but the early 1930s brought the realization that returns from such efforts were rapidly diminishing. Increasingly, the organization's turn would come to emphasize the permanent parts of what was defined as its technical side, which was focused on its permanent Secretariat. This emphasis also allowed the League to make overtures to actors that might provide it with renewed relevance.

Technical cooperation became a lure to entice nonmember states into the League and to retain those feeling pressure to leave. States like Brazil needed to be hauled back aboard, but the biggest prize was the one that had never been hooked, the United States. After the war, Avenol was quite candid about attempts to entice the United States into the League with the bait of technical cooperation.[3] The League's desire to embrace these wayward states was undoubtedly about enhancing cooperation (and budget contributions), but it was also an antidote to increasing international fragmentation in the 1930s. Not only had states like Germany, Japan, and, later, Italy withdrawn from the League, but also they increasingly flaunted liberal economics through an embrace of autarkic practices, at least in principle.[4] As the decade wore on, there was a raft of Latin American departures from the organization. The situation deteriorated so quickly that it compelled the League to send a special delegation to staunch the exodus.[5]

There was a related fear that the tendency toward regional blocs might further undo the promise of liberal universalism the League represented. In this context, trends in the Western Hemisphere toward neutralism and Pan-Americanism were disturbing. Some of this was institutional competition, but it also gave form to a looming fear that broader political fragmentation was threatening to permanently rearrange international life.[6]

From the beginning the League had a mission to assist in building the international commons.[7] World War I had produced a wave of liberalization. Many of those most committed to the League saw it as not merely an expression of internationalist dreams but as a mechanism to constitute and execute basic elements of a liberal order.

DATA FOR PEACE

It is no surprise that the League of Nations attracted those who sought to govern the variety of forces that had been unleashed or accentuated by the modern world. In fact, the work of the Geneva organizations and other international bodies belies the conventional assumption that appreciation of the complexity brought by the growing interdependence and speed of international life came only with late twentieth-century "globalization." This view tends to position such change as closer to the present, or as a fixture of it, a proximity that emphasizes the complexity of the present as compared to what are deemed earlier "pre-globalized" periods.[8] However, the rapid, vertiginous changes of the late nineteenth and early twentieth century were global in scope and portended much for the periods yet to come.[9]

A characteristic of numerous ideologies in the nineteenth and early twentieth century was their presumed global relevance. Communism, anarchism, and even fascism rested on the assumption that their principles had worldwide resonance and application. Anticolonial nationalism found expression and amplification in a variety of forms, and Pan-African movements united a global diaspora among a variety of pan-nationalist movements. Liberal internationalism was but one part of an expansive and competitive galaxy of internationalisms that, in part, reflected an increasingly interconnected globe.[10]

A spectrum of elites in the United States were thoroughly invested in a liberal version of internationalism. Like the modern world that version attempted to navigate, its nodes were diverse, requiring attention to economic issues, health, or the social reforms that societies required to adjust to demands of the industrial, high-technology present. Such issues often overlapped, and contemporaries often did not see them as distinct. Later scholars have been quick to draw distinctions between what contemporaries would have perceived as interconnected and permeable.

Liberal internationalists forged transnational links to cultivate the knowledge needed to engage issues on a world stage. Americans also acted transnationally and were active parts of movements attempting to shape opinion and even actions on a collection of issues from temperance to global health to international law.[11] As a community, those who were internationally minded understood that many concerns and problems surrounding modern societies were beyond the reach of a single state. At the same time, it was accepted that national states—the United States' counterparts around the world—were the primary means to actually act on these forces. Inputs from abroad could be just as valuable as those at home, and national interests and goals could be a reason to contribute to international efforts. To put it more simply, internationalists could think globally and act locally as much as they could act globally and think locally.

After the Great War, great stock was put in a "scientific peace." A vein of progressive thinking ran through interwar liberal internationalism and asserted that cultivating "scientific" research and analysis on a variety of issues could benefit global interactions and world order. The rush of institution building that came after the conflict reflected this urge. Significant sectors were supported by US foundations. This larger trend sustained interest in the League as a service provider. It was a central office woven into a realm of diverse activities that sought to govern a multiplicity of forces, even if it was only one institution among many.[12]

Health was one of these areas, and it showcases how the League of Nations Health Organization (LNHO) was far-reaching in both its geographical extent at the time and its influence on later institutions. In a world that had learned hard lessons about how human health in an interconnected world could be compromised by epidemics and dislocation brought about by war, revolution, and migration, remarkable efforts to survey and control disease were initiated in the interwar period.[13] The work of its epidemiological service and a campaign for standardization in medicine racked up a number of impressive accomplishments. Historians have hinted at why some of its successful programs have been overlooked. In the case of the LNHO's Standardization Commission, the efficiencies and collaboration it allowed are hard to quantify. Even in the case of formidable publications like the *International Health Yearbook*, the standards it encoded bled into the historical background.[14] Undoubtedly, the League offered a new means to contend with issues around health. But it did not and could not do the job alone. It needed the input of scholars, technicians, and advocates around the world.

The LNHO's potential drew international support that included cooperation from the United States. Beyond the collaboration of universities, the Rockefeller Foundation was an early patron. From its inception in 1913, Rockefeller had made significant commitments to global health. With the

LNHO a promising hub of activity, foundation officers were quick to see it as a good investment. By the 1920s, the foundation was providing a major portion of the League's funding on health issues. This indicates how important external contributions to the League's efforts were and simultaneously exposes the centrality of American institutions.[15]

The League's aggregation of data on disarmament is another forgotten tool of governance. This was another endeavor to create information and analysis for particular ends—"data for peace," as it has been called. The project produced a set of regular publications, particularly on armaments spending. Although the publications were considered uneven by contemporaries, an international audience of academics, journalists, activists, and policymakers nevertheless employed them as a baseline of information on a commanding international issue during the interwar years.[16]

The League was also attentive to topics that seem remarkably contemporary in the twenty-first century. An established international campaign to constrict transnational trafficking in women and children found a new ally in the League's Social Section, which offered a base for global governance, coordination, and information gathering on the issue. The League's International Criminal Police Commission and the International Bureau for the Unification of Penal Law worked to fight transnational crime, although these bodies could regularly scant a central tenet of liberalism, the rights of individuals.[17]

On another front, the League's economic organs gave early consideration to what would be later called environmental degradation of the international commons.[18] These and other endeavors were also global, attempting to link together international efforts to provide the means to govern transnational questions. When the variety of programs are considered, the collaborative nature of the League becomes apparent: it often worked with, and crucially *through*, various institutions in member and nonmember states.

The importance of the League to cultural and scholarly exchange is best represented by the International Studies Conference (ISC), itself a part of the League's International Institute of International Cooperation. The ISC was a roving set of conferences on international relations that mobilized a cross section of figures in the interwar period. The ISC and the International Institute of International Cooperation, when they are remembered, are recalled as a flowering cultural exchange.[19] They were certainly reflections of an imperfect system, but they illustrate the League's role as a sort of world university. They also opened up avenues for participation by experts from non-Western states, particularly those in Asia. At the same time, they reified the existing world order, as participants could candidly discuss the maintenance of an international system built around empire and colonialism. Rather like the collection of institutions in Geneva, the ISC could pull together a wide selection of figures—admittedly those from elite circles in global policy and academia. The topics it addressed were multifaceted, but during the 1930s there was a recurring emphasis on economic forces and how to govern them.

The ISC shows the interrelationship between the League, the ideas it assisted in cultivating, and the selection of groups and figures from liberal international society that employed them. As a League-sponsored forum, the ISC was an itinerant gathering of scholars and policy types who debated what were deemed critical international issues of the day. Their variety of personal and institutional backgrounds served the reach and legitimacy of the ISC. It also served as a nursery for some figures who would come to play a prominent role in postwar policy and economics. Participation was wide ranging, and one sign of the League's engagement with international society was the level of participation by US institutions, both activist and academic. Healthy numbers of American academics as well as a set of researchers and advocates who orbited new international affairs institutions were regular attendees.

The legacies of these meetings are deeper than many fathom and capture the contradictions of the liberal internationalism of the period. All the meetings were furnished with rafts of studies and analyses prepared by scholars and other prominent voices on international issues. Many of these reports would emerge as respected publications that, in the case of the United States, were propelled into public discussion by the Council on Foreign Relations (CFR), the World Peace Foundation (WPF), and other internationalist organizations.

Indeed, an underappreciated element of this is that the ISC was itself part of a transnational movement of scholarly collaboration. The US even had its own broad scholarly conference. The Institute of Politics, which met annually at Williams College, also convened an international slate of prominent officials, commentators, and academics.[20] While the institute would fade, other organizations that formed in the US after the Great War proved enduring. As in so many other countries, there was an active US League of Nations Association (LNA). Other influential groups had wider mandates. Among these was the CFR, which, while failing to fulfill its goal of sustaining transnational bonds between American and British elites, nevertheless became a defining voice of the US establishment.[21] Others like the Foreign Policy Association (FPA; conceived as the League of Free Nations Association in 1918) sought not only to further elite discourse but also to create the means to mold the perception of world affairs among the general public.[22] Founded in 1925, the Institute of Pacific Relations (IPR) fostered a selection of national groups; it nurtured a remarkable amount of dialogue between national representatives and conducted and published an extensive amount of research about Pacific Asia.[23] These new organizations joined ranks with prewar bodies, which included the Carnegie Endowment for International Peace (CEIP), founded in 1910, and the Boston-based World Peace Foundation, born in 1911 as the legacy of publishing magnate Harold Ginn. The WPF conducted advocacy in its own right, but it significantly furthered its own mission and message by serving as the de facto publicity and distribution arm of the League's research in the United States.[24]

Collaboration between scholars and researchers accompanied the rise of these organizations across international society, a sign that many of these operations were interconnected, if not mutually dependent. There was an interchange not merely of ideas but of personnel from an increasingly diverse array of nations. Of course, there were limits. Many programs, such as those gathering statistics or other data, were dependent on the contributions of governments and could be hamstrung by the information supplied (or not supplied) and the level of cooperation. Aspects of all the League's technical programs were marked by the reality that many peoples around the world were imperial subjects and could not participate, or their participation (even down to their being reduced to statistics) was circumscribed by colonial rulers or thickly drawn color lines.

THE AMERICAN SECTION

If the League served as a hub for a larger internationalist community, various segments of what would later be called civil society in the US were always linked to it. For many, this was a deeply personal connection. Behind the trappings of bureaucracy, institutions are dependent on the people who steer them.

American engagement in the League's affairs not only affected the US at home but also extended to Americans abroad and led to the rise of an American colony in Geneva. It was just one part of a larger international canton that had grown up in the city with the establishment of institutions like the Red Cross in the nineteenth century. This settlement was augmented by the appearance of the League and a set of related nongovernmental organizations (NGOs) after World War I. With its relevance to world affairs, Geneva became a haven for tourists and scholars. Several organizations, including an "American Committee," were established to cater to the hundreds of visitors from North America who made a tranquil section of Switzerland part of their European grand tour because of the League's presence.[25]

A colony in Geneva was one means by which the United States accessed and contributed to what quickly became appreciated as a font of "research data" on world affairs.[26] The information and analysis emerging from the variety of organizations was significant not just for education and policy but for whole fields of inquiry, particularly economics. A stint in Geneva became a prestigious, even necessary, credential for a budding international researcher. It is striking how many influential figures in American economic policy in the mid-twentieth century would pass through the city. Important officials who would later populate the State Department, notably Herbert Feis and Leo Pasvolsky, did tours in Geneva. Eugene Staley, whose publications populated the ISC as well as the CFR, studied there. The leading academic economists Jacob Viner and Fred Harvey Rogers drew from the League, as did New Dealers Winfield Riefler and Henry Grady.

By the 1930s there was a vibrant American community in Geneva, which reveals that both institutions and citizens of the United States were deeply invested in the internationalism that the League was woven into, even if their government was not. It also is a reminder that the US not only was present in Geneva but also constituted one settlement integrated into a pale of liberal internationalism.

While there was much US engagement with the League, there were prominent Americans *in* the League from the start. These personal experiences mattered. It is regularly forgotten that in 1919, Wilson selected Raymond Fosdick to be an under-secretary-general of the new body. Fosdick's own experiences as a progressive reformer drawn into war work primed him for the mission.[27] His carried with him a belief that modern life was something qualitatively different from what came before. As "machine civilization" rushed over society, it posed a set of decisive questions regarding human perceptions and interactions. Fosdick would repeatedly return to that point over the course of his multifaceted career.[28]

Plans to have Fosdick serve the League were frustrated by the United States' unwillingness to officially join the organization. After just a year in London (the temporary seat of the League), he was compelled to pack his bags.[29] Although he resigned the post, Fosdick did not abandon his internationalist views. Sliding into legal practice in New York City Fosdick maintained connections in politics and international affairs. He knew how to pick friends. He served as consigliere to the Rockefeller family and its brood of foundations. Bound up in these relationships was his early support of Franklin Roosevelt. Fosdick would channel Rockefeller donations to Roosevelt as he set up a polio therapy center at Warm Springs, Georgia, and reset his political career.[30]

Continued devotion to the organization led Fosdick to the LNA, which eventually made him its chief. There he remained a strong advocate for US membership. Fighting this uphill battle impressed those in the Rockefeller system, and in 1936 the Rockefeller Foundation (RF) selected Fosdick as its president. In that capacity he would continue and enhance support for research in the social sciences, appointing program officers like Joseph Willits, former dean of the Wharton School at the University of Pennsylvania. Willits was deeply committed to an activist social science and deepened the foundation's commitments in that area nationally and internationally. He would maintain and extend programs at the League that had already made it a center of global research on issues critical to liberal internationalist visions.[31] Fosdick and officers like Willits are a reminder that the RF was not a faceless bureaucracy; rather, its largesse was structured by personal beliefs.

In 1932 Fosdick suffered the aching trauma of his mentally ill wife murdering their two children before she took her own life. As the sensational tale splashed across newspapers, Fosdick retreated to Maison Mérimont, the Switzerland residence of Arthur Sweetser. Staying with Sweetser for an extended period as a guest allowed Fosdick to avoid a press frenzy and pull his life back together.[32]

That Sweetser knew Fosdick was no surprise; like so many of their peers they bore the stamp of the elite. For both men, their internationalism was a basis for a lifetime friendship. Importantly for Sweetser, like many of his generation, he was forever marked by world events. Looking back over his life in 1936, he could see a consistent global-mindedness forming early. At Harvard during the first decade of the twentieth century, he was tantalized by the possibility of international law, exemplified by the agreements churning in The Hague. During his youth he was also able to make a literal world tour that enabled him to "compare and contrast" Europe, Malaysia, India, China, and Japan. He later recalled that his wanderings inspired an enduring curiosity about "other men and peoples" that gave him a "faith that human beings, when given half a chance, are not really bad"—or, a touch glibly, that "'All God's Chillun,' though fascinatingly different, are yet fundamentally alike." After graduating in 1911, he fell into journalism.[33]

When fighting broke out in 1914, Sweetser scrambled to the battlefield, spending three weeks as a reporter following the German Army from the Belgian border to within "eyesight of the Eiffel Tower." Seeing modern war firsthand, like so many others of his time, he had the "futility, absurdity, [and] crime of it" permanently stamped on him. Sweetser published a book drawn from his experiences but found the United States remarkably disinterested in the catastrophe unfolding abroad.[34]

After bouncing from a "dreary" indenture at the *New Republic* to the Associated Press, Sweetser, along with others of his generation, was swept up in the US intervention in the Great War. He was made a captain in the Signal Corps and watched the war from a "swivel chair in Washington." Transferred to the cutting-edge Air Service, he managed only "one dreadfully air-sick flight," but he was savvy enough to transform that single sortie into a book on wartime American military aviation.[35]

The chance to run the press section of the American Commission to Negotiate Peace was an attractive change for Sweetser. His time at the Versailles Conference put him on a path to serve with the League. Drawn into its Information Section, he would serve the Secretariat in various guises for the next twenty-two years. Sweetser was a true believer in the ideas the League stood for, and this served him well in a role that made him a de facto public relations officer. His nationality made him head of an informal "American Section" in Geneva and an envoy to his fellow citizens. The man's enthusiasm for international cooperation was complemented by lucid writing and a jovial disposition. Connections, some emerging from Harvard, but most from energetic networking, were his best asset. His contacts straddled the left and right, the official and the unofficial. Every opportunity presented seemed an opportunity taken.

From Geneva, Sweetser ran an extensive correspondence and set of relationships. He was tied to a wide range of the influential in the United States and the international community. American internationalists were regular recipients of upbeat reports and letters on the state of affairs in Geneva. On a 1933 Atlantic crossing during which Secretary of State Cordell Hull was a fellow passenger, Sweetser managed, in his own estimation, to become "almost a member of the Secretary's personal party."[36]

Sweetser even managed to draw Franklin Roosevelt into his circle. He crossed paths with his fellow Harvard alum on a number of occasions, and they built enough of a relationship that the president later generously referred to him as an "old friend." Sweetser was quite comfortable corresponding with the president in detail—although the cagey chief executive was sure to vet Sweetser's communications before responding to them.[37]

Sweeter was devout, with a career and identity devoted to the League and the liberal internationalism it epitomized. He has even been written into fiction as one of the faithful.[38] However, his zealous commitment to the cause could work against him, with some forming an enduring view that he "was so thoroughly imbued with the League idea that he did not recognize the League's weaknesses" and that his "enthusiasm . . . was not quite matched by his realism."[39]

Similar charges have been levied against any number of liberal internationalists in the United States and abroad during the interwar period and since. A firmly held belief in international cooperation could be cast at the time as blind idealism or utopianism, and with historical hindsight, dismissed as foolhardy. However, it was never so simple. Views of the League and the liberal international society it served could be sophisticated and wrapped in attempts to reckon with a rapidly changing world.[40]

For so many figures of the era, and Fosdick and Sweetser were just two of them, their experience of the Great War and the peace that followed was an object lesson in the costs of conflict. Modern science and technology were intensifying risks to international life even as they held out great possibility to "humanity" (a term then coming into greater use). Both came to understand the need for cooperation on many levels internationally. This was not solely to advance the goal of collective security demanded in times of crisis, but also to foster the joint action to understand, knit together, and govern the modern world in all its power, velocity, danger, and potential. It was peace and security for which the League might provide answers, as well as the ability to control and harness the forces of the modern world itself.

The League was hardly alone in the endeavor to contain and explain these forces. Nation-states and empires, as well as various international bodies, were hard at work to the same end. Indeed, the late nineteenth and early twentieth century had seen a remarkable expansion of groups that provided organization and order to global interaction. Prosaic to the point of seeming passé today, they were an innovation and a response to a rapidly changing world. Supranational bodies hammered out agreements on postal systems, statistics, relief, and even time itself.[41] They are often rightfully thought of first in these endeavors, but there was also a concurrent growth in national services to measure and engage similar issues on the domestic front. The United States was a prime example of a state engaged in evolving a progressive set of metrics of social, economic, and cultural life, developing its own variants of these systems—a process that continued into the interwar period.

Here lay a powerful appeal for the League and the international cooperation embedded within it. It was one expression of a general urge to measure, coordinate, and standardize the international community. Many in the various public associations advocating for the League of Nations in the US and around the world never tired of making this point. However, it was not merely an issue that animated the most addled; it was also currency in wider political discussion in the period. The interwar international relations superstar Owen Young, author of the eponymous reparations plan, advocated for a relationship with the League on the basis of its technical work.[42]

Such views were not alien to leading political figures. In 1928, writing in *Foreign Affairs*, the house organ of the recently established CFR, Franklin Roosevelt readied himself for a return to national politics by marking positions on world issues. Despite the defeat of the proposal to enroll the United States in the League at the hands of Republican Warren Harding, FDR nurtured an affection for the institution. Yet he remained unwilling to take firm, unqualified stances on the body. Burned by the results of the 1920 election, he refused to relitigate the question of US membership. Still, he asserted that the League was useful as a "roundtable" to settle international disputes and that there was good reason to "offer a far larger share of sympathetic approval and definite official help than we have hitherto accorded." At the same time, FDR was careful to hedge this assertion with an equivocal rider that politically he was "opposed to any official participation in purely European affairs or to committing ourselves to act in unknown contingencies."

Asserting that the League was contributing to sprawling issues that, by their nature, "concern us" was less controversial. The US therefore had reasons far beyond the roundtable to "cooperate with the League . . . for the maintenance of peace and for the solution of common problems ever known to civilization," including "international health work, improvement of labor conditions, aid to backward peoples, the improving of education, the clarification of international law, assistance to world trade." A component of FDR's worldview was one that other American internationalists shared: while the League was a politically tender topic, it nevertheless provided technical tools necessary for the operation of liberal world order.[43]

It is no surprise that Democrats, the party of Wilson, would harbor sympathies for the League. However, interest in the League's ability to deal with issues of common concern crossed US party boundaries. One of the leading exponents of building up information-gathering capacity was a Republican, Herbert Hoover. Holding a common perception, Hoover saw that a modern world driven by science and technology that was enhancing the movement of people, goods, and ideas was also breeding interdependence. That interdependence demanded governance to solve problems and ensure stability.

Hoover was among a parade of liberal internationalists and progressives who saw the League as a means to achieve global stability. Hoover supported the institution in 1919 precisely because it offered a means to cooperative action. As he turned to politics, he accepted his party's dismissal of the League but was clear that its "rejection" did not mean that "America has lost interest in finding a solution" to problems requiring international cooperation. In Washington he acted on his belief that the scientific approach offered by quantitative analysis would allow the US to play a more effective role in world affairs. As Calvin Coolidge's commerce secretary, Hoover was devoted to developing national abilities to compile statistics that would facilitate cooperative action to solve problems. This would be apparent on the international scene. A US Commerce Department delegation to the Geneva Economic Conference in 1927 suggested a regime of data collection to solve a metastasizing global agricultural crisis.[44] Sweetser recalled that Hoover confided in him that the League's great global contribution was its generation of a stream of reliable information.[45] Publicly, Hoover accepted that US-League cooperation was a positive good—at least in some spheres. As his party's presidential nominee in 1928, Hoover stated that while the United States "refused" membership, it was "glad to co-operate with the League in its endeavors to further scientific, economic, and social welfare"—a nod greeted with unrequited anticipation in Geneva.[46]

As president, Hoover would enact his drive to map the social whole by commissioning a massive study of the state of the United States. The final report, *Recent Social Trends,* was the work of a host of scholars coordinated by the economist Edward Eyre Hunt.[47] The League was not alone in the cultivation of information and analysis in the economic and social field. It was just one part of a larger transnational community engaged in varieties of social and economic research that sought to relate it to policy.

THE VIEW FROM THE TOWER

A sign of how progressives in the US not only engaged the League but also cultivated it is Abraham Flexner's visits to Geneva in 1926 and 1927. Here was a model establishment progressive of the era whose influence ranged across disciplinary and national boundaries. His specialty was education reform, and the policies he championed shaped crucial aspects of American life. A 1910 report he authored on medical education remains a watershed moment for the training of physicians in the United States. Flexner's advice and criticism had a continual impact on the broader landscape of US higher education.[48] The cluster of Rockefeller foundations as well as the family itself counted him as an adviser on a variety of issues. He never had a specific portfolio regarding international organization and has not been cast by scholars as one of the League's boosters. However, precisely because Flexner was a commanding progressive figure, his views on the import of the organization are all the more revealing of what the body meant not just to self-nominated internationalists but to the progressive mind broadly.

Flexner's missions to Geneva in the late 1920s underscored the possibilities percolating there. He was in touch with the League's highest officials, and in the back and forth he was exposed to the boundless enthusiasm of Sweetser. A perceptive Flexner "feared that Sweetser is so *ardent* that he may do harm." The reformer proposed a technical solution: "Can't he be given a sedative?"[49]

Behind Flexner's visits lay discussions emerging from the Rockefeller philanthropic orbit, enriched with the input of a constellation of internationally engaged Americans, about the formation of an international institute of research.[50] As did many Americans at the time, they appreciated that Geneva had the potential to fill the gap in crucial sectors of inquiry. They felt that the United States, in particular, had to awaken to the glaring lack of capacity across society for research on national and global issues. There was an ongoing push for the creation of all sorts of new institutional sinew to foster an international consciousness that connected with efforts in other parts of the world.[51]

It did not take much to convince him that "the League is the Thing." It was a prime candidate to supply the facts, figures, and ferment necessary to a larger campaign to confront the problems of modernity. Like many figures of the time, Flexner was no naive positivist; he could spell out clearly his view that "facts" were based on perspective as well as ideology and politics. Precisely because of this there was a need for serious, in-depth inquiry.

Armed conflict was a lens that focused Flexner's views on reform, as might be expected in the years following the Great War, but he did not solely look at violence. He was optimistic that the new regime of inquiry that was international relations could deal with the panoply of concerns modernity brought, and these were much more than war alone. The League could be part of a larger campaign to provide solutions to those social and economic problems that led to conflict rather than mounting "a frontal attack on war as such." He worried that a desire to sponge out war "is likely to be overemphasized as compared with the attainment of a clearer conception of the real problems of modern life and the experimental cooperative efforts seeking their solution." He speculated that "more will perhaps be accomplished in maintaining the peace by the study, comparative and absolute, of the social, humanitarian, and economic problems of the modern world, and by deliberate effort to solve these problems, without for a moment considering that we are thus either avoiding war or building up an organization."[52]

Flexner was hardly blind to the League's weaknesses. He saw real flaws and dismissed as "lip service" many of the "fine words" spoken about the institution. Nevertheless, he appreciated that the League was something distinctive in world affairs, yet part of a wave of institutional innovation. It stood among brand-new institutions like the FPA and a rising set of "international relations" programs. In this environment, progressive interest in the League should be understood as one part of the international urge to foster the institutional muscle to not merely grasp what was happening internationally but to grab hold of means to govern those forces.

One thing that impressed Flexner about the League was that it was a permanent "Board of Directors Room" where representatives of states could meet "regularly in the open." Here the Secretariat was the thing within the Thing. Although the League stood as a permanent convention of nations, its political activities were fleeting, with sessions convening only to break up as the "directors" regularly "scattered, playing politics

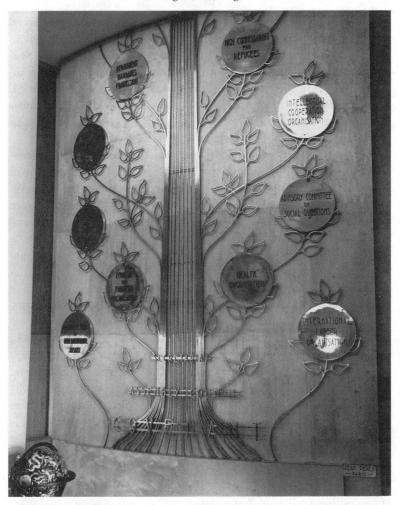

FIGURE 1.1. *"Sits like a tower, surveying the entire situation." A representation of what made the League "the Thing," with the trunk of Secretariat and the branches of technical services growing from the roots of the Assembly, Council, and Covenant, as displayed at the 1939 World's Fair. (Courtesy of United Nations Archives at Geneva)*

and golf." But its permanent Secretariat "holds together. It sits like a tower surveying the entire situation." That tower held a new caste: international civil servants who "move about ceaselessly . . . enlightening themselves, and of course, modestly but inevitably, enlightening others." All of this made the Secretariat the site at which the fundamental contributions of the League could be made, providing the perspective and the means to intervene that modern world affairs demanded.

Reluctant to back the proposed institute, Flexner nevertheless urged that the pocketbooks of the Rockefeller philanthropies and family remain open. Funds were needed to create the infrastructure to support the Secretariat's core missions, particularly the cultivation of its invaluable human capital. It needed a library—"the best equipped, the best supplied, and most readily usable in its field in the entire world"—as well as family-friendly accoutrements to make Geneva a sought-after post, including an international school to sustain a growing international colony.

Flexner's views circulated around the American and Geneva internationalist networks. No "Institute for International Research" would ever emerge as such, although a massive $2 million grant from John D. Rockefeller himself would allow a library wing to sprout from the planned Palace of Nations. The analysis would also fertilize Raymond Fosdick's general approach to supporting international studies in the US and internationally in the coming decade, and it emphasized foundation interest in the permanent economic research sustained in Geneva.[53]

The interventions of Flexner and Fosdick show how broader trends in liberalism and progressivism provided a scaffolding to support the League. Fosdick was connected to a range of mainstream reformers who were eagerly extending institutional capacities to deal with the extensive and multiplying problems brought by industrial modernity. Indeed, their very conception of a liberal regime of international relations and its demand for research and information led them to Geneva. This helps explain why not only Rockefeller acolytes but also many internationally minded figures gravitated to the League and stayed in its orbit. This instrumental view is also why the foundation and other Americans turned to the Secretariat when the Depression struck: it had already been marked as a site that could offer diagnoses for the ills of international affairs.

Proof that all the organizational suggestions were part of a wider pale of transnational progressivism was that Flexner himself would soon leave the Rockefeller orbit for the next phase of his career. While elements of Flexner's prescriptions were filled, there was resistance within the RF. For the foundation, the idea that grant making was to be focused on the promotion of knowledge rather than fostering capacity to attack specific problems still prevailed—although this would change when Fosdick assumed the reins. Outside the Rockefeller system, Flexner would get a chance to construct a hive for high-level research, albeit closer to home, further revealing capacity building as a transnational urge. The wealthy Bramberger family tapped him to plan a "university without students," which would become the Institute of Advanced Study (IAS) in Princeton, New Jersey.[54]

The importance of the scope of League work was repeatedly confirmed among American elites. A young Herbert Feis, who himself had worked in Geneva with the International Labour Organization (ILO) and would later serve as an economic adviser in Franklin Roosevelt's State Department, surveyed the variety of activities continuing to germinate in Geneva in 1929 at the behest of the Social Science Research Council (founded in 1923). He explored, too, the activities there as part of a conception (which he thought unoriginal) of "international relations." Feis could see the importance of the League as a hub for such international relations research, as essential "features distinguish it from most current research undertaken by private students and national governments." Its activities supported not only the construction but also the maintenance of international order. Hence the "area of interest covered by the League's research is world wide." Feis appreciated, too, the importance and novelty of this broad scope: "In this respect, what was exceptional before the creation of the League has become usual. . . . The League is more and more documenting contemporary life throughout the world. . . . [I]t is continuously scrutinizing fresh proposals which offer the hope of stimulating the development of an international society."[55]

EMPIRICAL ZEAL

The League's growth was part of an international trend in institution building from which the US was not exempt. Domestically, the interwar years saw the rise of the Social Science Research Council, the National Bureau of Economic Research (NBER), and the Brookings Institution, all meant to collect and analyze information as a means to offer solutions to the problems raised by modern society. Within the academic world the pitch of activity was growing as social science departments fledged, new methods coursed into fields like economics, and entire schools in the new interdisciplinary field of international relations were conjured into existence. All this work in the United States paralleled similar activity abroad.

The international collaboration on quantitative analysis had real impacts on research and held possibilities for action on policy. With the onset of the Great Depression, policymakers in the United States, desperate for reliable and comparable information to respond to the financial crisis, pleaded for new economic measures, particularly for national income, on which to base a response. Simon Kuznets, a researcher at the NBER and statistics whiz, answered this call. The report he compiled for the US Congress in 1934 was an unexpected best seller and was employed by FDR himself to assess the crisis and the effectiveness of the response. Kuznets's research stood out among efforts around the world to employ national income measures, demonstrating how data and analysis could be deployed to structure policies to salve the Depression.[56]

The rise in the importance of national income was part of larger changes in the field of economics. Kuznets could be florid about the need for more and better data to make economics more scientific. He cultivated a "zeal for empirical observation and for data" that could serve the "need for more intelligence in the solution of social issues." His rapturous commentary was flush with the progressive faith that if the right data were captured, social scientists could provide the analysis necessary for effective responses to pressing social concerns. At the same time he wrestled with the problems in creating a "scientific" economics. He realized that "while much of the present day economics is not science, a great deal of it approaches such a status." But the discipline did have some distinguishing characteristics, particularly when it came to its all-important inputs. Economists "need a supply of raw data vastly larger" than researchers in other realms.[57] Unlike peers in, say, physics, economists did not generate their own experimental data. Economic statistics are "not obtained as a result of [the economist's] designed arrangement: they are given to him by other agencies that may or may not take his interest into account." Indeed, Kuznets realized that these figures were socially and politically constructed artifacts, because "these data are given ... by the subject of observation itself. We study the behavior of man; and all our economic statistics are essentially responses by the people who are themselves the perpetrators of their economic behavior."[58] Added to this was the fact that "reliable and comprehensive data . . . have become available only recently."[59] Yet the available data, including government statistics, were often collected for reasons and in manners that did not directly suit economic analysis. This led to a "lack of comprehensive and continuous" information that hampered inquiry. Accordingly, a ready supply of planned and thorough economic statistics was vital to "social science and social planning."[60]

Kuznets's view that data were essential to engaged economics and that reliable and comprehensive information was limited was one shared by peers around the globe. The mission of remedying the shortfalls by collecting the necessary information and weaving it into something useful in the troubled 1930s was a transnational one.

It was not solely Americans who were attempting to sort out the riddles of national incomes and economic health. Kuznets's own work owed much to contemporaneous efforts on the topic. Closely related was the research of Colin Clark, an English economist who transplanted himself to Australia in the 1930s. It shows how one response to the crisis was a transnational urge to measure and define. With related agendas and a common aspiration to collect informative economic statistics, Clark and Kuznets corresponded about their research and shared their information and methods.[61]

Clark would take national income further and begin to sketch a global schema of economic health. His framework consummated the view that with comparable national statistics it would be possible to analyze the economic performance of various countries as individual units but also to view these units collectively—that is, globally. The new scheme was not necessarily a tool for ranking countries but for seeing the vast economic trends playing out worldwide. This perspective made it conceivable to trace how general policies of investment, trade, or social security played out in different economies. The results of analysis then could be used to answer the questions of how to improve the income and the standard of living of various peoples around the world. In an era of stagnation, a global view could begin to diagnose problems and propose solutions that might work in a variety of situations.[62]

Because researchers like Kuznets and Clark were working on globally relevant analysis, they were sought out internationally. One figure who found this new work relevant to pressing questions was Jan Tinbergen, a Dutch economist working with the League. Tinbergen himself was conducting pioneering statistical work on the pressing question of business cycles.[63] Tinbergen pumped Clark not only for concepts but for his data as well, and Clark in turn cited Tinbergen's work and leaned on data compiled by the League to draw the conclusions for an influential 1939 study.[64]

These interactions and critiques show that the League was far from the only hive of activity on the burning economic and standard-of-living questions raised by the Depression and fanned by growing political and social strife. Yet the Geneva institutions were actively tied into basic as well as influential transnational research and enduring debates on the world economy.

While hardly a cure-all, the appearance of new economic measures and analysis, and the data these rested on, was a distinct improvement. Looking back from later periods that were both besotted and infatuated with data and information, it is a surprise to see how limited the tools available to actors in the early twentieth century actually were. It is striking what policymakers lacked in the early days of the Depression, even in large, wealthy countries. The United States simply did not have the comprehensive economic information needed to fully grasp its own domestic economy, let alone a rolling global crisis. Despite the impulses to gather information that had marked the preceding decades, the Roosevelt administration groped through its early days in office. It tried to tease out economic trends with unreliable and mismatched data, such as stock prices, freight-car loadings, and an assorted collection of indexes of industrial production.[65] This appreciation was why a variety of endeavors to improve the economic situation and create comparable indicators, including the expanding efforts of the League, drew such attention both in the United

States and in the world at large. New analytical concepts such as national income became a measure and also a goal—something for government policy to increase. For this reason, figures across societies eagerly grabbed at the analytical innovations of the era.[66]

Emblematic of what international collaboration could accomplish was the 1928 International Conference on Economic Statistics hosted by the League. It was hardly the first effort to improve international statistics on trade. The desire to coordinate and compile such data already had a reasonably long history, and the conference included many organizations, including the International Statistics Institute, that had long labored for better numbers. It trussed the effort as a secondary and self-evident effort for peace: "All statesmen and economists are aware that good statistics are an essential condition of good economic policy." Participants rather grandly asserted that if reliable statistics were available, good policy could be made that would inspire peace.

The president of the proceedings noted that strides had been made in generating these data since the nineteenth century, but there was still a great distance to go. He discussed the shortfalls in information that would soon bedevil policy makers confronting economic disaster, noting that national statistics held dramatic, even comical, gaps. Official statistics of the United States decreed that 48 million bushels of wheat had been exported to Canada in 1927, but its northern neighbor acknowledged importing only 155,000 bushels. Even when disparities in amount were not orders of magnitude apart, there could be large discrepancies in value. Portugal claimed to have exported 388,000 hectoliters of port wine valued at £1,550,000 to the thirsty British in 1926. The United Kingdom acknowledged importing a somewhat more sober tally of 356,000 hectoliters but, betraying expensive tastes, appraised the value at £2,670,000.[67]

These may seem trifling comparisons, but in the aggregate they show how poor information distorts the outlines of trade and production, and with them, policy. Without an accessible understanding of what was moving and being produced, observers and policymakers could not see aspects of world economics and could not govern it with the efficiency and rationality that boosters sought. Good information of this sort provided the ball bearings for the wheels of commerce.

The conference emphasizes that the League was inserting itself into an ongoing international trend. The creation of the means to measure national capabilities and illuminate global trends, however flawed—Kuznets had grasped the limits imposed by the inherent subjectivity of data from the beginning—yielded outstanding innovations to put in the hands of policy analysts and makers at the national and international level. By the start of the 1940s, some of those most invested in creating new tools and understandings of how the global economy fit together, namely the staff at the Rockefeller Foundation, offered abundant praise to figures like Kuznets, who was ranked "out in front in the field and indeed has contributed more in economic research in the last ten years than any other economist." They should have been pleased: they had supported his work, and he had actively framed Rockefeller's understanding of the evolution of the concept of national income and the role of economics as a social science.[68] More to the point, national income had emerged as a *transnational* tool with *global* relevance. In the words of Willits, it had become a "basic measurement and the perfect tool . . . for policy makers, for scholars, and others."[69]

National income also made the impersonal, abstract, and inherently metaphorical issue that is the economy legible for wider audiences. In combination with other concepts such as standard of living, national income quickly found an outsized place in public discussion for an audience beyond policy elites. In the United States alone it became a tool enabling various actors to frame the basic outlines of an economic crisis that showed no sign of abating.

The concept of national income permeated discussion early and often. In 1935 the FPA employed such analysis for a program of "public education." National income could be used to illustrate how far and fast collapse had occurred internationally in a "scientific" and comparable manner. It could reveal how "living standards" had declined in areas of consumption and nutrition. It could even be used to question whether, even in prosperous times, the national income was structured to meet the needs of most Americans. Most of all, it confirmed the internationalist mantra that US "well-being is closely tied up with that of other nations."[70]

Behind efforts to improve the information available on world trade were the hands of large US philanthropic foundations. The internationalism of officers and trustees like Fosdick and Willits (among others) was bedrock for the foundation's outlook. Their support was both national and international in its scope. A motivating assumption behind many of these organizations was that the collection of data and the promulgation of analysis could be used to promote more objective, and therefore better, views on issues that needed to be understood before they could be tackled. In a world where basic tropes about international affairs centered on increasing interdependence, the RF was regularly involved in supporting humanistic and social-scientific endeavors toward that end.

Indeed, Rockefeller and others continued to see Geneva as a bright star in the constellation of institutions contributing to international education, policy, and understanding. Foundation officials were alive to the possibility of using research fostered in Geneva to assist in the coordination of national efforts on many pressing issues. They retained Flexner's view that the "role of the Secretariat is naturally of great significance" and that its "fact-finding role . . . [is] of primary significance." However, in a discussion in the mid-1930s that hints at why later structural reforms to the League were so well received by the RF, they lamented that "its research activity can only be secondary and are limited in scope by the nature of the organization of the League."[71]

Of course, when it came to agendas and goals, even of in the gathering of information, there were motivating ideas. Scholars have seen wealthy foundations as outriders for the rise of the United States to global dominance.[72] That overstates their intent and sees too unified a purpose, but organizations like the RF were undoubtedly globally minded. However, this perception was deeply rooted in established structures. The Depression only drove home how tightly the United States was linked to global trends and pushed the RF to redouble efforts to foster solutions within liberal political boundaries.

The Depression pushed many to dwell on the issues of living standards and quality of life. In important respects, these were outgrowths of long traditions of reform. However, the crisis had given them new and global relevance. There was an appreciation that the era revealed the innate interconnection of the world, even in breakdown.

FASCIST STATISTICS

Advocacy for data and attention to its analysis reveal the truism that numbers do not speak for themselves. Statistics and the varieties of research they can be bound up with are not innately apolitical. A contemporary of the individuals who were orbiting the League was Corrado Gini. His devotion to statistics was as deep as that of any of his peers, and through it he sought to create a quantitative social science. This wide-ranging effort led him, as it did others, to international engagement. In fact, he authored an early and influential League study on what was to be an influential and ongoing topic, raw materials.[73] His name lives on in the "Gini coefficient," a statistical measurement that tracks wealth inequality within nations allowing for comparison by global observers.

Gini was also a committed fascist. Benito Mussolini's acknowledgment that "statistics has expanded its jurisdiction over all phenomena of life" showed that the movement was well aware of the power of such data. Gini evangelized for the ideology, offering a "scientific" justification of the "fascist experiment" for elite American audiences in the late 1920s.[74] Gini shows that intellectual innovations do not flow in one direction and that the tools they generate often can be used by a variety of movements and actors. Just as liberal international society instrumentalized statistics and ensured that they were applied in a manner that suited its views, others could use the same resources to different ends.

A NEW DEVELOPMENT

As new regimes of data began to gird international affairs, new analytic methods were broadly applied in various forms. The League's technical efforts had already branched into international assistance and targeted Nationalist China, then in the midst of what would later be defined as its "Republican Decade." The Guomindang regime, as part of a strategy to leverage the League to enhance China's international status, was particularly enthusiastic in accessing a new option—direct development aid offered by the international organization. Struggling to forge national authority and build capacity, the government turned to the League of Nations. China requested and received varieties of aid from the League. This assistance spanned economic, transportation, health, educational, and agricultural areas that comprised development and state building, and it demonstrated that international bodies already had found a role in supporting the process.[75]

For a polity in need, it was a logical choice to approach an international body that did not impose some of the constraints that came with aid from other states. The spectrum of assistance was striking, with missions from Geneva consulting on roads, health, agriculture, hydraulic projects, and other issues during the late 1920s and through the 1930s. The League was pioneering efforts to promote development that successors would also embrace. At the same time, it would encounter some of the frustrations that later programs would face. As visits by foreign specialists continued, there grew a feeling among the Chinese that the comparatively short visits and types of reports issued had limited value in the face of the complex problems facing the Republican regime.[76]

Nevertheless, technical assistance to China would be referenced over the coming years and billed to international publics as a sign that the League had a particular role to play influencing social and economic change on the world stage. It also reinforced a basic assumption that international cooperation could and should play a role in supporting economic reforms and development in various parts of the world.

ORDER OUT OF CHAOS

As aid to China suggests, the purpose of much international collaboration was to generate means for action by policymakers at a state level. This points to a contradiction in the international generation of facts and figures, which were not necessarily tools to achieve harmony or cooperation in the most generous senses of those terms. Yet they were very much grist for a transnational community of activists. There has been growing appreciation of how various countries were all grappling with problems brought by modern life that were seen to be shared across boundaries. This was never so true as during the Depression.[77]

Nevertheless, the reality was that the facts and figures generated were often sought after by those seeking to inform or motivate changes at a national level. They were sometimes tools to advance business agendas and other types of competition.[78] What many supporters were seeking were instruments to read global change, to see what policies worked, and to track trends. This might seem parochial, but it was a basic lubricant for the desires of internationalism.

With the onset of the Depression, economic issues and their governance became a decisive factor in national and world affairs. As the reality sank in that the Great Depression was not a dramatic spasm but a nagging norm on the international level, the ability of the League to serve as a hub of international inquiry became increasingly important, even a point of emphasis.

Increased attention to the permanent organs of the League in the early 1930s was partly a response to the Depression and partly a response to the limits of the League's ability to directly influence economic policy with large international conferences. Although there had been success on issues such as statistics and other more technical topics, returns were diminishing by the early years of the 1930s. The failure of the 1933 London Economic Conference was one sign of this. The conference was not convened by the League (although sessions had been held and much data gathering and analysis had been done in Geneva to prepare for the meeting), but it was a blow to the idea that large conferences to foster intergovernmental cooperation would be the forum for governance on these issues.

Nevertheless, crucial actors had already gleaned the importance of the potential for monitoring and analysis latent in the permanent economic organs in Geneva. Although the League had only recently positioned itself as an important site for gatherings on significant international issues, it had already oriented some of its research toward pressing international questions. The work of Geneva institutions on standardizing economic measures fed other transnational concepts, such as the "standard of living," that had increased relevance in a worsening economic situation.[79] As it had on other issues, the League used its leverage to gather experts in Geneva in 1931 on the already-gnawing issue of the Depression. The United States eagerly participated.

A sign of how seriously the possibility of international insight was taken was that Edward Eyre Hunt was sent as US representative. A better representation of the US commitment to information as a means to grasp national and international concerns would have been hard to find. Hunt's ongoing work coordinating the research that would lead to *Recent Social Trends* meant he was well versed in how information gathering could be used to shape larger views of social and economic units in preparation for action.

In Geneva, Hunt found himself among kindred spirits. He was impressed that the League was able to draw together a set of impressive national delegates, all seeking to address a global issue. This impression was partially generated by flattery. European counterparts explained how they had been influenced by American work on economic issues, and they were familiar with the project Hunt was leading for Hoover. Hunt recalled that as the participants recounted their perspectives on how the crisis unfolded, the narration of the march of the Depression through their respective countries showed a "geographical progression" of the crisis. An astute observer, Hunt was able to identify the Depression as the transnational crisis it was, waves spreading out in all directions, breaking in different places at different times but always striking with stunning force. Hunt also captured the international nature of national data collection and how the results could be compared to other sources.[80] Like many others, he appreciated that economic questions were catalysts in world affairs. He portentously wrote to Wesley Clair Mitchell (a policy entrepreneur instrumental in the establishment of the NBER and a moving force in the *Recent Social Trends* project), "It is surely a most dangerous situation, the economic depression deepening as political conflicts accentuate.... History is not prophetic but it holds the germs of prophesy. We fear what may be because of what has been.... Surely there would be no Second World War if there had not been a First."[81]

Hunt's reports were broadcast to numerous figures and institutions. Particularly attentive was the Rockefeller Foundation. While the foundation had already given considerable monies to the League and related bodies, the interest in economic research on the Depression was a new and critical front. Like many others, the foundation made "stabilization" its byword. Along with supporting domestic work, the RF was seeking international mechanisms to create the information and analysis that could offer blueprints for policies that might bring the crisis, then near its depth, to heel. How those mechanisms were lobbied for and constructed reflects the institution's international and transnational nature.

Rockefeller's goals merged with the League's own agenda. Members of the Secretariat were quick to appeal to this increasingly critical funder on the basis of these benefits and the agenda of the new director of the Economic and Financial Section (EFS), Alexander Loveday. He had taken over from the well-regarded Arthur Salter. Loveday had long experience with the League, but part of his intellectual background was in political philosophy, a topic on which he lectured at the University of Leipzig briefly before World War I.

Even after Loveday turned to economics, part of him always remained a political theorist. This orientation would also frame his understanding of the forces at work in the world and the challenges posed to the liberal, democratic societies with which Loveday identified. From an early moment he understood that the political forces—often driven by an acute sense of economic insecurity—unleashed globally by the Depression were a threat not merely to the League but also to order itself.[82] In 1933, following Germany's departure from the League after Hitler's ascent to power, the political theorist within Loveday sketched a larger picture: "I have always thought that . . . the 30's-40's of the present century would be a revolutionary period." Born of these decades were a set of revolutionary movements driven not by leaders but by ideas. These were "the result largely a) of economic changes and conditions and b) of national psychology." Regimes steeped in these ideas had taken hold in Germany, Russia, Italy, and Japan and were overtly nationalistic, anti-individualistic, antiparliamentary, anti-internationalist, and even in some forms "antieconomic." He understood them as opposed to much in the liberalism and internationalism that he held close. This hostility predisposed those regimes to disdain the League, which meant the putative universalism of its recent past would be impossible to maintain going forward. The only way to navigate this was to "swing . . . emphasis from work connected with differences to work in common." Technical work offered potential common ground, but the overall outlook was ominous, as these movements were on the move and there was "no reason why they should not spread."[83]

Despite the temper of the period, Loveday would remain a liberal in terms of both economics and politics. Broadly, he shared many views common to liberal internationalists about the importance of free trade, individual liberty, and the vital input of international institutions. A view of the importance of an open regime of international exchange was not simply ideological; it was also a response to events of the era. Late in the 1930s, as the world economy again swooned, Loveday shared apprehension over the "grave danger of the system of economic autarchy, with all its political implications spreading both much more widely and much more rapidly than it has already."[84] All the while, he carefully nurtured contacts in the US. He appreciated not only the input provided by American funders and colleagues but also how the US itself was experiencing and responding to a global crisis.[85]

The intensification of focus on the Depression that flowed with Loveday's tenure also highlighted the increasing attention to the Secretariat's permanent organs as the sites of research activities, rather than infrequent international conferences. The EFS held the potential to be a hub for a constant stream of information as well as analysis. Embodying this function was a new member of the Secretariat, John Bell Condliffe. Born in Australia and raised in New Zealand, as a teenager he joined the latter nation's Customs Service. It turned out to be an education in the importance of information. One of his early tasks was recording export entries. He would recall with pride that his work in economic statistics began with this immersion in "primary material."[86] Like so many people, he was sucked into World War I and badly wounded. After recovering he studied economics at Cambridge University and began to plug into the internationalist networks of the time.

A thread running through Condliffe's career was that change in a modern world was a constant.[87] That change could be perceived through keen measurement and analysis, and his affinity for statistical analysis gave his work credibility. In the second half of the 1920s, he mustered regional statistics to sketch the emergence of an "industrial revolution" that was reshaping East Asia. It was part of an "epochal" shift that was transforming those countries, the region, and the world. Indeed, in a manner that would frame later discussions among modernization theorists, he saw processes that played out in nineteenth-century Great Britain and Europe flowing to and through an industrializing Asia. The West had hammered out a template that other states would follow and eventually converge upon.[88] Like the West, countries in Asia would have to adopt their societies and politics to absorb these massive changes. A recurring point was structural changes brought by accelerating global interchange that were making the earth smaller and ginning up industrial growth in smaller economies. More generally, Condliffe understood that international relationships were moved by tectonic forces rather than particular controversies roiling the surface of political life. Broader economic trends exposed the realities of world affairs.[89]

These trends, along with recent history, conspired against European, particularly British, primacy. This view intensified over the course of the interwar years. Continually reading economic data, Condliffe perceived that a "new economic system" was emerging. One country, above all, was positioned to benefit not just from recent history but particularly from longer historical shifts: the United States. While the new Leviathan was only fitfully moving into its new position politically and socially, there was no doubting its primacy. It was clear by the second half of the 1930s that "no effective international organization is now possible without the cooperation if not the leadership of the United States." Condliffe did not think such a profound transformation would be easy, particularly as the Depression continued, and he shared Loveday's view "that the world's economic future is likely to be a bumpy one."

Even if the US actively asserted its power, the growing complexity and diversity of global interactions could not be bent to the will of any single state. This meant "international co-operation is more necessary than ever." As did many others, Condliffe knew the economic was not a sphere apart but linked to defining issues. Effective response to global economic shifts and instability meant a commitment to the right political and social systems. Leadership was imperative to confront a changing world, but it had to be "based upon and drawn from an educated and stable democracy."[90]

In the 1920s Condliffe found a niche and exposure at the newly formed IPR, where he became director of research at the headquarters of its secretariat in Honolulu, Hawai'i. The IPR was a pioneering organization that put the perspectives of a selection of national councils side by side. Condliffe's labors with the IPR provided him an international profile. They also brought him to the attention of the Rockefeller Foundation, which counted the IPR among its stable of grantees. As the regional NGO's operations began to attract attention, the League's Secretariat took pains to show that its work was relevant to the regional organization and the Pacific Basin it sought to represent and understand. In the IPRs first major publication, the serial *Problems of the Pacific*, the League offered a contribution. It the case that not only its mandates commission—which maintained a large portfolio in the region—but also its health programs, intellectual cooperation, and economic research mattered in that part of the world.[91]

The League was entangled in the operations of a proliferating set of institutions in liberal international society in the decade after World War I. But it was not simply a question of organizations turning to the League; the Geneva institutions were actively trying to make their capacities relevant to a variety of actors.

As with many peers, Condliffe would find his professional path and perceptions altered by the Depression and its global economic consequences.[92] As an early addition to Loveday's team, the Kiwi joined the League at the Depression's nadir. It was also the moment when the Financial and Economic Organization of the League was split. An Economic Relations Section under the Italian Pietro Stoppani was tasked with broader economic policy and was "administrative" in its outlook.[93] Loveday became the new chief of the EFS with its waxing Economic Intelligence Service (EIS). The EFS would establish itself as the premiere research arm of the League and a permanent engine of international economic data gathering. Condliffe noted how far Loveday took the EIS beyond its official mission. Rather than providing economic, financial, and statistical materials as grist for deliberations of League bodies, it sought to insert them into world affairs.

The New Zealander was instrumental in this turn. With established international credentials and acceptable liberal politics, his would be a decisive voice in lining up US support for these efforts. As Condliffe had built a relationship with RF through his work with the IPR, his views of the value of the League programs to "systematize" statistical work on the economic front carried considerable weight. This would make the desperately sought "raw materials for the study of international economic problems" more readily and regularly available. Rockefeller largesse was necessary as League efforts were hampered by limited resources—Condliffe could not recall ever seeing offices so cramped and staff so overworked. Yet there was plenty of work to do on numerous topics.[94]

Overall, Rockefeller staff were comfortable with these League officials. They liked the "studious" Loveday, even if they thought his more academic bearing might not carry the same public weight of his predecessor. His emphasis on data creation was a major factor in Loveday's appeal. Thus, in the early 1930s, with the encouragement of figures like Hunt and Condliffe, the Rockefeller Foundation, already a League supporter, moved to systematically assist its economic sections in shaping a response to the Depression with a large multiyear grant.[95]

Since the League dealt with global issues, Loveday set out to collect statistical information for the world as a whole. In important respects, his was the first such effort to do so, and his project faced yawning inconsistences and gaps in the data. Nevertheless, the noble goal was to "bring order out of the chaos of national statistics."[96]

The work was complicated. National statistics, such as balance of payments, are taken for granted in the twenty-first century. In 1931 the League could calculate this balance for only thirty-three countries. Improvements came with time, but the numbers that came to Geneva often had to be reworked, converted into a common base, translated into common measures and currencies, and recorded. It was a painstaking alchemy, transmuting sketchy national figures into something globally comprehensible. None of this was helped by the fact Loveday was a "perfectionist" who refused to print a number unless its provenance was known, how it was calculated, and what it meant. He held up publication of the proposed *Statistical Year-Book* for years when he was uncertain whether the project met his stringent standards.[97]

Condliffe felt privileged to have had a role in the creation of the comparable statistics that marked the inflection point in what really mattered to many internationalists and policymakers—the application of the data to international questions. Condliffe later explained the historic significance of this effort: "For the first time, this small group of economists documented, measured and interpreted the ways in which the national econom-

FIGURE 1.2. *Alexander Loveday and one of the products of his "remarkable system of economic intelligence." (Courtesy of Nuffield College Archives, Oxford)*

ics were interdependent." He thought that "historians may conclude that its contribution to world understanding was not the least of the League's achievements."[98]

The EFS's efforts yielded numerous products that would achieve extensive international reach. The permanence of this part of the Secretariat allowed data to be reworked into knowledge in the form of analyses of trends with sustained global resonance. A throng of serials emerged from the economic section: *Review of World Trade, World Production and Prices*, and the *Statistical Year-Book of the League of Nations*. Of all of these, perhaps the most emblematic and influential was the *World Economic Survey* (*WES*). It would outlive the League itself. Published annually, it ran from 1931 to 1947, it was folded into its successor and, in modified form, is still published today.

Condliffe would devote his six years in Geneva to the laborious serial. It was largely his work, even if he drew heavily on the data and methods generated by his colleagues. The *WES* was not mere data but a usable interpretation of it, devoted to offering a synthesis of the information the League had collected and presenting it in a global framework. Throughout the 1930s that framework was dominated by the specter of the Depression.[99]

Because it was analysis and not merely numbers, Loveday was worried from the start about the serial's political implications. He discouraged Condliffe from publishing an examination that suggested—rightly, as Condliffe at the time and others later asserted—that financial speculation in New York in the late 1920s had been a basic cause of the Depression. Fearing repercussions from this sort of analysis in the *WES*, Loveday departed from League protocols and had Condliffe named as the author of the volume.[100]

The risk of having his name attached to such a publication paid compounding dividends for the New Zealander. The *WES* quickly became "indispensable" in Western academic and policy circles for those seeking a "tolerably well-informed picture of the events of the depression throughout the world." Specialists, seeing that it unified the statistics published in serials such as annual "volumes on *World Production and Prices*, the *Review of World Trade*, and the *Statistical Year-Book*," appreciated that it was "much more than a work of reference" and recognized that at its core an "attempt is made to appraise the significance of the different tendencies at work, to disentangle underlying causes from the more obvious factors near the surface, and to suggest tentatively some of the conclusions which appear to follow from the experience of recent years."[101]

Culturally, the *WES* became a marker of seriousness. The doyen of the American establishment, former secretary of state Henry Stimson, accidentally left a hint of its importance when he borrowed a volume of the serial from Feis and marked it up. After the damage was discovered, Stimson's personal secretary rushed the economic adviser a replacement, embarrassed by the damage done to something of such value.[102]

Along with other information flowing from the Economic Intelligence Service, the *WES* had wide impact across academia and in the press. It became increasingly commonplace for US media outlets to compare Americans' fate in the Depression with that of others around the world by using varieties of League data and analysis. This helped to frame public discussions about dislocation and inequality. How the global economic crisis straddled borders to affect individuals could be more easily seen and compared. In the European and American press, League documents became windows on the impact of the Depression abroad and at home. For example, media across the United States used the statistics gathered by the League to apprehend the lot of American workers as compared to their international counterparts. The cost of living in different countries could be readily and easily compared. The value of the seven-dollar daily wage then paid by the Ford Motor Company could be measured in an international context.[103] Assertions by League economists that global industrial production was growing in 1934 underlay hopeful commentary that the world, and with it the United States, was headed "out of the Depression."[104] The *New York Times* called the League's 1937 nutrition report the most important book of the year. League research provided the "first study ever made on a global scale of the relation of nutrition to health, agriculture, and economic policy," showing that the tangible distinction between the "Haves and the Have-Nots" was food.[105] The statistics and analysis emanating from Geneva provided a singular means for the Depression to be understood as a shared global experience.

WEBS OF KNOWLEDGE

As the author of a premier exegesis on world economic concerns, Condliffe extended an already-expansive reputation. The impact of the *WES* was quickly registered and would earn the New Zealander not merely accolades but also tangible rewards down the years.[106]

With the remarkable popularity of the *WES*, internationalists realized they had a hit—at least in terms of economic literature. The Boston-based WPF exploited this. As each new edition appeared, the Brahmin bastion issued glossy promotional materials. It could do what few other publications could do, namely provide a perspective on a world economic crisis. Obtaining a copy promised a "world's eye view of business conditions . . . literally crammed full of comparative measurements and estimates." In 1935 the WPF asked, "Do you know the answers?" to pointed questions such as "Is private enterprise dead in the United States?" "What are the lines of the new economic structure?" "What is happening to the 'New Deals' in other countries?" "What is the greatest single obstacle to Recovery today?" Now such questions had answers, found in the data organized and interpreted by Condliffe. National economic concerns could be solved with data that illuminated other countries' responses to the global question of Depression. Advertisements sighed that with so much material between the covers of the *WES*, it was "impossible to sketch the whole panorama that is revealed by this exhaustive survey."[107]

Self-adulating promotional materials aside, the advertisements were right: the materials filled a pressing need, which is why they were praised and sought after. Nevertheless, as much as it was a League publication, it should be seen as part of those efforts internationally, particularly in liberal circles, to understand the world not only as a whole but also as parts that could be compared to one another.

Exploiting the popularity of the annual, in 1935 the League turned to the new media of radio to further extend the reach of the *WES* in the hungry US market. Great effort was taken to put Condliffe on the airwaves of the National Broadcasting Company during a visit to the United States. The actual outcome was somewhat of a disappointment, due less to the economist or the contents of the *WES* and more to atmospheric conditions and the then-brutal competition between print media and the upstart wireless.

FIGURE 1.3. *Global audience: Condliffe's views reached a swath of the international public through a variety of media, facilitated by various institutions. This is Condliffe on the radio in 1950. (Courtesy of Alexander Turnbull Library, Wellington, New Zealand)*

Print outlets snubbed the latest version of the League's analysis when Condliffe chose to make his appearance on the upstart new media. Press rivalry aside, there was an international audience hungry for this sort of information and analysis from the start.[108]

Condliffe's misadventures on the air were only a fraction of the attempts to use his analysis to shape American views. That same year, the WPF and FPA, eager to educate the middlebrow public, had commissioned him to write *War and Depression*, a pamphlet on the coming of the economic crisis (interestingly, he was not billed as an international civil servant but as visiting professor at the University of Michigan). These sorts of pamphlets were given wide distribution through a variety of schools, clubs, and other institutions. Condliffe's own followed a basic template, providing a straightforward explanation that still echoes in scholarship in the twenty-first century. Disorganized production, along with "saturation of the market in many countries for even elaborate industrial products such as automobiles," was exacerbated by a breakdown of credit and the international monetary system. This led to a cascading collapse of international trade.

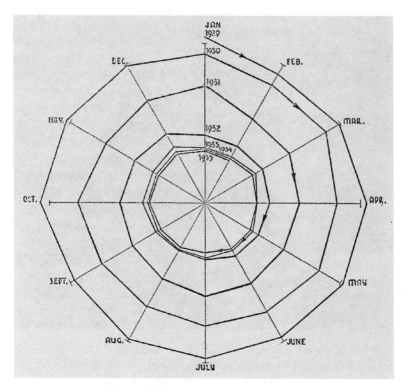

FIGURE 1.4. *The "spider's web" of economic analysis. Condliffe's visualization of the collapse of world trade during the Great Depression based on League data, as presented to US audiences in 1935. It has since become a staple of scholarship on the global crisis. (Courtesy of World Peace Foundation).*

What gave this discussion lasting impact was how Condliffe presented his analysis of the data the League had generated to support his argument. Tucked in the book was a gripping visualization of the collapse (fig. 1.4).

Condliffe's coil made palpable to audiences how dramatically world trade had been flushed away in a very short period of time. It was an extrapolation of an illustration placed at the front of the 1932–1933 *WES* and composed from information compiled for the serial.[109] What Loveday called the "spider's web" was a global version of the economist Oskar Morgenstern's own evocative death spiral of exports from Austria and Germany in the same period, created at the Austrian Institute for Business Cycle Research.[110] It fit into some other trends in other representations of global affairs in the period, including cartography, that were reshaping not just the reportage of events but how they could be perceived.[111]

The web has since become a striking representation of what made the Depression "great." Generations of scholars have appreciated and ac-

knowledged that it was based on League data (although they never credited authorship of the actual illustration to the League). But they often do
not appreciate something that many contemporaries did, namely that the
League was essentially the only source of such globally comparable data
that could be bent to such conclusions. In the fraught 1930s it was, in key
respects, the only game in town.[112]

As much as the *WES* and the litany of other valuable statistical and analytical publications flowing out of the economic organs of the League,
Condliffe's web represents how profoundly this work resonated not only in
policy but also in the scholarly and public imagination. It was not simply the
raw numbers and charts compiled that mattered but also how this newly
available information could be marshaled, represented, and presented to
audiences around the world. The popularity of the web also contextualizes
the place of the League within international society. It held an important
place because it could do vital work that no other organization could do.
At the same time, to accomplish and publicize that work, it had to draw on
talents cultivated in a variety of institutional backgrounds (governments,
universities, and NGOs) and required the assistance of a variety of groups
in various countries. The web and Condliffe's analysis would not have been
propelled as far into international public (and scholarly) discussion without a network of contacts. Organizations like the FPA and WPF increased
the range of audiences exposed to this sort of information and analysis because it overlapped with their own agendas.

Condliffe, like others in the League and among those partial to his work,
saw the revival of world trade as a treatment for the symptoms of worldwide economic disease and for the causes themselves. His views, like much
in the League's work, were understood as a profoundly liberal view of the
maladies afflicting the world and the prescriptions for its recovery. This was
apparent from Condliffe's earliest versions of the *WES*, and it continued
into his wartime writings. Scholars have since seen the League's economic
analysis as "liberal fundamentalism." This may be an overstatement, but
the basic tenets that bounded much League work were unquestionably
liberal.[113]

The "spider's web" offers an illustration of why and how putatively technical information was not only registered but also valued, and why it had
import. This was the sort of resource and ability that many would esteem
and see as a means not only to grapple with the Depression but also to
contend with conflict as it began to loom. Such data were essential to an
internationalist community struggling to find answers to a chronic world
condition. The League was a focal point because it was producing some
of the best information overall and the only globally comparable data at
a moment when the increasing interconnection of national economies
was becoming impossible to ignore. Nevertheless, the League's activity

was sustainable because it was rooted in international society. Part of the reason such analyses had the reach they did was that other bodies in international society broadcast them further into national publics as part of their own participation in transnational discourse. Looking solely at the League overstates the importance of the organization while limiting the impacts of the work it did. These various activities show how such new resources and analyses took root within internationalist culture and became a staple many thought vital—indeed, indispensable. These sorts of tools were what so many sought to sustain and to beef up as world conditions worsened.

THERE IS NO WORLD ECONOMY

Interest in the utility of new analytic methods lay behind a July 1936 gathering at the French lakeside city of Annecy, just down the road from Geneva. The gathering, itself at a moment when the League's own technical turn was gaining momentum, convened a slate of specialists—almost entirely from Europe and North America—on international economic topics. They were all committed to liberal economics, but their views nevertheless ran a gamut.[114] On one end there was a godfather of neoliberalism, Ludwig Mises, as well as Gottfried Haberler, who would end his days at the American Enterprise Institute. These were balanced by the pragmatic hand of Condliffe, who was flanked by the American Keynesians Alvin Hansen and John Clark, as well by the New Deal tribune Winfield Riefler. The League offered a delegation led by Loveday, and the ILO sent Lewis Lorwin. Bertil Ohlin, Jan Tinbergen, William Rappard, and a selection of other international figures added depth as well as breadth. Their personal as well as institutional connections underlined the interdependence of international society. They also betrayed the necessity of patronage, shown by the set of RF officers in attendance at the conference they convened and funded: "Encouraging Coordination of Fundamental Economic Research on the Problem of Economic Change."

The central question on the agenda cut to the quick: did a world economy even exist? No was the obvious answer from participants. Such a response shows the different conditions of the time. The answer was hardly a denial of global interactions, which were understood as very real and important. Rather, it was an acknowledgment of the primacy of political and ideological divisions. These had distorted any idealized worldwide economic interchange. To the figures at the conference, there was no unified world economic system in the "strict sense," but there was undoubtedly "a play of international forces in the international sphere from which no national economy can isolate itself." This interplay and the impact that a few national economies could and did have on the international sphere further dramatized the need to foster research, hence the focal point of the meeting.

The League was seen as a critical part of a regime of data collection that also included national governments, domestic research institutions, and the labor of individuals. Annecy again showed the deep investment around the internationalist ecumene in the procurement of information. There was particular desire for an "improvement in the quantity, quality, and comparability of relevant data" to feed the activities necessary to bind together international research regarding the problems of world economy or, as it was phrased, the "level of problems of economic change."

However, suggestions made at the conference also betrayed the limitations of what existed. They pointed toward what would be a persistent demand in the decade that followed for the sort of surveillance and analysis already accepted as essential. Loveday offered a further no when attendees asked whether the necessary international coordination of national research centers could be conducted through the League. This led to some discussion of an international institution that could provide such coordination among a raft of subjects to study, including the "range of problems inherent in the supply of raw materials." There was also concern over what was being measured. Much of the extant data emerged from industrialized states. With a growing appreciation of the trend toward industrialization in agrarian "out-lying areas," there was a need to foster research on this type of "economic change" (efforts to assist Nationalist China were singled out as valuable in this area). Perhaps the biggest question was not data-driven at all. There was a need to understand political movements and their "influence on economic systems," specifically the effects of "the newer ideologies in Europe."[115]

As the attendees offered their suggestions for ways to enhance capacity, they pointed to ongoing studies, particularly Haberler's. They considered it emblematic of the sort of research that could be conducted collaboratively. Annecy, then, emphasizes the importance of information and how the EFS was able to leverage its relationships with various institutions and scholars to produce some of the research that burnished its reputation and position. But it was able to do that because individuals and institutions within international society accepted and cultivated its role as a hub.

The work of the EFS was such that even as the political wing of the League entered a pronounced stage of political decomposition at the end of the 1930s, its research was reaching a pitch of influence. After attending the Annecy meeting, Haberler took a position at Harvard University and finished *Prosperity and Depression*. Although Loveday had to urge him to tone down the "professorial polemics" against John Maynard Keynes and his followers in the book, it was another coup for the League. After the war Loveday would laud it as the single best-selling study the League had produced. Passing through several editions, it remains today an influential statement on the business cycle and depressions.[116]

Soon after Haberler's publication, Tinbergen published his *Statistical Testing of Business-Cycle Theories*. It was another influential sortie in the effort to explain how the crisis upset economic trends. Presaging a career devoted to econometrics, Tinbergen's analysis was dependent on crunching numbers that the League had provided to clarify the impact of the Depression on such rotations.[117]

Generated cooperatively by the League through collaboration with institutions and individuals in international society, this research showed the growing commitment to a regime of information generation. Nevertheless, the push to see the world through lenses grounded in data generated pushback. Members of what has been called the Geneva school of economics, which was centered on both Mises and Friedrich von Hayek and would harden into a basis for neoliberalism, harbored doubts. By the end of the 1930s, people in this circle had become skeptical that information could be generated and analyzed that would provide a perfect response to the inherent variety and complexity of economic life. This was a reaction to the mainstream currents of a sort of liberal internationalist economic policy that many around the League, the United States, and international society generally were endeavoring to build.[118]

The distaste was not confined to the right. Tinbergen's book drew the attention and criticism of Keynes. He and his acolytes, rather like members of the Geneva school, nursed suspicions of economic theories that put too great an emphasis on intense statistical analysis. He cheekily sketched how Tinbergen's reaction to their disapproval might be to "engage ten computors [*sic*] and drown his sorrows in arithmetic." He did pay Tinbergen and his research a backhanded compliment: "It is a strange reflection that this book looks likely, as far as 1939 is concerned, to be the principal activity and *raison d'être* of the League of Nations."[119]

Keynes's puckish view was not far from the mark. By the end of the decade, economic research and analysis sustained much faith in and support for the League. This posture echoed in policy. In 1937, there were hopes that a regime of "Peaceful Change" would allow a broad condominium built around economic reforms to appease revisionist states while jumpstarting a liberal international economy. Leo Pasvolsky suggested to Assistant Secretary of State Sumner Welles that the economic organs of the League presented a viable means to assist in implementing such plans, particularly if the organization was to be reformed. Pasvolsky was a Brookings Institution and Geneva veteran who attended League Economic Committee meetings as a US representative in 1936. His influence on economic and organizational issues would only grow in the coming years, as he had the ears of key people in Washington. In this manner, the tendrils of international society—of both personal contacts and the realm of policy—reached into basic discussions in the United States. Pasvolsky's experience also demonstrates that the assumption that international institutions were a necessary part of global economic relations was well established before the war, and that the League provided a basic (if imperfect) proof of concept.[120]

Regardless, the information generated by the League had (and continues to have) a bearing on discussions of world economics and, critically, its periodic breakdowns. One measure of the importance of this information is that it continues to be used in current debates over the cause and course of the Depression, often for the same reasons it was generated, namely to diagnose causes and prescribe solutions. Not only is it enmeshed in scholarly literature; a set of twenty-first-century commentators still uses it to tease out the lessons of the Great Depression.[121] The value of the sources the League and its collaborators could generate became all the more important as the organization's political profile retreated as the world scene darkened in the second half of the 1930s.

THE THING LIVES

Flexner returned to a staggered League in 1938. It was one stop in a longer trip across Europe by the head of a now operational IAS. Flexner's visit was, in part, prompted by Riefler. A superbly credentialed and influential New Dealer, Riefler epitomizes US links to international society. As head of the US Central Statistical Board, in the first months of FDR's administration he had been one of the first recruits for the president's "brain trust." After much speculation in the press, Riefler turned out to be the administration's mysterious "interpreting economist." He made this into an influential position during FDR's dramatic first term. In 1934, Riefler proposed a program of federally backed mortgages.[122] It was a plan that would eventually produce the Federal Housing Authority and the deep and abiding commitment of the US government to the housing sector, with its outsized impacts on economic policy and society at large. This effort earned him the praise of Keynes and an international reputation.[123]

Riefler's prominence (and possibly Washington squabbling) led him away from government and onto the first roster of scholars at the IAS in 1935. Like so many other economists were, he was soon drawn to Geneva. After attending Annecy, he became the US representative to the League's Financial Committee in 1937, reflecting Riefler's view that the Depression was a world event needing international cooperation for solutions. This led to the League's Committee on Depressions, where Riefler, used to circulating in signal circles of government and academia, was impressed by dis-

FIGURE 1.5. *"The ablest young economist." New Dealer Winfield Riefler exemplifies the links fostered between varieties of liberal reform by international society. He would be instrumental to securing the League's Economic and Financial Section asylum at the Institute for Advanced Study, where this photo was taken in 1947.* (Life *magazine via Shutterstock*)

cussions "on as high a level as I have experienced." They revealed that "the fact that the League has lost political influence seems to have thrown it back on the one asset left, namely its ability to serve as an intellectual center. In this case it seems to be reaching the level of a super-university."[124]

Flexner agreed that "the League has recooped [*sic*] its influence in one direction after losing influence in another" by becoming what others called a world university.[125] His own mission during his visit was, in part, to understand how this "super-university" fit into the international regime of economic inquiry linked to the United States and the IAS. His trip centered on the force believed to be at the root of every crisis in the grim 1930s: economics. The tour emphasized the Eurocentrism of liberal international society; nevertheless, it showed how interconnected various aspects of inquiry could be. During the journey and before moving on to Geneva, Flexner met with a set of leading figures in Great Britain, including Albert Beveridge, Henry Clay, Carr Saunders (head of the London School of Economics), and Harold Laski.

Flexner's return rated a personal tour by Sweetser of the League's gleaming new headquarters, the recently completed Palace of Nations. Flexner was shown the imposing multistory library, constructed with Rockefeller funds. The grandeur and scale of a building that remains impressive today inspired the progressive to mull the future. While clear-eyed about its problems, Flexner believed that hope remained for the hobbled institution. He undeniably understated the reality that "it has unquestionably not achieved 100% success in every problem," yet those who dismissed the League were "taking snap-judgment." Seeing the new library cradling a number of researchers, he recalled the abortive Institute for International Research and mused about an expanded center devoted to solving pressing world problems. Such possibilities made him think that the League had simply not had enough time. Many intractable problems were "the problems of life and could not be foreseen." Disasters like that over Abyssinia might have been a success if not for political intrigue. Flexner speculated that the League's costs and failures would look small if, a century hence, war was abolished.[126] That, of course, assumed the League had a century to act.

Flexner was more interested in those who populated the offices in Geneva than in the offices themselves. At the ILO Harold Butler awakened Flexner to how the new concept of the standard of living had global relevance and hinted at what would later be called international development. Butler asked the IAS chief to consider "what is going to happen in the next twenty-five or thirty years. India, China, and Japan are just beginning to realize that people in those countries are miserable and that they have in their own hands the weapons with which to obtain better conditions." Butler saw these "weapons" as mostly economic. He overstated their ability to level the disparities between the nations of Asia and the industrialized hubs of Europe and the United States. Still, in a manner that echoed Condliffe, he foresaw that this structural shift would bring "great adjustments and readjustments" in world economics and world politics. Economics, with its telescope-like ability to see broad trends, would be vital in this changing world.

At the palace, Flexner sought out Loveday for his thoughts on the state of economics and finance. The Englishman drove home how the League had been integrated into the pale of liberal economics, a settlement that included the IAS. Exposing his political theorist within, Loveday explained how ideological shifts of the period were already reflected in the discipline. The sort of economics the IAS was attempting to cultivate (and that he adhered to as well) "exists in only a few countries"—a sentiment shared by Butler. In Italy, Russia, and Germany, economics had been subordinated to what he obliquely described as the "arbitrary political conception" under the regimes in those states. To be sure, he saw economics as something subordinate to politics, but Loveday believed in a liberal state like England the political realm was open and could accommodate economic change. In places like Russia, however, politics—and therefore economics—was "doctrinaire," meaning that neither could be truly "rooted in the spontaneous development of the people." The implication was that only liberal societies could foster effective economic research.[127]

Loveday nevertheless believed economics was a force that necessarily traversed national boundaries, ergo economists had to stay in motion and needed the freedom to do so. Foundational issues could not be illuminated if they were to "stay at home." A serious scholar had to visit the great centers of London, New York, and Paris, and, of course, "must come to Geneva." Broad global movements and problems could be fully grasped only by maintaining a transnational network that was fostered by institutional as well as personal contacts between researchers scattered about the globe who labored on these issues.

Loveday supported Flexner's idea of forming a school of economics and politics, as it acknowledged "the importance of linking economics and politics and history and . . . doing these at a high level."[128] When Loveday later was asked for his views on finance, he declared it a different regime than economics, stating, "As I see it, [finance has] the same relation to economics [as it] has to chemistry." Despite claims to the contrary, "finance is a quantitative science floating in a medium of ideas," meaning that "it requires of those responsible for its direction an understanding of the philosophical environment." A sensitivity to the realities of the day "for the policy adopted by those responsible for finance will largely be determined by the . . . general politico-philosophical opinion and by the current teleological conception of the State" (a message still relevant in the twenty-first century). As much as Loveday's comments are a reminder of his connection to a transatlantic community at work, they also show that he firmly appreciated how putatively "technical" research was deeply enmeshed in and influenced by politics and ideas, something readily apparent in a fiercely ideological age.[129]

Loveday knowingly complemented Riefler, calling the New Dealer "perhaps the ablest young economist in the world." He was impressed by Flexner's idea of bringing groups of younger researchers together for short terms to foster networks. He even expressed a desire to someday come to Princeton. The head of the IAS was swayed by what had turned into the very sort of networking session both men sought to patronize. Joining the club of Americans impressed by the EFS and its chief, Flexner's official report described Loveday as a "man of great ability and large experience . . . and knowledge." Whatever Flexner's visit accomplished, it certainly strengthened links within international society.[130]

BRICKS WITHOUT MORTAR

The appreciation of the League's economic organs as important contributors to the overall understanding of core global issues was not lost on other parts of American society. Internationalist groups had not failed to cultivate the view in the public mind. As part of its broad program of "public education," for example, the FPA instructed the American public on the evolution and importance of international cooperation. It tapped Varian Fry to sketch the evolution of collaborative efforts over time for middle-brow audiences. Fry's view was undeniably determined by the received assumptions about the forces shaping the world. It was the Industrial Revolution and the brand modernity it brought that accelerated and intensified human activity worldwide. This perspective had elicited a response in the form of a raft of international conferences and unions in the nineteenth century to govern the slew of issues that arose in this new world. The ferocity of the Great War only dramatized the need for cooperation, and the FPA (itself a postwar creation) presented the League as a logical progression. It emphasized that the organization's "technical" activities were an extension of what came before, and that through its "coordinating the work of the pre-war international unions and encouraging international cooperation of a non-political sort[,] the League has achieved its most brilliant successes."[131] Even in an ominous 1938: "We can say without hesitation that there has been a steady growth of international cooperation in these fields; that the League has been responsible, directly or indirectly for much of this growth. . . . [Progress] was somewhat more rapid between 1920 and 1930 than it has been since 1930. But it has continued to be an advance, it has not turned into a retreat."[132]

But the FPA's voice acknowledged a truism about the League's place in a liberal ecosystem: "Much of it would have occurred even if the League had never come into being." Fry was not reticent about the League's failures to maintain political order. In this sense, the constructive "bricks" of

technical efforts laid on the transnational terrain of health, communication, and economics lacked the binding "mortar" of security and order.
This led Fry to other possibilities for governance beyond the League, but
his summary of international cooperation reinforced aspects of conventional wisdom. In the three years after its publication, the FPA scattered
nearly 31,865 copies of *Bricks without Mortar* around the country to schools,
clubs, and discussion groups.[133] The FPA's view that the League remained
a hub for the sort of governance indispensable to a functioning modern
world was able to reach into conventional wisdom. At the same, it exposed
the liberal internationalist view that Geneva was a means to an end, not
the end itself.

Still, bricks had a variety of uses. By the end of the 1930s, a decade
marked by upheaval directly linked to persistent economic crisis, the economic capacity of the League was one talent seen as directly relevant to
world affairs. It stood among a set of technical programs and accomplishments, from disease control to refugee work, that had real international
resonance (the work of its Nansen office on refugees earned the 1938 Nobel Prize). By the end of the 1930s, among the League's technical organs,
Loveday's Economic, Financial, and Transit Section (the fruit of a 1938 reorganization of the EFS; for convenience these bodies will continue to be
referred to as the Economic and Financial Section, or EFS) was its most
respected and its largest, outnumbering the rest of the technical staff at the
Geneva headquarters combined.[134]

Increasingly, the economic components of the League had focused on
providing a picture of the great international question of the era, the Depression. Aggregated comparable data became invaluable to actors at the
time seeking to understand what was unfolding around them. Many of
these officials realized they had information that was quantitatively and
qualitatively superior to what had been available just a few years before.
The League's work was only part of a broader international movement to
measure and analyze the trends and forces that set loose on the world stage
and to muster policies to ameliorate them.

However, such constructive materials were increasingly seen less and
less as means to promote an international comity but as a way to buttress
various, and increasingly hostile, ideological encampments. Mechanisms
of international cooperation were being drawn into the stew of militant
nationalism, international strife, implacable ideological hostility, and urgent calls to reform the world economy and, with it, world order.

ABOVE IT ALL

In this tense time, as a symbol of an international order that other forces
were actively working to dismantle, the League endured great slights. It

was increasingly sidelined as new crises crowded the world docket. Negotiations surrounding the Munich crisis and the fate of Czechoslovakia consciously excluded the League.[135]

As the world sat tensely in late 1938, Sweetser sent off one of his regular surveys of events to contacts at the RF. The missive brimmed with spin. Even though the League had formally been sidelined, he celebrated activity in Geneva. Hundreds of delegates "paced anxiously" about the palace, waiting for scraps of information. Turning the fact that the League was "practically completely outside the negotiations" into something positive, Sweetser transformed it into the claim that the League was actually the "most impartial observation post in Europe."[136]

"Above the fray!" was the derisive note jotted in the margin by a Rockefeller staffer. Those who read Sweetser's report tore it apart. In their responses, Rockefeller staff anesthetized an eruption of "Sweetserian philosophy." One derided Sweetser for having the "soul of a Jesuit," which condemned his evangelical scribblings to "ineffective propaganda." Willits, frustrated by obfuscations, scribbled a telling blow: "Was or was not the League established to play a political role and *primarily* to prevent war?"

Still, the believer knew his audience and knew the notes to hit. The second half of Sweetser's memo turned to "constructive work," the most "substantial" aspect of which he (like so many others) thought was in economics and finance. Previewing some ideas and terms that would appear in the war years, he thought the League's diversity of work added up to "a kind of economic General Staff" that was "approaching its vast problem from three angles; the gathering of facts, information and statistics, the coordination of intergovernmental cooperation, and the development of a new international social-economic policy in fields such as nutrition and housing. Nothing comparable has ever before existed in international life; there can be no question but that today it is only at its beginning." He repeated the League assembly's ingratiating praise of Hull, whose commitment to free trade was held up as "one of the most powerful forces on the side of economic sanity in the world today." Supporting that goal were the broad social and humanitarian aspects of the League's activities that had knitted themselves into the fabric of liberal international life.[137]

However slick his presentation, Sweetser could not diffuse the noticeable odor of political decomposition hanging over Geneva. The drubbing his fellow American internationalists gave the PR man is a sign of their realism—for want of a better word. Stereotyped interwar utopians they were not. While supportive of the League in principle, they were quite aware of its political limits and failures.

And yet even as they shredded aspects of his memorandum, the same RF staff continued to generously support the technical services Sweetser had been careful to laud. Their comments demonstrated that they no longer looked to the League as a political body, but they did support it as a source of usable information to serve political ends. Its data, surveillance, and analysis could be put to use by those working to secure a liberal world because they were already indispensable to other national and international endeavors to come to grips with instability. On this point there was patience with Sweetser, as this was an area in which Rockefeller and others in international society shared his views.

The continued focus on the League's economic section was the product of this confluence of interests. It lay behind a campaign to insert the League's new technical posture more directly into the political and social discourse of leading actors, especially the United States. There was already a major cultural initiative under way to court a bigger slice of American public opinion. This move reflected the distinct need to do more than preach to the converted activists in nongovernmental groups or work with politically reticent officials and diplomats. New media had to be explored and exploited to make the case and convince those who had kept their distance from the League that the sort of endeavors it supported played a decisive part in supporting liberal internationalism. They might not guarantee peace, but they could protect an endangered liberal international society.

This sense of mission is the reason there was great eagerness when an invitation arrived in Geneva. It was a call to participate in one of the rash of international expositions dotting the period. Despite the fact that the international organization had studiously avoided other such events, the League quickly assented. This new opportunity would allow it to make a case for its relevance, even importance, in a graying world scene. The aim was not so much to highlight the League's ability to foster collective security but rather to affirm that it could still contribute to international order through its technical activities. Because American advocates had participated and invested in these projects through international society, they fully comprehended their scope and importance.

But the cultural campaign waged by members of international society to redeem the League was only part of the story. It marched in formation with (and helped provide cover for) a surreptitious diplomatic effort to bring the United States government into closer collaboration with the League on those technical subjects that it had long found valuable. The technical regime had expanded to meet a nagging economic crisis, but as world conditions worsened, that plowshare of cooperation was beaten into a sword of confrontation. This led to a remarkable effort to bring down to earth airy ideals of liberal internationalism—itself threatened with the ash heap of history—through a spectacle for the American public on a former landfill in the borough of Queens.

2: PLOWSHARES INTO SWORDS

KNOWLEDGE, WEAPONIZED

*It is not improbable that when, a century hence, the impartial historian
writes the story of these days, he will pass quickly over some of the news
sensations that have filled the world's press and concentrate on the fact
that, behind all the post-war readjustments, the economic upheavals,
and the struggle for power, more was done for creating a philosophy of
permanent international cooperation than in the preceding century.*

ARTHUR SWEETSER, 1938

*The millions of people that will come to the Fair would far rather
see . . . the League . . . than some commercial interest, let alone a
pickle company.*

ARTHUR SWEETSER, 1939

*If an international system is to be restored, it must be an American
dominated system, based on a Pax Americana.*

JOHN BELL CONDLIFFE, 1940

It was work! It was fun!

MARIE RAGONETTI, 1939

WHO'S BURIED IN GRANT'S TOMB?

The 1939 New York World's Fair sprawled across 1,216 acres in the city's
borough of Queens. To see its sights in comfort, visitors could board Grey-
hound trams that shuttled fairgoers around the grounds. All the pro forma
invocations of peace and cooperation repeated at the fair could not hide
the contradictions becoming all too apparent in 1939. Tram riders could
not have missed the Peace Plow that had been installed in front of the

FIGURE 2.1. *Plowshare or sword? The Peace Plow outside the League Pavilion in Queens, New York (Library of Congress)*

League of Nations Pavilion. An Old Testament aphorism given form, the plowshare had literally been beaten from the swords of US Army veterans of the Mexican-American War and the Civil War. Donated to the City of Geneva, it was loaned to the League for the fair. But by the time the plow was positioned in its place of honor, means to achieve harmony were being recast by internationalists into weapons of war.[1]

Perhaps these and other contradictions explained why tour guides often departed from their scripts as they approached the far end of the grounds, which harbored international exhibits. Visitors and staff heard flippant comments: "Here's the League of Nations Building. You've probably heard people say, 'Where have I seen that building before? Oh yes—Grant's Tomb.'" Or, "Here is the League of Nations Building built like Grant's Tomb to commemorate the death of the League." As these biting ad-libs became routine, the commissioner general of the pavilion, the American Benjamin Gerig, complained to the fair's administration. Admitting that such graveyard humor was indeed "jocular," Gerig stiffly protested that "if our building looks like Grant's Tomb . . . it is only fair to point out that it[s] external shape and design was deliberately made to carry a special message." Specifically, he reminded officials that the structure was an attempt to put particular visions of internationalism into physical form. The frustrated Gerig could not bring himself to register a biting protest, instead articulating his displeasure gently in the "interests of good understanding and mutual cooperation."[2]

Like many important elements of the relationship between the League and the United States, the League of Nations Pavilion at the New York International Exhibition has been overlooked, misunderstood, or simply forgotten. Gerig was correct; the building was "deliberately made to carry a special message." Actually, the edifice constructed in Depression-wracked Queens was transmitting multiple messages. It was an articulation of larger, transnational assumptions that were at the heart of a then arrhythmic liberal internationalism. At the same time, it sought to remind the US public that global forces could be knitted together and governed by information gathering and the application of the technical knowledge generated thereby. It offered a concrete representation of technical elements that were indispensable to keep a brand of internationalism alive. The exhibits gave form to abstract narratives of interconnection and interdependence that were seen as a hallmark of modern life, as well as the forces that threatened to disrupt it. In describing these, the League was making a claim to be an instrument for fostering and controlling them. It aimed to show that it had a role in sustaining the sort of liberal global governance that the United States was increasingly asserting its power to protect.

CARRYING MESSAGES

That the League chose New York to take its first and only stand at an international exhibition is revealing. Beyond telling a story of the League's importance to an internationalist agenda, the pavilion also fit, formally and informally, into a larger campaign that held out its propagation of globally relevant information in an appeal to the United States.

What was on display in Queens was literally and figuratively bound up in broader trends of world affairs. Recovering the schemes behind the pavilion's conception and construction provides insight into how liberal internationalism, itself built through international inputs, could be made comprehensible to the American public. The pavilion was a crucial element of a broader strategy to reform the League to emphasize its technical attributes and justify its continued existence as a member of the international community. Equally important, it was a physical representation of some otherwise abstract ideas about the global interconnections that drove liberal international society. The pavilion was an advertisement that an ailing League, if treated with the right therapy, could continue to provide resources critical to sustaining and defending an equally infirm liberal internationalism.

The League Pavilion was constructed to make the sometimes abstract and diffuse cause of liberal internationalism tangible, even tactile, to a broad and specifically American audience. Here it held yet another message. It was not merely informational; it was a transparent piece of public diplomacy attached to a deliberately opaque backroom campaign to tie the United States more tightly to the League. It was a crucial part of an agenda pushed by officials in Geneva and a set of supporters who sought to enlist the United States directly in the League's technical work. It also showed the interlinked nature of internationalist activism. This was not something done solely by foreign agents to appeal to the United States. The program depended on the patient assistance and commitment of US citizens, organizations, and officials. This interest grew as Americans realized that mechanisms to measure and understand things like the global economy might be recast as the means to do battle with competing regimes.

Throughout, the League was transforming itself to tackle new issues and problems. There was an embrace of new activities and concepts, such as the standard of living, that offered means to tackle the instability brought by the Great Depression. These issues would eventually be thrown at concerns about what kind of world would follow when the conflict went from looming to reality. Woven into this was an attempt to restructure the League, a campaign that would accomplish little for the institution but, ironically, would structure its successor. Collectively, these efforts codified the view that liberal internationalism required various sinews to hold it together, and one of them was information. Americans agreed. They were willing participants in this campaign, because they saw League not as an end in itself but as a means to an end. Increasingly, that end was conflict.

THE DUSTBIN OF QUEENS

For decades the League Pavilion was consigned to the rubbish heap of history. Historians have only recently recycled it.[3] Then again, many exhibits built on a fairground carved from the smoldering garbage dump immortalized in *The Great Gatsby* have drifted from memory. The League constructed a modest pavilion that competed with a carnival of high-tech exhibits. These included Norman Bel Geddes's Futurama, designed for General Motors, a vision that still dominates the memory of the fair. There was a forest of imposing national and imperial, as well as corporate, pavilions offering hints of a life brightened by technology through flashes of the home of the future, robots, and television. In its buildings and programs the fair made physical the power of industrial modernity to transform human life. Those who saw the fair in their own present were offered a vision of a better tomorrow, which is now yesterday.

The lean League Pavilion snugly fit the fair's stated theme: "Building the World of Tomorrow." While the idea of "tomorrow" has crowned its memory, one dominated by stock images of futuristic structures like the Trylon and Perisphere, the fair was not and could not simply be about a world to come. There were strong references to the past. A stated purpose of the fair was to celebrate the 150th anniversary of the inauguration of George Washington, but it also became a means to laud the democratic process. While honoring the past, this point of emphasis helped draw distinctions between an idealized history and the modern present that so enamored the fair's organizers.

With attention focused on worlds gone by or worlds to make, it can be easy to forget that the fair was firmly rooted in what was represented as a high-tech present. As much as possibilities to come, the fair sought to offer visitors an education regarding a basic liberal internationalist refrain. From the start, boosters promised that it would demonstrate the "complicated interdependence in which we are all involved today." The planet of the present predominated, with its plethora of potentials, perils, and prejudices. Obscured by the glitz of the fair's own advertising and the gloss of memory, the exhibitions focused on actually "building" that world of the future, suggesting that there was work to be done in the present. This future orientation also explains the fair's constant invocations of interconnection and interdependence. A high-tech present, let alone future, was not possible without inputs from around the world.[4]

That present was a deeply ideological time, and the fair reflected it. The World's Fair was another canvas on which various shades of internationalism, liberal and otherwise, were splashed. American newsreels were keen to let the public know the fairground was a propaganda battleground.[5] The Soviet Union built its own pavilion, as did Italy, each extolling the accomplishments of its respective ideology. Nazi Germany's withdrawal from the exposition, lest its presence create a focal point for American protests (the official excuse was a measurable economic indicator: shortage of foreign exchange), reflected the increasingly chilly international atmosphere.

However, the majority of the American and international exhibits shared reflexive liberal tropes of the time: technology was shrinking the globe and compelling interdependent relationships between peoples around the world. They also explained that the growing connection between peoples and places was something that would forge the future.[6]

Although it holds a singular place in the American imagination, the New York World's Fair was just one in a long procession of world exhibitions stretching back into the nineteenth century. Many of the themes found in Queens were staples of that genre. Largely Western in orientation and location, the fairs universally shared a faith in science and technology and the progress they were assumed to bring. At the same time, tension and conflict were also apparent. While claiming to nurture international harmony, exhibitions played to nationalistic feelings. For many of the hosts, an international exhibition became a site to highlight a staple of liberal internationalism built on exclusion and racism: empire.

New York kept well within the conventions even as it reflected its times. Nevertheless, the content of fairs did change over the years, and the 1939 exposition reflected this. The Depression made theatrical optimism about progress a harder sell. It also saw a shift in the portrayal of colonies and colonial peoples. The cause of empire was comparatively muted in comparison to previous fairs, although it was undoubtedly present. The scale of bawdy attractions in Queens was part of a pronounced turn toward cheap amusements and the bottom line seen at US fairs of the decade.[7]

Further exposing the New York fair's politics is the catchy nickname that public relations wizard Edward Bernays affixed to the provisional metropolis: "Democracity." Despite the other views visible on the grounds, the dominant message was that the liberal capitalist order remained the best means to organize modern life and achieve a brighter future. The life-sized but not-to-scale diorama of an interconnected world staged by the fair was a sympathetic forum for the League, and here the League provides a point of entry into this larger discourse. The pavilion built in Queens was a plea that the League remain a franchised member of this larger liberal realm— a domain the United States was increasingly seeing as its job to maintain.

Rooms in the League's pavilion sought to endow abstract notions of liberal internationalism with physical form. The exhibits emphasized the technologies—not just mechanical but also social and analytical—that allowed the complicated modern world to be understood, scrutinized, and governed. The League could put forward images of its own work as part of a montage glorifying liberal interdependence. For the embattled organization, it was a chance to make a plea for relevance by dramatizing the activities it sponsored, which made a complicated globe legible to observers and, most important, were valuable to its operation. Following the crowds inside that pavilion reveals aspects of how the culture of liberal internationalism could be expressed. It physically represented how the League attempted to show that it fostered the interdependence that so many internationalists took as fundamental to their creed. At the same time it was a sign that culture, in the form of popular appeal, was not something separate or opposed to other sectors of international affairs but an instrumental part of a larger ideological, diplomatic, and institutional campaign.

On the ground in Queens, the mechanisms of the technical services could be portrayed as gears for dynamic and expansive interaction, moving things toward the glimmering world to come. In an attempt to court the United States and its public, the League employed a lingua franca to interpret global processes. As a summary of important parts of a liberal internationalism that was under threat, it served as a reminder of those things that had given and continued to give the wheezing League relevance in a crisis-wracked present. Tailored to an American mass audience, the pavilion served to remind the crowds that the technical work the League continued to perform was emblematic of the liberal world the public should value and might just want to protect in a world quickly sliding toward war.

More than just a physical expression of vital elements of liberal internationalism, the pavilion was also a component of a larger strategy adopted by the struggling League to draw the United States into greater cooperation. Much effort was spent in courting the US by reframing the League to make cooperation palatable. The attempt linked institutional diplomacy to cultural appeals to publics. While scholars often treat these as sealed and separate spheres, those conducting such efforts in the past did not make such distinctions. A desperate throw on a fairground becomes a snapshot of evolving aspects of liberal internationalism in a world where it faced very real threats.

A SPECIAL MESSAGE

The opportunity at the New York World's Fair unfolded as the League was attempting to scratch out its apolitical, technical path. The diplomatic debacle of the Ethiopia crisis in 1935–1936 and the League's precipitous fall from a position as a presumptive linchpin in the international system forced the institution to emphasize new rationales for its existence and enlist new supporters. Increasingly, it looked to the United States. Justification for this course and even for the continued existence of the League was a live wire in the second half of the 1930s. The League had long made attempts to emphasize its relevance and it still had legions of supporters.[8] But there was a need to preach to those who were not already converted. Like so many other organizations, the League turned to those revolutionary technologies that were seen as remaking time and space and with them human interaction.[9]

Among these "revolutionary" technologies was radio. It was already serving the League through the wireless reports transmitted worldwide by the Health Organization's epidemiological service. Motion pictures were also part of the strategy. Several motion pictures were planned as part of the strategy and some made it to the screen. *The League at Work* (1937) documented how the technical turn had become a justification for existence. It focused on "the Thing," the Secretariat. While the film is a remarkable artifact, it is unlikely that the stiff recitation of its operations by staffers, digressions about frugal institutional budgets, and awkward introductions by Avenol energized great swaths of the international public.[10]

Still, that a campaign to rebrand the League was already under way meant that officials in Geneva were alert to any options for publicity. The established form for courting and informing international publics, the international exhibition, was enlisted as well, particularly as plans for a fair in New York City began to germinate. As early as 1936, Avenol received encouragement from organizers to insert the League into the proceedings in Queens.[11] When the official invitation materialized in June 1937, it was quickly accepted.[12]

International society was well versed in international exhibitions. Many in Geneva had visited the 1937 Paris International Exposition of Art and Technology in Modern Life, which vividly demonstrated how participation in such an event might benefit their cause. Eagerness to join the pageant is all the more telling when it is remembered that the League had not participated in an international exhibition up to that point. This shows the importance of the endeavor and reveals that the presence of the League was not merely some formality. Rather, it was part of an extended courtship of a nation that had formally turned its back on the organization. An exposition was an ideal venue to highlight the League's work. Any pavilion built by the organization would figuratively stand with other component parts of the world system. International interconnections could be dramatized on the ground in the largest city in a nation-state the League was eagerly courting. The fair offered a moment in a longer internationalist procession to try to draw the United States closer, possibly even entice it into a quasi membership, on the basis of technical relations.[13]

Before any of this could happen, a great deal of work had to be done. Things moved remarkably quickly for the League. An initial budget and early plans for New York were ratified by the League Council in January 1938. Still, the League was very much behind the curve, considering that fair authorities wanted construction on all exhibitions to be completed by April 1939.

With time short, the League cast about for architects and designers suited to the task. Fortunately, expositions were a minor international industry, and with the Paris expo winding down, there was a surplus of capacity. Veterans of Paris who had built or managed prominent exhibitions were hurriedly interviewed. Several of the designers assumed that most of the audience would not be bright ("perhaps only 15 percent intellectual type"). They also assumed that the masses would most likely be distracted and rather tired after their journeys to and around the fair. Because of this, emotional appeals, particularly concerning the "welfare of children," would best hold the attention of the general public. Of course, visitors would still have to be enticed with flowers and fountains, as well as personal comforts such as moderate temperatures, nonslip floors, and a limited number of stairs leading up to the League's pavilion.[14]

Not all agreed on these views. The commissioner of the Swiss Pavilion at Paris, a Monsieur Lienert, thought that appeals to the heart alone were not sufficient. Success came from stimulating the visitor's sense of curiosity and desire to learn. At the same time he advocated something that League officials themselves were angling to do: make the fair a site for "good propaganda" for the organization. Lienert felt this should be done without too much concern for the political implications of this advocacy. But Avenol, with his growing focus on a technically astute, apolitical League, inserted himself in the discussion to declare that "only a restricted attitude" regarding "politics could be taken."[15]

Needless to say, Lienert was not offered the job. Instead, the designer of the Vatican's Paris exhibit, Father H. P. Reviers de Mauny—who shared other designers' dim views of a dull public—was given the commission.[16] Initially, League staff thought that the content of the exhibit should concentrate on the political. They envisioned a site that would portray their institution as a culmination of efforts to promote human cooperation and the rule of law. It was the clearest, surest path on the "high road of history." Logically, the League was part of a journey to "world unity and . . . universal peace."[17]

However, this vision did not reflect what high-level officials, specifically Avenol, wanted to emphasize about the League. Perhaps more importantly, it was out of step with how the League itself was perceived and the course its own leaders and supporters thought it should take by the second half of the 1930s.

Revisions were made. The design that emerged in 1938 retained space for political activities but put the greatest weight on the technical work of the League.[18] The final plan produced an exhibit that did not ignore the League's political potential or its claim to be a culmination of human political organization. However, the pavilion this ultimate draft produced was focused on the technical efforts necessary to make great swaths of international society function.

A

FIGURE 2.2. *Grant's Tomb? (a) Grand plans for the League Pavilion in Queens and (b) its more humble reality. (Courtesy of United Nations Archives at Geneva)*

GLOBAL PIVOT

A visitor entering the pavilion was confronted with a larger pewter shield with the biblical invocation "Peace on Earth—Goodwill to Men." The first room kept visitors on that putative "high road" of history, showing an "evo-

B

lution of humanity from the smallest possible group (family) up to the unity and complete understanding of peoples (Federation)." The exhibit did have an expanded historical view that included non-Western mileposts. It evoked Ramses II and Confucius, as well as Dante, the Council of Trent, Benjamin Franklin, the International Postal Union, and the Hague conferences as milestones in the march of governance and order. After this recitation of accomplishments, guests were left with the impression that the birth of the League was the destination to which this high road inexorably led. The reality, of course, was that its political and diplomatic path had been a rutted track.

FIGURE 2.3. *Rooms with a global view. (a) A plan for a central room of the League Pavilion and (b) some of the public it attempted to reach (Courtesy of United Nations Archives at Geneva).*

Accordingly, as visitors were pushed onward, politics was whisked from sight and alternate avenues came into view. Tone and subject matter changed to the putatively apolitical as they moved into the second room. The League's work on international health materialized. "No health without international co-operation," the exhibit decreed. The transnational question of disease and hygiene was presented and the League was of-

B

fered as the answer for collective action necessary to deal with the problems it raised. Programs were highlighted in alcoves to give Americans an impression of the scope of the League's work: its struggle against malaria, its work on "biological standardization," the diagnosis and treatment of syphilis, and its expanding focus on nutrition.

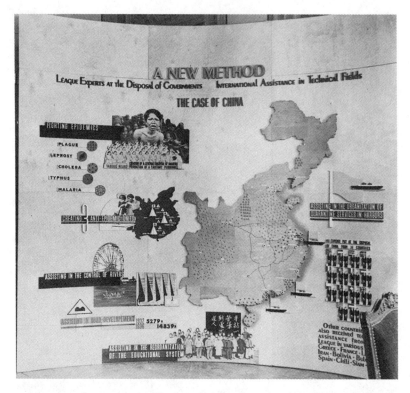

FIGURE 2.4. "A new method." The League's representation of the variety of development assistance offered to Nationalist China (Courtesy of United Nations Archives at Geneva)

Adhering to the advice of exhibition experts, the crowd was served something on children's welfare: how groundbreaking nutrition research was reforming their diets. There was also attention to "collaboration with governments" on these issues, particularly the League's "international assistance in Technical Fields" to Nationalist China. Here the pavilion made legible a regime of economic and social development that the League was helping to sort out.

The technical emphasis continued into the third room, organized around what was termed "human aid" that took as its byword: "No Social Progress Without Solidarity." The exhibits focused on the League's mandates system and on slavery, refugees, work against drugs, its campaign against trafficking in women, and—ringing that crowd-pleasing bell once again—child welfare.

"No Prosperity without Peace" introduced the fourth room. It took as a starting point a liberal internationalist dictum that governed the fair: humanity shared "A Shrinking World." Visually the room conveyed how rapidly new technologies had altered perception of time and space. Crowds could see graphically how it took the liner *Queen Mary* four days to reprise Columbus's seventy-day voyage across the Atlantic, or how Howard Hughes circumnavigated the globe by air in three days and nineteen hours, in comparison to Magellan's three-year voyage by sea. These charts illustrated the liberal refrain posted in the room that as "the world shrinks, human contacts increase, new problems arise. International cooperation is the only solution."[19]

Intensifying interdependence was Janus-faced. After a decade of wrenching economic crisis, this central exhibit reminded viewers of what had become established fact: "In a world growing smaller no nation escapes depression; all share prosperity." It stressed that the League was already a hub that made this necessary global cooperation possible.

Sitting literally at the base of an exhibit that filled an entire wall were the economic organs that so impressed American elites. The Economic Intelligence Service became a literal pivot on which gears of interchange and interdependence could turn. The vital information it "collects, analyses, and disseminates" was illustrated by a blossom of its various publications and serials, which seemed to seed the various charts and maps of world exchange sitting above. The compilation and coordination of economic data and the study of economic problems like the business cycle, double taxation, and the gold standard—as well as the standardization of traffic and communications regulations—were displayed as means to get a handle on complicated issues. The exhibit also noted that the League's Organization for Communication and Transit helped set standards for passports, inland navigation, and road and rail traffic. It had even begun considering the problem of oil pollution in coastal waters. Radio Nations, the League's wireless station, was lauded for its ability to instantaneously communicate with a worldwide audience. The implication was that these existing tools already gave the League a key role in global reform and governance and could aid in a return to prosperity and normalcy.

Designers took care to show that all the elements on display were liberal and in line with mainstream ideas flowing through the United States. Strategically, the designers quoted Cordell Hull. They prominently highlighted his decisively liberal view that "steps should be taken toward promotion of economic security and stability the world over through lowering or removal of barriers to international trade." On the whole, the exhibit made the case that the League was a gear in the machinery moving the economic interdependence on which the liberal world order was premised and hopes for peace and prosperity were pinned.

The fifth room, the "hall of peace and justice," used "No Peace without

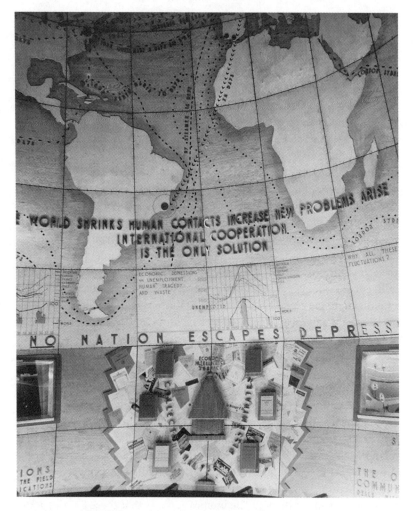

FIGURE 2.5. *Global pivot. The exhibit in the League's Pavilion suggesting how the League's Economic Intelligence Service through its data and analysis formed a base on which global interdependence and international cooperation could turn. (Courtesy of United Nations Archives at Geneva)*

Order" as an organizing theme. It documented moribund efforts to control armaments, which bled into the peaceful settlement of disputes, as demonstrated by the Council of the League, the Permanent Court of International Justice at The Hague, and the Institute of International Cooperation.

As they entered the final room, visitors received a warning that referenced fears all too real in 1939. The public was exposed to "all the catastrophes due to disorder, violence, and misunderstanding." As they continued

FIGURE 2.6. *American Pavilion. The final room of the League Pavilion. Allegorical figures defending the "Tree of Peace" are in the foreground and Roosevelt's quote in the background. (Courtesy of United Nations Archives at Geneva)*

on, they confronted "a dark wall plunged in shadow on which are four frescos representing the scourges of war, famine, epidemics, and exile." These horrors were challenged by the hope that the peoples of the world could form a "constructive union . . . [for] ensuring peace, security, and happiness." Embodying this union were five brightly lit female figures. Representing five continents, their arms were linked in a collaborative, defensive circle around the tree of peace. As visitors passed this allegorical scene and toward the exit, they were offered a quote summing up the room and stating part of the League's case for itself:

Peace must be affirmatively reached for.
It cannot just be wished for.
It cannot just be waited for.

It was an apt sentiment but one not uttered by a League official. The quote had been lifted from one of Franklin Roosevelt's fireside chats.[20] This was yet another in the series of less-than-subtle attempts in the pavilion to tie the League's mission to American traditions, goals, and political rhetoric.[21]

Altogether, the pavilion sketched a world that could choose either to harness the winds or to reap the whirlwind of interdependence. Problems that cropped up within the shrunken and troubled modern world, as it was astutely put, were everyone's. The League's justification for its existence was that international governance had to be at least part of the solution. It sought to assure American visitors that Geneva was not merely theorizing; it was actively seeking the means to solve the world's problems. At the same time the vision of interconnection and understanding put forward was avowedly liberal and connected to the interests of influential constituencies in the United States and beyond.

TO TOP IT ALL OFF

As exhibits were being composed in 1938, officials faced the realities that came with actually constructing a building on the complicated terrain that was the borough of Queens. One impediment was the fair's president, Grover Whalen, who was more showman than administrator. Promises made by the fair administration were quickly and regularly broken, leading to continual trouble, particularly among international exhibitors.[22] The League would be one victim of this gangly management. The first lot promised to the League had to be rescinded, but Whalen substituted a prominent spot on the grounds that had been offered to the H. J. Heinz Company, which had placed a lien on the plot without making a final commitment. Given this inaction, Whalen offered the site to the League. The location would have made the League exhibitions a hub among the American government's displays and larger commercial exhibits, hinting at its relevance to the United States. Another spatial feature seemed to guarantee the public's attention: the site was just across from a planned concession area.[23]

However, once this swap came to the attention of Heinz himself, he exerted ownership. Through Heinz's underlings, fair organizers were told that they could either use the plot for their own purposes or insert another exhibitor deemed "satisfactory" by Heinz. It was clear that the industrialist "definitely" did "not want the League in the plot."[24]

Heinz's dollop of distain and the milquetoast response of the fair's leadership to his demands left a bad taste in Sweetser's mouth. To be sure, much of this was due to the gangly management style of Whalen. Incompetence aside, Heinz's action topped an awkward situation with a spurt of reality: there were sections of American society that found the League unsavory. Sweetser remonstrated that "the millions of people that will come to the Fair would far rather see . . . the League . . . than some commercial interest, let alone a pickle company." But there was no squeezing Heinz for a compromise and there was too much at stake for the League not to attend. In the end, League meekly accepted what it considered an "inferior" spot in a comparatively remote corner of the government area, not far from what is today the Billie Jean King National Tennis Center.[25]

Slights had to be put aside, as there was little time to waste. With the completion of the design and the end of the hubbub concerning the lot, there came the urgency of construction. Here the international ran headlong into the local. All exhibitors faced problems, particularly dramatic cost overruns that seemed to flow naturally from building in New York City. Nevertheless, there were some benefits—from the perspective of an owner—to building in Queens in the late 1930s. Organizers offered their own unintentional exhibit on a subject scribbled all over the fair: interdependence. They unwittingly modeled how the vast transnational forces of the Depression played out on the local level when they reassured the cash-strapped League that building costs would be affordable. Lingering economic lethargy meant local labor could be found cheap. Despite these pressures, unions fought back with work stoppages and strikes that increased costs and slowed construction schedules across the fairgrounds. The League had to pit its inflexible budget against dynamic contingencies and expenses.[26]

However slim, the resources the League allocated show the desperate seriousness of efforts to entice a broad American audience. Paralleling the worsening global situation, the League's had a budget with unrelenting red ink that presented an existential crisis. There were real effects as strained budgets limited programing and austerity peeled staff members away. Resources were scraped together to complete the project. Altogether, 1.2 million Swiss francs were budgeted for the overall effort (approximately $264,000 in 1940, and more than $5.3 million in 2022), with the pavilion and its landscaping costing $135,000 alone.[27]

Although Adrian Pelt, a Dutch citizen, was named commissioner general of the pavilion (an honor that would eventually devolve to Gerig), Sweetser was the prime mover. With his flair for public relations, he was in his element. The reverses of preceding years and a slew of nagging problems had not squelched his belief in the League. He ginned up interest in the project and made sure Americans across key institutions of international society were reminded that the League, or a facsimile thereof, was coming to US shores.[28]

Sweetser was the face of the League at the laying of the pavilion's cornerstone on November 10, 1938. He took pains to note that it was the eve of the twentieth anniversary of the conclusion of the Great War, the impetus for the League's creation. Weaving together a tale that, despite difficult chapters, remained an "inspiring, almost romantic story," he suggested there was still much to be written. Failures were in part attributed to unnamed enemies, "unscrupulous, even grotesque" in their rhetoric. Sweetser did repent for the League's own sins of both "omission and commission," but these did not invalidate its principles and goals. In fact, they made the necessity of commitment stronger.

Although the League's political blotter showed, at best, mixed results, its critical importance was that it expressed international cooperation in ways "undreamed of before its creation." Sweetser fell back on the mantras of internationalism and interdependence to justify its presence at the fair and its continued existence as a body. He explained the League had to be seen as an outgrowth of the very interdependent modern world it could serve. Radio and the airplane—even the older train and steamer—were conspiring to create a world "which make [an] agency like the League absolutely indispensable." Like so many others, he asserted that if an international organization did not exist, one would have to be created to contend with a scrum of globe-straddling questions besetting law, labor, armaments, human trafficking, narcotics, economics, health, and nutrition. He mused, "It is not improbable that when, a century hence, the impartial historian writes the story of these days, he will pass quickly over some of the news sensations that have filled the world's press and concentrate on the fact that, behind all the post-war readjustments, the economic upheavals, and the struggle for power, more was done for creating a philosophy of permanent international cooperation than in the preceding century."

The building was offered as a physical expression of those "concrete measures" that moved humanity toward the necessary cooperation that itself bred peace. But even the optimistic Sweetser had to admit that the League had become a spectator to current events. Only if the great powers stopped driving the world toward a looming "holocaust" and instead took the "road to sanity" would the League have an opportunity to act.[29]

BURN AFTER READING

Sweetser's speech fit within the larger endeavor of positioning the League as an integral mechanism able to rein in the wild forces of the modern world and hence relevant to the United States. He used the fairgrounds to begin to address the interested American public directly. Of course, the pavilion, a mechanism in a campaign of cultural and public diplomacy, was also very much a gear in some traditional diplomatic maneuvering. It would serve as a sort of League embassy to the United States, offering a platform from which to officially and unofficially engage outposts of American international society as well as officialdom that were already hospitable.

Shrewdly, Sweetser used construction as a new excuse to meet with FDR. Like so many others, the president was already on Sweetser's contact list and had received regular dispatches about goings-on in Geneva. FDR had already signaled that he was receptive, encouraging Sweetser to visit when in Washington and write "from time to time" so that he might communicate "thoughts on the situation from the Geneva end."[30]

This became a license for Sweetser to approach the president. In September 1936, after the Ethiopia crisis, the president confided to Sweetser that "we must keep the League alive" but that its existence "should move more into economic and financial matters and that the United States should cooperate fully in all non-political matters." Others were treated to a similar message that happened to closely track a route being marked out in Geneva.[31]

As construction of the pavilion began, Sweetser met with an FDR officially "delighted" that the League was participating in the fair.[32] Their conversations went far beyond the details of exhibits. An April 1938 discussion quickly broached the issue of League reform. Sweetser thought that the need reflected the increasingly "evil disorganization of international life." Sweetser was fishing for a US statement on the importance of the international organization in relation to world affairs, but instead he reeled in a series of dramatic suggestions from FDR. One of the farthest-reaching proposed that the political heart of the League, its council, be cut out. Another was that the League's Assembly focus each year on one particular issue, and another that the League even change its name. But the president's most radical proposal was a "top to bottom" change: removing all political questions from consideration.

Sweetser balked, objecting to the striking of all the League's mediating and conciliatory responsibilities. For all his talk of things technical, he still thought the nations of the world needed a "quick, automatic meeting place where they can bring their disputes, if only for ventilation." Unsettled by the president's dramatic proposals, Sweetser speculated whether

they were "deep convictions." However, he knew FDR had long appreciated the League's technical value. Only now, like others, the president was
suggesting the political be downplayed, even smothered, while the technical was highlighted. Sweetser was so worried about the implications that
when he wrote a summary of the meeting for the White House he made
the extraordinary request that the letter not go through normal channels.
Once FDR had a chance to read it, Sweetser requested the document be
destroyed. There were undoubtedly reasons to be concerned. The leader
of the major power on which the League had pinned many of its hopes
wanted it fundamentally rebuilt. Of course a copy was kept, and Sweetser
conveyed FDR's thoughts to Geneva.[33]

For all Sweetser's worry that memos needed to be burned (literally,
if not figuratively), the president's riff echoed earlier views. More to the
point, FDR's suggestions were an opportunity that mirrored some aspects
of the League's own agenda. Sweetser's meeting with Roosevelt was one
moment in the larger dialogue about deepening the US government's engagement with the League via technical cooperation. Removing the veneer
of formal politics hardly diverged from the direction in which the Avenol
regime was already moving. The United States had a stake in League services as means to support and increasingly defend liberal order.

DARK MIRROR

This interest in the League was shared outside the White House. Sectors
of US officialdom appreciated the fact and cast the League in new roles.
One voice was Howard Bucknell Jr., the chief of the US legation in Bern,
which served as a locus for much interaction with the Geneva organizations. Bucknell composed a memo in late August 1938 gauging the health
of the international body lying in Geneva. In important regards it was a
recitation of a pitiable situation. Not only had the institution's reputation
slumped; faith in collective security had also "been greatly diminished if
not abandoned." The organization that was once hoped to embody that
approach had become a liability. The American asserted that attempts to
actually kick the "political machinery" of the League into action "would
mean either its complete disintegration or war." Any hint of controversy
might lead those European states still clinging to the institution to abandon
it. Its warped position in international affairs made it "a mirror in which
European politics are reflected."

Regardless, Bucknell did see a use for the League in a tense time. Worth-
less as an implement of peace, it was "potentially an effective instrument
for carrying on a war." To be sure, much of this potential lay in the realm of
perception and propaganda. If the League retained anything it was "moral

influence"; the body might still denounce aggressors to a world public, and the ideas behind it could support a coalition by legitimating its cause as that of "law and order." International (for Bucknell that meant intra-European) tensions made collaboration difficult, restricting its scope. Nevertheless, Loveday's vaunted EFS could continue its statistical and technical studies of financial and economic questions and help "states solve their specific problems." But more than that, any war that did break out would be on a "totalitarian basis," meaning for the participants "that the whole state would be mobilized in the common effort." Here the trained "political and technical machinery of the League would be of considerable value in facilitating the coordination of the states fighting on the side of the League." While war ironically offered the relevance so long sought, there was a serious catch. If the League were to be seen to be taking sides, it might well cause the eviction of the Secretariat from Geneva.[34]

Bucknell's commentary had a different tone from much of what had come before. International organization, the primary example of which was the League, remained instrumental in international politics and could serve the ends of various actors. The memo also shows that the question of whether the League or key parts of it would need to relocate was being discussed officially as well as unofficially at an early stage. It was a sign that Americans increasingly saw the League as less than the sum of its parts, yet something to serve their particular interests in a divided world. Unstated was that it might be made to serve the ends of others.

How completely Washington absorbed Bucknell's missive is unclear, but elements of its message were already appreciated. Just a few weeks after Bucknell's memo, the League's Assembly adopted a resolution that the Americans found appropriately appealing. Falling into line with the campaign to recast the institution as a service provider, it stated that since its foundation, "a series of technical and non-political activities have been established of which the scope is in some cases worldwide." This work had always included the possibility of collaboration by "non-member States." Because it was a "universal interest" that such cooperation be extended, the Assembly welcomed any "comment or suggestion for the wider development of such technical and non-political collaboration which non-member States may care to make."[35]

The resolution was a plea to retain and to recruit. Skittish member states concerned that work on technical matters might eventually drag them into some sort of potentially inflammatory political situation would be reassured that a preventive firewall was in place. At the same time, it was an opening to a number of North and South American states to join (or rejoin) the institution. For US officials looking to draw on and contribute to the expertise of the organization, the prospect was clear. You could officially work *with* the League yet not be *in* the League, at least not in a standard political sense.

Of course, the whole exchange revealed a truth about what was referred to as technical work. It *was* political—not only in the sense of the perception or the import of a particular program but also in light of the existence of particular strains of research and activism in support of particular regimes and causes.

Regardless, the effort succeeded in part because the US government was waiting for just this sort of opening. On February 2, 1939, Hull commented, responding to Geneva's entreaties with a statement that captured why many Americans saw the League as relevant to international society:

> The growing complexity of the modern world has for many years made increasingly clear the need for intelligent co-ordination of various activities and the pooling of information and experience in many fields. The International Postal Union, the International Institute of Agriculture, the International Office of Public Health, and other international organizations were created to meet this need in specific fields before the creation of the League and continue to carry out their tasks. The League, however, has been responsible for the development of mutual exchange and discussion of ideas and methods to a greater extent and in more fields of humanitarian and scientific endeavor than any other organization in history. The United States Government is keenly aware of the value of this type of general interchange and desires to see it extended.
>
> Encouraging as has been the progress already made, much remains to be done for the promotion of human welfare in health, social, economic, and financial fields. This Government regards each sound step forward in these fields as a step toward the establishment of that national and international order which it believes is essential to real peace. The United States Government looks forward to the development and expansion of the League's machinery for dealing with the problems in those fields and to the participation in active efforts to solve them. It would not be appropriate for it to make specific suggestions for the development of the League's activities, but it will follow with interest the League's efforts to meet more adequately problems relating to the health, humanitarian, and economic phases of human activities. It will continue to collaborate in those activities and will consider in sympathetic spirit means of making its collaboration more effective.[36]

It was a memorandum designed for public consumption. When it hit the international press, the *Times* of London noted that its "warm and appreciative tone" was "greatly appreciated" in Geneva.[37]

Though staid, Hull's memo was to become a remarkably influential document, backstopping much US-League engagement. The statement would be clutched tightly and referenced repeatedly by League supporters over the coming years. It defined American interest as firmly rooted not in politics but in technical services in the service of global interconnection. To the hopeful, it more than suggested that interest might be expanded into some sort of involvement, even membership. It made a renovation of the League's technical arms, and by extension the League itself, into a priority. This official interest hinted that the technical services had already established the strategic bona fides for the sorts of ends Bucknell articulated. They could begin serving those preparing for global conflict. This helps explain official US government interest in maintaining at least part of the League's formal activities as world conditions worsened. This interest reflected a continued demand for the sorts of governance of the liberal international order that those services had grown out of and sustained—only now they might be turned to defend that order.

COLD WARS

Hull's memorandum on the League's technical services appeared during the final flurry of activity surrounding the opening of the fair. This hubbub allowed a series of League officials to circulate around Washington in early 1939. Disguised as commissioner general of the pavilion as well as representative to the Congress of the International Association of Recognized Automobile Clubs, Adrian Pelt arrived just after the fair opened that spring. Using this cover, he met with Hull and Llewellyn Thompson, formerly US consul in Geneva at the State Department. Both Americans thought the League had been "very well advised to accept" the invitation to the fair and were particularly pleased that its outpost "laid stress on non-political activities of which the American public is generally unaware." They assured Pelt that they served the League by encouraging other states, particularly smaller European ones, to support it as they could, stressing the importance "which the United States Government attaches to the continuation of the League in these difficult times." Thompson, careful to label his comment as personal, was encouraged by the renovation committee stirring around Stanley Bruce, which he saw as a direct reply to Hull's February note.

Thompson hinted at the complications for American participation, suggesting that any reforms be tailored in a way that defanged criticism from Congress or the press that the United States was being dragged in by "a back door." Indeed, he felt it desirable that "proposals must preferably be formulated in such a way as to exclude refusal by Congress." They even discussed appointing an American to Bruce's committee. Hull generally agreed with Thompson's "personal" points—which were then passed along to those individuals reforming the League.[38]

Pelt's meeting reflected the contacts that had grown between the United States and the League on an official plane, running through the pavilion to the larger question of technical cooperation. As part of this campaign, Avenol put himself in closer contact with the US government. There was regular communication, in person or through intermediaries at the US legation in Bern. These conversations were premised on the idea that the secretary-general would visit the United States in spring 1939 to attend the opening of the pavilion along with meetings with high-level American officials, including FDR and Hull.[39]

Staff at the League and the ILO spent an increasing amount of time discussing what their work meant in a world riven by ideological conflict. This led to the question of where their institutions would have to situate themselves figuratively and—frighteningly—literally if the battle of ideas became an open clash of arms. Avenol was keenly aware of this himself. He was attuned to worries that the presence of the League in Switzerland could serve as a pretext for violating that country's neutrality—another sign of how the League was implicated in a liberal order that fascist states sought to raze. In fact, Avenol told the Americans in early 1939 that he thought events showed "the ordinary principles of order and international law were suspended." World affairs were in a state of "demi-guerre."[40]

The secretary-general was not alone in feeling that the temper and temperature of international affairs had changed. During a visit to Great Britain during the "Phony War" in March 1940, Sweetser felt the last breeze of this ideological chill before the whirlwind. Rather than a conflict of peoples, the Western confrontation with Germany was part of an ongoing "cold war against a regime and method."[41] But this pre–Cold War cold war, according to Avenol, put political activity out of bounds for the League. With what he and numerous others termed "totalitarian" states arrayed against the democracies, he feared that attempts to make the League into a political site "might be taken by the totalitarian states as a despairing effort to belabor the dead body of the League into a further instrument of encirclement."[42]

Avenol did think the "dead body" still had some functioning organs. He reaffirmed its technical activities. There was praise for Hull's memo as well as some of Roosevelt's relevant statements. With the threat of war a chronic condition by spring 1939, in strictest confidence, Avenol broached the question of relocating the League if its haven in Switzerland were to be threatened. A momentous decision to move the organization would be contingent on circumstances, but he was careful to dangle the fate of the venerated EFS in front of the Americans. Avenol thought it "impossible for this section of the League to operate under war conditions" in Europe.

FIGURE 2.7. *Showing the flag. Sweetser, left, raises the "hastily improvised" League flag for the first time on US soil at the opening of the League Pavilion, April 30, 1939. (Library of Congress)*

With few other locations seriously considered, he mused that it might find a home "somewhere on the American continent."[43]

THE FAR PAVILION

In April 1939 Avenol, worried about the international situation, canceled his trip to the United States, even if his presence in Europe made little difference. It was probably for the best that the League Pavilion opened without the equivocating Frenchman on May 2, 1939. The speech he had planned to give was a pessimistic document by a pessimist. Nevertheless, he stuck to an established script, arguing that the "League's technical work . . . [was] inseparable from general peace effort," and he sought to include it in the liberal line of battle as an "outpost of democracy."⁴⁴

Without Avenol, the opening day was hopeful, even if not uniformly optimistic. It fell to Adrian Pelt to address the crowd on a day when Sweetser raised the "hastily improvised" League flag for the first time in the United States.⁴⁵ He read Avenol's speech and gave an address of his own that also toed the line that Sweetser had drawn earlier. Pelt acknowledged the League was "in an intense crisis" and "paralyzed" in its "fundamental task of maintaining peace." However, while failures marked the past, the future might be shown by the technical organizations, which could provide collaborative solutions for common problems. The pavilion was an attempt to set forth "clear and striking" examples of key issues where the League remained the international center of work, "for the promotion of human welfare and in the economic and financial fields." Sentiments were clearly keyed to American attitudes and opinions; Pelt quoted Hull's memorandum twice as part of a larger plea to notice "the growing activities which we hope the American people will appreciate."⁴⁶

Pessimism among League officials in spring 1939 is unremarkable. What *is* remarkable is that the US officials who came to salute the League's first official outpost on US soil were distinctly upbeat. It demonstrates how they, along with like-minded colleagues in the academic and philanthropic worlds, understood the role of the League in an integrated globe.

Although FDR and Hull chose not to attend, a hefty chunk of the president's cabinet did participate in the ceremonies. The most substantial voice was that of the high-profile and sometimes controversial Henry Wallace (followed by Secretary of Labor Charles McLaughlin and Surgeon General Thomas Parran). The presence of these officials emphasized that it was the League's technical efforts that gave it value in American eyes. All chanted the internationalist mantras that an interdependent, modern world required institutional machinery to bridle the dangerous forces industrial modernity had unleashed.

On the third day of the fair, with Woodrow Wilson's widow at his side, Wallace delivered a speech at the opening of the pavilion that became front-page news.⁴⁷ Wallace took up the challenge to portray the League in a positive, utilitarian light. This was no surprise. Wallace was an internationalist of deep conviction. His views were fodder for international society, a market the WPF and FPA actively cultivated, by publishing and publicizing his thinking. Wallace was clear where he stood: "My own bias is international. It is an inborn attitude with me."⁴⁸ This perspective was tied

FIGURE 2.8. *Inborn internationalism. Edith Wilson and Henry Wallace at the opening of the League Pavilion, 1939. (Library of Congress)*

to long-held views of the power of information. Like many progressives, he looked to data as a lever to move reform. A refrain in his career was that as better information on issues became available, better solutions could be found and then administered over time. His 1920 book *Agricultural Prices* was an early and influential econometric study of the farm sector and substantiates his later assertion that in statistics lay truth.[49]

As he spoke, from his vantage point in the forum of nations in Queens,

Wallace could see an international order in crisis. In the secretary of agriculture's estimation, the League conformed to many assumptions and ambitions dear to American internationalists. Like Pelt, Wallace acknowledged that the League had failed to maintain order but replayed the argument still heard today that the international community at large was culpable. Yet at the core of this disorder lay a poor understanding of the world economy. It made it hard for the League's nations to be "good neighbors" as they put "temporary national expediency" over the "long-run international welfare." The failure of democracy brought a concomitant rise in dictatorship. The transformation of the world from "a neighborhood . . . [to] an armed camp" bred cynicism toward the "vision" of peace and cooperation for which the League stood.

The backdrop to this crisis of world order was longer global and historical trends. Wallace repeated the liberal refrain sung at the fair—and illustrated by the pavilion's exhibits—that "science and invention have made the earth a very small place." Because of this, the United States had to admit, "We are closely associated with the whole world, whether we know it or not and whether we like it or not." A high standard of living in the US and worldwide was dependent on extensive international trade. New technologies, particularly the airplane and radio, could bring benefits or dangers to every corner of the world. These realities could not be denied, and the League, through its technical activities—Wallace said little of its diplomatic efforts—aided the "struggle of mankind toward a finer civilization." Hailing the League as a reflection of a desire to "create a world community, composed of free nations and free individuals living in peace and order," might seem trite. However, in the spring of 1939 this was an anxiously political statement and an assurance to Americans that there was an asset abroad to help them preserve a liberal order under threat.[50]

Wallace and his compatriots reflected a particular segment of American officialdom. Specifically, he was a left-wing New Dealer and a darling to those who adhered to its promise. Wallace actively leaned on the League's existing technical work to support his own visions for agricultural reform, a better quality of life for the common man, and renewed international trade. It is no surprise that he had a portfolio of contacts with internationalists at home and abroad who were themselves enmeshed in the variety of questions illuminated by the League's work on multiple technical issues.

Wallace's enthusiasm is a reminder that the New Deal, as a reform effort, was transnational in its orientation.[51] Many Americans saw fulfillment of the League's ideals not simply as part of a dream of collective security stitched into fantasies of international cooperation but also in operational and reformist terms. They understood technical capacities within the organization as vitally necessary to govern modernity and realize its potential. Technical achievements assisted with governing the modern world, particularly one beset with chronic problems. It is a sign that the technical services of the League, which over the course of the Depression had increasingly become identified with a growing discourse on social welfare and a desire for raised standards of living, were tied into a larger transnational community of reform. That Wallace understood this posture demonstrates how American reformers linked their own agenda to those of the League and hoped that international work could benefit the New Deal agenda at home.

AN AMERICAN PAVILION

Right after the opening, Sweetser wrote Avenol about the festivities. He also assured the secretary-general that finances were holding together largely because a "good deal of essential work has been carried by our American friends."[52] If it was Americans who extolled the pavilion when it opened, it was also Americans who played a decisive role in keeping it in operation. Mirroring the increasing pull of the United States in the liberal sphere, the pavilion's operations became increasingly dependent on American interest and largesse. American institutions aided in disseminating League messages, Americans helped staff important operations, and critical funds came through US sources. The Carnegie Corporation of New York, the CEIP, and the WPF paid for the flyers and brochures distributed at the building.[53] Much of the outpost's staff was American. The college students who constituted much of its garrison were recruited by the US League of Nations Association in conjunction with the American Committee in Geneva. They came from around the country and from institutions as varied as Harvard University and St. Mary's Junior College to staff exhibits, guide tours, and provide a dose of enthusiasm. As one guide, Marie Ragonetti, recalled, "It was work! It was fun!"[54]

For all the difficulties and concerns, once the exhibits opened there was an unquestionable payoff. From May to October 1939 the "electronic eye" at the building's entrance registered 1,013,203 visitors (shortcomings of the "eye" meant the tally might have been higher).[55] This number pales before the eight-figure ones that other more dramatic or salacious venues attracted. Still, it was no small accomplishment. Ragonetti was proud of how she and her compatriots handled the large crowds, but she admitted, "Naturally cranks also came." One visitor authoritatively took issue with the Peace Plow, informing staff, "[That] ain't no plow, that's a cultivator." Another, perhaps sensing the pavilion's quasi-embassy role, attempted to apply for a Nansen passport. A gentleman particularly interested in the second room, when "button-holed" by staff, turned out to be

Dr. Ludwick Rajchman, former chief of the League's Health Organization who had been stripped of that job by Avenol (and who would later help found UNICEF).

Guides thought the exhibits "were frank and honest" about the short-comings of the "failures" of political efforts while the "successes of the non-political work were recorded." This candor had a positive effect, as "the majority who came to scoff, remained to praise." The League's failures were general knowledge among the public, but guides claimed to hear comments along the lines of: "I thought the League was only a political body. I never knew that it did such important health and social work! Why do the newspapers always play up its failures? Doesn't the technical work have any news value?" That Ragonetti and others highlighted reactions to the technical side suggests how the staff itself was primed. But the pavilion's design and message indeed had its intended effect on visitors: it graphically demonstrated that the League remained relevant to the sort of liberal international society the United States sought to maintain.[56]

A limitation faced by the pavilion was the fair itself. The outsized space it holds in American memory perhaps reflects the massive advertising campaign, media coverage, and New York mystique more than actual public interest. It never truly enthralled the American public. Attendance failed to meet promoters' promises. FDR even confided to Bruce that he was more interested in the fair's competitor, the San Francisco Golden Gate International Exposition.[57] Regardless, the New York World's Fair heaved itself into a second season in 1940 in a fruitless attempt to make a profit.

Another season was both an opportunity and a curse. It allowed the League to continue to proclaim its relevance, or just remind the public that it still existed, as the Western Allies and Germany glowered at each other in the Phony War and the Soviet Union attacked Finland in the grimly serious Winter War. For an organization whose brittle budgetary situation had worsened with the start of the European conflict, further expenses were not pleasant to contemplate. With costs estimated at $20,000, there was legitimate concern that the League's already-stretched budget did not have the slack to maintain its outpost in Queens. As the spring reopening approached, there was a significant backlog of maintenance. Some tasks were standard brick-and-mortar issues. Others were more substantive, including updates to the exhibits. Even the list of members of the League had to be renovated. Numerous states had left or, in the unique case of the Soviet Union following its aggression against Finland, had been expelled. But with the League budget in tatters, there was "no money" for such changes.[58]

Therefore the operation, and even continued existence, of the pavilion depended on US attention. The "American Group" of boosters came up with significant funds to prop the pavilion's doors open. The final deal they struck, in fact, left the Americans with "the financial responsibility for operating the pavilion [and] all pecuniary liability connected therewith." The League did agree to pay the group $10,000 and cover the fire insurance premium. While the League was still formally the owner and custodian of the pavilion, it now fell to the Americans to do of much of the necessary work, including bankrolling repairs and making edits to the League's membership roster.[59] The League's outpost in the United States had become an American pavilion. That it stayed open until the end of the fair was an indicator of the American interest, enthusiasm, and funds supporting the liberal internationalism the League represented.

BATTLING WITHOUT BULLETS

These efforts to continue the campaign to highlight the potential of the technical League in New York ran in conjunction with actions to actually revise the organization to emphasize its role that was taking shape in Geneva and Paris. Political impotence further cultivated the growing ambivalence about the organization. Even members in regions where the League idea had been strongly held were less and less willing to be bound by its decisions. Once enthusiastic Scandinavian states were becoming leery, lest they be dragged into confrontation with "revisionist" states that had no love for the organization.[60]

However, for the United States there remained a shared interest in having the League serve international politics, albeit in a redefined role. Increasingly these tools were being seen less and less as means to promoting an international harmony or collective security and more as serving mutually hostile ideological encampments.

What is interesting is that the Americans increasingly used the Economic Committee (as distinct from the EFS) to speak with clarity on the economic problems threatening the peace. Indeed, by the middle of 1939 a tone was set that would reverberate into the Cold War. The hard line came from Henry Grady, the US representative on the committee. For Grady economics was the fulcrum of international relations. Having given up the call of the Catholic priesthood, Grady embraced another faith, the liberal marketplace. He became a professor of economics at the University of California, Berkeley. He would later join the US government, becoming a member of its Tariff Commission—an important post in the Depression years.

Grady was also a long-standing partisan of the League, although such enthusiasm was not shared in every corner of the State Department. He was a member in good standing of an alumni association of economists and policymakers that had passed through the American colony in Geneva. Not all of these veterans thought alike or shared Grady's affinity for the League, but most accepted broadly drawn liberal principles as crucial points for organizing the international economy.

This was one reason Geneva retained its status as the best platform from which to divine and measure how international economics intersected with the realities of politics and ideology. It was there that Grady gave voice to an American liberal internationalism clearing its throat to confront ideological systems it saw as dangerous. Grady primed the March 30, 1939, meeting of the Economic Committee with statements that were frank and withering. Appeasement, in all its forms, was dead. He "expressed the opinion that recent developments in Europe had made totally useless any consideration of an economic *rapprochement* with the 'totalitarian' states whose trade methods are so inextricably tied up with their political ideas that the result is tantamount to economic warfare" (emphasis original). Although he did not suggest that pressure should be applied to Germany, he was "emphatic" that the League body should consider condemning the use of trade for what he decreed were "aggressive purposes." Grady summed up by stating his own raw ideological view that "he had been unable to find any evidence that the control systems could succeed in the long run." It all led to the daunting conclusion that "two diametrically opposed economic systems could not be maintained in the same world over any extended period."

Other members of the committee were less inclined to be confrontational. As an official record of the meeting noted, Grady's "more forceful" statements "aroused the general interest of the Committee as well as a certain uneasiness." The British representative, Sir Fredrick Leith-Ross, was reluctant to add to the inflammatory rhetoric. This was, of course, reflective of pressing European tensions—something that the uncommitted United States and its tough-talking representative did not have to navigate. In European ministries Grady's commentary was less a call to arms than a statement on a shattered global order whose shards threatened to draw blood.[61]

Still, the American view that the League could be useful in prosecuting an ideological conflict was correct. Its corridors were already echoing with the language of "cold war." Grady was later open about how he saw the League's Economic Committee as a means to contain claims by challengers about the shape of the world economy. He would claim that one of the heralded products of the economic committee, the 1937 raw materials report, undercut a major claim by "revisionist powers" that they were "have-nots" when it came to vital commodities. This assertion of a shortfall, putting them at a putative economic disadvantage, was often served up as justification for their expansionist and colonial ambitions. The raw materials report, however, tut-tutted this point and asserted, quantitatively, that this was not the case. It concluded, on the basis of information collected by the League, that colonial dependencies accounted for only 6 percent of global production. Most raw materials were produced within the boundaries of sovereign states. The implication, for Grady and others, was a liberal one. Those making demands for redress were not merely suspect, they were incorrect. Equity did not require the forging of new empires but rather an improved system of global free trade.[62]

This was not a dialogue that simply reverberated through hallways in Geneva. The "raw materials question" played into larger debates about how a warped global economy was distorting world order. A remarkable amount of commentary was sired by the issue. American economists plugged into the foreign policy establishment were wrestling with the issue as well. Their interventions on the issue targeted both American audiences and the League-sponsored International Studies Conference.[63] By 1939, analysis meant for wide public consumption asserted that growing economic warfare was the defining characteristic of world trade and, by extension, international affairs. The presumption was that a world economy was breaking down into a crowd of actors vying for control of raw materials. This descent into mob action would necessarily lead to violence.[64]

The strident statements by officials like Grady were undoubtedly a product of what he and others were able to divine of the impacts of German trade policy, increasingly seen as emblematic of economic warfare waged by an ideological competitor. Grady's Geneva visit in the summer of 1939 provided a portal into southeastern Europe to gather further data and impressions. This led to a confidential report that measured the dynamics of the trade relationships between the Nazi regime and Greece, Yugoslavia, Bulgaria, Romania, Hungary, Turkey, and Italy.[65] Economic statistics enabled Grady to draw a clear picture of trade policies enhancing Germany's position in the region. Most of these countries exported raw materials to Germany in exchange for ASKI marks. These were kept in country in clearing accounts that were blocked—meaning they could be spent by the holder only on purchases in Germany.

Angled to create dependency on the part of Germany's trade partners, this sort of relationship granted considerable political and diplomatic leverage to Berlin. Aspects of this statistical analysis were leaked to the press to show how Germany's gains were political as well as economic, and were shutting other "free systems" (particularly Great Britain) out of important quadrants of European trade, skewing general economic activity. But the State Department, which had requested the report, was more interested in how German policies could detach states from other regional arrangements and even from the world economy. Understanding such tactics had a strategic import, for there were growing American concerns that the Germans might attempt similar moves in Latin America.[66]

These views, sharpened by transnational analysis and discussions in Geneva, were not fringe. What is more, backed by credible data and analyses, they were easy to convey to general audiences.[67] North Americans were told in 1939 how ideological systems and the economic competition they promoted had left the world economy rent by conflict. They were shown that the ASKI mark was on the march. In Eastern Europe its advances portended a "trade war" in the region between Germany and Great Britain. That ASKI marks might be deployed in trade with Brazil was ominous. The US defense was the liberal Hull trade program, demonstrating that the United States had not "by any means conceded the victory to the totalitarian regimes." But even this assertion framed the international economy as a theater of ideological conflict. Without an "open, international economy" such "battles without bullets" portended a shooting war.[68]

In such a discussion Grady was no outsider, but the appointed representative of the United States government. After his jaunt to Geneva he returned to become an assistant secretary of state for economic affairs and later filled prominent troubleshooting roles in American foreign policy. He later became a first-string player in American diplomacy: the first American ambassador to an independent India, the ambassador to Greece when Marshall Plan and military aid began to flood in, and the ambassador to Iran in the years before the CIA-sponsored coup against Mohammed Mosaddeq. When Grady returned to private life in 1941, he took lessons of economic warfare with him and did not stray too far from state imperatives. As head of American President Lines, he worked in collaboration with the US Maritime Commission to snatch strategic raw materials from Pacific Asia.[69]

For Grady, economic data and analysis of the sort that Geneva excelled at producing was a starting point to understand the scope of a potential threat and, crucially, fit it into an ideological context. Grady would look back on these actions as part of a larger trend in interwar politics toward economic warfare that would become commonplace between ideological encampments. He saw economic containment as part of what he called a "cold war" against Germany and its partners in the late 1930s.[70]

Once again, the League and the sort of aggregation and analysis it was performing made visible something fundamental in peace or war—the world economy. It was not only the information that the League generated but the variety of analyses, which were becoming more and more useful to various actors defending the liberal pale. Debates about raw materials, the standard of living, and the recovery of world trade turned on liberal principles. Basic elements of these discussions were easy to fit into a variety of aims that were directed toward defending a liberal bloc. That they could also be readily adopted by the United States was not merely a sign of their liberal pedigree but that American ideas and actors had been intimately involved in their evolution.

It was these sorts of views that might have kept some hopeful in the difficult months of mid-1939. There were enough signs within US official-dom that some sort of mutually beneficial relationship could be stitched together. At the meeting of the League Council on May 23, 1939, Avenol pulled out Hull's now-dog-eared memorandum. This US interest was used to buttress a call for a committee to study measures to make technical ser-vices more effective. Avenol was frank: the "task is urgent." "Skill" would be necessary to produce a blueprint to "enable the League to escape from the 'impasse' in which it stands." This blueprint needed to be much more than a bureaucratic schematic; it had to be a plan that would entice pow-erful nonmember states into collaboration. Avenol openly admitted, "I am thinking especially of the United States and Brazil." Four days later the council handed the task to the Australian Stanley Bruce.[71]

DYNAMIC DUO

Bruce was an obvious choice to execute such a plan while making it more appealing to the United States. He was no mere functionary. Former prime minister of Australia, in 1939 he did double duty, as his country's high com-missioner in London and representative at the League. In both positions he maintained an extensive portfolio on imperial and international economic issues as well as a broad understanding of how the League could serve as a hub for crucial issues that were global in resonance.[72]

Bruce's reach and authority were enhanced by Frank Lidgett McDou-gall, his economic adviser and alter ego. McDougall cut an interesting figure. Beginning as a fruit farmer in Australia, he had transformed him-self into a trusted voice on a set of imperial and international economic issues. While building a close professional relationship with Bruce, he had emerged as an influential voice internationally on issues around the nexus of agriculture, nutrition, and living standards. Moving to Geneva, he be-came a fixture of League commissions and studies investigating that set of interrelated economic issues. McDougall's thinking on economics evades easy categorization. He was no simple technocrat and was remarkable in his ability to see the broad yet intimate interconnection between issues and to understand that their scope stood beyond Australia or the British Empire. Food and nutrition were international issues that had global res-onance yet remained critical national concerns. His career shows how the information and analysis percolating in Geneva became an indispensable part of a larger dialogue on interlocking issues that themselves were seen as keys to unlocking the economic gridlock of the Great Depression and the variety of problems it inspired.

As it did for so many others, the Depression marked a turning point in McDougall's professional life. McDougall had burnished his reputation at the heralded Ottawa conference on economics in 1931, but increasingly his work hinged on the world crisis. Experience as a farmer and on agricultural issues facilitated his immersion in the rapidly evolving field of nutrition, which abutted major economic and political questions that were necessarily international and global in their scope. He accepted as a truism that international governance of these issues was a sine qua non. Like many internationalists he was firmly committed to not merely the idea of the League but also its technical capabilities. He too grasped that the League, for all its possibility, was a means to an end.

As they navigated these issues, McDougall and Bruce remained empire men. They understood Australian interests as fundamentally national and distinct but rooted in an imperial system (and they recognized real tensions between the two). This was an ideological viewpoint; empire can often be treated as an end in itself and separate from global issues, but it was a basic component of the existing liberal system. Thus, McDougall, ghostwriting for Bruce (something he did regularly) in 1933, could see the British Empire as a "League of Free Nations." Of course, the "free nations" in this formula were the "white dominions." This exclusionary club included McDougall's own country, New Zealand, as well as South Africa and Canada. India was portrayed as approaching the threshold of the "free" without having crossed it. However tendentious the formulation, there was a need to position the empire as an entity that could solve pressing problems, given that "intelligent people today are greatly interested in great experiments to alter and to shape world affairs."

The imperial system, then, had to experiment to prove its legitimacy, in competition with "communist Russia [and] the Corporative state in Fascist Italy" and even with "Roosevelt's America." Much of what McDougall would propose was aimed at reforms that could show that empire and the larger international order it was integrated into could contend with crisis. Still, McDougall and Bruce viewed Australia's needs as distinct, fostering interests in trade and security that increasingly gravitated toward the US.[73]

McDougall always pitched his appeals within a liberal internationalist frame. This is in part why his ideas had pull with many of those within the League's orbit in and around Geneva. While reflecting the national needs of Australia as well of those of the British Empire, his proposals were tethered to the impulse to reform that others nurtured. Reform, in terms of governing global problems with a particular brand of international cooperation, was a lingua franca in Geneva. It guaranteed a common ground between liberal internationalists, all of whom sought to find the means to reform not only their countries but also the global system in the face of unrelenting economic chaos and rising ideological challengers.

McDougall regularly turned to the League as a means to implement broader schemes. This was the tactic of choice for someone from a smaller and weaker state (Australia was a country of just six million in 1940) who saw the organization as a means to gain leverage as much as to foster cooperation. This pragmatic view aligned him with many people who shared his view that international bodies could serve as stabilizing elements in a reformed liberal world. In this, he was not far from others who had passed through the world's "super-university."

RALLYING TO THE STANDARDS

Liberalism connected questions that cut across national boundaries. It was McDougall who made an early call on the League's capacities on a set of linked issues that had gained nagging prominence: nutrition, food, and health. As the Depression ground on, health and nutrition problems gained increasing significance in international affairs as science made increasingly stark how food intake and quality affected individual's lives. Food production itself was tied to the crisis in the agricultural sector worldwide, which directly affected global economic questions. This nexus meant all these concerns had pressing political relevance.[74]

In 1935 McDougall authored a broadside on the question of nutrition that was to become a foundational document for international governance. The Depression had only accentuated the deprivation many people faced in their diets. Sensible policies would ensure that people could consume more nutritious, "beneficial," and "protective" foods. Such policies would go some distance in giving succor to various national agricultural sectors (particularly exporters like Australia) but also in improving international trade and, with it, the world economy.[75] Bruce drove these ideas home in a well-regarded speech (again, ghostwritten by McDougall) to the League assembly in September that year—an important moment that effectively linked nutrition to agricultural and economic policy on the international docket. It would lead directly to the League's exceptionally influential 1937 report on nutrition that had a noticeable influence on larger international discussions on food and the standard of living.[76]

The nutrition speech was a significant reason that McDougall was made a representative to the League's Economic Committee in 1937 (and its Committee on Depressions), which steered him only deeper into international issues. He engaged with the cross section of appointed figures on the committee and the permanent staff in the Secretariat. His work on improving nutrition merged with other initiatives that were grouped around increased consumption that underlay a wider international push to improve the standard of living.

In 1937, in part due to McDougall's agitation, the League Assembly set out to deal with the contradictory elements of modern life that saw the "progressive increase in the world's power of production on one hand, and, on the other the existence of severe poverty with its inevitable ill-effects upon health, happiness and life of large sections of the population." The hope was to utilize that leading technical service provider, the Economic and Financial Organization, to catalyze "measures of a national or international character for raising the standard of living."[77] The call to action was covered with McDougall's fingerprints, stocked as it was with some of his well-tried examples. Fundamentally, this statement was to be about the mobilization of that raw material that internationalists found so valuable and that the League produced in surplus: information. A primary goal of the inquiry was "to bring together existing data for comparing different groups of people and observing changes in their standards."

An English academic, N. F. Hall, was drafted to prepare a preliminary report. It was to contend with the problems of the Depression and the continuing economic dislocation by "giving a clearer sense of direction to economic activities generally, and by inducing and deepening a sense of conviction that technical progress in industry, agriculture, and transport has created for the world as a whole unique opportunities for promoting human welfare by wisely balanced increases in production and by well-planned measures of economic cooperation between nations."[78] Hall's salvo on living standards was in line with other emerging concepts in economics internationally, where marshaling statistics and analytical products such as national income could make legible and comparable the outcome of national policies. The idea was to reveal global patterns that could inform national policies to solve basic problems. Hall's analysis put great stock in economic policies that would foster consumption—which was focused on increasing the ability of populations to purchase vital items (e.g., clothes, necessary foods). In turn, these policies were meant to have impact across various economic sectors and to assist in a revival of world trade. This approach accepted that there would have to be direct interventions to push innovations that could improve living conditions. The guiding hand of state planning was seen as a means to this end. A whole section was devoted to programs to foster the "economic development of primitive countries" that mirrored colonial welfare agendas (Hall based much of this analysis on "dependent" components of the British Empire) and segued into contemporary discussions that themselves hinted at what would later be called "modernization."[79]

Hall's wide-ranging report was an important international benchmark on the emerging concept of the standard of living, compelling to economists, reformers, and politicians in many places. However authoritative the League's work was, it was hardly the sum of liberal internationalist activities on issues like these. Nevertheless, the League was a critical hub that facilitated and extended research. Hall's report and the League's turn to standard of living was not a singular development but an important part of a rising discourse that was struggling to address the problems that surged from the Great Depression. Even as Hall's report was promulgated, McDougall highlighted a parallel suggestion from Gunnar Myrdal. The Swedish economist independently proposed that increased consumption of nutritious, protective foods through social programs like school meals could solve problems of overproduction in his country's agricultural sector.[80]

As much as it fostered research, the League also facilitated the membership of figures like McDougall and Bruce in international society. The Australian duo's analysis had been circulated through networks around international society. Reformers, particularly those in New Deal Washington, shared affinities with the pair. They all had faith in the ability of statistics and other hard data to offer a script in which new chapters of reform could be written.

Like their American counterparts, Bruce and McDougall believed in the League, but they were not blind idealists. As late as 1938, Bruce condemned the Anschluss on the basis of the Locarno Pact and articles of the League Covenant.[81] Nevertheless, he knew that failures to maintain the established order in the 1930s had staggered the organization. He accepted that the League could realistically influence world affairs (and British imperial policy) as a technical instrument. Even restricted abilities retained utility for Bruce and the like-minded.

Such utility was seen to be particularly strong on the economic front, where it had the ability to move international affairs. In 1936 McDougall and Bruce assisted in hammering out a plan of "economic appeasement" for Germany. Appeasement, as part of a regime of what a set of transnational liberal activists framed as "peaceful change," was a bid to franchise "revisionist" states in the established order. They would be offered assistance in raising their standard of living in return for tamping down territorial (that is to say, colonial) and raw materials claims. At the same time, this was the sort of program that would legitimate the "free nations" by demonstrating that they could deliver the goods of economic and social improvement.

McDougall has been given credit for loading the term "economic appeasement" with much of its meaning. By late 1936 he was circulating this agenda around high levels of Australian, British, and, surprisingly, US officialdom—leading Anthony Eden to wryly note on a copy, "Is this not unusual?"[82] Regardless, his plan, which integrated ideas about trade, consumption, nutrition, and standards of living, was a deeply ideological project: "A direct attack upon low standards of living conducted both on the national and international plane is here advocated as providing dynamic economic and social policies for the Governments of the democratic countries. Such policies are required to demonstrate that the democratic countries can achieve for their peoples greater comfort and wellbeing than can the Fascist or Communist States."[83]

It is no surprise that McDougall cast the League's technical organs in a supporting role to implement the plan. Such a role was seen as both a way out of European and international tensions and as a means to demonstrate the value of international cooperation and governance in legitimating and implementing liberal economics and politics. The program McDougall championed used existing technical relationships in Geneva to suggest how the United States, under a Roosevelt administration that was itself eager to energize international trade, might be included in such a scheme. Although McDougall's vision met with wizened skepticism when a less confrontational version was circulated in Geneva, the broader economic appeasement agenda was pushed for some time by the British government. It was used as a currency in discussions around international society to suggest how global problems could be bought off until German disinterest and world events consigned this tack to oblivion. It was just this sort of effort that Grady was formally declaring dead in his comments at the League in 1939.[84]

Bruce and McDougall were active on other interconnected fronts. Profiles enhanced by their League activities allowed them to cultivate connections with American sectors of international society during visits to the United States in the late 1930s. Loveday was sure that their trips had "increased the cordiality of the response" of the US to League calls for greater cooperation.[85] McDougall's work and commitment to concepts such as appeasement and standard of living linked him with like-minded American reformers like Wallace whose ideas about reform also pivoted on questions of agriculture and consumption. The two would forge an enduring relationship during a two-week visit that McDougall made to Washington in 1938.[86]

Bruce visited Washington in May 1939 as League reform was gaining momentum. His tour was part of a larger move by Australia and the United States to forge a strategic relationship.[87] This opened doors to key figures in Washington, including FDR, James Dunn, Sumner Welles, and Cordell Hull. There was a great deal of talk about the world situation, but reform was not forgotten. According to Bruce, Hull "made it clear he was aware of

FIGURE 2.9. *S. M. Bruce and his committee. Carl Hambro is third from left; Bruce, fourth; Joseph Avenol, fifth. (Library of Congress)*

the work I was doing on the economic side and expressed his admiration of it."[88]

Undoubtedly, Bruce agreed with the sentiments expressed to him by McDougall just before his trip that, in case of conflict, "the importance of securing the most complete U.S.A. support cannot be exaggerated."[89] Australia carefully fostered US engagement with the League. McDougall's growing attention to the US was not, then, solely the effect of networking. In crucial respects it mirrored Australia's (and New Zealand's) increasing sense that the United States was assuming an outsized prominence in many spheres of international affairs. Bruce's journey demonstrated that, increasingly, many internationalist roads led to the US.

At the same time, the Australian mission is a reminder that affinities for technical reform in liberal international life were not confined to Switzerland or the United States. Many views nurtured by the League that the US found compelling were shared by other constituencies internationally. Liberal international society was one way McDougall and Bruce were introduced to American counterparts, and their ideas were integrated and legitimated within broader economic and political discussions. As the question of reforming the League to meet the expectations in European and American capitals came to a head in 1939, their work on overlapping issues, as well as their reputations in Geneva, London, Paris, and Washington, made them both favored voices on numerous topics. This was a significant reason Bruce was made head of the committee to reconsider the corpus of the League.

BRUCE REPORTS

In May 1939, fresh from his conversations with leading US political figures, including FDR, Bruce settled down for meetings in Paris. He and his collaborators could not fail to sense the acceleration of world events as they struggled to come up with a statement on the League's future. They were attempting to mold Avenol's suggestions and the interests of other powers into a program of action to enmesh nonmembers, particularly the United States, in League activities. They grasped that one of the troubles with direct participation in League technical activities was that it fell under its council's authority. Trepidation was palpable among nonmembers. If they joined the League simply for technical ends, they might be dragged down dark political alleys.[90] This was part of the organizational conundrum the committee sought to solve. But it was clear from the start what these reforms really targeted. The deliberators considered a number of options, even one focused on creating an entirely new League. In the end, discussion gravitated to the idea of creating a new body divorced from the council and devoted to technical questions.[91] All participants knew that constitutional change would be difficult, as there would be open discussion before any change could be ratified. Considering the tender state of the League, such openness was best avoided, as "it gives an opportunity for public debates on the very principle of League membership, particularly risky at the present time."[92]

Participants shared assumptions and were focused on preserving the League. It was agreed that the aim of reform was to extend the scope of the League's nonpolitical work, "particularly to secure the full participation of the U.S.A." If other wayward states, like Brazil, were enticed, so much the better. Critically, reforms would ensure that those states that joined would "pay their proper share of general expenses" into the League's vacant coffers.[93]

The Paris discussions centered on the question of saving the institution rather than establishing a clear plan to dramatically enhance the capacity of those technically oriented League organs that had become so lauded. A major problem was finding the most palatable means to draw new members into the League with little political friction. Even if too much participation was to be avoided, Bruce's program was another initiative aimed at winning over international public opinion. It shared with the pavilion another goal—namely to augment the "insufficient knowledge" in public and elite circles of the economic and social efforts of the League. Although technical services were often held up as the great redeemer, Bruce lamented that even the most devout, such as members of the League of Nations Union, were often ignorant of the work in these fields. At the same time the committee was hardly naive about the deeply political nature of these issues, which had long been discussed as "technical" and "apolitical." From its early meetings, Bruce's committee appreciated that many issues under this rubric naturally fed into dynamic political issues that governments had to contend with. It was decided to abjure the term "technical" in favor of "economic and social questions."[94]

The final report of the committee recited the liberal internationalist mantras that had been given form in Queens. Bruce's argument for the League was built around core liberal beliefs that the complexity of "modern experience" demanded the "exchange of experience and co-ordination of action between national authorities." No single state could solve the transnational questions cutting across realms of health, housing, drug trafficking, prostitution, child welfare, transport, demography, migration, finance, and economics. Bruce and his collaborators outlined global trends, making international cooperation essential. Bruce also borrowed emergent analyses of figures like Condliffe and showed that he had read the stream of memorandums McDougall had sent him over the years. The fundamentals of the report rested on liberal truisms. First, "the world, for all its political severance, is growing daily closer knit; its means of communication daily more rapid"; and second, "at the same time the constituent parts of the world for all their diversity of political outlook are growing in many respects more similar."[95]

Varieties of analysis discussing the standard of living, and even economic appeasement, were echoed in the report. In a manner that anticipated (and in certain ways seeded) Cold War modernization theorists, Bruce suggested that the core economic structure of all nations was converging toward one basic type of modern industrial society. This raised persistent commercial questions about fiscal, trade, tax, and credit policies, as well as the flow of raw materials. But this shift brought massive social concerns as well. A transformation of agricultural life was ongoing worldwide, driving a profound reordering of societies. More people were mobile and flooding toward cities, and with that came new problems. How would states cope with migrants, with the hygiene and health of people crowding cities and towns, and with their new demands? Or with their the growing awareness among their people of the vast differences in standards of living that quantum leaps in communication (particularly radio and movies) did not merely dramatize but also fostered? All these trends had been intensified by the Depression. Urbanization showed that the shrinking of the globe and the intensification of contact among populations inflamed by a persisting economic contagion put solutions beyond the reach of any solitary state.

Bruce's report repositioned the League, fairly asserting that it was not and had never been an institution *solely* concerned with the prevention of war. It did have a mandate for "the promotion of economic and social welfare." The committee highlighted the health work of the League and how it tracked diseases and attempted to halt their spread on a global scale. It did so across 148 countries and territories, most of which were not League members (many "territories" were colonies or mandates barred from formal membership). The report also acknowledged the reality and the centrality of support from the United States. The Rockefeller Foundation and its "liberal grants" were praised by name.

This established role promoting "economic and social welfare" merged with a stream global troubles to revise and extend the League's role. Economic depression was presented as its own kind of disease that the League could help to contain. The ills it unleashed not only affected people globally but also threatened "national and international order." Revised to optimize its technical assets, the League could be a hub of information and knowledge that states could draw on and use for their own policies. On the whole, the League was presented not as a substitute for national governments but as an essential supplement for state action. It was a vital tool for coordinated action by the community of nations facing the multitude of complex problems that came with the modern world.

These capacities needed to be further developed, and part of that development was providing the opportunity for nonmember states to participate in this work, which was putatively indispensable to humankind. Reformers saw earlier discussions about widening the activities of the Economic and Financial Section as the basis for enhancements. However, the proposals were extensive. An entirely new "organism" within the host of the League was suggested: the new Central Committee for Economic and Social Questions would supervise all work considered as falling under that rubric. This would siphon much control over the technical services away from the Assembly (although it still retained some authority) and crucially from the council, leaving both as primarily political bodies. Divorcing responsibilities in this way cleared space for nonmember states to collaborate on technical work "on the same footing" as members and, importantly, contribute to expenses.

Although the committee rightly saw its program as "far-reaching," its members sidestepped any question of revising the League Covenant, which might require significant debate, by simply asserting that "it does not involve any fundamental constitutional question." Again, Hull's February 1939 communiqué was waved about as proof that important states valued the League's services. It was also surely interpreted as a sign that the technical operations referenced by the Bruce Committee already had a sort of official US government blessing. Indeed, from the start of their deliberations, the committee planned to cite Hull's missive.[96] It was a sign that while the reforms had numerous goals, the core ambition was to create openings and inducements for the United States to officially contribute (in both an intellectual and a financial sense) to the redeemable elements of a troubled institution.

REDEMPTION ROAD

The Bruce report was a critical moment in a larger campaign to reposition the League as a service provider for a larger liberal order. Evasions in the document aside, it offered a major restructuring of the League. By enhancing the place of "economic and social work," which could be pitched as nonpolitical, it shifted the institution's focus and recast basic claims to legitimacy. It was an acknowledgment that the League's political efforts and its own internal organization were inadequate to contend with the issues it faced. The report supported assertions that information and coordination were indispensable to international life. At the same time, the League's recent work on interlocking issues surrounding appeasement, standard of living, and raw materials demonstrates that liberal-minded policymakers (McDougall being emblematic among them) saw its technical capacities as useful to implement policies integral to liberal order. By suggesting reforms to emphasize such capacities, the League was nominating itself for a continued role in the care and maintenance of a liberal world.

As the report was hurried into print, appearing as a special supplement in August 1939, Sweetser rushed to access his network. A barrage of letters struck American supporters as soon as the report was published. To this audience the always-hopeful Sweetser described the reforms as an opportunity for greater official interaction and also a moment to provide nongovernmental bodies like the Carnegie Endowment with "a completely new line of approach" and a "wholly new impetus" to engage the League and foster greater American cooperation.[97]

There was considerable interest in the Bruce proposals across international society, and certainly in the United States. State Department officials parsed them, and those predisposed to the League—whose numbers included Hull—counted themselves pleased. Such feelings were not universal, though. The chief of European affairs, Jay Pierrepont Moffat, and Assistant Secretary of State George Messersmith had been skeptical of earlier reforms to the Economic and Financial Organization, and of colleagues whom they felt enthused too much about the League.[98] Regardless, the figures who populated internationalist mainstays like the LNA and WPF were pleased. By and large, those Americans who saw the League as a service provider critical to the maintenance of liberal order approved the blueprints for a renovation that might sustain efforts in which they were heavily invested. At the Rockefeller Foundation there was satisfaction with the report, as it followed a path the foundation had long blazed. It was "distinctly a step in advance," Willits told McDougall. "I only wish it could have come years ago."[99]

The larger political and international context shows that the Bruce reforms were not sterile bureaucratic theater. They were part of a broader shift in liberal international society. The very attempt to restructure was a political act, aimed at creating an opening to draw the United States into the institution while maintaining and extending capacities to contend with issues exposed by the world crisis. At the same time, the restructuring should not be seen as dryly diplomatic. Its appeal rested on concurrent cultural attractions, personal contacts, and a sophisticated, transnational understanding that modern life was complicated and interconnected, demanding engagement and cooperation in spheres beyond the nation-state.

The effort to secure the technical League depended on internationally minded and connected individuals like Bruce (and his perpetual collaborator McDougall), who understood how useful—indeed, indispensable—knowledge generation centers were. Their involvement in the process enhanced the legitimacy of the reforms in the eyes of Americans who shared affinities on important issues. Their participation also further demonstrates the wide-ranging acceptance of certain liberal assumptions about what was needed to preserve, defend, and extend liberal life. The reform effort had formalized discussions of technical services that had been ranging about international society and cast them in an important and permanent role. As war loomed, this endeavor became one further measure of how the United States and its resources were a draw for figures in Geneva but also for those in far-flung places. This is a major reason the basic elements and conclusions of the report would be regularly revisited during the coming decade.

By the time the international community had a chance to consider Bruce's official recommendations, the European war that many had anticipated had amputated the September meeting of the Assembly. Only in December 1939 did the rump gather in Geneva, voting Bruce's proposals into force on December 14, in a session during which the League also expelled the Soviet Union for attacking Finland. The reforms were the "greatest change in the history of the League," Sweetser wrote in a bubbly letter to Grady.[100] He was right—they were a profound shift in the structure of the organization. Their success depended on more pedestrian calculations.

Could a financially hobbled and politically bankrupt League actually put the ambitious program into action?

THE LEAGUE IS DEAD,
LONG LIVE THE CENTRAL COMMITTEE

After the unanimous decision by the Assembly to reshape the League in Bruce's image came the actual planning of how the new body might be created, structured, and populated. As if to emphasize the difference between what was an old League and a new system, meetings were held outside Switzerland in The Hague. Bruce did not attend, but a spot was reserved for his doppelgänger, McDougall.

The meetings included another important figure in Carl Hambro, a prominent Norwegian conservative politician. His participation is a further sign of how internationalist attention and activity were being pulled toward the United States. He had invested in the League in a roundabout way. During debates in 1920 Hambro had opposed Norway's membership, but over time he saw international organization as a means to the end of supporting the rights and enhancing the position of smaller states. Equally important, a pillar was set into the foundations of his internationalist worldview: the importance of the League's technical services to the global commons. While remaining president of the Norwegian Storting, he served the League in a variety of capacities, culminating in his ascension to the presidency of the Assembly in 1939. With his growing portfolio, a colleague joked that staff would soon say "Heil Hambro" before entering the Palace of Nations. This was in poor taste, as Hambro, who was Jewish, long appreciated the threat presented by totalitarian regimes. He understood that their challenge was not simply about creed or nationalism but about ideology.[101]

What is more, like his Australian counterparts, Hambro nurtured US connections and understood the country's importance to the League. He was long curious about the Leviathan to the west, and his travels there inspired attempts to explain its power and contradictions to Norwegian audiences.[102] His position brought him to the attention and even to the home of FDR. During a 1938 visit to the United States, Hambro was scheduled to meet the president at the White House. Roosevelt, preferring Hyde Park, sent a car, with sirens blaring, to scoop Hambro up and run him to the Hudson Valley. It did not hurt that the internationalist, "world-Hambro" (as a biographer labeled him), spoke English, which made him a valuable interpreter in internationalist circles.[103] Nevertheless, Hambro was an independent mind, and by the end of the 1930s, he had realized that Europe, and world order generally, was headed toward the abyss.

The commitment of Hambro and McDougall to the technical agenda and the strategic agendas behind it signals that this was an international effort based on the transnational allure of information that could be bent to particular ends. Increasingly one of these ends was containing competing systems. The voices of these men show that the possibility of US participation through a reformed League was not a one-dimensional American initiative or some intrigue rooted in the Palace of Nations. It found support from various figures and nations because they, too, sought similar means for similar ends.

Behind a high Dutch police cordon (a rank of officers all "over six feet"), the meeting convened on February 7, 1940, to considerable press coverage at the Peace Palace in The Hague. A reminder of the (by then) perpetual ideological tension infusing world affairs was provided by Nazi denunciations of the meeting as an attempt to revive the Versailles system. Others heard the death knell of one part of that settlement. Observers claimed to almost hear chanted down corridors, "The League is dead, long live the Central Committee."[104] Even if such words did not pass delegates' lips, a candidly expressed assumption was that, even if the United States refused the seat offered, it would still cooperate with the new committee.

During the formal sessions, there was a percolating optimism that the Bruce reforms had piqued the interests of member and nonmember states alike, including those, such as Hungary, that were in the limbo of preparing to leave the League. But it was the spirit of the United States that loomed over the discussions. Avenol made the exciting point that the US was "thoroughly interested." He then doused any enthusiasm this comment ignited, noting that it was highly unlikely that it would accept any invitation before the 1940 presidential election. Swiss and Dutch delegates nevertheless stressed that a program of work of "first-class importance" had to be outlined to "attract Non-Member States and particularly the United States of America." McDougall, eyes firmly trained west, suggested that it might be wise to leave official and unofficial seats open at the committee's table until the "views of the United States Government could be more fully ascertained."[105]

Outside governmental circles there was guarded optimism. The Bruce reforms promised to cover the "main flaws" in the old League system and make technical collaboration "autonomous." They accepted the difficulty of political cooperation while acknowledging that the "vast social and economic interconnections of the modern world . . . if they are not to bring disaster, must be considered collectively, studied in common and co-ordinated by international effort."[106] Commentators also perceived that the restructuring could actually create space for revived political activity by exorcising the "remnants of the Versailles spirit [that] still hang over" the

League.[107] The *Economist* cautioned against "over-optimism" but backed Bruce by declaring that the "new line of approach is obviously sound." The realities of war and the prolonged crisis that had brought it now offered a new technical mission: "collaboration to oppose economic and social upheaval after the war," or, in plain terms, postwar reconstruction.[108]

In the early days of 1940, League reform looked to be a legitimate and, more importantly, useful means to the end of fostering a revised liberal world order. Indeed, the effort was ranked among a growing roster of international proposals for the world to come.[109] The Hague meeting promised a plan of action, but any efforts would require funds for a cash-starved organization to implement. Eyes turned westward again, not toward the evasive US government but to US civil society, particularly the Rockefeller Foundation. The foundation, which was well informed of League activities (often by the indefatigable Sweetser), was already predisposed to provide funds.

PROFESSOR AT LARGE

The very technical questions that the Bruce reforms and the Hague meeting promised to foreground were already being aired. Discussion of the state of the world economy as well as figuring out how to guide reforms (and prepare for conflict) that leaned on the resources of League bodies became urgent as conflict became unavoidable. The ISC had been engaged on economic issues throughout the decade. Its 1939 meeting, "Economic Policies in Relation to World Peace," promised to tackle that timely question.

Although its citizens and institutions had been heavily engaged in the ISC throughout the 1930s, the Bergen meeting was disproportionately populated by Americans. This reflected US interest but also because it convened on the decisively inauspicious date of August 26, 1939. Even with the oversized US contingent there were a diversity of voices, mostly from East and Central Europe, as well as a smattering from Latin America and one from Japan. Ominously, the German delegation never materialized.[110]

Serving as general rapporteur, Condliffe was in the driver's seat in Bergen. His position reflected the New Zealander's continued authority on global economics and his prominence in international society. After leaving the League in 1937, he took a post at the London School of Economics, where colleagues soon referred to him as "our professor at large." In a sign of Rockefeller's continued devotion, it gave him direct control over the funds it had provided for the Bergen meeting, which was only a segment of his "at large" duties. A preliminary meeting for the coming ISC session in Norway brought him to Prague in early 1938, where political tensions seemed everywhere, and thence to Paris for the famed "Colloque Lippmann."

Condliffe saw how that symposium wallowed in political squabbles of the time, and he wrinkled his nose as participants agitated for a manifesto that was aimed at the welfare policies of France's Blum government. When F. A. Hayek (then an LSE colleague) gave a "characteristic" speech, Condliffe counterattacked with a firm defense of the social state. Although he liked Hayek personally, the New Zealander never agreed with the Austrian's "involved" theories or "extreme reactionary views." Pragmatic, Condliffe remained critical of an intellectual posture that would eventually morph into neoliberalism because of its dependence on a "mysticism which endows present organization with something akin to the divine powers of Adam Smith's 'Invisible Hand.'" The two continued their dispute en route to a conference on business cycles (and epicurean delights) hosted by Gilbert Rist at Pontigny. Then it was off to a conference at the Geneva Research Centre, an important node of contact with the United States. Yale University was a final stop, where he received the Henry E. Howland medal in recognition of the *WES*, demonstrating the importance of that amalgamation of information and analysis for US audiences. All of this before the important meeting in Norway.[111]

Condliffe's itinerant expertise, along with his involvement with the ISC, shows how the League's program depended on the extended networks and resources of liberal international society while remaining an expression of it. Preparations also turned him into a talent scout. Among those he recruited to contribute to the coming conference were the American Henry J. Tasca, a student at the LSE, who would offer the ISC a meditation on *World Trading Systems* (his critiques of the British variant provoked ire at Chatham House).[112] Condliffe also discovered Albert Hirschman, exiled and sheltering at the Institut de recherches économiques in Paris. Excited to find paying work, Hirschman took up the Kiwi's offer to write on Italy's economic policies and their consequences for the 1939 ISC.

What grew from Hirschman's statistical analysis was a commentary for those at Bergen on the challenge posed by bilateral systems. Italy's policies, centered on massive military and public works spending, had led to successes, but they also brought increasing dependency on clearing systems. Growth in exchange controls put more and more of the economy under the purview of states that were prone to bully trading partners and act aggressively on the world scene.[113] It was an exegesis that helped launch a career, but it also reflected Condliffe's own views and the general liberal anxiety about the fragmentation brought by the Depression and the innate aggressiveness of "totalitarian" regimes.[114]

Beyond these strivers, an international chorus of thinkers offered analyses for the meeting. Among the numerous US contributors was Staley, an avid participant in the ISC. He had contributed to an earlier meeting with a report (later a book) on raw materials. Staley's missive to the 1939 ISC enunciated ideas that many liberally minded figures shared. It was premised on the growing contradictions and conflict between "power" and "welfare" economies, categories that were aliases for the ideological divisions framing the competition in world politics.[115] These competing types of economic systems advocated different means to achieve modern ends. Yet all of them could benefit from science and technology, because "knowledge, together with the productive arts based upon it, is the most potent of all the resources we have for improving the economic lot of mankind." Harnessing these forces for the correct ends promised to raise the standard of living around the world to spur growing demand for industrial and agricultural production. International efforts, dovetailed with the concept of planning, offered what was seen as a cohesive way to advance various efforts to accelerate and channel changes that were already under way. A coordinated international effort focused on "the improvement of equipment and knowledge in regions most lacking these . . . by means of loaned funds and capital goods and trained men from the countries that have these in abundance." He pointed to the Tennessee Valley Authority as a mechanism that could implement such plans. Distinctively liberal, Staley's overall agenda had a political goal, to "help bring real appeasement by offering . . . [an] attractive alternative . . . to the risky gains of aggression." He called his scheme an "International Development Program."[116]

Staley's contribution pointed to more explicit programs to guide economic change internationally toward particular ends. This was no surprise, considering his immersion in the international discussions fostered by the League and the ISC. That these ideas were incorporated into international society is logical in light of the efforts of figures like McDougall and Bruce, whose appeasement and standard of living initiatives were themselves developmental. There was also increasingly a legacy of experience, as the League itself, including some staff engaged in the ISC, had been attempting to foster economic development in places like Nationalist China.

The conference was a reminder that intellectual activity can never escape the pressures of its times. Despite the caliber of contributions, Condliffe, like other participants, could see that hostilities were imminent and tried to slip away from the ISC. He sought to emulate another attendee, Jacob Viner, who was given passage on a US Coast Guard cutter sent to retrieve the US secretary of the treasury from a Norwegian fishing excursion.[117] Condliffe attempted to secure passage on the cruiser HMS *Newcastle*, lying in Bergen harbor to recover a British delegation slinking back from failed negotiations with the Soviets. Its captain, however, curtly refused to turn an officer out of his berth for a mere professor.[118]

With no other means of escape, Condliffe stayed, offering comments in the final session, which also marked the closing moments of peace. At the rump session itself there was considerable discussion about the impact of the sorts of bilateral clearing agreements that were agitating liberals in the United States and beyond. In Bergen, analysis of this problem, founded on the sort of information gathering that Leaguers like Condliffe had been instrumental to conducting and promoting, was buttressed by the voices of officials and academics from Eastern Europe.

Condliffe repeated something that had long propelled efforts in the internationalist universe. He noted: "We have all been laying great stress upon the fact that economic policies are founded in national institutions and national policies and national situations, and that those are shaped by the inate [*sic*] and psychological backgrounds of the national institutions. Therefore, national economic policies must work and must continue to be the dominating factor in the international economic relationship." Yet there remained a danger if national economic policies operated "unilaterally."

Despite this focus on individual nations, Condliffe believed "it is necessary to state that even if we place most emphasis on national economic policies, there are certain technical services, clearing services, which are necessary and involve the use of institutions of international character." He sought, even at that late hour, "perhaps to draw attention to the experience of the technical services of the League that do persist and that are illuminating examples of the necessity for some place to meet and discuss the subject of international relations."

He concluded his contributions with a comment on what he termed the "negative" value of those services. The Health Section had conducted a survey on yellow fever, and its mapping showed that India, while at the time free of the mosquito-borne illness, was vulnerable to the spread of the disease. This had led to some precautions that Condliffe believed would keep India free of the disease. The combination of analysis and prophylactic measures became the proverbial dog that did not bark (or mosquito that did not bite), for "no one will know the negative result of . . . technical work." But it was this type of "negative," invisible activity that was vital and "could never take place unless there was a technical machine at Geneva whereby you could do that work on the general aspect of the problem and by which you can call attention to the interested governments to the matter." He posited an axiom that he and others would carry forward: "The necessity of an international spirit in the international institutions, even if the decision in important matters arise out of national economic policies."[119]

PAX AMERICANA

After the conference, Condliffe departed on a ferry that delivered him to the port of Newcastle one day before Britain declared war. The Rockefeller Foundation encouraged him to employ the remaining funds from the ISC to publish a synthesis of the research compiled for Bergen. In the months following his departure from Norway, and then Europe, the New Zealander pulled together the participants' work, which he mated with some of the growing crop of international literature on the "technical" question of postwar order. Condliffe's own view that forming a more perfect international society required international governance led him to favorably cite J. E. Meade (his successor as editor of the *WES*) on the need for an international organization to deal with postwar economic questions. A confluence of trends led Meade toward a regime of international development in which conscientious programs would foster growth and improved standards of living in poorer areas of the globe. This system could also have an "International Authority" to contend with ongoing economic problems that bedeviled what had abruptly become the prewar years.[120]

Condliffe readily turned to the League as an example of the sort of technical governance required for such reformed order, reflecting a tendency to connect desires for international governance to the existing accomplishments of the Geneva institutions in executing a technical internationalism. Condliffe's discussions of international governance on the economic front from the interwar years were already being channeled into the war years and show how liberal international society was already taking up the question of postwar order before the battle was fully joined.

By the time he wrapped up his writing, he was forced to confront what a "rapid and complete German victory" might mean. Suddenly, ideas about global integration and reform were inverted. Germany's success would lead to a reorganization of Europe's economic relations but on a "totalitarian" basis. A "cluster of satellite, puppet states" would grovel "around the industrial heart of the great German Reich." The power of this core would be enhanced only by the dependence of raw material suppliers on European markets, which would shift colonial territories into dependency on a new master. Latin America was certain to share such a fate. Without European markets, Latin America, too, would be locked into immiserating clearing agreements with the Germans. Condliffe sketched a picture of five remaining economic zones grouped around industrial cores (a framework similar to some articulated in the early Cold War).[121] Germany would dominate two zones, as the "extended Italian and Japanese empires" would exist by its "grace." Britain, with London replaced by Berlin as its economic hub and "drained by the collapse of international trade and finance," faced vassalage. Only the United States and the Soviet Union might remain unfettered by this maladjusted system.[122]

This nightmare scenario was laid out in the midst of geopolitical disaster, but principal elements were drawn from the information and analysis accrued during the crisis years. A functional international economic system was vital for stability, but any economic system demanded security. Marshaling a variety of statistical information that fed established analysis that was itself sponsored and drawn from international society, Condliffe articulated many mainstream assumptions. His conclusions show where a variety of streams of liberal internationalist thinking led, all channeled through organizational structures that included the League. The culmination of his analysis showed that these technical labors on economics brought an irrefutable geopolitical conclusion. Recovery and economic development required a guarantor of "collective security," and there was only one choice. The "United States must assume a large share of responsibility and make far-reaching political and military commitments. It is simply unrealistic to blink this fact. If an international system is to be restored, it must be an American dominated system, based on a Pax Americana."[123]

THE LURE OF EXILE

Even as postwar ideas and plans germinated in a variety of international forums, more immediate worries blossomed. War, even a phony one, made Geneva an unenviable spot. Fears lingered that Switzerland and its international colony would likely be invaded (or at least blockaded) if the conflict intensified.[124]

Major reforms to a struggling organization that was speculating about moving critical segments of its operations to other parts of the world might have seemed ambitious to the point of absurd. In the winter of 1939 and spring of 1940, however, the Bruce reforms did not seem utterly fantastic and had even staked a claim to necessity. Emphasizing the technical while keeping those activities compartmentalized ensured the League's relevance in visions of postwar settlements conjured in minds across Europe and America during early 1940—visions that presumed a victory favoring the Western Allies and a liberal world order. For these and other reasons reform continued to have resonance in the United States.

The League Pavilion faced liquidation in summer 1940. For once, a sad end was not due to international upheaval or the League's shortcomings. The exposition itself was winding down and much of the fair was to be razed. However, in an attempt to salvage something from the destruction, there were efforts to salt American universities and institutions with positive images of the League. Institutions of higher education and research, including Swarthmore, the University of North Carolina, Haverford, Princeton, and the IAS were offered fragments of the pavilion, and the Peace Plow was shuttled to the Franklin Institute in Philadelphia for safekeeping.[125]

Boosters had reinforced conventional wisdom that the League's technical work mattered in an interdependent world. Many concepts that matured through its role as a hub of international society continued to gain traction in international discussions. American officials inside and outside the government remained sensitive to that work's scope and importance as the international situation went from bad to war. Yet final efforts at the fairground to foster engagement did not fundamentally change the official relationship between the United States and Geneva. Dynamic public support did not spring from the static exhibits in Queens or other attempts to reach a mass audience. Despite all the tantalizing, symbolic, and occasionally substantive contacts and actions, the US government remained cagey, maintaining deniable distance from the League even as it stoked the issue of technical cooperation.

THE FINAL TURN

In another ironic turn, as the pavilion was readying to close its doors the League itself faced dissolution. At the same time, the relationship between the League and the United States abruptly became closer than ever. Speculation about relocation suddenly became a very real issue. As spring unfolded, world events systematically demolished carefully laid plans to build the world to come and, by extension, to reposition the League. By the summer, events would irrevocably shatter international order. In the midst of disaster, an odyssey drove home the ultimate diplomatic decay of the League, whose political paralysis in the face of a deteriorating situation left it not just an impotent spectator but a victim of world events.

Much as the pavilion was broken up and scattered, the League itself would be dismembered by the war, its appendages strewn across warring nations. The course of global war brought an abrupt end to the League's failed attempts to tempt the United States to Geneva through a shared focus on technical cooperation via personal contacts, diplomatic maneuvers, the reforms offered by the Bruce Committee, and the cultural appeal at the World's Fair. But important goals of this campaign would be fulfilled. It was not the whole League that warranted saving. Rather, the technical services lionized by the pavilion and the Bruce report and nurtured in concert with international and American support had shown themselves to be worth saving. In a moment of geopolitical flux, great effort would be made by international society to save something quite valuable—information and knowledge.

The rescue again demonstrated how the League was a dependent part of liberal international society. What would be saved were components that had shown their value as tools to facilitate modern life and, as Americans and others had foreseen, were of use in an ideological war. In order that capabilities touted and increasingly employed by internationalists might be turned to the defense of liberal life, finding asylum for them became urgent. That imperative inspired a remarkable reversal. Refuge was sought in a country that had officially turned its back on the League two decades before. The United States did not come to the League; the League came to the United States.

3: INTERNATIONALIST DUNKIRK

INTERNATIONAL SOCIETY IN EXILE

The world as we knew it seemed to be coming to an end.

ARTHUR SWEETSER, 1940

The creative science of the group of men who can do this work should be fostered, for the benefit of civilization, by the one nation which is now clearly in a position to provide the necessary sanctuary.

FELIX MORLEY, 1940

In so far as work is to be done, it will be done at Princeton.

FRANK MCDOUGALL, 1940

An odd outcome indeed.

ARTHUR SWEETSER, 1940

THE BURDEN OF WILSON

On a stunning late summer day in 1939, a large truck lumbered through the entrance to the Palace of Nations in Geneva. It carried a heavy burden, the legacy of Woodrow Wilson. A long journey was finally at an end. The Woodrow Wilson Foundation, itself honoring a president who had anguished to establish the League of Nations, had donated a monument in the shape of the globe to the man's memory. Like its namesake, the statue had a tortured past. Ten years and considerable haggling had finally transformed $25,000 into sculpture. Respect for Wilson earned the monument a prominent spot at the League of Nation's gleaming new headquarters, with its striking views of Lake Geneva and Mont Blanc, where it remains. On that sunny day in 1939, three Italian workers set it down in the Court of Honor before the League's Assembly Hall. The two wings appended to the hall containing the Council Chamber and the imposing library—erected on a foundation of Rockefeller money—stretched toward the memorial globe, giving the impression that the building was reaching out to recover something lost.

The sculpture was not greeted by celebration but by grim solitude. Only a few curious Americans and those who chanced upon the scene witnessed the hurried work of the Italians. Rather than a herald of a new beginning, the installation was an overture for the dismemberment of the League. Few were at the palace anyway to view this reminder of the support and interest that US organizations had sustained for the idea of the League over two decades. A formal ceremony to mark the occasion had to be canceled, as many delegates were hurrying home and others never materialized.

Officials who remained in Geneva found troops everywhere, even in their gardens, as a nervy Switzerland joined much of Europe in general mobilization. Wartime seemed to have already arrived; in the city, rationing of food and fuel had already begun to bite. Perhaps even more disconcerting was the wait for events to take their final turn.[1] The entire setting served to emphasize that a basic element of Wilson's legacy, the experiment in collective security, had met a dismal end. That very morning, the litany of political failures to maintain the peace came to a head. A crisis of the very sort the League had been created to prevent flared into violence. Lacking the ability or credibility to influence decisive events just hundreds of miles away, it stood passively as the German invasion of Poland cast Europe into the abyss. For Loveday it was the "end of hope."[2]

The road to war made plain the decomposition of the League as a political actor. It is telling that when France and Britain declared war on Germany in coming days, they did not bother to involve the League or invoke the Covenant. At the same time, war and the problems it unleashed underlined the importance of the technical work that had increasingly come to define the organization in the eyes of liberal international society. As global order was torn to shreds, those strands that held any promise to help stitch it back together again rose in value. Paradoxically, the world war that sounded the death knell for the League itself made its globalizing work vital to a nation-state seeking to reshape that world. The global crisis would convince actors in the United States that they needed to move quickly to preserve those branches of the League that supported the larger goal of liberal world order. In this moment, Americans fully appreciated that aspects of the League's technical work could aid the refashioning of the liberal world order into one increasingly tailored to fit American specifications. A spectrum of agents representing powerful interests in international society but also characterized by its diversity—advocacy groups, universities, foundations, international organizations, and individuals as well as governments—would mobilize to save one of its displaced members. The flight of the Economic and Financial Section to the IAS in New Jersey in August 1940 immersed the League in a stream of exiles. Asylum in the United States was the end of a long odyssey, one that began long before the fighting started.

NOT ACCORDING TO PLAN

For League reformers, the start of the European war in 1939 was assuredly inconvenient. Their internationally sanctioned program to restructure the League to emphasize its technical services, given form by the Bruce report, was only just gaining traction. Yet the conflict was both expected and, in its own way, opportune. Even as the report was promulgated, there was talk about using technical services to contend with the problems raised by war and its aftermath. This plan was another plea for the League's relevance, but it would also position the organization in a larger and vital international discussion of the postwar world. The aim was not only to make technical prowess central to the institution but also to turn it into a tool for the Allied cause.

US postwar planning is often portrayed one-dimensionally as an attempt to herd the world in its direction. In the initial phases of the European war, however, planning for the aftermath was a plural enterprise and reflected the interconnected nature of liberal international society. While not coordinated, existing networks did ensure that information could be shared as a rush of postwar planning swept across the internationalist community. A slew of university, advocacy, and government bodies straddling the Atlantic opened discussions. Even as the US State Department began to marshal its resources while subcontracting vital functions to the CFR, a collection of other nongovernmental groups also began to explore how to structure the world after the conflict.[3] But efforts were already taking shape across the American scene; they included the World Peace Foundation and the Committee to Study the Organization of the Peace, among many others.

Condliffe was rushing to join the American discussants. The Rockefeller Foundation let him subsidize his own statement on postwar challenges with funds remaining from the Bergen ISC. However, Condliffe's report was delayed when the gravitational pull of the United States itself became inescapable. It was not the imperative of exile but the lure of opportunity that drew him. Just weeks after the Kiwi was ferried from Norway, he relocated to the University of California at Berkeley to occupy a chair vacated by Grady. The process included a tumultuous transatlantic voyage in October 1939 during which the veteran got a taste of yet another world war. Aboard the liner, Condliffe and his family reached the point at which abstract discussions of the global economy, transportation, communication, and commerce were enveloped by the stark imperatives of war. He watched (and his son filmed) a French tanker afire following a U-boat attack. Once in the Bay Area, he would assemble an international selection of economically minded scholars who would have much to say on the world to come.[4]

Planning activity stretched far beyond the United States, however, dotting the internationalist ecumene. In Britain a variety of university and government groups, including the Royal Institute of International Affairs (Chatham House), began to ponder the issue. Some of this work was done with the blessing and support of the Rockefeller Foundation.[5] As a transnational dialogue it quickly attracted figures who had orbited the League. True to form, McDougall, who migrated to the Australian High Commission in London, was firing off memos on the subject before the war began.[6]

On the continent there were related efforts. Despite an uneven mobilization, which swept many scholars and technocrats into the ranks, there were early contributions from the French. European neutrals also put forward their own views. Specialists in the Low Countries and in Scandinavia turned their attention to the question of how the globe would be reformulated when peace came. Similar planning activities in Italy and Germany were also monitored.[7]

While there was interaction, and even some coordination, these various national planning groups articulated ideas of the world to come that were in line with their own perceived national interests and ambitions. Of course, there was considerable speculation about what a settlement might look like and how the presumptive defeat of Nazi Germany would be handled. But after a decade of chronic economic and political instability, the restoration of peace was also often viewed as an opportune moment to implement reforms, long speculated upon, to mend a broken international system.

For those mulling a new order in the first months of World War II, both the lessons of reconstruction following the Great War and the structural problems revealed by the Depression loomed large. These made some sort of supranational body not merely advisable but actually gospel. For many in the internationalist community, there was a firm belief that some intergovernmental organization on the pattern of the League, if not the League itself, would be necessary to maintain stability and perform certain tasks. At the very least, its ability to help master the thorny technical questions surrounding relief, economic reconstruction, a peace settlement, and the global order following the struggle demonstrated its relevance. All these issues assumed or even demanded some sort of international means for coordination. Such assumptions provided an opening for Loveday and others to position their contributions as relevant to a major issue on the international agenda. The economic planning that Loveday and others advocated was only part of the postwar role that League staff hoped to assume. Nevertheless, within the Rockefeller Foundation there was considerable eagerness to preserve the League's economic capacities to aid in general reforms to world order once peace was restored.[8]

As the Bruce reforms were weighed, the League hurried to engage the possibilities of the postwar. These dialogues emphasized that the organization was not the end in itself. Rather, it was a mechanism to bring diverse parts together. Bruce himself spoke at Chatham House, explaining how the League's new Central Committee was an ideal organ to coordinate the official and unofficial efforts on postwar reconstruction that were emerging in a variety of countries. Allowing input from other nations—particularly nonmembers—could produce a durable settlement and prevent a repeat of the economic upheaval that brought the war. Bruce's mention of nonmembers was an only slightly veiled allusion to the United States.[9]

An emphasis on international bodies as possible points of cooperation reflected how postwar thinking was evolving in the United States. There was no single view, as numerous groups were angling to interpret the possible outcomes of a conflict that, while long in coming, had hardly begun. Nevertheless, even in official circles in the United States there was a desire to participate in the peacemaking as a means to further global stability. As 1939 ended, figures including Assistant Secretary of State Adolf Berle speculated about reform to the international monetary order and the State Department began to outline ideas for the peace. Such speculation acknowledged a postwar role for the reformed League. This segued with Under Secretary of State Sumner Welles's view that neutrals, with the US in the lead, should have a role in any settlement. A growing desire for the United States to contribute indicated that international bodies seemed the most logical and politically palatable opportunity. In January 1940, Hugh Wilson, who had served as a US minister in Switzerland for much of the 1930s, primed discussions in the State Department and the FDR administration. One assumption was that if "world order" was in the United States' national interest, then the country needed to "study cooperation with the powers of Europe in matters of economic reconstruction." To avoid the appearance of involvement in "purely political problems," which would be unpopular with the public, it was best to use international institutions to this end.[10]

From the start, boosters on both sides of the Atlantic maintained that the League's analysis supporting the elusive goal of "stabilization" was even more important in wartime. Many economic questions raised by a possible postwar settlement were just the sort to which the technical services of the League and the ILO, particularly their economic sections, had long been seeking answers. However, if conflict increased their value, it also raised the stakes. Realities of modern war also threatened to tear the EFS apart. Watching from the United States, Riefler pleaded with Loveday, "Do keep it together, if you possibly can." In fall 1939, the Englishman reassured his American counterpart that his section, along with the ILO, was hard at the task of postwar planning. But the labor only emphasized that they were part of a network. Loveday anxiously sought a US perspective, as he believed it "very important that international organizations . . . should keep in the closest possible touch with national thought" on such issues, including nations across the Atlantic.

Calls to sustain operations raised questions of sustenance. As he reset the course of the EFS's research program Loveday again turned to the Rockefeller Foundation to support this tack. Regardless of continuities flowing from prewar reform to thoughts of postwar planning, Loveday grasped that the nature of the reconstruction would depend on the length of the conflict.[11]

The orientation of the League's most respected body toward postwar issues does reveal that it had purchase at a critical moment. Deputy Secretary-General Sean Lester was quick to remind the British Foreign Office of this in January 1940. Lester believed that Allied war aims for a world to come were best based on the prevention of aggression through the peaceful settlement of disputes and broad improvement in individuals' standard of living. To achieve these aims, Lester shared the view with peers that an international body would be required. This had an added benefit. It could provide the very means and cover to invest the United States in efforts for European and world reconstruction. Whether the League and its Covenant would be preserved was an open question, but the present required that "existing League machinery ought . . . to be preserved as far as possible, this implies for H.M.G. [His Majesty's Government] not merely that they should do nothing to destroy it but that they should do what they can in a positive sense to keep it working."[12]

STATE OF EMERGENCY

Even as the League merged into the new cause to which it could contribute, and could thereby use to justify its existence, structural problems continued to rattle the palace. The descent into crisis and war further strained already-precarious finances. As the war began, high-level officials began to speak of a financial "State of Emergency." This was not hyperbole. The League's budget, never plush, had plummeted from $7,413,800 in 1933 to a threadbare $4,933,730 in 1940 (and a scant $2,218,810 by 1941).[13]

Crisis forced hard choices. Keeping with trends over the preceding several years, technical work was pushed forward. Even so, finances dictated difficult decisions about which cuts would have to be made to the Secretariat. A breakdown of the proposed 1940 League budget made that plain: 81.2 percent of expenditures were earmarked for nonpolitical activities. Much of this was invested in the technical bureaus, demonstrating how far the League had journeyed toward the vision of becoming a technical service provider.[14]

Loveday and others were satisfied that this emphasis was correct, given that the League's "political activities have almost ceased and its ideals have become, at least for the moment, largely detached from reality. In consequence it must live on its technical work." The various bureaus remained well respected; the leader among them in both size and reputation was Loveday's economic section. But this status could easily change. Keeping the human capital that allowed the EFS to function at the pitch it did required maintaining decent salaries and keeping talented individuals in Geneva as war service in their home countries beckoned. Overtaxed budgets raised pressing questions about retaining staff. While the League was focusing resources on its nonpolitical elements, war had made those elements ever more vulnerable.[15]

With the League budget in tatters, the vital economic bureau depended on American money to maintain its pitch of activity. The Rockefeller Foundation remained the most important patron, showing the critical importance of US engagement in sustaining the League. But the larger and more important point was the growing centrality of the United States to sustaining the pale of liberal internationalism. Up to 1940, Rockefeller contributed a total of $403,000 (over $8.2 million in 2022) to the economic work of the League. Its most recent grants served as the basis of Loveday's postwar work. They also served another purpose: by financing one of the largest and leading bureaus, foundation money had done much to ease the burdens of an already-overtaxed budget. Even the reforms in which many placed great stock—the establishment of the Central Committee and the general implementation of the Bruce proposals—created demands on stressed finances. In the increased stringency of wartime, the implementation of these plans came to depend to an even greater extent on American support. McDougall repeated the hope that the US government might contribute directly. Realistic prospects rested on Rockefeller.[16]

WOOLLEY HEADED

While the League quickly gravitated to the question of the impact of the war on global order, the issue of the conflict's repercussions for the institution were already being considered. Worries about the position of Switzerland would ebb a bit as 1939 wore on, but overall concerns about the impact of conflict on the League continued to flow. Throughout that year, members of the League and the ILO had discussed their future in Europe and their role in the world. The international institutions were wise to the problems brought by the collapse of the order they had embodied and supported. Neutrality looked like a weak shield in a Switzerland surrounded by combatants. Even with the conflict lolling in the Phony War, earlier discussions about relocating activities to other parts of the world, including North America, must have seemed prescient.

Concerns about the status of the League's technical work were not solely the property of cliques of ministers and international civil servants. The wider NGO community had noticed its precarious position as well. Women's groups were among the most attentive. As part of international society, they shared in the wider liberal internationalist assumptions about the necessity of technical activities. As part of the international colony in the city, a panoply of NGOs could clearly see staff and budget concerns sapping capacity. The Women's International Organization, which coordinated a number of nongovernmental groups in Geneva, was soon calling for the preservation of these technical and cooperative programs. By the second month of the war, a set of groups were appealing for increased protection of these unique capabilities.[17]

There were real concerns about the status of the League in a Europe at war. Fascist states had little love for the League, a reality of which its officials were painfully aware. Germany had left the organization quickly after Hitler came to power. It was not just the nationalities and other policies the League promoted that agitated the Nazis, it was the fact that the League stood for a world order they were fighting to demolish.[18] The Soviet Union, in contrast, long frustrated with its relationship with the institution, was stung by its expulsion after its assault on Finland.[19]

Such positions chafed the League's host. Swiss discomfort with the League had begun even before the war. In the late 1930s the Swiss government began to apply pressure on the League to curtail parts of its operations. One of its more ominous actions came in 1939, when the host government began to agitate to control Radio Nations. Its high-powered transmitters publicized the work of the League, and they were also instrumental to the operation of its technical services. The epidemiological service used wireless communication to pass on regular global updates on disease. In a Europe careening toward war, such communication resources were a strategic commodity and concern. League broadcasts had embarrassed Mussolini during the Ethiopian crisis and held the possibility of being a separate source for information in a Europe where diversity of views was increasingly at a premium. For American officials, Swiss pressure on the League after the war began was a further sign that the neutral state could be compelled to toe the fascist line. It was also a reminder that even remarkable, distance-annihilating media such as radio are nevertheless sub-

FIGURE 3.1. *Woolley headed. Like other internationalists Mary Woolley had a long history of seeing the League as a means to an end. Woolley's appreciation of the role played by its technical services catalyzed efforts to rescue them in 1940. This is Woolley at the Conference on Reduction and Limitation of Armaments, Geneva, 1932. (Courtesy of Mount Holyoke College Archives and Special Collections)*

ject to control by political forces. This vulnerability also alerted the internationalist community inside and outside Switzerland to how easily the flow information out of Geneva, technical or otherwise, could be choked off.[20]

These and other issues worried Mary Woolley, former president of Mount Holyoke College. Her impressive internationalist portfolio included prominence in the peace movement and serving as Herbert Hoover's representative to the 1932 armament limitation conference in Geneva. Woolley quickly insinuated herself into Roosevelt's circle, becoming one of those correspondents he used for testing ideas and to gauge support for his policies. Intriguing proposals such as her 1936 idea for a "truce of God" gained her a degree of access to and attention from the chief executive. This familiarity meant that at the start of the war, Woolley felt she could offer an "appeal from Geneva" to the president.[21]

Well-connected Woolley was aware of the attempts to reform the League around its technical activities. She knew their value, but also their vulnerability, something that was apparent even during the Phony War. In March 1940, Woolley took the lead. With the aid of Clark Eichelberger, the head of the LNA, and the interventionist William Allen White, she convened a committee to lobby for the support and preservation of the technical services.[22] Although this was a private initiative, they undoubtedly knew it reflected official government concerns. Woolley wrangled a meeting with the president on March 8, 1940, officially "bearing a message from organization in Geneva, Switzerland to bring about international understanding."[23]

The advocacy of established and networked American liberal internationalists like Eichelberger and Woolley was one node of international society's activism on crucial issues during the war. Indeed, allies in Geneva knew some behind-the-scenes details regarding what would become known as the "Woolley Committee" through connections of international society. Here, the League Pavilion at the New York World's Fair continued its service as an informal embassy. Gerig, then commissioner general, passed along reports on the activities of US partisans. When Woolley suggested an appropriation from the US Congress to support the technical organizations of the League, Gerig was able to report that Roosevelt was said to fully agree with the idea that the bodies should be maintained to "rebuild and reconstruct the necessary post-war machinery in the technical field." At the same time, Roosevelt cautioned Woolley that in the current fraught political climate, and in an election year, he had to avoid appearing to embrace the League. Unwilling to ask Congress to directly bankroll relocation efforts, the president instead proposed a "public appeal" for the $100,000 thought necessary to sustain a League in transition. The foundations were reported to be "interested and are ready" to commit funds. Gerig, perhaps overstating, noted that "with the President and the State Department taking such a direct interest in the matter, it comes almost as a command to Americans to help carry out this appeal."[24]

Such funds were seen by a variety of people instrumental to sustaining the technical services while continuing down the path marked by the Bruce report. But more immediately they allowed the waging of war by promoting plans for peace. Even before Woolley and FDR met, Grady, by then an assistant secretary of state, had spoken with Willits about "making some contribution to Loveday's department."[25] That had come after McDougall's prodding of the RF at the start of the year to "step into the breach" until "certain Non-Member-States have decided to contribute." The Australian was eager to have assets in Geneva available to trumpet Allied war aims offering "improvement in the welfare of the individual, here including the standard of living" as a means to secure "greater equality among all nations in . . . economic opportunity." So it was clear whose cause such efforts were to advance.[26] At Rockefeller, staff were keen to see emphasis placed squarely on the Economic and Financial Section, considering its value regarding the question of postwar order.

A few days after Woolley saw FDR, Tracy Kittredge, head of the Rockefeller Foundation's European office, met with leading officials from the Geneva institutions. Money was high on the agenda. That concern fed other basic institutional imperatives. Although impressed with the Bruce reforms, the foundation had concerns that the Central Committee had been delayed. An economic department to be headed by Loveday had been sketched out, but little else of substance had been considered. More worrying was a concern that it might be years before the United States would formally join the technical efforts of the League (if ever). However, word had gotten around that Rockefeller officials had been approached by the State Department. It was clear the foundation was an ideal agent to keep vital League machinery like the EFS running. One crucial justification for a Rockefeller grant was to allow the section to serve as a hub of postwar planning, connected to other organizations supported by the foundation that were themselves turning to the issue.

Kittredge impressed on Loveday that any award would be more of "a grant in aid of the League budget than previously made." That is, the funds would not be earmarked for specific projects but allotted to generally prop up "the non-political side of the League's activities." Loveday confidently stated, "This is clearly the desire of the State Department," as Grady had been "particularly active" to this end. Loveday was keen on the opportunity but fretted that Avenol's "idiocy" might spoil things.[27] Kittredge was more circumspect in his report back to New York (perhaps because it could be read in transit), but after his meetings he was acutely aware of the larger meaning of a RF grant. Smaller states were particularly attentive to US actions; many had come to see the Central Committee as a fundamentally American initiative. That meant the grant was something more than a RF action: it was an "exceedingly important" statement of *American* interest.[28]

In New York during the first week of April, Eichelberger approached Rockefeller. He sought permission in meetings he was having with Woolley, as well as with Hull and Berle, to openly discuss the support that RF was considering offering the League. Eichelberger let the foundation know of rumors circulating in Geneva that, despite anticipation and assurances, there was apprehension that the United States would do nothing regarding the Central Committee. Eichelberger thought that the US had to underline its desires with a positive action that would further the program while quashing such rumblings. Although Rockefeller urged discretion about their deliberations, there was no question of their willingness to step in to fulfill the "public appeal." In fact, several days before Eichelberger inquired, the foundation's executive committee had moved to commit $100,000 (over $2 million in 2022) to the League for the Central Committee.[29]

The haggling over a grant expose the various interests at play. The foundation's award served the ends of a number of actors. Coincidence is a possibility, but everyone involved in this discussion had long been part of a syndicate supporting the League. This award shows how the nongovernmental elements of international society overlapped and acted, if not in conjunction with, then at least to the same end as the US government.[30]

Regardless of Washington's hand, the Rockefeller monies were more than a continuance of a long-standing trend. The early 1940 grant was an intervention to help maintain the League at a critical juncture by easing it into a long-considered transformation that could serve the planning and implementation of a particular version of postwar reconstruction that could include neutrals like the United States. The money undoubtedly eased the relentless financial pressures on the EFS and, indeed, the League's budget as a whole as the Phony War plodded on. It also served as a preface to the long-discussed move of the League or segments thereof to the United States. More importantly, the funds would be of great use as events took a turn for the worse.[31]

Overall, the Rockefeller Foundation's support for the League underscores that the Bruce reforms were something more than an expression of institutional renovation. The League had become a cog in the postwar planning undertaken by a swath of liberal international society. This planning was increasingly perceived as a way of forming, advertising, and implementing Allied war aims. In this framework, a League reorganized around its technical services, particularly its economic services, was indeed becoming a weapon of war for the Western powers and those that supported their cause. The strategic value of the League's technical abilities was a significant reason the reforms received the attention they did and lodged themselves in ongoing discussions of international organization.

Whether the munificent Rockefeller grant was officially solicited or sanctioned remains (perhaps purposefully) unclear. The US government, however, was quite pleased. Of course, despite all his earlier opinions on the League, Roosevelt had good reason to avoid anything that looked like a formal embrace. Vocal noninterventionists in the United States posed a direct political threat—it was an election year.[32] What seemed simple collaboration with technical service was viewed warily by many in the United States who continued to view the League with skepticism.[33] This broad constituency was vigilant to any change in relationship. Opposition was not limited to the halls of Congress or figures in the diplomatic corps. Numerous media outlets nursed views that were, at best, suspicious of the organization. The *Chicago Tribune*, a vehicle for Roosevelt opponents, may have been wise to these and other maneuverings. The paper studiously followed the possible relocation of the League from 1939 onward.[34] The president and his advisers were forever aware that the *Tribune* and other disapproving eyes were watching.

IRONIC FOOTNOTES

For all his evasions, the president did offer something tangible to the cause of protecting and preserving the technical services. On April 4, FDR delivered the promised personal letter endorsing the Woolley committee's aid to the "non-political and humanitarian activities of the League of Nations."[35] Here, too, there were connections to international society highlighted by the League's unofficial embassy in Queens.

Although signed by FDR, the letter was credited to Berle. However, it was drawn up with the assistance of "a ghost writer for the White House," Gerig.[36] The note wished Woolley's aims would get "full and adequate support." It emphasized liberal mantras repeated on the fairground while underscoring the fact it had been "the continuous policy of this government for many years to cooperate in the world-wide technical and humanitarian activities of the League. Certain of them indeed are not only worthy, but definitely essential."[37] Hull's by-then-dog-eared 1939 memorandum was cited as proof of American appreciation, but Berle (or was it Gerig?) added a universalist coda to his support for the technical work of the League: "However Governments may divide, human problems are common, the world over." At the same time FDR's statement maintained a healthy political distance, carefully noting its hopes to see League resources preserved were made "without in any way becoming involved in the political affairs of Europe."[38]

Regardless of who drafted the memo, it was an important, if officially noncommittal, statement bearing the imprimatur of the president. Rather than issuing a diplomatic communiqué or privately expressing his sentiments, FDR had publicly stated a rationale for the preservation of the League's technical structures based on larger liberal assumptions. Even a qualified intervention had real uses. As much as it allowed the president to support the League without spending much political capital, it did place the survival of the technical bodies of the League on the public agenda, smoothing the ground for a possible move that had already been discussed. The attention given to nongovernmental groups was further heightened, and they had something like official sanction for their activities from the president. The Roosevelt administration felt it had made a compromise that suited the situation. However, it could succeed only if everything and everyone stayed on the same course.

Regardless of motives, Roosevelt's intervention was certainly a coup for the team of internationalists considering the transplanting of League organs. However, Woolley would not release the letter to the public for nearly two months. This was almost certainly to allow partisans to further develop plans behind the scenes with American and League officials.

Assured that foundations were committed to efforts to safeguard the League, Eichelberger and Woolley busied themselves with stage-managing the public posture of the committee, all the while keeping the Roosevelt administration informed through regular contacts with Berle. They were particularly careful to give their organization a bipartisan flavor by recruiting moderate Republicans such as William Allen White and "real Republicans" like Charles Taft.[39]

The League's man in New York, Gerig, remained franchised in these discussions. From the unofficial legation on the fairgrounds he responded to requests from Rockefeller staff to sketch the needs of the technical bureaus on the basis of their previous activities. Party to an emerging plot, Gerig could comfortably, and for the most part accurately, inform counterparts in Geneva that he was "aware of everything that is going on [in] connection with this campaign and I am advising and supplying information in regard to it."[40]

The growing cast and scope of this intrigue, as well as the acceleration of world events, guaranteed that it would not stay hidden. On May 19, 1940, the *Tribune* broke the story that the League was contemplating a move to the United States. The paper correctly surmised that this would be "in line with the desire of the Roosevelt administration to promote the nonpolitical activities of the League—such as economic studies. . . . Well informed persons felt this portion of the League would be the most logical to transfer to the new world." Further proof lay in Hull's oft-cited 1939 memorandum. Should the move go through, the *Tribune* noted, it would be an "ironic footnote" to the history of the League.[41]

AN UNDEAD LEAGUE

In a period laden with irony, the final fate of an organization that had made great claims to serve peace would be decided on the battlefield. The opening of the German offensive in the West on May 10, 1940, irretrievably altered the situation. With the struggle joined, it was ever more apparent that the League's destiny floated on the whims of the great powers. That day, Loveday understatedly noted in his diary that "'Totalitarian' war has presumably begun."[42]

Preexisting concerns exploded into a full-blown crisis with the stunning events of spring 1940. German military victories rapidly brought an Allied rout. The end of May and beginning of June saw the unthinkable become reality. Belgium and Holland surrendered; the British fled the continent; the French army collapsed; and Italy entered the fray. Internationalists could feel tectonic shifts shaking the geopolitical order. Plans mulled before and during the Phony War were condemned to irrelevance, and speculation about the vulnerability of Geneva became an alarming reality.

Neutrality looked to be a flimsy shield against what had become a fascist continent. In the spring there were fears that the Germans could briskly conquer Switzerland. Even if this did not happen, any latitude for truly independent action in Geneva was quickly disappearing. Once France was fully digested, Axis states would have near total control over ingress and egress. Communications, as the Radio Nations controversy portended, were indeed threatened. Loveday and others nervously watched as cable connections with other parts of the world were gradually cut.[43] A skittish Switzerland, worried about hosting institutions disliked by the victors, gibbered about their future.[44] Harsh realities compelled officials and supporters to consider that the experiment begun in the wake of World War I might be extinguished by the second one.[45]

There was another possibility that was even more disturbing: the League might live on. But it would survive under drastically different circumstances—and masters. As a season of disaster wore on, it was painfully clear that Nazi visions were shaping the world of tomorrow. League officials and partisans had grown convinced of German eagerness to transform the institution to serve a fascist order. Hitler had declared the League a "dead thing" in October 1939, incapable of fostering the revisions to international order that the Führer saw necessary. However, other German officials made it known in neutral circles that a league, if not the League, might be employed for other ends. A Dutch journalist recounted conversations in Berlin that autumn. In a quest to "perpetuate peace" after a "real consolidation of the political situation," a place could be made for a "new League of Nations." This body would not rest on the "injustice of Versailles" but reflect a "new system of collective security."[46]

The "consolidation" of 1940 made such speculation portentous. Loose tongues of German diplomats around Geneva further accented rumors swirling that spring and summer. The Nazi regime had shown it was not above utilizing existing international bodies to further its interests. It had already co-opted the International Criminal Police Commission and would retain and utilize its membership in the Bank for International Settlements for its own ends (breeding distrust and a desire for its replacement among the Allies).[47] This made ominous suggestions that the bodies of the League and the ILO might be revived. Their remains might be fused into some sort of economic skeleton that would buttress Nazi economic and labor philosophy, based on *Kraft durch Freude* (strength through joy) for a pan-European audience.[48] Fears were validated by emerging efforts to reorganize European culture around a Nazi hub.[49] Reich Minister of Economics Walther Funk, articulating official views of how Germany would foster European integration, made frighteningly real what had been anxious speculation. Flushed with victory, in July 1940 he announced: "We shall, after the victorious termination of the war, apply those methods in economics which brought us great economic successes before the war. . . . We do not intend to allow the unregulated play of forces that cause the German economy the greatest difficulties."[50]

This made plain that autarky—buttressed by the sort of subjugating trade and currency relationships that Grady, Condliffe, and others in and around international society had anxiously sketched from Geneva, Bergen, Berkeley, and beyond—would become a European norm. This would institutionalize the trends seen as anathema to a stable international economy and begin a cascade of effects that would reshape the globe.

Although the fate of the League did not touch a raw geostrategic nerve comparable to questions around the fate of European empires or the disposition of the French fleet, it nevertheless had resonance in the grim summer of 1940. Internationalists appreciated how the League provided crucial data and institutional mechanisms that allowed a liberal version of the world to cohere and maintain trappings of legitimacy. At the same time there was the nagging worry that the League's services could assist in binding together a fascist Europe in the same manner it could stitch together an unraveling liberal world order. Part of the liberal nightmare within these German dreams was that the recently completed palace, with its grand Rockefeller-funded library brimming with vital data, might become a column supporting this "New Order."

THE END OF THE WORLD

Fear energized efforts to salvage what remained of the League. Plans to succor the technical services swung completely toward the rescue of key parts of the League from Europe. Much of this would center on Sweetser, who had made plans before the German attack in the West to visit the United

States in May. With the opening of the offensive, Sweetser accelerated his travel plans. Although he begged an unofficial leave from Avenol, he had an official agenda. Before departing, he dined with Loveday and Lester, discussing issues their respective preoccupations. Without question, one of these was the possible relocation of the EFS to the United States. Hurrying his goodbyes, Sweetser was unsettled by the uncertainty that had enveloped the palace. Conversation there had turned to its possible seizure by German paratroopers and whether the newly constructed headquarters should be abandoned. As Sweetser bid farewell, Lester asked to be kept informed of his movements. The deputy secretary-general almost unconsciously added, "I'll let you have ours when we know what it is."

Sweetser made his way through Switzerland to Genoa, Italy, where he waited three and a half days to board a ship. As they waited, they were joined by several acquaintances from France who carried fragmentary reports of unfolding disaster. When patched together, this news indicated "four empires seemed crumbling, British, French, Dutch, and Belgian." It made for a "nightmarish trip through the Mediterranean, past Gibraltar, and across the Atlantic," leaving all thinking, "The world as we knew it seemed to be coming to an end."[51]

As other parts of world order broke down, links of international society held. This was apparent as soon as Sweetser's liner docked in New York City on May 28, and he flew into that internationalist hive. He phoned Riefler, who said that the IAS was willing to assist. Sweetser then lunched with Willits, who made plain that Loveday's "Section constituted one of . . . the foremost centers of economic research in the world" and that it would be a "crime" if it were "crippled" by the crisis. As they ate, Fosdick breezed over to their table and, when asked, said he "felt sure the foundation would cooperate." After such promising news, Sweetser contacted the League of Nations Association, which dutifully put him in touch with members of the Woolley Committee. It would keep him in the loop as their own efforts with FDR evolved.[52]

With these fruitful meetings under his belt, Sweetser headed for Washington, where he caught Feis, then economic adviser to the secretary of state, for a discussion. He made the rounds of close counselors to the president, although it seems that the "old friend" of FDR never made it to the White House. Regardless, this extensive slate of meetings showed Sweetser how the war in the West affected a swath of officialdom. By early June he was "*amazed* at the change of opinion here. . . . There is a lot here for encouragement if there is only time."[53] He informed Lester of these changes in American attitude (noting a reception held for him and other League officials at the pavilion and the increased number of visitors it was attracting—eight thousand on one Sunday in May) and that they reinforced the possibilities of the move. He also hinted that there might be even deeper and more profound benefits from relocating to a roused United States:

> I need not stress again . . . the importance such a transfer would have for the future. It would open the most interesting possibilities and personalize this work to a degree otherwise impossible. Even apart from all other considerations, if we see the future in a large and long view, this alone would justify a bold and, after all, a temporary step. . . . I feel most strongly that, entirely apart from any technical reasons, there are other and more compelling reasons that would make the gamble very much worthwhile. Everything is now fluid; all of us need movement and fresh air; I'm sure this would be invaluable in opening a new chapter both for us and our friends who only ask to help.

Sweetser, ever the optimist, saw in the crisis of the spring an opening for the end toward which he and others had long been working. If plans went forward, "the country would, in a sense, become identified with, and part of this work," supporting a "belief that if this country gave asylum now in this moment of emergency, it would be integrated for ever."[54]

As important as the agitation of League staff was, the real possibilities came from a broader internationalist recognition that fascist victory in Europe had global implications. Attitudes were certainly shifting but political complexities remained. Sweetser found support in many quarters, but the most immediate and tangible came from nongovernmental groups, which had their own views and goals. Even as Sweetser darted around New York, Rockefeller staff were coming to terms with the larger, grimmer situation and what it portended.

On June 4, Willits offered a sober analysis of what was in store "If Hitler Wins." It would mean the "amputation" of the British and French empires, economic subordination of Europe to Germany, the forced migration of millions, and "suppression of all independent expression" contrary to Nazi ideology. Beyond these upheavals, Willits thought that the "intellectual consequences are no less appalling." A German victory would undo much of what the foundation and others had sought to cultivate. Western Europe would cease to "offer the kind of milieu in which social science research can flourish." Willits's memo was no impotent lament but a commitment to the larger cause of refugee scholars: "an opportunity—greater for the United States and greater for civilization."[55]

Those displaced from the "super-university" were a significant part of that opportunity. There were numerous groups and individuals converging to snag them. One "fell out of the blue" and into Sweetser's efforts. That was Carl Hambro, by then a refugee himself. The Norwegian remained president of the League Assembly—an official position that would prove vital as events developed. He had narrowly avoided his own internment in fascist Europe. Hambro was in Oslo as Germany launched its surprise attack on Norway on April 8, 1940. An eruption of resistance at a Norwegian fortress staggered an assault force, delaying the *coup de main* to seize the capitol and the royal family. Hambro used this brief respite to assist the king and parts of the government to escape just before the Germans landed. Events would force Hambro to flee to Sweden but he continued to advocate resistance.[56]

Remarkably, he reached the United States just months after the invasion, with the cause of his own country but also that of the League's technical services in mind. His advocacy on the part of the League would only be a first act in a longer campaign to court American opinion and urge intervention in the war. Hambro's newfound status as an antifascist exile along with his official position as president of the League Assembly enhanced existing relationships with key US officials, including an individual he referred to as "No. 1," Franklin Roosevelt.[57]

In July, Hambro joined Sweetser in a journey to Princeton to tour the facilities offered there by the university, the Rockefeller Institute, and the IAS.[58] Sweetser was immediately taken with the institute. Coupled with Princeton University, the IAS had world-class scholarly resources that would allow the EFS to continue its work. It was a hospitable spot—both geographically, situated between New York and Washington, and philosophically, born of the same progressive urges that recognized that "the League is the Thing," in line with its first president, Abraham Flexner.

Critically, the IAS, built on progressive reform, was laden with committed liberal interventionists. Frank Aydelotte, Flexner's recent successor as chief, became an early member of the Committee to Defend America by Aiding the Allies when it formed in spring 1940 and was an active participant in efforts to get the United States to contain fascist power. Under his leadership, the IAS had already begun sponsoring a series of projects to link scholarly expertise to policymaking. With the aid of another major foundation, the Carnegie Corporation of New York, the IAS hosted a military and foreign policy seminar explicitly aimed at reframing American grand strategy to contend with world disorder.[59]

From Princeton, Hambro and Sweetser shuttled to New York for further meetings with Fosdick and Kittredge as the foundation offered its assets to the campaign. When they spoke to Eichelberger of the LNA and the Woolley Committee they heard how plans to broker an official invitation had come to naught. But frustration morphed into ready interest for a plan centered on Princeton. Increasingly, the efforts of itinerant League advocates were dovetailing with the efforts of domestic American internationalists already invested in a rescue plan. On June 1, in the middle of this shuttling and scheming, Woolley announced the existence of her committee, detailed its goals, and released FDR's letter.[60]

It was high time: the military tide in the West was flowing remorselessly in Germany's favor. The committee made sure that the letter got wide play in the press, but it did not change the public posture of the administration toward the League. It was yet another reminder that Roosevelt was unwilling to openly embrace the League. Still, there was much activity just beyond the pale of the official serving the interests of the League's technical services.

ASYLUM REQUESTED

The indirect and limited support given the EFS by the Roosevelt administration should be measured against the outright lack of support, formal or otherwise, given the International Labour Organization. ILO staff had been just as worried about the deteriorating situation but found the US government unreceptive. It too had advocates in international and American civil society. As the Western alliance collapsed, Johns Hopkins University offered sanctuary.[61] In June, its chief, John Winant, an American, approached US representatives in Geneva asking for official help.[62]

The State Department's unwillingness to extend an invitation led to an appeal by William Green, president of the American Federation of Labor—again showing the wide support the Geneva institutions had in a diverse international society.[63] An increasingly anxious Winant made an impassioned plea, steeped in the rhetoric of ideological struggle, to Hull. He cast the ILO as an "agency of democracy" that the "totalitarian states" had spurned. Created to further "social justice," the body had adhered to the "democratic principles upon which it was founded." Perhaps equally important, Winant reminded Hull that its staff had ensured that the ILO "without deviation has supported the international policies you have advocated." This was in part because the United States was a powerful member and both the chairman of its governing body and the director were US citizens.[64] He asserted that the ILO still had "real work to do . . . [that] can be best accomplished in North America." Considering that both the secretary and the president approved his appointment to the organization, he felt Hull was compelled to bring the issue to Roosevelt.[65]

Hull did speak with FDR, but the conversation aided in the dismissal of Winant's argument. For the secretary of state it was not a question of US commitment to the organization or Winant's leadership that decided the matter, but the fact that half of the nations represented on the ILO's governing body were under some form of German domination. Plus, any international body that demanded an independent existence in the United States would have to have congressional assent. Hull was clear that "we could not request such agreement at this time."[66] As in the case of the League, an official invitation for the ILO was out of the question; the labor body, however, did not rate the unofficial maneuvering that was already under way for the EFS.

ASYLUM OFFERED

Even before the ILO's petition foundered in Washington, plans to rescue the League were under sail. As part of his internationalist circuit riding on June 7, Sweetser visited Princeton and toured its facilities. He came armed with general commitments from Loveday and Lester about transferring League functions to the United States, although nothing, apparently, from the secretary-general. Aydelotte convened a meeting in his IAS office between Sweetser and an ad hoc set of academic officials who had a stake in the preservation of the League. Vice President George Brakeley of Princeton and President Carl Ten Broeck of the Rockefeller Institute for Medical Research tendered their institutions as sanctuaries. Fortuitously, the trustees of Princeton were meeting just a few days later on June 10. The relocation plan received their unanimous approval.[67] That same day, Sweetser confidently informed Avenol that while complexities remained, "if worst came to worst" the "door could be made to open," and "it could be arranged for the technical sections to come over here and find hospitality."[68]

The whole scheme provides a window on how aspects of liberal international society functioned. It was a signal that nonstate groups had considerable flexibility institutionally, legally, and financially to quickly act. They were also free of many of the political fetters with which government officials had to contend—something FDR, Hull, and others in Washington certainly appreciated.

Nevertheless, the scholars' cabal still needed permissions that only the US government could bestow. After the meeting, Aydelotte hastily departed for Washington with an ad hoc delegation from these academic institutions to meet with Hull and other State Department officials to secure official blessing. While the nongovernmental groups had the latitude to easily issue an invitation, they still had to face the fact that states controlled borders and travel, a power intensified in a time of war. However, considering the US government's appreciation of the importance of what was considered the League's premier technical body and being well aware of the stakes, Hull readily granted passage. With hosts, money, and government approval all in place, a plan could be put into action: issue the invitation, pack up the bureaus, and move.[69]

A joint letter launched the operation on June 11. President Harold Dodds of Princeton wrote Avenol at the behest of his university, the Rockefeller Institute for Medical Research, and the Institute for Advanced Study. Their offer extended to all the bureaus involved in public health, opium control, and economic work, because supporters were "fearful that the trained personnel of these sections, so carefully built up, may be dispersed, and that the records so painstakingly accumulated may be destroyed." To prevent this, they extended "a most cordial invitation to the technical sections of the Secretariat to move from Geneva to this place."[70]

It was an offer that fulfilled many proposals to secure the technical bodies that Avenol himself had floated in the preceding two years. Although there were murmurs and the secretary-general harbored reservations, all Avenol had to do was accept.[71]

ASYLUM DENIED

He did not.

Deflecting the invitation, Avenol trotted out a legalism. The day after Paris fell, June 15, he wired that the seat of the League was Geneva and that it was beyond his power to transfer "all or part of the Secretariat unless the initiative were taken by one or more states." Dispatching the offer, he extended brisk thanks to "American friends" for their "sympathetic concern."[72]

Avenol's dismissal of an escape to North America of the sort he had discussed just months before might seem puzzling, considering the resources already invested to cultivate a technical relationship with the United States. Indeed, the framers had written the possibility of a move into the Covenant. Although article 7 decreed that "the Seat of the League is established at Geneva," it allowed that "the Council may at any time decide that the Seat of the League shall be established elsewhere." The complicating factor was that the League Council was not sitting, meaning a timely decision was hardly possible. A final decision on a move of the whole organization was formally something the secretary-general could not make on his own. This provided an officious shield that Avenol used to cover his decision to deny the EFS to the United States. His position inflamed concerns that other major changes were in the works.

Rumors flashed around the palace that Avenol was making room for Germany and Italy in the League, or at the very least hammering out some sort of agreement for technical cooperation. As the battlefield fortunes of France sank in June, Avenol had descended into defeatism. To subordinates in Geneva, his behavior became erratic and, to some, treasonous.

He was never entirely candid about what exactly he had hoped to do, but he denied—to the point of "changing color" out of exasperation with one postwar interviewer bold enough to ask the question—to his death such a scheme and any contacts with the Germans on the issue.[73] But only the Germans. In 1940, he reached out to the forces that would coalesce into the Vichy regime.[74]

Avenol's action fanned the infighting that had started in the halls of the palace. For Lester, Geneva had become a cage. He confided to Sweetser on June 19 that "the world is crashing round our ears" and could not hide that "there have been some terrible disillusionments (Avenol) and anger at times has helped me through difficult days; one may put up with pomposity when it is backed by a quick intelligence, but when one has to put up with pompous futility coupled with demoralization, the last shred of respect goes." He stated something German military success had laid bare: "Our future is for the moment very far from being in our hands."[75]

Such palace intrigues might be seen as the convulsions of a dying organization. But the final disposition of the League, its staff, and resources mattered, including in the court of international public opinion. As he maneuvered to contain Avenol, Lester appealed to the British, dramatizing the fears that the League could just as easily legitimate and offer technical support to the fascist New Order. The Irishman reminded the British minister in Bern, David Kelly, that the secretary-general, acting alone, could convene a meeting under League auspices. Whether done at the behest of the Germans or any of their clients, the propaganda implications were obvious.[76]

In the United States, Avenol's refusal signaled worst-case scenarios were unfolding. There was still hope that FDR and American officialdom could be moved to take the political risk they had, up to that point, studiously avoided. On June 15, just after the refusal, Woolley was back in Washington, meeting with Berle. She presented him with a memo prepared by Frank Boudreau summarizing the case for bringing the League to the United States.

Boudreau, veteran of the LNHO, was then chief of the health-oriented Milbank Fund. He was deeply invested in international endeavors to create the means to govern transnational forces influencing global life. His was the perfect voice to explain why supporters in the United States clung to the idea of the League even after its abject political failure. Boudreau did not articulate fuzzy fantasies of international harmony or a belief that the League was the realization of the dream of collective security. Rather, he explained how the urge to preserve the League reflected a fundamental internationalist urge to contend with and control the dynamic elements of the modern world.

Geneva constituted one part of a "system of world cooperation" offering the means to contend with a planet that science was shrinking into a tightly linked but complicated globe. "Woven into the fabric" of the League were ambitions to understand and analyze this world. The work these League fragments could do was "not academic," because their efforts impacted the "daily life of many people." This helped explain the "public esteem" that these technical efforts had garnered, even from those nations that were not part of the organization. Boudreau reminded the president that the roster of Americans contributing to this success was long and varied. The knowledge and expertise generated were invaluable. But just as important, it could be a strategic resource. If the League personnel were left in Geneva, this capacity was endangered, not only because they would be unable to effectively do the work that was so valued but also because "Germany and Italy will do everything in their power to destroy it." Boudreau hoped American views were changing, which would allow League organs to be comfortably transplanted to a place in Washington to connect again to US government agencies and representatives of other League member states. He shared a view that Versailles' failure was in part a failure of expertise. Keeping these shards of the Secretariat in existence would augment the reserve of people versed in the international questions that would frame any settlement. They could assist in sorting out the complicated issues that would arise in a postwar world. The United States could do its duty by serving as an asylum for this servant of humanity and get a useful tool in the bargain.[77]

Boudreau's missive received attention. From Berle's communications with Roosevelt, it can be established that the president was clearly aware of the issues to which it spoke as well as Avenol's refusal of the Princeton invitation. In their exchanges, Berle stated for the record something the president assuredly knew: the transfer of League technical activities was no simple request. The crisis raised the "question as to whether the whole machinery can exist at all, unless it finds asylum." The amputation of League members for the move to Princeton, therefore, had to be selective. With economics the priority, various humanitarian and health activities were undoubtedly going to be "left hanging." Even with the clear division of the nonpolitical from the political organs for the transfer, Berle understood the political baggage they would carry to the United States. Any request, even one limited to the economic section, involved "an obvious political decision of some importance, which can only be decided by yourself, the Secretary of State, and the Cabinet."[78] Things would never progress this far. Again, Roosevelt dodged the hard question of open, official commitment. But tribunes of international society had already moved into the breach.

Despite the president's formal inaction, Woolley did not let up. Through

June and into July she continued to plead the case for an invitation, considering the "critical situation" facing the technical services. In the last days of June she echoed the view that the League, in fascist hands, could be manipulated to aid a new European (or world) order. Hitler might be "inspired to seize the League . . . to be added to his 'Triumph' and finally be shaped after the Nazi pattern," adding legitimacy to his conquests. However, the president did not meet with her and did nothing more than thank Woolley for her contributions.[79] But this is not to say the administration ignored the issue or did not understand the conundrum presented by the League. In the days that followed, the State Department did begin to mobilize what resources it had in Switzerland in the cause of the technical services.

BOOKS OF TOMORROW

By late June, following Avenol's refusal and the lack of overt action by the US government, frustration and resignation might have been in order for American supporters. League staff seemed likely to be "imprisoned" in Geneva for the foreseeable future. However, appreciation that the League and the valuable materials it controlled might be locked in a fascist Europe merely inspired more radical plans. At the IAS and Rockefeller, thoughts immediately turned to the most valuable items still held by the League—data.[80] In the backwash of the secretary-general refusal, Willits sent a wire asking about the status of a project that would use the relatively new technology of microphotography to film a substantial proportion of the EFS's invaluable records. Loveday quickly responded that this was already under way, but only partially completed. With the staff of the section possibly trapped, there was at least a hope that some of their work could be rescued. Willits, in concert with Aydelotte, began plotting to keep the vital economic data they had done so much to cultivate out of fascist clutches. A conspiracy formed to complete microfilming reams of economic data residing in the palace.[81]

What might seem an overwrought suggestion born of armchair or cinematic espionage was an astute use of what was then a cutting-edge technology that can seem prosaic, even dowdy, to later generations—microfilm. The Rockefeller Foundation had a pioneering hand in what was then a new and revolutionary information technology. Microphotography had only recently come into general use, in part because of investments by the foundation. Seeing its potential to save space and improve the accessibility of a wide range of resources, the RF had supported microfilming programs undertaken by the American Library Association and the University of Chicago. Excitement back then that text was on the verge of a revolution because the "books of tomorrow" had arrived parallels much later excitement for the power of digital technology to transform reading and research. At the League, the technology's ability to scale down massive amounts of material seemed a godsend at a moment of crisis.[82]

Just days after receiving Loveday's message, the foundation allocated money from its April 1940 grant for the microfilming to be completed, a task that was rapidly accomplished. Once in this compact form, the information that so many valued and had worked to cultivate could more easily be smuggled out of Europe. Even if the husk of the League could not be saved, the fruits of its labors could be preserved.[83]

Much of this took place behind the back of the head of the League. By June what shaky trust remained had disappeared among the leadership. Avenol was making key decisions without discussing them with key subordinates, particularly Lester and Loveday. In June, Avenol went as far as to dispatch the organization's secret archive to Vichy without consulting senior staff. Lester took the unprecedented step of countermanding this and demanding the materials be returned to Geneva.[84] This was emblematic not only of Avenol's embrace of the emergent Vichy regime but also of the rancorous distrust infesting the palace. Among subordinates, respect for the secretary-general dwindled to the point of disdain. Loveday and Lester increasingly found themselves not only opposed to Avenol's policies but hostile to the man himself—feelings shared by supporters abroad. Increasingly, when US patrons sent a message to the secretary-general they were careful to see that Loveday or Lester received a copy. On some issues Avenol was completely cut out of communication.[85]

Even more thorny was the disposition of the human resources of the technical sections. By early July, the situation of the international civil servants in Geneva was approaching critical. Limited communications enhanced confusion and anxiety. There was a real problem of finding financial sustenance for the cadre of international civil servants. Loveday was struggling to scrape together resources to keep important members of his section "on the books" and in their positions. Dissolution might come not from warfare or political pressure but simply for lack of pay. Indeed, austerity and the need to shed staff remained a ready excuse for Avenol, an experienced bureaucratic infighter, to dispose of those who were politically problematic or failed to conform to his vision.[86]

Collectively, developments in Geneva disturbed the remaining Allied powers as well as partisans in the United States. It was no idle time. It was another element reflecting the global transformation of geopolitics in 1940. There was no desire to hand Hitler and Mussolini anything else that might enhance their legitimacy on the world stage. There were great issues on the table as a new phase of the war opened, and indeed many saw that a new era in international life had commenced. The Western alliance that had gone to war in 1939 had been destroyed, and the forces of fascism were at flood tide. The disposition of France, its empire, and its military were an open question. The very independence of Great Britain and its empire was in doubt.[87] That the fate of the League and its economic section mattered in that summer of upheaval is testament to the importance of information to any vision of liberal order. An international constellation of individuals appreciated just what the EFS could do to aid in planning a war and supporting the order that could follow. At the same time, they recognized that their opponents might use it for similar ends.

STRONG WORDS

On American shores, the response of these internationalists demonstrated a commitment to fight for a liberal world. Machinations to keep the respected parts of the League out of a fascist grip should have been no surprise, considering the loyalties of the conspirators. Eichelberger, Aydelotte, and Woolley had already heeded a May 17 call to join the new and explicitly interventionist Committee to Defend America by Aiding the Allies.[88]

In a busy summer, Aydelotte took time from his scheming to convene discussions of how to react to the radically changed world situation. His extracurricular activities show that if EFS were to make it to New Jersey, it would be in the custody of those already tipped toward intervention. The IAS hosted a seminar by the National Policy Committee on June 29–30 that discussed the implications of a Nazi victory for the United States. Its influential roster included IAS colleagues Riefler and Edward Meade Earle as well as Kittredge of the RF and Jacob Viner, already an influential member of the CFR's War and Peace Studies.

When the conclusions of the seminar were published the evidence cited to show the grim implications of German victory included the bilateral agreements trialed in Eastern Europe. The worry now, like those expressed at Bergen and Geneva just months before, was that the agreements would be employed to yoke Latin American economies to a German-dominated Europe. These assertions drew directly from established analysis. Condliffe, simultaneously sounding the alarm about the global economic consequences of German victory, cited the IAS meeting conclusions because they repeated his own. There were other fears expressed, but this example demonstrates how economic analysis emerging from international centers was integrated into higher echelons of US strategic thinking. It energized Aydelotte, who chided others in the interventionist camp to support the "destroyers for bases" deal to place fifty of those versatile warships in British hands.[89]

These were all signs of how the switchboard of international society

lit up in response to the crisis. British and American collaboration intensified. A critical member of the exchange was Philip Kerr, Lord Lothian, the
British ambassador in Washington. Among the portfolio of issues he con-
tended with that summer was the status of the League. Like so many in the
internationalist ecumene, he was well aware of the value of EFS. He shared
the British government's desire to see the technical services extracted from
Geneva. He also assiduously cultivated relationships with the influential
inside and outside Washington. Fosdick, Willits, and Aydelotte were reliable, regular contacts, and they eagerly informed him of their plans to
transplant the EFS. Lothian relayed the details of the American initiative
to London. He kept his American contacts informed of British actions,
particularly when the Foreign Office decided to wade into the fight with a
"strongly worded message" to Avenol on the Princeton option.[90]

Lothian reflected the British government's grave view of developments
in Geneva. After the Princeton invitation was refused, Loveday and Lester confidentially told Kelly that they were "seriously disturbed" by the
secretary-general's actions. They believed he was moving to "reinsure himself" with some sort of "accommodation with Axis Powers." Hence Avenol
"needed close watching."[91]

Suspicion of the secretary-general's decision to pass on the Princeton
offer, along with word that the "liquidation" of the Secretariat was being
considered, brought a stern British response. Halifax drafted a letter that
stated, "His Majesty's Government are unable to understand how [Avenol]
felt able to do this without consulting the members of the League. . . . The
refusal . . . should be rescinded pending further discussion."[92] The British
action was seconded by the United States, which mobilized members of
its Bern legation to confront the secretary-general about his decision.

To contest Avenol's obstinance, the British minister and his American
counterpart subjected him to back-to-back visits on June 27. It would be an
education. Avenol was no political neophyte and had long operated at the
highest diplomatic levels. He quickly and adroitly divided the two powers.
The British minister, Kelly, arrived at 11 a.m., bearing Halifax's prickly letter. The note stated that the British government considered the Princeton
invitation an "official proposition." As the "preferred" option favored by
the British government, it was "wise" for Avenol to accept it "at once." The
letter bluntly stated that if the invitation had indeed been turned down,
that decision should be "rescinded."[93]

Avenol, in his element, easily deflected the missive, noting that it could
"not be said he had refused the invitation." He claimed the concern keeping him from acting on the Princeton offer was not the invitation per se,
but the status of League officials. Avenol used the British desire to see
Princeton as an "official proposition" to complicate matters. Without US

government sanction, any staff dispatched to the United States would have to be treated as private persons. Of course, Avenol claimed to have no authority to change the status of these "international officials" and debase their labors to the level of "unofficial academic publications." Those backing the proposal, he chided, would "have to see whether the American authorities would be willing to recognize the international status of these officials." Even more important, the secretary-general asserted, were the thorny constitutional questions raised by the invitation. The transfer of all or part of the Secretariat could be undertaken only if a request was made by one or more states. Avenol, long acquainted with US government trepidation, turned this to his advantage.

Shifting responsibility, Avenol left it to the United States "to decide whether it could, if not actually invite all or part of the Secretariat, at least to authorize such transfer as is implied by the invitation of the Princeton University." Such action would safeguard the international standing of League staff. Yet even as he made this suggestion, Avenol derided the Americans behind their backs, telling the British representative that it was "improbable" that the United States would take "any initiative" on the invitation.[94] According to Kelly, when offered British assistance in negotiating the US status of officials—a problem that Avenol had just evoked—the secretary-general "flared up violently" and declared this unsatisfactory.[95] Avenol dismissed the idea of spending League money on relocation, deeming it an investment from "which one could not expect any returns." He also rejected Kelly's offer of British credit to pay for the move because Princeton was an "uncertain" proposition.[96]

This was all expressed in a high-handed manner, but Avenol held the upper hand. World events were moving rapidly and not in Great Britain's favor. Avenol's behavior reflected this turn. Those privy to the meeting noted that they had never seen a representative of any government treated so shoddily by the secretary-general.[97]

Having disposed of Kelly, at noon Avenol was presented with the softer target of Harold Tittmann from the US embassy in Bern. The secretary-general regaled the American official with a summary of what had just transpired, mentioning that the United Kingdom was treating the Princeton invitation as a formal offer. Avenol stated that since the British had made it a formal question, the League needed formal assurances before it could consider decamping for the United States. Prepared to answer this sort of objection, Tittmann suggested that the United States merely had to authorize the functioning of the technical services and the international status of their staff, not formally invite them. But considering the legal concerns he had emphasized, Avenol put a question to Tittmann that he likely could have answered himself. Would the US government, the secretary-general leadingly asked, extend the much-discussed formal invite? The American was pushed off balance and answered that he would have to ask his government. Avenol had muddied the waters, transforming the British demand that the Princeton offer be seen as an official proposition into a means to compel the United States to clarify its official position on the League.[98]

Tittmann duly made this request of Hull. The response was what Avenol predicted: the Roosevelt administration would take no such overt action. It was not prepared to bear the political costs of an "obligation to make possible the continued functioning of the technical services of an international and intergovernmental organization of which this government is not a member." More to the point, this could not be done "without the approval of the Congress and we do not consider that it would be possible to seek the agreement of the Congress at this time."[99]

Well-connected networks immediately transmitted the news. Willits was made privy to Hull's response to Tittmann's request for clarification. Willits spoke with Aydelotte, who in turn had apparently gotten the scoop from Llewellyn Thompson at the State Department. Willits let the IAS chief know that "Avenol wired to the State Department asking whether technical services could transfer and if they did could they still function as an international organization. The State Department or the President seemed to feel that this bureaucratic procedure implied some political guarantees that they were unwilling to give."[100]

A diplomat with practiced abilities to deflect and obfuscate had outmaneuvered the British and American governments. Avenol had the advantage of a turncoat, understanding intimately the limits of those now arrayed against him, particularly the Americans. Avenol was familiar enough with his former friends that he expected Hull's response would validate his obstruction. The upshot was that by the end of June 1940, it appeared that the opportunity to rescue the technical bureaus and secure the League itself had been lost. This could not be kept from the international press in Geneva, particularly the *Tribune*, which gleefully pronounced the League "Ready for Death."[101]

UNLIMITED HOLIDAY

As July began, there was little room for maneuver. An anxious Loveday confided to what had become his most resolute supporter, the Rockefeller Foundation:

> On the chances of the Service functioning I can hold at present no final view other than that there are very serious risks ahead. I do not know

what communications there will be between Switzerland and the outside world in a few days' time—already we are shut off from the British Commonwealth except by cable. The Princeton offer in spite of my
protestations was unfavorably received here and it now appears cannot
be supported in higher quarters on your side. . . . The Health Section—
leaderless—hardly exists. Nothing remains but the epidemiological intelligence and opium, or nothing that is worth preserving. I have been
fairly successful in pushing my key men so far. But they may be thrown on
the streets at any moment and if they are they may be financially forced
to accept resignation and in that case never be recollected as an official
group.[102]

Complicating matters, many staff felt the pull of home while personnel
from countries that were still at war with—or worse, conquered by—the
fascist powers, became an object of concern. On top of this, perhaps twenty
of the staff of the ILO were "wanted" in some form by the Germans, a cir-
cumstance that might complicate any departure, should it happen. Willits
was deeply concerned about where the EFS might end up, or when it would
meet its end. Nevertheless, he was clear that while the EFS, "does not contain all the elements needed for such continuing study [of world economic
developments]. . . . [I]t is the best going center of such study and knowledge
in the world."[103]

The international resonance of the organization generated anxiety
around the globe. Among the agitated was McDougall, who paced the
floors in London. Shaken by the events of June and injured by a fall taken in
the blackout, he slackened his usual brisk pace of work and took to reciting
somber Shakespearean snippets. He was preoccupied with the fate of the
technical services on which he had staked so much. That spring he was in
contact with both Loveday and Willits, to little effect. Officials in Australia
were told by their High Commission that McDougall was "very eager for
some action to transfer part of the League of Nations to America."[104]

In the United States, apprehension was no less acute. Willits, whose
Social Science Division had invested so much, tied the EFS's fate to the
larger issue of refugee scholars and scholarship. Writing on July 2 after
learning of FDR's decision on the invite, Willits asserted that if the "Nazi-
fication" of Europe continued and Britain was subjugated, the "intellectual
task which becomes the responsibility of this country is as important as the
military one—ultimately perhaps more so." He felt that the EFS "does not
contain all the elements needed for each continuing study as seems to me
desirable but it is the best going center of such study and knowledge in the
world. Elementary considerations of conservation would seem to dictate
that RF should see that the nucleus of this organization is salvaged for the

future service of mankind." Deliverance for the sake of humanity came with a steep price tag. Willits's offer of salvation required an investment by the foundation of upward of $100,000 (over $2 million in 2022) for up to two years.[105] In the end, it would be much more than that.

Meanwhile, hope continued to ebb as Avenol leaned on the two heaviest counterweights to his schemes, Lester and Loveday. The Frenchman attempted to maneuver Lester into resignation through a bit of bureaucratic jujitsu. When that failed, he outright offered his deputy an "unlimited holiday" with full pay. For Lester it was a tantalizing chance to escape and return home before that possibility dissolved. The resolute Irishman refused this temptation.[106]

In the United States efforts to secure the League's technical services continued. An idea emerged in mid-July that turned the legalism of Avenol's refusal against him. Riefler called on connections in Washington to discuss the issue. With the "guidance and approval of his friends in the State Department," he drafted a letter to Avenol. Riefler suggested that instead of claiming that the full Secretariat or even the entire EFS was decamping for New Jersey, those sent could merely be considered temporarily on mission. This proposal was immediately conveyed to Lord Lothian, who rallied British support for the idea.[107] The Princeton institutions followed up with a further letter to Avenol, again offering the technical services a haven. Princeton's president asserted that "most of the difficulties we feel are formal rather than real" and pleaded: "Surely the League has the power to authorize part of its personnel to proceed to the United States on mission and thus to work physically out of Geneva. Would not the proposal we have in mind be thoroughly analogous to this situation?"[108]

Hambro's presence in the United States paid dividends when he put his heft behind a follow-up message to the secretary-general. He called Avenol's legalistic bluff by advocating acceptance of the Princeton invitation in his capacity as the sitting president of the League Assembly. The Norwegian made it clear that officially the EFS would be establishing only a "branch" office in Princeton (even though its director and most of its remaining staff would be going), there was no need for approval from the member states. Hambro's initiative helped disarm any reservations primed by references to the Covenant. Geneva would officially remain the bureau's seat. Hambro emphasized that Princeton would be a hospitable and well-equipped country retreat where the technical service could continue its efforts. He also let it be known that the issue was being followed by the American media with "great interest"—which was not an exaggeration.[109]

PRESS FOR SANCTUARY

Leading American newspapers had closely followed the drama in Geneva. As the crisis reached a head in July, leading outlets announced their support for turning the United States into a safe harbor. In mid-July the *Washington Post* and the *New York Times* threw their support behind relocation of the technical bureaus. Felix Morley, outgoing editor of the *Post*, had been prompted by a number of those conspiring to move the economic section. Well informed by advocates of that action, he wrote a solid summary of the events of the spring. Morley tiptoed around Avenol's refusal, instead claiming the secretary-general had sent "no definite reply" to the Princeton invitation, which made it seem the option was more viable than it had appeared in mid-July. Among the Secretariat sections, the EFS was singled out for its "importance to reconstruction . . . vital regardless of the outcome of the war," because its analyses "supplement, coordinate, and give a broader viewpoint to the publications of . . . various national governments." Overall, "if we assume a world in which there will continue to be exchange of products and financial transactions between nations then the factual and statistical studies of this League agency will also continue to be of great value." Morley put himself and his paper behind "temporary settlement" of League agencies in the United States, because "the creative science of the group of men who can do this work should be fostered, for the benefit of civilization, by the one nation which is now clearly in a position to provide the necessary sanctuary."[110]

The *New York Times* was even more direct, in a missive that reminds us that it was not simply partisans who believed the League had value. It articulated a vein of what had become conventional wisdom: "The truth is that though the League failed in its main political objectives, it has done splendid work, with American aid and cooperation and sometimes with American personnel, in the vast field of public health; in the study of economic and financial problems; . . . and in other social and scientific areas." Because of this, the Princeton proposal was "commonsense": as "more and more this country becomes the refuge of creative minds," there was "every reason why a temporary shift should be made from Nazi-threatened Geneva to this peaceful sanctuary."[111] While opponents remained, a vocal constituency had appeared to publicly articulate the case for asylum. This was not because of the political potential of the League, but because its technical abilities seemed even more valuable to repair a fractured world.

Nevertheless, sanctuary was possible only if leverage could be found to spring the bureaus from their European prison. As the Battle of Britain began in earnest in July, British influence on the continent withered. German dominance over France was certain, and a collaborationist regime was gaining authority, complicating any escape. Despite all the intrigue in London, Washington, New York, and Princeton, Avenol appeared to hold the best cards. He was able to continue to defer and deflect the entreaties from the United States and elsewhere. Sweetser continued his lobbying in Washington for some sort of direct US government action, yet a July 8 meeting with Berle witnessed how even his own reservoir of optimism was draining. The assistant secretary recorded that Sweetser "sees twenty years of work going down the drain, and naturally is unhappy. I could not console him very much."[112]

A VICHY BETRAYAL

The first weeks of July promised that the issue would come to a head. Persistent rumors intimated that the secretary-general was preparing to remove British staff as an overture to handing the League over to the "totalitarian states."[113] Fresh assurances from Avenol that he intended to continue the technical activities of the League—at whose behest was not specified—left an already-wary Tittmann suspicious.[114] A report to Washington recorded that the secretary-general had provided little substantive detail about the future of the League itself. Talk that liquidation of the Secretariat was at hand continued, and the "obvious difference of opinion among the higher ... officials" on vital issues was becoming hard to ignore.[115] Tittmann clearly had some other confidential perspectives on a situation that Lester believed was "approaching a crisis." Secretariat staff had shrunk to just one hundred—sixty-five from around the world and thirty-five from Switzerland. Many were from nations that were conquered or still combatants. Among these there was considerable anxiety, as Avenol, wielding the hammer of austerity, looked to chisel away international staff. By July 17 it looked as if the secretary-general would finally be able to compel an exodus of a significant portion of the remaining staff, potentially clearing the way for his agenda.[116]

Abruptly, one of the masters Avenol apparently hoped to serve foiled his plans. René Charron, a French official with the EFS also shocked by his nation's defeat, returned from Vichy with the news that its decision to leave the organization had been reversed. France would stay in the League but would not take an active part in its activities. As part of this policy, the government ordered Avenol to resign his position on account of his nationality.[117] News swept through the palace and was almost as quickly placed in Tittmann's cables. It was a gift to Lester, who delighted in watching Avenol's "bumptious bubble be burst." Constraining Lester's glee was the question of whether the secretary-general would "try—even from spite—to put his plan into force before he goes."[118]

Spite did not prevail. Although Avenol attempted to hide Vichy's order from subordinates, his views—particularly toward the Princeton plan—had to shift. He floated the possibility of sending Loveday and Rasmus Skylstad to "investigate conditions" at the university. Staff began to actively formulate the logistics and costs for a possible transfer.[119]

On July 25, under pressure from various countries, struggling against his own staff, and abandoned by Vichy, Avenol finally resigned. His self-justifying and far-from-candid resignation emphasized the virtues of technical collaboration (rather than collaboration with Vichy). He lauded his own efforts to further the "great economic, social and humanitarian work" undertaken by the League's technical bodies. He highlighted the Bruce-inspired Central Committee as one of his leading accomplishments, an attempt to bring technical work to the forefront of the League's mission. Implementation, he admitted, had been a problem, and he lamented that since the start of the war, he had been managing an organization in decline. Obscuring critical reasons for his departure, Avenol claimed he could no longer execute the mission for which he had been appointed or justify holding his office.[120]

Whatever Avenol's true motivations for leaving, most of the remaining member states eagerly accepted his resignation, and pro forma acknowledgments of his service followed. There was relief among those who had hung on against the Frenchman. Lester's opinion was best expressed in his diary by a poem tucked beneath a copy of Avenol's resignation:

> For while the tired waves vainly breaking
> Seem here no painful inch to gain,
> Far back through creeks and inlets making
> Comes, silent flooding in, the main.
> And not by eastern windows only,
> When daylight comes, comes in the light.
> In front the sun climbs slow—how slowly!
> But westward look! The Land is bright.[121]

TO A BRIGHT, WESTWARD LAND

The day after his resignation, July 26, Avenol publicly assented to moving the EFS to the United States. Princeton was cabled. Dodds immediately shot back "Delighted."[122]

Acceptance, however, was not an exit. There was much to do in an unsettled and dangerous Europe to get valuable persons and information to the safety of New Jersey. With the door opened, staff faced the challenge of booking bus, train, and boat passage through France and Spain—no easy task in the aftermath of bitter military campaigns and political collapse. This was duly completed, although the lack of an official invitation might pose problems; it left open the question whether the United States would provide the necessary visas.[123]

The League staff need not have worried. On the day of the announcement there was action at the highest levels. Hambro and the Norwegian minister in Washington, Wilhelm von Munthe af Morgenstierne, met with FDR at the White House.[124] The following day, key figures in the State Department dismantled all legal and diplomatic barriers to entry. Sumner Welles quickly approved visas that would allow for the "prompt clearance" of the detachment and any data they brought along. With the politically fraught question of a formal invitation no longer relevant, the US government took the official actions crucial to open its borders to the League.[125]

Although hesitant political calculations on the part of the Roosevelt administration had contributed to the near-failure of the Princeton plan, the United States did not alter its position toward the ILO, which it still formally refused to aid. However, just as things were falling into place for the EFS, the Canadian government extended to the ILO an offer of sanctuary at Montreal's McGill University on July 26.[126]

Of course, institutions are made up of people, and several sets of individuals had to actually travel to North America from a shattered, shaken Europe. They were embarking on a journey thousands of others would make, and even more would attempt. They were joining a stream of migrants in flight from ideological realities into exile.

For organizations that lived by documentation and memorandums, there was a generous serving of paperwork to digest before departing Switzerland. But the exodus was swift. The international press covered the August 6 departure of EFS members from Geneva on a chartered bus. ILO staff left the next day.[127] Swiss newsreels even captured the evacuation on film. The long-deferred process that was at last in motion, though, was soon interrupted. What could have been a summer motor tour in a calmer time quickly took a wrong turn. That night, outside Grenoble, France, the bus carrying the EFS collided with a tram, crashed into a pole, and flipped into a ditch. Media attention to the section's departure ensured that the accident was reported by French newspapers as well as the Associated Press. Word of this quickly reached the United States and those invested in the journey. Almost every member of the group suffered some sort of injury, and three people were sent to the hospital. While none of the wounds was mortal, valuable time was lost.[128]

Bruised and fatigued, the group made it to its next hurdle, the Spanish frontier. Transiting Spain was complicated. The international civil servants

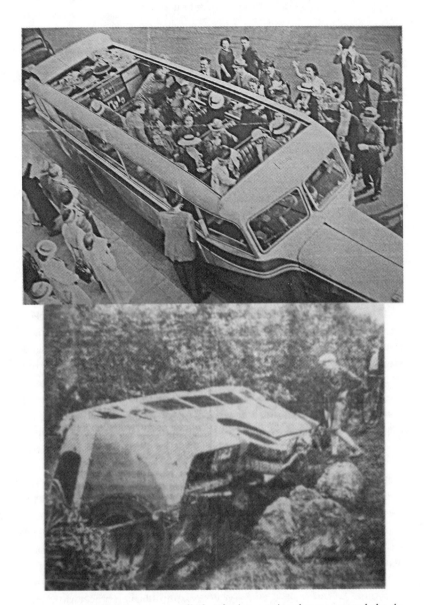

FIGURE 3.2. *Exit Geneva, enter ditch. The international press covered the departure of the Economic and Financial Section from Geneva by bus in August as well as the accident that left the bus in a ditch outside Grenoble. (Library of Congress)*

found themselves on inhospitable ground. The Spanish government was aligned with the political order that disdained the Geneva organizations. This attitude was visible at the border. Even before the EFS's trip, Spanish frontier guards had taken to telling international civil servants that they no longer rated diplomatic privileges, and staffers had suffered the indignity of having their luggage searched.[129] Just months earlier, contempt had reached the point where Spanish border guards brandished bayonets before Winant while he was traveling on ILO business.[130] Formal harassment was only part of the complications. Spain still had open wounds from a civil war that had ended only the year before. There were strict controls on currency, and visitors often found US dollars indispensable. With cash tight and the Spanish government rationing many consumer items, travelers found that many daily transactions were best conducted in cigarettes.[131] The frontier of France and Spain might have seemed to present another barrier, but to the relief of all, they were allowed to pass after a relatively short wait at the border. Despite all sorts of worries and inconveniences, the EFS contingent managed to cross Spain in good order.

It was a short journey, but it ended in a different world. The refugees straggled into Lisbon on August 12. Coming from anxious Geneva, they found a city where prewar conditions and attitudes prevailed. Controls and rationing were absent. Food was abundant, with the Portuguese expecting visitors to sit down to "fish and two meats at every meal." They also savored the "pre-pre-war coffee" that could be found at the city's better cafés, even if such pleasures were "surprisingly expensive." The city had become an impromptu migratory hub, and its lively atmosphere was further enhanced by a growing colony of refugees. Some considered the ambience "fatiguing," although this verve was "delightful" to others.[132]

Despite the relief that came with reaching Portugal, there was still the very real difficulty of getting to North America. The plan the League refugees had hatched in Geneva was to arrive in Lisbon, obtain the necessary exit permits, and then wait for a berth on a vessel out. Passage was not ensured. With so many queuing for escape, space was at a premium. Compared to others, the League migrants did not suffer too badly. Loveday and at least part of the entourage found lodging at the grand Avenida Palace Hotel (not far from the Rockefeller Foundation's Lisbon office, which was finding a new role assisting refugees), a spot that was earning a reputation as a haven for migrants and spies. The travelers had to trust that they had enough "subsistence" to support them while they idled.[133]

They could take heart that the faithful were working for their deliverance. The US offices of the American Export Line and Pan American Airlines found themselves "besieged" by Riefler, Sweetser, and Aydelotte, who were seeking space for their charges. Aydelotte was particularly shameless in his efforts, even using the news of the bus accident to curry sympathy and favor. But their various ploys worked. On August 20, Loveday and his family, along with several other members of the staff, were given berths on the most prized (and costly) of escapes, the Pan American Yankee Clipper (chartering a flight for the EFS was discussed).[134] The rest of the section would remain in Iberian internment for several more weeks, but when Loveday's time came to embark, he fulfilled standing instructions to send a final cable to the US consul in Geneva: "Sailing to day . . . Clipper." The US legation in Switzerland, which had tracked the progress of the section closely, dashed off a message to Washington.[135]

The Clipper brought Loveday's small detachment to New York with a rapidity almost unthinkable just a few years before. Their arrival was a moment of near jubilation for the various individuals who had schemed to bring them across the Atlantic. Press reports of the journey's end were hard to miss in the newspapers and notified those in the United States that they had valuable peers on their shores.[136] It was not until September 4 that berths for the rest of the staff, including the influential economist Ragnar Nurkse, were found on the SS *Excambion*, which arrived safely in Jersey City on September 14.[137]

News of the expedition's successful end in the United States undoubtedly warmed Sean Lester, who had been left to keep the embers of the League alight in Geneva. Officially acting secretary-general after Avenol's resignation, the understudy Lester would play the leading role well for the rest of the conflict. Although he had come to detest the Frenchman, Lester implemented one of Avenol's emergency contingencies. The new secretary-general retreated with a small group of about twenty remaining staffers to the Rockefeller-funded library in a wing of the palace, sealing up the rest of the building. From there the Irishman retained titular control of the League, but in practice he had little power.

The League budget remained a shambles, and Lester spent a great deal of time struggling to find economies. As predicted, communications were limited and censored. Increasingly, letters were sent in simple codes (cheekily, France became the "Restaurant Company" and Hambro "our northern friend"). Lester often wrote more about personal concerns and nagging bureaucratic issues than the momentous issues of the day, lamenting to those outside his monumental prison, "I wish I could write with freedom."[138] Particularly in the early years of the war, the Swiss government continued its tense relationship with the League. It did little to hide its displeasure as the host of an institution that had become a foreign body, inflaming its relations with continental Europe's new rulers. Lester clung on, sometimes grimly, in the face of these problems and prevailed in his mission. That the League headquarters remained in operation (at least officially) and loyal to its liberal origins is a credit to its last secretary-general.[139]

This show of fortitude was a consequence of Lester's own run-up against closed borders. He remained in intermittent contact with the far-flung organs and supporters of the League. In fact, on the heels of Loveday's departure, Lester attempted to convene the League's Supervisory Commission in Lisbon in late August. Officially, this meeting in what had become the departure lounge for escape from Europe was to deal with the thicket of issues still facing the League. Despite his position and having obtained the correct papers, Lester was denied passage across the Spanish frontier. He and his entourage were victims of a general order issued by Spain's government on August 13 that barred international officials from crossing its border—just after the ILO delegation had crossed en route to its own exile in Canada.[140] Others had become aware that vital components of the internationalist bodies were making good their escapes. The order might well have been the Franco government's attempt to bar a gate, but only after most of the proverbial horses had bolted.

Just after Loveday departed on his journey to America, Sweetser more than hinted at the confluence of interests that had surmounted the political and logistical barriers to the transfer:

> The first steps here worked out with a rapidity, a completeness, and a cordiality which I had not dared hope. Everything that could be done from here seemed to have been done, though, as you can imagine, I would have liked a more formal official attitude than proved possible in the circumstances. The sincerity of the welcome left no doubt, however, and the form seem to me less important than the substance. . . . Our people are perhaps a bit formalistic; they feel that they can do a great deal privately, but that, with our form of government they could hardly go to the extent of formally inviting an official international agency based on a treat to which the government is not a party to come here without at least consulting Congress. That would have taken time and cause complications at this moment of delicacy both at home and abroad and seemed unnecessary in the circumstances. People felt they could do that was necessary without this, and, curiously enough, more easily with the League than for the ILO, because the League would be a completely foreign agency simply seeking asylum here while the ILO would in addition number the US amongst its most active members and thus have a double relationship . . . an odd outcome indeed.[141]

The departure of the EFS and ILO was just one scene in the larger drama of intellectual migration brought by the chaos of the period.[142] It was a spreading affliction in international society that enveloped many. Emblematic of the stricken was the ISC contributor Albert Hirschman, whose safe harbor in France was wrecked by the German triumph. Hirschman would find an ally in Varian Fry, who had left his writing job with the FPA to become a key figure in the Centre americain de secours. The organization aimed to get as many endangered individuals as possible out of occupied France. Here Hirschman's research for the ISC and his connections with Condliffe changed, and perhaps saved, his life. When contacted by Fry, Condliffe, by then based in Berkeley, used his connections in Washington and with the Rockefeller Foundation to lobby for assistance not only to refugees generally but also to Hirschman specifically. A timely letter from the Kiwi promising a fellowship facilitated attempts to provide Hirschman a "nonquota" visa that brought him to safety in California.[143]

EXILE IN NEW JERSEY

Evacuation was an end and a beginning. The League organs that had done pioneering work toward understanding the transnational forces that made the world economy a global system had been successfully transplanted. The value attached to this kind of understanding explains why American patrons saved this particular segment of the League. Its activities fit well into their view of what was necessary to govern the forces of the changing modern world. The EFS would again adapt to changing world conditions and aid in US and Allied postwar planning. Its members were already primed for postwar inquiry, and their expertise would prove invaluable to the United States and the Allied camp as they faced the expanding imperatives of global war. Now, however, they would assist a nation-state to which they were firmly attached as it sorted out its own visions for a world order to replace one that had degenerated into violence and chaos.

Aydelotte gloated over what had come into the hands of the United States:

> We had rescued one of the most important of the technical sections of the League from the rapidly advancing Nazi destruction. We had outmanoeuvred the puppet government of Vichy. In the darkest hour of the League the United States, whose defection in 1919 had been partly responsible for the League's weakness, was offering to important activities not merely sanctuary but a chance to continue work. The group of economic experts, gather and trained slowly over the course of twenty years, were either here or safely on their way, with the most important part of the records copied on microfilm.[144]

It is reductive to call the clumsy operation a coup. It was something bigger. The emergency effort in 1940 grew out of a longer campaign to coordinate US and League technical activities. More importantly, the urgency of support was rooted in the general internationalist belief in the vital need for the technical means to understand and govern aspects of modern life.

Therefore, a set of different constituencies worked to the same end, to preserve those elements of the League that had international resonance and deny them to the other side. The collaborative nature of the effort shows the interconnection and interdependence of international society. The American government and nongovernmental groups that were interventionist in intent worked together with peers to preserve what they all knew was a valuable strategic resource—knowledge.

There was further significance. As part of their credo, liberal internationalists accepted the importance of international organizations for their coordinating role in world order. Concerns in the tumultuous days of 1940 about fascist plots to seize the League and turn it to their ends might seem an example of liberals creating an image of their own ambitions in a dark mirror. However, in the face of Avenol's machinations, internationalist fears that the League might be turned into a propaganda pillar, an arm of Vichy, or technical support for German and Italian hegemony were not entirely baseless. Even though only putatively technical components of the League had escaped, their relocation had a political resonance and ensured that the League would not be completely co-opted by a fascist New Order. Its largest and most respected technical body was harboring in Princeton, the ILO was settled in Canada, other components had found havens in the Allied camp (its treasury went to London and the Opium Bureau to Washington, DC), and Lester was still hanging on in Geneva. This dispersal of elements of the League provided assurances that it would not serve another master in either form or function. Yet it is interesting to speculate on the impact a co-opted or even pro-Axis League might have had, particularly on plans for a postwar international body. Had the League been bent to serve the other side, it assuredly would have complicated the war aims of the disparate coalition roused to face fascism, an alliance that would name itself the United Nations.

From the moment of the exiles' arrival in New Jersey, labor awaited them. As with other evacuations in 1940, there were questions of reorganizing and reequipping. However, in the case of the EFS these were a touch mundane. Thriftily, the new "Princeton office" at the IAS was furnished with needed business equipment from the closing League Pavilion.[145] This was fortunate, as section members were already being handed tasks. Recovering from his malaise, the irrepressible McDougall filed requests from London at the height of the Battle of Britain, noting that although "things . . . are far from pleasant morale is . . . very high . . . and we shall all get used to a certain amount of bombing." He revealed a truth about the relocation: "Lester will hold the fort at Geneva, in effect doing nothing save maintain a facade. In so far as work is to be done, it will be done at Princeton."[146]

Even under fire, McDougall was keen to restart that work. Now it was even more apparent to him that tasks the EFS could perform were central to prosecuting the war that was at his doorstep. As the section was in transit, he dispatched a message to them in America. After perfunctory acknowledgment that Loveday had endured "an extraordinarily difficult time," McDougall bluntly pressed for the EFS to get on with the problem of postwar reconstruction. This was a tad presumptuous, as the Australian, aware of the Grenoble crash, remained uncertain whether Loveday and his section had actually made it to America.

Nevertheless, he impatiently included a memorandum (that Loveday marked up) laying out a "revolutionary" program. As a basic war aim, the democracies—a coalition into which he had already drafted the United States—promised to harness advances in science and technology in order to raise international standards of living. Like others, McDougall increasingly deployed the political rhetoric of the nation where he would soon carry out a mission. The United States was the indispensable partner for a revolution the Australian framed as a "'New Deal' for our own people and for all nations who are prepared to cooperate with us."[147]

International society was regrowing its connective tissues. American institutions inside and outside the government were quick to seek out the data and talents that the EFS staff had brought with them. Loveday would heed various requests and waste no time updating plans to attack the problem of postconflict reconstruction days after the rest of the staff reached Princeton.[148] It would be this task that the League exiles and a related band of journeymen would busy themselves for the rest of the war. Their ideas, primed and legitimated by interactions facilitated by international society, would stoke many of the ideas to reforge liberal international order in a postwar world dominated by the United States.

Even as these monumental questions waited, in the safety of their elite and ostensibly neutral environs, there was time for reflection. Sweetser was particularly appreciative of Aydelotte's actions. He later expressed gratitude "from the bottom of my heart" for the IAS chief's efforts to ensure that "out of the tragedy of the present moment," the League's services would soldier on in the United States. But establishment of the League outpost in Princeton was something larger and deeply personal for Sweetser, who confided to Aydelotte, "You know how much this means to me not only substantively but even emotionally after all these long years and particularly after . . . the disappointments that have come from this country."[149]

There was also space for relaxation. Sharing the satisfaction of bringing their charges to safety, Aydelotte and Sweetser escaped their responsibilities for a summer round of golf. Aydelotte recalled their time on the links together under the August sun as particularly sweet.[150]

4: THE ROVER BOYS OF RECONSTRUCTION

INTERNATIONAL SOCIETY IN THE AMERICAN WORLD

Do not give the animals paper or other harmful material.

SIGN POSTED IN GENEVA, 1930S

It's all extraordinarily interesting. I like these Americans.

FRANK MCDOUGALL, 1941

How to reorder world trade after the war, how to plan new international economic relations—these are favorite topics to-day both with the stratospheric politicians, economists, and sociologists, and also with the Rover Boys of Reconstruction, who will plan for the future with good will in their hearts and memories of the Versailles Treaty in their heads.

C. HARTLEY GRATTAN, 1942

January for health . . . February for economics.

FRANKLIN D. ROOSEVELT, 1942

EATING THE PAPER

By 1944, discussions of a postwar settlement were a constant hum. Institutional plans—and new international institutions—were moving from speculation into reality. Into this din the worldly Royall Tyler, an American veteran of the League's Secretariat and the European art scene, then in the service of Allen Dulles's intelligence syndicate in Switzerland, inserted his own commentary on the critical question of international governance. Sent by courier to the president of Johns Hopkins University, Isaiah Bowman, a member of the steering committee of the CFR's War and Peace Studies program, Tyler's set of memorandums was dutifully introduced into the US internationalist ecosystem.[1]

These unsolicited insights addressed an apparition that had long stalked discussions: the League. Tyler's experience there made him skeptical of it and its legacies. He recalled that in the late 1930s, as the ailing League moved into the hospice that was the freshly built Palace of Nations, a sign was posted near the llamas and a Moroccan sheep that were the last hold-outs from the previous occupant of the grounds, the Geneva Zoo. It commanded:

DEFENSE DE DONNER AUX ANIMAUX DU PAPIER
OU TOUTE AUTRE MATIERE NUISIBLE.[2]

He felt the sentiment about who should be fed paper was so apt that it should have been plastered in "six foot letters" in the Assembly Hall.

Such doubts shone through Tyler's missive on the Secretariat. He dismissed the technical turn as a mere evasion. It avoided the tough choices the body should have made after a first phase of "youthful enthusiasm" descended into a midlife crisis of frustration and failure with the Great Depression. Rather than take the realistic course of paring down and biding its time, the Secretariat sought to justify its existence with a stream of conferences and inquiries. This "work-making at Geneva" was the product of a "mysticism" that thought peace could be built by furthering "Health Surveys, Intellectual Co-Operation, Inquiries into Rural Life, Nutrition . . . Behavior of the Business Cycle . . . and Publicity in the League Pavilion at the New York World's Fair." All of these claims contained an element of truth but were beside the point. Tyler decreed that they fundamentally served to justify the continued existence of sectors of the Secretariat and only proved that "paper breeds paper as rabbits breed rabbits." This make-work "might have the economic section busy for years, giving birth to committees and sub-Committees, endless journeys and junketings and tons of documents." Fundamentally, the "Secretariat-tail came to wag the League-dog."[3] Tyler's was a view that would be recapitulated down the years. The last phase of the League's life was largely spent justifying its own questionable existence.

The pages Tyler himself fed into the debate found their way into the hands of the guru planning that "new international organization" at the State Department, Leo Pasvolsky. Long immersed in postwar planning, he had taken on a commanding portfolio on the question. This was an outgrowth of Pasvolsky's long-standing progressive and liberal views and his own experiences, which convinced him that the creation of tools for international governance was part and parcel of a stable order. Weeks before

Tyler's missives reached him, Pasvolsky delivered a speech noting how in the "vast and complicated field of economic, social and related activities, there is great need, now more widely recognized than ever, for specialized functional agencies." These would see that the new organization could conduct and coordinate the elements crucial to sustaining global order and peace.[4] Mechanisms such as those housed by the League Secretariat were not a tail wagging the dog but vital organs in the international body politic. So while Pasvolsky was served Tyler's papers, they were likely not digested.[5]

SOCIETY AT WAR

Pasvolsky has been dismissed as a "colorless bureaucrat" by histories of the United Nations. Called "Friar Tuck" by his peers, he might not have been flashy, but as an engaged economist throughout his career, Pasvolsky certainly was not lacking in substance. Some of these same histories have often given short shrift to the broader internationalism that lay behind not just the UN organization but also the UN alliance.[6] Yet Pasvolsky's inclusion of technical services as a cornerstone of the postwar settlement should have been no surprise. His time in Geneva, complemented by work at the Brookings Institution, was another variation of the progressive urge to measure and analyze problems to offer policy solutions. This all franchised him as a member of the international society that had long seen the League's services as offering at least a partial solution to the economic problems exposed by the Depression.[7]

Thus, Pasvolsky intimately understood the value of the EFS sheltering at the IAS, as he was one of the expansive set of Americans who saw the importance of information and analysis to govern a modern world economy. Such interest was itself a reflection of the fact that World War II was, as Paul Samuelson said, "an economists' war."[8] This was no boast. Total war demanded a broad view of the productive capacities of societies and economies—both enemies' and friends', and also one's own. Facts and figures were vital tools in these surveys, and many of the innovations in data and analysis that had appeared just a few decades, or even years, before had dramatic import. But Samuelson's tag also suggests how well the liberal internationalist ideas and concepts that had been filtered through the League before the war suited the needs of the prosecution of what has been called a "war for international society."[9] It was also a war waged *by* international society. The Allied war effort was necessarily collaborative, and in certain realms of economic thinking—particularly those related to the creation of a postwar liberal order—it depended on ideas and figures whose origins and legitimacy were grounded in international forums. Journeymen brought and sustained ideas crucial to a United States that was rejiggering international liberalism in a world at war.

The operations of the League and its exiles, along with those who had worked through and around it, provide an opportunity to observe how earlier ideas were retooled for wartime. There has been growing appreciation of the replication of imperial priorities that suffused the League in its heyday into the settlement that was framed during and after World War II.[10] But this is only part of the story. By tracing the wartime experience of League officials and a network of supporters, as well as the ideas and agendas they furthered, the emergence of the United States as an exponent and hub of liberal internationalism becomes clear. The UN alliance grabbed existing ideas from a variety of sources linked to debates and individuals that had long circulated in the larger internationalist universe. These figures embodied and embraced the technical capacities that liberal international society valued so deeply. Liberalism had already accepted the need for the skeletal supports of technical work, which provided a whole host of activities that rendered its concepts palatable—indeed, necessary—to a new global hegemon. This interplay exposes the multifaceted nature of many ideas incorporated into a renovated world order.

It was not the League itself that was decisive in establishing this new order, but the views and individuals that had flowed through it. The League's analysts investigated how crucial issues springing from modern life could be engaged and governed. However, wartime experiences in the US would ruthlessly diminish the League, even as the host embraced concepts the organization had done much to cultivate. It increasingly ceased to be an institution in its own right and was reduced to grist for discussions of a postwar world. Instead of being reinstalled as the leader of a liberal world order, the League would be distilled down to the sort of information in which it had trafficked. But this diminution itself shows how information was currency for vital planning and strategy and provides another sign of how information and analysis were seen as necessary mechanisms to sustain liberal order.

AN AMERICAN REVIVAL

The Geneva institutions were a welcome asset from the moment they arrived in North America. Their reach into American society was made apparent on April 19 and 20, 1941, when nearly one hundred Americans met in Princeton to hold a "reunion" of League associates along with a series of discussions dealing with important international issues and the means to govern them.

It all had a revivalist air. President Dodds noted that he was preach-

FIGURE 4.1. *An eddy of exiles. A profile of a strategic resource, members of the Economic and Financial Section at their asylum, the Institute of Advanced Study. Loveday is at left. (Library of Congress)*

ing "to the converted" in his sermon to the congregation. The readings were mostly the gospel of technical services. Still, the meeting did reveal the extent of the League network in the United States.[11] It had been easy to compile a list of over 250 names from vital sectors of academia, advocacy, philanthropy, and government, demonstrating how tightly knit Geneva was to US international society. The reach of an alumni association was clear in the embassy that the government sent to the conference. It included Feis and Pasvolsky. Even so, the event registered that the war had "changed fundamentally" the course of this relationship. Now, rather than streaming to Geneva, "the flow of American technicians ceased and a counter-eddy set in of international technicians to the Americas."[12]

That the refugee League easily fit into a niche in that interventionist habitat was a sign that it had evolved to fit a larger liberal ecosystem. The Princeton the EFS settled into was no neutral zone. What might have seemed a quaint academic village fairly bristled with analytical weapons pointed outward at world instability. Princeton University hosted a Rockefeller Foundation–funded listening station, which absorbed worldwide radio broadcasts to analyze the views that were streaming over US borders (a project that would inspire the establishment of the Foreign Broadcast Monitoring Service).[13] A security seminar initiated at the IAS with money from the Carnegie Corporation of New York was attempting to reorient American society to deal with an unstable world. The weaponized EFS had found its way into a miniature arsenal of democracy that emphasized how parts of US international society were already mobilizing for war.

At the IAS, Loveday and his fellow refugee scholars nestled among other exiled luminaries such as Albert Einstein and Kurt Gödel. A 1941 *New York Times* profile extolled the institute as a vital wing in the asylum the United States had become for the best of humanity; it was "the repository of the lore of time, not merely for herself but for the whole of the race." But the scholars' accomplishments were not assessed solely in academic terms. They were seen as assets for the nation in an uncertain time. The IAS director was not coy about his feelings about world affairs or, by extension, his goals for the institute's contributions to American security. He saw "neutrality [as] an excuse for not thinking." Totalitarianism was not merely a threat but immoral. It was impossible to "be neutral between right and wrong."[14]

Aydelotte was so convinced of the continued importance of the capacities the EFS brought to American shores that he sought funds from the Woodrow Wilson Foundation to build it a permanent home on the IAS campus. This abortive plan had been intended to preserve a resource for the interventionist liberalism that Aydelotte subscribed to, and it is yet another example of how progressive reform became a weapon in a global war.

Settling in at Princeton was remarkably easy, considering the drama of the wartime transatlantic evacuation. Swaths of the IAS's main building were handed over to Loveday's refugees. As always, the Rockefeller Foundation was in the background footing the bill. Grants-in-aid supported the settlement of the League staff in New Jersey, and the weighty $100,000 grant allocated in an already-distant April 1940 was repurposed for North American operations. More was to come. Over the following five years, Rockefeller would provide an average of $50,000 per annum for EFS operations (an annual average of around $1 million in 2022).[15]

The policy community in the United States was quick to make use of the exiles. There was little doubt of the utility of the resources the EFS had brought on microfilm. But even more important were the human resources that had been preserved, of great value to a government and society struggling to create the resources necessary to contend with its new global role. Soon after arrival, Loveday found his schedule crowded. Simon Kuznets would invite him to join studies on national income. Pasvolsky was soon attempting to shape the exiles' program. He solicited and praised a variety of reports generated by the EFS on "relief, commercial policy, and stabilization funds." He was "grateful," as such analysis was of "great help" to a harried State Department. Rockefeller staff approvingly noted that beyond academic and media organizations he was soon consulting with the Labor, Treasury, Commerce, and State Departments in Washington. They were hopeful that Pasvolsky's established expertise on Depression-era failings would provide needed perspective to foster the "peaceful reorganization of the world (if ever)."[16]

Although the arrival of the bureaus of a dismembered League had been widely covered in the press, Sweetser made sure to publicize the presence of the League itself on American soil, and he was given pages in the CFR's house organ, *Foreign Affairs*. In the dark days of 1940, Sweetser hurried past political failures that distracted "from its solid but less conspicuous successes." Rather, he thought it best to look to the nonpolitical work of the League. He repeated Flexner's view that it provided a permanent site of exchange. If nothing else, the League provided "a center where all international activities, particularly those of a technical and non-political nature, could concentrate and draw strength."[17] The war had "suspended" these efforts, but the "most highly developed" body—a "kind of specialized economic and financial league within the general League," namely the EFS—was safe in Princeton. Such technical activities had only increased capability and legitimacy by including inputs from nonmembers like the United States. This demi-league had proved its value with the variety of statistical data and holistic analyses contained in the "popular" *WES* series. These bodies had also advocated the "liberal policies" of "free and unrestricted trade" that "in the end . . . will prove to have been the right ones." Sweetser acknowledged that the League had "proved inadequate to avert the great catastrophe" rending the globe, but it showed a way forward on the "solution of day-to-day" problems besetting a modern world. It was a signal that following the relocation of the EFS, the United States had in its possession the best example of how to contend with the ongoing problems of modern life.[18]

The connections in international society that the League had helped to forge would prove enduring when transplanted to North America. What is more, these links facilitated the interests of some of the smaller actors. As a result, the ideas and individuals who had worked up concepts in transnational dialogues would have ready access to centers of power and authority in the United States. And the United States, with limited capacities and facing potentially limitless global commitments, was eager to employ them.

SOCIAL JUSTICE WARRIOR

Other figures who had been instrumental in shaping key concepts would soon feel the gravitational pull of the United States. McDougall—who retained his seat on the League's Committee on Depressions—embraced it. From an embattled London, he entered the intermural British discussion of whether the peace would rest on an Anglo-French alliance or a British-US condominium. This had been settled by the spring's catastrophe. A future offered jointly by the "British Empire and U.S.A." would have to be pitted against one imposed by Nazi Germany. Long appreciative of ideology in economic questions, McDougall knew that promises to build a better world would be decisive in what had always been a "war of ideas."[19]

Much that dotted these weaponized memorandums was not new. What had become wartime initiatives were drawn from programs McDougall had worked up in the dying light of "economic appeasement." Also cannibalized were ideas from his attempt to articulate a British plan of action to support a general international settlement in the months before the European war began.[20] Nevertheless, the new joint plan was vast, touching on trade, colonies, and monetary relations among a variety of subjects. Fundamental was the need to foster "social justice" as "inspiring our own people with a crusading zeal. . . . We must be prepared for positive action . . . to associate our defense of liberty with the re-dress of economic inequalities." This required turning the productive power of science and technology toward "raising the standard of living." The scope of the endeavor extended to include even the relation between the state and the individual, and McDougall accepted that state action was necessary. Acting on these propositions in the light of 1940 required international coordination, and fortunately there was already a bank of experience to draw on. McDougall closed his report with an exhortation: "It seems clear that whether the name 'League of Nations' is used or not, the experience and machinery of the Economic and Financial Organization of the League, the Health and Social Organizations should be used as a basis upon which the future World Authority should be built."[21]

July 1940 might have made any liberal pessimistic, but the former fruit farmer remained irrepressible. McDougall suggested the need for the liberal powers to "become the leaders of a beneficent revolution by associating with our defense of liberty and International [*sic*] law effective proposals for securing economic freedom and social justice." This required "boldness" and following paths "however far reaching and even revolutionary." Co-opting US reform jargon, he declared that this would mean a "'New Deal' for our own people and those nations prepared to cooperate with us."

However, this "revolutionary" change was to be built on established elements. McDougall's suggestions were intended to win the war, but that could not be done without winning over the Americans. McDougall's views were intensified and extended by the tendrils of international society. The international circuits he had already established ensured that they reached figures like Pasvolsky. Friar Tuck was already deeply invested in postwar planning that funneled nonstate expertise into the US government. Appealing to this connected member of the US establishment, McDougall suggested, "Once the Blitzkrieg gegen England is over ... (if it comes) I should very much like to come to Washington and discuss these problems."[22]

His wish would be granted. Australia would make the United States the site of its first overseas legation in 1941, part of its own attempt to forge a strategic relationship with the Pacific leviathan.[23] Sent to Washington as a delegate to an international wheat conference, McDougall would find a niche rallying the forces of liberal international society for the cause of world order.

He quickly made the most of contacts fostered through Geneva. Indeed, the people McDougall accessed were a literal who's who of important quadrants of international society. His patron, Bruce, had a society contact who was even closer at hand after the events of the spring, John Winant. After shepherding the ILO to Montreal, Winant was tapped by Roosevelt to serve as US ambassador to an embattled United Kingdom. He became one node in a shifting set of contacts that moved discussions about economic warfare in a variety of directions, but all the proposals depended on international institutions to support liberal order. Bruce's stature, as well as his position as Australia's High Commissioner in London, granted his ward access to Welles and Wallace. As the latter was vice president, McDougall was particularly attentive to rekindling their relationship. He also made a point of seeking out the panoply of other actors who influenced planning. He contacted Willits to renew bonds with the RF. Figures at the Brookings Institution were also in his sights.[24]

Circuit riding brought the itinerant Australian to preach at Princeton. There he found the League exiles and Riefler (who popped up in Washington as well). The EFS would play the part for which it had been cast, providing intellectual heft for rapidly developing plans on the economic front. The Australian pressed Loveday's section to do a "scientific" study that would cement an already-keen US interest in transforming the phrase "Freedom from Want" into a substantive program via an international conference on the issue.[25] Tied into the network of liberal international society, Loveday's section would repeat this function throughout the war. It regularly provided intellectual and informational sinew for internationalist concepts being transmuted into reality by the United States and its allies.

Throughout, McDougall remained his own hub of international society, keeping the Australian and British governments briefed. He also made a point of letting other nongovernmental groups outside the United States know which ideas (particularly his) were germinating within, continuing cross-fertilization across international society even under the pressures of war. He kept in touch with an economics group at Chatham House. It included Paul Rosenstein-Rodan and his protégé H. W. Arndt. This outpost was itself part of an extended British community pondering reconstruction.[26] From afar, McDougall prodded a British collaborator, John Boyd Orr, to declare at an international conference on science and the postwar world in London that Allied aims should include a "committee to work out worldwide food policy based on human needs."[27]

This was part of a larger campaign to establish "US-Empire" cooperation as the basis of the world to come. McDougall leaned on the standard-of-living concept to organize his agenda as he tied it to American jargon. As the League Pavilion had shown, internationalist concepts could easily be sugarcoated with US political rhetoric. Glazed in that way, standard of living became a signal theme for digesting the US-UK relationship. Exploiting the "Four Freedoms" mercilessly, in late 1941 McDougall took up Lord Halifax's call to link "Freedom from Want" to the Allied cause: "Freedom from want has two interrelated facets, national and social. The first requires that nations should have full opportunity to develop their resources, ready access to raw materials, and should not be deprived by the action of other nations from acquiring the means of payment. The second requires that each nation should make a progressive improvement in standards of living." It was assumed that international cooperation was indispensable to achieve these goals. Success would require a diagnosis of the problems through the compilation of statistical information on populations and economies. Analysis of this material would, in turn, inform the policies that provided solutions. The endeavor would also require international assistance for relief and reconstruction, which the United States and Britain could supply. The hope was that a conference would yield a body to conduct any surveys that might be required. The League and ILO exiles provided a template and support for those who would do the work. Because the questions were large and persistent, there was a need for an international "Council on Food Problems," but the whole issue suggested that larger, permanent international machinery would be required.[28] Through efforts to improve diet, the standard of living became the means to an end that McDougall and others christened "social justice." This was an earnest hope, but it could not help but be a political weapon in an ideological war.[29]

Presence does not automatically confer influence, but it was telling how easily McDougall's ideas and initiatives rode the wires of a networked international society. It is remarkable how many offices and figures in Washington were served his memorandums. McDougall's offensive on the standard of living was well timed. It opened when there was a pressing need to spell out what the Western democracies, back on their heels, offered the world. As McDougall noted, there had been painfully little from Britain on the question, and the United States was not officially a combatant. What is more, Germany was already bending European economic, political, and social relationships to its own desires.[30] This reality and the grim legacies of the Depression meant that a return to the *status quo ante* was unpalatable to great swaths of the world's population.

While McDougall was an energetic voice, his message resonated because it was part of a conversation where the participants shared many terms and assumptions. As an Australian he was able to communicate intimately with London. This identity had uses in the United States as well, where he was perceived differently than British officials. As McDougall literally and figuratively spoke languages the Americans could understand, he found a ready market for his agenda. As for others, his status in international society, burnished by time in Geneva, paid a further dividend. McDougall, using a shared lingo of reform, was able to move between the various encampments in Washington and the American establishment, even those arrayed against each other. In this way, individuals with connections built via international society facilitated work within a sometimes-fragmented US government.

MINISTRIES OF WARFARE

Americans needed no introduction to nutrition and food as a social and strategic issue. Yet McDougall's agitation does expose a rising discourse around the importance of international development within the larger goal of reconstructing a liberal global economy. Fed by concepts and ideas from the interwar years, this discourse germinated in tandem with other related agendas in the strategic hothouse of Allied war planning, where ideas were weapons of war. Still, it is telling how early and quickly the matrix of concepts to generate improved living standards were pressed into both government planning and public discourse in the period before and immediately following the US entry into the conflict.

At the highest levels, the Roosevelt administration related these issues to the swelling dialogue on a postwar world. In a January 1941 address FDR articulated the Four Freedoms, those "essential human freedoms" that were to be secured for peoples "everywhere in the world": freedom of speech, freedom of worship, freedom from fear, and freedom from want. FDR acknowledged that internationally the "strength of our economic and political systems is dependent upon the degree to which they fulfill . . . expectations" of a "constantly rising standard of living." One of the four, "freedom from want," became an easily referenced benchmark for improved "economic understandings" extending a better, healthier life to all.[31]

Roosevelt's highly unneutral act of meeting with Churchill in Placentia Bay in August 1941 underlined the global nature of this commitment. The joint communiqué issued, the Atlantic Charter, was collectively a set of principles, a promise, and a projectile in an ideological war. Aggressively assuming the "final destruction of the Nazi tyranny," the document's points referenced interwar discussions while extending promises of equal access for all nations "to the trade and to the raw materials of the world which are needed for their economic prosperity." It also promised "the fullest collaboration between all nations in the economic field with the object of securing, for all, improved labor standards, economic advancement and social security." It was, as some have called it, part of a New Deal for the world, but rather like that initiative, it would be implemented with formulas generated internationally.[32]

The rhetoric of the Four Freedoms and the Atlantic Charter spelled out global visions. Welles, who assumed a leading position in explicating American desires for a postwar world, employed these hopes as well as concepts McDougall and others trafficked in. In a series of addresses in the months straddling the US entry into the war, he explained the need of international cooperation (with a tone hospitable to the League).[33] In October 1941, he offered a vision of a renewed liberal international economic order. Abstract rubrics of trade and standards of living were harmonized with the easily grasped issues of nutrition and consumption. These two issues were highlighted as means to bring airy reform visions down to earth: "Both from immediate post-war needs and in the longer range aspect, we must give serious attention to the problems of nutrition." Referencing food and nutrition squared the circle of broad ambitions to restore trade that would benefit individuals in a manner fulfilling promises in the Atlantic Charter. Welles also emphasized that plans for the peace should not wait until after the war (or even until the United States was in it).[34] Treasury Secretary Henry Morgenthau Jr. drove home the point that food reflected larger aspirations to improve living standards: "In order to build a better world—and that goes for our own country as well as for those abroad—we must recognize the citizens' right to have a minimum standard of food with which he can live the life of a free man."[35]

There was more than rhetoric. As part of the pell-mell US mobilization to prepare for and then wage a global war after the fall of France, FDR turned to Wallace to head the high-profile Economic Defense Board in July 1941; in December it would become the Board of Economic Warfare (BEW). Heralded at its creation as "a sort of Ministry of Economic Warfare," the board was to conduct "investigations and advise the President on the relationship of economic defense . . . to postwar economic reconstruction."[36] It was to plan the world to come. Around it, what outsiders came to call a "Wallace school" cohered as a nucleus of American economic and postwar planning during a formative period.[37]

The board's broad mandate incited controversy. While the BEW was a means to the economic warfare the Allies waged, it would also be a theater of bureaucratic combat that characterized the Roosevelt years. The very extent of its responsibilities meant it overlapped and conflicted with the State Department and other bureaucracies. This led to bruising rounds of Washington infighting where it (and Wallace) would be battered, beaten down, and eventually buried in 1943.[38]

However, in the BEW's early phases, when it had pride of place, it provided the context for some of the vice president's well-known and influential rhetoric. Early on, Wallace used his strategic position to promote his desires for a renovated world hospitable to the "common man." He has regularly been relegated to the realm of idealism or roads not taken. But at that critical and formative historical juncture, Wallace's ambitions and rhetoric coincided with the transnational New Deal and gained traction internationally. Once again the internationalist views so well articulated by the Geneva crowd were internalized by a set of American advocates and institutions.

Like Wallace's 1939 League Pavilion speech, his administration of the BEW revealed that internationalism was indeed his default setting. Wallace's comments came from the left wing of the New Deal, but they were fully enmeshed in and took legitimacy from an established internationalist economic discourse. Even so, his speeches were calls for US global leadership to take up the role that power, position, and history demanded. Wallace's "Foundations of the Peace" speech in December 1941, later appearing in the *Atlantic Monthly*, was fundamentally an economic argument that repeated staple internationalist views and established agendas that were being refitted for warfare. Wallace defined a "century of the common man" built on elevated standards of living as one of the "foundations of the peace." He foresaw fostering industrialization in places where capital and technical knowledge were scarce as a means to such improvements. However, his calls for programs to promote progress and prosperity as basic war aims prompted the question of how just how this would be done.[39]

Behind such rhetorical flourishes were action and implementation. Wallace himself was already deeply invested in international initiatives to improve nutrition and standards of living by boosting agricultural production through new methods and crops. One place where he was engaged was Mexico, where a long-standing Rockefeller Foundation interest in agriculture would lead to programs to improve wheat production. One fruit of these efforts would be the dwarf wheat bred by Norman Borlaug, inspiring the first phases of what would become the "Green Revolution."[40]

A sign of the BEW's seriousness was that it was stocked with talented minds attempting to offer substance to ambitious agendas. At its formation, one figure the vice president immediately snatched was Winfield Riefler, who became the BEW's executive director.[41] Riefler's work in summer 1940 to save Loveday, the EFS staff, and microfilmed data was the prelude to a deep investment in economic warfare and overlapping questions around postwar order. These interests were an extension of his views about the interconnected world economy and its relationship to global order. The same information and analysis would become grist for the economic warfare Riefler would wage on a number of fronts.

Proof that information and analysis knitted rhetoric to policy was offered by Riefler. In the desperate months of early 1942, he emphasized the vital importance of statistics to the US war effort. Such tools were honed during World War I, but economists could see the maturation of data gathering and analysis in the United States over the decades that had followed, much of it in response to the pressure of the Depression. At the same time this evolution of data creation and capture merely placed the US within a larger global pattern. Even so, worldwide data gathering had been bounded by national categories and boundaries. Such emphasis during a global crisis became a problem. Riefler worried that the national had been emphasized at the "expense of the international organic whole of which it is but a part." This was a key issue, as he explained: "Economic warfare calls for intimate knowledge of critical elements in the economy of the enemy. Support of friendly powers requires information on which to base decisions with respect to priorities, to sustaining purchases, and to loans. For all of these purposes economic data are required that consist of more than a summary, nation by nation, of purely national statistics." Riefler lauded the work of the League and its economic section for providing what means there were to understand these crucial questions. It was a reminder that the United States fought a global war (and even apprehended the scope of it) in part with weapons stamped in Geneva.[42]

The plowshares of economic data and the concepts they helped cultivate in the 1930s were being swung as weapons. Economic warfare could be prosecuted on several levels, including preemptive purchases of materials, blockades, strategic bombing, and smuggling. Subtler tactics could be utilized toward various ends.[43] Economic data was one means to understand the enemy's capacities and, crucially, to learn where to apply pressure to squeeze its vitals by denying or destroying crucial matériel for their war efforts. Combined with the growing capability of modern weaponry, particularly airpower, data could be utilized to target the most vulnerable spots of an economy. It is no surprise that the fields of management and economics pumped a large number of credentialed personnel into the Allied strategic bombing campaign.[44]

Ideas about building a new world were bound up with ferocious wartime campaigns to tear down the economic and social structures of the enemy. Riefler would spend much of the war in the United Kingdom conducting the "Big Blockade" of economic warfare. It was an unglamorous regime of leaguer, intimidation of neutrals, and preemptive buying, as well as sometimes shadowy and secret activities to track opponent's efforts. Although this work once again allowed him to rub elbows with prominent figures like Keynes (and to continue attending meetings of the League's Depression Committee), Riefler's contributions to the postwar have been obscured, in part because he disappeared into this secretive wartime realm.[45]

Nevertheless, Riefler's activities with the BEW illustrate that, just as economic warfare could destroy, it could build. The promise of an improved global economy that could deliver the benefits of the modern world to the balance of humanity was central to the political warfare that enveloped the economic. Postwar plans for a better world were a seminal part of the war of ideas. Larger questions of the world economy pressed on Riefler not because of some guild identity, but because they were central to the wartime portfolio he and others had been given. In mid-1941, well before the struggle engulfed the United States but while the war of ideas was raging, Riefler grappled with a larger question besetting liberals concerned with the legacy of the global impacts of the fragmentation of the world economy. This brought him to a narrative that had merged with the discourse of "peaceful change" and the standard of living in the 1930s: a worldwide vision of development.

Riefler, like other internationalists, believed that global economic reform necessitated cooperation and governance to guide needed change in many parts of the world. His mid-1941 plan, served up at the request of Wallace, included an "International Development Authority" that would oversee investment meant to improve poorer areas of the globe. Riefler was aware that this required not only providing capital but also building capacities in poorer parts of the globe. Investment in development was in part a reaction to the fragmentation of the Depression, but it was also a means to advance postwar plans. These centered on an effort to enhance a stable, liberal capitalist world order over the long term by firmly linking poorer areas of the globe and their raw materials to the capitalist industrial centers in the West.[46]

Wallace was impressed with the idea and circulated the report at high levels in Washington. Riefler, feeling that such projects were critical to postwar reconstruction, nevertheless understood US capacities were limited. To remedy this, he proposed creating a program of "basic training" for Americans on the questions of reconstruction, relief, and demobilization at the IAS. This would provide opinion leaders, administrators, and officials with the "*minimum* background essential for the intelligent consideration of pressing international problems" that the United States would have to confront with its limited abilities.[47]

Riefler's thoughts were amplified because they were shared by a growing ensemble playing a very similar tune. Another performer was Condliffe. After playing maestro in Bergen, he got his own band together at Berkeley. In Condliffe's case, the war along with his considerable international reputation assured that his troupe at Berkeley grew. By the time of the United States' intervention in the war, he had put together a remarkable collection of thinkers on international economics. Tasca repatriated with him, and Hirschman was given sanctuary. Alexander Gerschenkron also attached himself to Condliffe's seminar.[48]

The Berkeley band were among those embracing international development as a means to maintain a liberal world economy. Their ideas were drawn from the mix of internationalist discussions on global economics, key parts of which had funneled through the League and into international society. Members of Condliffe's ongoing Berkeley seminar, including Hirschman, cut their intellectual teeth on questions around the increasingly fashionable concept of international development.

As the figure who made the *WES* a sensation, Condliffe retained considerable cachet. Prominent publishers distributed his post-Bergen synthesis, keeping him visible to East Coast power centers. Wallace and the BEW were quick to recruit him to prepare a series of memorandums on the problems of postwar planning and world reconstruction.[49] The ironies of pairing economic warfare with the issue of reconstruction were not lost on the New Zealander. International development became a means to meet a slate of imperatives that sometimes could appear contradictory. Condliffe, like many others who had grappled with the collapse of international trade in the 1930s, had a clear vision of what needed to be done to "reconstruct" a functional world economy. He agreed with his fellow Leaguer Riefler that raw materials needed to flow freely in a reintegrated world economy. Condliffe continued to advocate for a functional international body to provide coordination, information, and expertise. In conjunction with McDougall and Riefler, he saw the best extant example in the United States: "The idea of an international supervisory body in the field of economic development is at least as old as the creation of the Economic and Financial Organization of the League of Nations with its standing Economic, Financial, and Fiscal Committees and numerous ad hoc delegations, committees and subcommittees. This Organization, once divided, was reunited in 1939 and, combined with the Transit Organization somewhat similar to that of the International Labor Organization. It still functions through its Economic Intelligence Service, now located at Princeton, New Jersey."

In 1942 Condliffe offered many of the suggestions he had made to the government directly to the public. He argued that to sustain a revived world economy, "it is important to devise plans of development and modernization in industrially backwards areas." Like many advocates, he was appealing to Western constituencies who might balk at such commitments. He believed that raising standards of living was positive in its own right but would also provide an outlet for pent-up resources, talents, and investment after the war. Having seen the spectrum of activities conducted by the League in places like China, Condliffe cast international organizations in a pivotal role. Capital was not the only thing required; "technical aid," in the form of trained administrators and technicians, was the "main need of the undeveloped industrial countries."[50]

Condliffe later nursed a sour view of his work with the BEW.[51] Nevertheless, the post did put him in immediate contact with Wallace and other powerful figures in Washington and in an influential position in the public discussions over postwar plans. More than that, his views were in harmony with the ideas that other influential policy entrepreneurs were introducing to postwar planning. While none of the proposals simmering in the BEW would ever be implemented as such, the ideas behind them drifted about key circles in Washington, leaving very definite impressions. Riefler's and Condliffe's interrelated ideas on international development—to be facilitated by international agencies modeled on the League's economic section—had appeal. These Wallace school proposals were a sign that the concepts they advocated had wider and deeper resonance than they are usually taken to have, yet they reflected ideas that were both malleable and acceptable.

Such views pleased not only New Dealers; they would also catch the eye of Jacob Viner, a gatekeeper for the CFR's War and Peace Studies. He has long been seen as a member of the transnational dialogue between British and American elites, animated by new ideas for the international economy. Viner was one of those who saw to it that such ideas were embedded into broader conversations that were waking to the need for international organizations to further international stability in any postwar scenario.[52] In short, ideas from the technical debates and scholarly meetings that the League had facilitated in international society were shaping not merely Allied aims but also the institutional visions to fulfill them. They were becoming strategy.

EXILE IDEAS

Increasingly, prescriptions built off the array of analyses emerging from international society wound their way into the evolving discussions of a new international organization. McDougall provides a window. Through the summer and fall of 1942, he bounced around between the White House and the Wallace school. He learned to navigate the Washington social scene and built relationships with a who's who of the influential. In the months following Pearl Harbor, McDougall gained the confidence of Alvin Hansen. Hansen was putting on the mantle of the "American Keynes" and a doyen with the War and Peace Studies project. As 1942 progressed, the two discussed many issues around nutrition that quickly segued into larger issues of postwar reconstruction. As McDougall and Hansen traded ideas on how to institutionalize the promise of "Freedom from Want," their discussions turned to the intertwined question of the structure of an international organization. Both felt that "we [the UN alliance] need to have an Economic Authority with a series of specialized organizations under its supervision." This family was to include an "International Bank . . . a Development Authority, an Agricultural Office, a Nutrition Office . . . and an Economic Intelligence Service."[53]

Here the reshaped contours of liberal international society cast in relief the connections that fostered a dialogue on the "world to come." They show that not only was it a transnational dialogue but also one that rested on earlier international ferment on questions of nutrition, international organization, and standard of living. That many ideas had already been legitimated by earlier research and had well-regarded boosters is part of the reason international proposals gained traction and began to accelerate after the United States entered the war. But the more they were discussed, the greater the need for tangible elements to turn them into policy. International society had offered not only the concepts but also some of the existing examples of how they might be implemented. For this reason, advocates regularly turned to the League mechanisms recently landed in North America for inspiration.

It was taken for granted that a plan to reform the world along the lines being sketched out would require international cooperation. In some ways it is unsurprising that an international network would generally urge such a path; this was a lesson the planners drew from their own collaborations and research. As the Bruce report had underlined, international resources were necessary for national governments to grasp world conditions and then conduct their own reforms. These early discussions, of which McDougall was only a part, underlined the collaborative dimension with their regular invocation of international institutions and actions. The opinions of the exiles in Montreal and Princeton would regularly be invoked, but they were also personally recruited to support these plans with raw data and analysis, furthering new structures that would be built on a foundation of earlier ideas.

Planning the postwar also further ginned up the question of international development, which is why the issue would be defined during the war. A guiding hand would be required to provide the data, expertise, and resources to implement these goals, all of which had to accord with a liberal agenda. The question of investing any Allied effort with an international institution was a continuation of interwar debates and discussions that infused postwar planning from the outset.

The other set of refugees, the ILO harboring in Montreal, were quick to see an opportunity. As the ILO moved to position itself to be a mechanism to implement postwar plans, it solicited input from the usual suspects, such as Pasvolsky and Loveday.[54] To tie itself to postwar questions, it sponsored conferences in New York and Philadelphia. Like those in Princeton, such meetings emphasized existing US connections to the hubs of international society and what they could do for a nation that was not in the war but had picked a side.[55]

Despite these efforts, the ILO would not become the chosen, central mechanism to plan and implement the peace. The US government was ambivalent, and others, including elements of the British establishment as well as McDougall and the Australian contingent, were not fans. Regarding the question of which internationalist elements could best support the process, Bruce and McDougall felt that the EFS was "far superior in ability and outlook" and the Bruce reforms a "far better basis" for international reconstruction.[56] However, the fact that the ILO, like the EFS, was turned into a site to explore significant policies shows how important the Geneva bodies were in a North America that lacked both the experience and capacity to engage pressing international issues. Both offered the ability to generate information and technical capacity to plan and, critically, implement the agendas international society already understood as central to global conflict.

None of the ideas the exiles would seek to implement were cut from whole cloth. Rather, they were stitched together from interwar ideas from a variety of sources. They were pieces that Americans had sized themselves, but in context and sometimes in consultation with international society. The question of implementation made this readily apparent. These proposals were not a new set of ideas conjured for total war, but the redeployment of existing (and deeply ideological) concepts. The hybrid nature of these concepts points to how networks generate, legitimate, and transmit ideas. In the case of the variety of proto-international development ideas, they would be threaded into the dialogue on standard of living. Indeed, one reason international development would become so tightly linked with concepts of international organization was that it belonged to a discourse that itself had been formed and sustained by the existing international organization, the League.

Validation for sweeping visions was sought by linking them to the Four Freedoms. While there was a shift in the transnational dialogue around development, the basic concepts continued to have an attentive audience among New Dealers in Roosevelt's America. These progressives were accultured to international inputs on reform and increasingly agreed that for a liberal economy to function effectively, a global regime of development was necessary. The entry of the United States into World War II underlined this commitment. What is remarkable is how early and quickly development ideas were injected into government planning and public discourse in the period straddling the US entry into the war.

Advocacy for international organizations or international development reveals the interests of smaller and weaker powers at work. The support of the United States was not an end in itself; the smaller nations saw their own interests in these concepts. The Australians, like other countries in the Allied camp, had seen how the League and connected bodies had offered means to enhance their voices and legitimate their national concerns on such issues. They, like other states around the world, would work toward new institutions as mechanisms to secure their own desires in the order to come.

None of this makes Australia the puppet master of Allied postwar planning. But the agenda McDougall furthered again shows how a cross section of ideas already in circulation could be made to complement American rhetoric and strategies even as they served other masters. While shaded by national and imperial imperatives, such ideas nevertheless represented an already-established internationalist view on these subjects. Accordingly, these views mated easily with emergent American views on the shape of the postwar world. Figures like McDougall found a ready hearing on issues that ranged from nutrition to standard of living because American officials were predisposed to concepts that had been aired and given legitimacy through the organs of international society.

The Americans' speculations included a roster of institutional candidates to populate the "World Authority" that was being mulled in circles of power. What is more, the evolving program for a war of ideas increasingly came to include the "industrialization of underdeveloped areas." This program also envisioned an international bank to provide needed capital and other resources, incorporating suggestions that had begun to circulate in other quarters.

American ideas were part of a maturing discussion across the UN alliance that also included views from Latin America and Nationalist China, which were partial to a regime of international development and to international mechanisms. These bodies offered them levers to pull to ensure the continued flow of the technical aid and financial assistance that they had learned could be provided by international organizations. It was hardly surprising that a government like the Guomindang would support this. It had experienced proof of concept of development assistance—as well as its limits—provided through an international organization (which had provided a highlight in the League's Pavilion). The full spectrum of aid that China had received in the 1930s showed that postwar thinking about international development aid did not spring from the ground. It was linked not only to growing thinking about the concept but also to how mechanisms of international society could be employed to facilitate development.[57]

Thus, when they tackled the question of international development and international organization, the League alumni were not inventing something entirely new in the early years of the war. Condliffe's and Riefler's ideas overlapped with those of others, including a clutch of figures around the Foreign Policy Association. The two men built components of international development into their plans for postwar order that reflected other ideas being promoted in public discussion by American figures. The policy entrepreneur Raymond Buell saw a regime of international aid as necessary to world reconstruction, proposing in 1940 an "international development fund" to provide capital for war-torn Poland, as well as Asia and Latin America. His former colleague at the FPA, Vera Dean, saw it as instrumental to the struggle to create a viable liberal world order.[58]

Informing these and other views was the initial experience of international control. Early endeavors for international intervention on global economic issues was something these and other figures had gotten to see firsthand in Geneva. It is not surprising that some of them explicitly invoked the earlier example or even the current experience of the League's economic organs for their postwar implementation. More importantly, these ideas were linked to international discussions of an "expansive" world economy and the organizing concepts of standard of living and raw materials that had been pumped through the League in the second half of the 1930s. The pointed raw materials report of 1937, assorted nutrition efforts, and the standard-of-living inquiry of 1938 and its wider discussion of the uplift of "backwards" people fertilized the ground that Riefler, Condliffe, McDougall, and others hoed in the early 1940s. That the League had played a role in promoting and extending such ideas shows how it was invested in mainstream liberal internationalist ideas that were larger than itself and could be turned into vital mechanisms for war aims as much as tools to win the peace.

The imperatives of governance, guidance, and control that information and analysis offer had not changed. They were still instrumental parts of a liberal order in the process of being and becoming. The League may have been broken into pieces but these demands remained. That the war years, in part, were a search for the concepts and mechanisms to deal with such issues explains why various figures were always harking back to earlier efforts.

Wartime plans began to assume something that McDougall and others saw as vital, namely that international governance and coordination were essential to any postwar reforms. That coordination was based on mustering data and analysis. There were calls for new mechanisms to ensure the promotion of prosperity to fuel stability, and more immediately to provide for an improved, international organization as a basis of a settlement and liberal order. Sumner Welles was so keen on the Australian's views that he wrote Bruce requesting that McDougall return to the US.[59]

THE APT PUPIL

The question of international organization was evolving in other quarters. Drawn into the debate was Sweetser, who had ended more than two decades of service with the League and decamped for service with the Office of War Information (OWI). It was a bittersweet moment for Sweetser, but he turned it into another moment to renew contacts. His last letter on League stationary went to Roosevelt.[60] However, with his knowledge of international governance, the OWI would be only part of his wartime work. This included cooperating with the CFR, a center of postwar planning.

The importance of the CFR in international society has long been apparent, but its role in the "war of ideas" was particularly intense. Its War and Peace Studies project has long been held up as a signal part of the US reach for global power with the coming of World War II.[61] This appraisal, however, is one-dimensional. The CFR was an American organization synchronized to US interests, but it had also been crafted to link elite explorations of international questions across international society. An early attempt to meld it with Chatham House did not take, but the CFR would nevertheless remain an influential clubhouse for many who populated a transnational world.[62]

When war broke out, the CFR became one outpost of international society's mobilization for postwar planning with the formation in September 1939 of its storied War and Peace Studies program.[63] The need for such planning was one of the hard lessons learned from the peacemaking that had followed the First World War. Back then, the US government had lacked expertise and resources and had left postwar planning for after the conflict. When conflict brewed in Europe twenty years later, there were many who thought planning should begin with the conflict itself. It was hardly a surprise that the Rockefeller Foundation, deeply interwoven into international society, provided funding for the undertaking. The CFR tapped universities, advocacy groups, and exiles for their knowledge and prescriptions. The project was explicitly welded to the State Department and allowed official Washington to draw on a selection of elite expertise in civil society. Pasvolsky would become its central contact at State.[64]

Unlike many shoots of postwar planning that had grown in the first stages of the war but were cut short by the dramatic shifts of 1940–1941, the CFR's program continued to expand. The War and Peace Studies program, organized into committees, focused on particular topic areas: political, territorial, economic, and disarmament. Each committee was stocked with a set of leading mainstream figures who could claim some expertise on the subject. With its status and reach the program gained considerable sway in a Washington scrambling to keep up with changing world events and expanding global commitments.

The vast constellation of individuals Sweetser had cultivated during his time in Geneva ensured that he was pulled into these critical discussions. He was a valuable source, an American with intimate insight regarding the internal structure and operations of an international organization who also was conversant with the US government. Sweetser was tapped to be a core member of the CFR's Political Group. CFR records of attendance show that Sweetser was a star pupil, particularly in its foundational early years. This offered him the opportunity to vest internationalist views in a discussion of US global commitments.[65]

Sweetser's own assumptions aligned with those of many globally minded figures who believed that "America is living in a crowded, dangerous, explosive world." He summarized US interests as a demand for security through the eradication of war; however, this would require "a far-reaching extension of America's outlook on its place and interests in the world" as a set of ongoing lessons drove home that "America's interests are completely universal, not confined to any one area, but dispersed over Europe, Asia, Africa."[66]

Others in the War and Peace Studies program recapitulated assumptions Sweetser held. For a global role to firmly root in an unsteady America, the hard lessons of recent history had to be learned. Peace meant more than the absence of conflict. Ensuring long-term stability demanded "the progressive development of a world order designed to promote economic, social justice, and cultural freedom, for all national groups, races, and classes willing to accept their proper responsibilities as members of the world community."[67]

While a firm commitment by the United States itself to such goals was a sine qua non, their implementation demanded international cooperation. This would have to be institutionalized as part of the war effort and of the world order to follow it. International organization, as a means to facilitate such cooperation, was thus indispensable not only for general security and establishing means to settle disputes but also for the things that sustained a broader peace in the economic and social spheres. Others at the CFR shared the conclusion that fulfilling what were defined as basic American goals required the "fullest use" of existing machinery, specifically the exiled ILO and EFS. But the examples they cited also pointed to specifically economic reforms for improved access to raw materials and mirrored ongoing discussions outside the CFR's headquarters that privileged "promoting the development of international financial institutions" for currency stabilization but also "facilitating programs of capital investment for constructive undertakings in backwards and under-developed regions."[68]

Commitment to such agendas underlined the strategic importance of technical bodies to the war of ideas and to ideas to build the world to come. As the Americans cast about for the means to implement the ideas articulated in the Atlantic Charter, the technical bodies that had been pulled from Geneva offered needed capacities to implement war aims. Rather like the roving set of internationalist voices that had found a place in early discussions, the technical abilities to contend with the litany of questions connected with raising standards of living in the areas of housing, nutrition, health, and refugees were indispensable to a revived liberal order.

Establishing technical services was necessary for any durable settlement. Sweetser noted that the League maintained a "large nucleus of expert personnel for various kinds of international activity." This pool had the benefit of being active in variety of fields and places and could be reassembled for future tasks.[69] For all the talk of the new, there were valuable extant resources that did more than

> merely suggest how much help for the future can be drawn out of the past. Occasionally there is a tendency to start wholly new, as though the slate were clean and nothing had been done before. The path of wisdom, however, would seem to be to draw upon the past as heavily as possible, bringing out both the good points which should be preserved and the weak points which should be buttressed. . . . It should be . . . the interest of the Allied governments to encourage and stimulate every undertaking, from whatever source, which may provide useful data and experience in dealing with these problems. Americans are available who have had wide experience in nearly all these fields.[70]

Those Americans had largely learned their trades through international society.

Sweetser also considered the less pressing but critical question of how a new global role would impact the United States itself. A hint of this transformation was visible in Washington, DC, a provincial city being thrust into the role of international capital.[71] As someone who had spent much of his adult life in the internationalist canton of Geneva, Sweetser was sensitive to changes that would be apparent to any attentive person. The extended world crisis left the United States in a commanding position and thus in a position to issue commands. What is more, he assumed many people were looking to the United States, with hope and apprehension, for leadership. Sweetser, having seen how the post–World War I order had been reflected by the growth of the international colony in Geneva, was sure that the nation's new posture would require the transformation of Washington, DC, into an "international center." Demonstrating to allies and partners that the United States would make space for them would be part of the war effort and beyond.[72]

This catalog of interests not only agrees with those of many other internationalists; it frames Sweetser's set of contributions to the War and Peace Studies program. One of his interventions was even on "international society." Sweetser understood the term in the more restricted sense of his day and focused on international organizations and relations between states, but nevertheless he saw the interlocking and collaborative nature of that sphere.[73]

There were others who looked to the possibilities of international organization, sometimes with more jaundiced eyes. Despite the enthusiasm with which Sweetser and other partisans inserted their assumptions about the League into conversations and the written record, there were skeptics. The political committee of the War and Peace Studies program was treated to views similar to those in the late 1930s that held that restarting the League's Assembly or any of its other political engines might cause other gears to freeze. This would suggest a revival of the reviled Versailles order, potentially giving a propaganda boost to enemies (foreign and domestic) who had inveighed against it—not to mention that a keystone of the UN collation, the Soviet Union, had been summarily expelled from it. Indeed, the Soviet Union's distaste for the League is an underappreciated reason the organization was not rebooted.[74] But above all, a full reconstitution of the League implied sliding back to the *status quo ante* and failing to fulfill the promise of a new, renovated world.[75] There were good reasons to keep the political image of the League at a distance from a liberal world order, even as the example of its technical services was discussed as instrumental to its restoration and operation.

Nevertheless, the importance placed on a functional international organization that could measure and analyze the international commons to support liberal reforms was clear from the start, not only among exiled Leaguers but at the very center of the US establishment. The Americans already understood many of the basic views and ideas (even if they didn't always see the hand of the League in them).

While Sweetser was apparently the only veteran of the League Secretariat to be placed at the core of the CFR's studies, "super-university" alumni dotted them, including Staley and Riefler. Their personal portfolios were also understood and valued. What is more, the War and Peace Studies program drew on the resources of the rump League to prime its discussions. Loveday, though never appointed as a member, was invited to participate in various workshops. His analysis of critical economic topics was therefore delivered in front of many of the usual suspects whose views held cachet across business, academia, and a variety of Allied governments.[76]

In January 1942, Loveday shared with the CFR his answer to the nagging question of how world capital needs might be met. One means was a "Central International Bank of Central Banks," a spigot for nations thirsty for capital. Such structures were likely to be permanent, as Loveday predicted "vast" demand for foreign capital would continue well after the conflict, in part because there was sure to be a "radical reorganization of industrial structures in certain areas, in Southeastern Europe, in China, in the Caribbean, and elsewhere."[77]

Beyond his direct interventions, major publications of Loveday's section were always available to the CFR's brain trust. The input of the League exiles was particularly important in the early phases of the war and emphasizes how the United States needed to supplement its limited capacities with voices from international society. It is a sign that the League's connection to the internationalist network, which had matured in the interwar period, had been reformed and redirected by the demands of war. It also shows that suggestions for international organizations to support the world economy and provide resources for economic development were entering discussions from a variety of directions.

TALKY-TALK

As was his wont, FDR was evasive on the issue of international organization. He played his cards close to his vest in the early stages of the war, allowing Welles to be the administration's standard bearer on the issue. Nevertheless, in May 1942 he did experiment with some of his ideas about an international organization built around the "four policemen"—the United States, the United Kingdom, the Soviet Union, and China—on his "old friend," Sweetser. Roosevelt ruminated on how the major powers might maintain world security. His remarks might be dismissed as off-the-cuff speculations, except that he pursued this train of thought in a long meeting marked by extended interruptions. Historians have long struggled to piece together what FDR thought about international organization. Many have attempted to tease out his views regarding security and the role of great powers at later moments in his presidency. His comparatively early conversation with Sweetser reveals that he understood that technical services would have to be part of any institution that would itself be a component of a larger settlement seeking a stable liberal world order.[78]

A cagy internationalist, FDR did see a defined role for "something like the League" to "carry on all those things that the League did so well"—meaning technical work. He envisioned continual meetings with monthly sessions on vital global issues—"January for health . . . February for economics." However, Roosevelt told Sweetser that even if this rump League was maintained, "police" tasks were out of the question: "It didn't do it and can't do it; you'll have to have something stronger." The president recalled telling Churchill that there had been too much "talky-talk" with "no force or action." Revealingly, he recalled how it had scarred his career: "I campaigned for the League in 1920 . . . but can't get that conflict started all over again."[79]

FDR's musings are part of the narrative of the rise of a new "world authority" during World War II. Among the new ideas he tossed out were some very much tied to established assumptions about liberal internationalism, assumptions to which the president himself long assented. It is not surprising that he understood that cops on the world beat would need an ability to measure and analyze.

Sweetser was one figure, but his singular international experience made him a valuable member of the US establishment with enough standing to serve as a sounding board for the president. His contributions to postwar discussions reveal how the technical activities of the League were present at all levels of discussion in international society in the United States. His observations framed an understanding of what would be required in a reborn liberal international system. They also showed how the League was beginning to shift from a living institution to an archive for liberal order.

AN INTERNATIONAL SCHOOL

As much as there was a need to build understanding at a highest levels, the presence of the fragments of an international organization provided a granular comprehension of the requirements of liberal order. As information generation was built into the postwar settlement, the existing League was broken down into information to inform that construction. Even so, making its experiences and lessons visible to a United States increasingly invested in a global mission required the interlocking efforts of international society.

Once a new international organization became an accepted part of war aims, there came a raft of issues that needed exploration and analysis. Exploring bureaucratic schematics and operations is not the sort of topic that presents scintillating terrain for scholars (or perhaps their readers). Nevertheless, it is the sort of work necessary to support policy implementation, and equally important, it represents the *conceptualization* of how order will be sustained. In the twenty-first century, international organizations have deep roots in global life, with ample precedent in law and practice for their operations. It is forgotten that the League pioneered many of the elements that today are accepted norms on the world stage as it worked to establish the status of an international organization and the international civil servants who staffed it. The US government, however, had dealt with the League only as an outsider. The great power's mulling of how to implement a globalist agenda that included a world organization had never formally been a part of such a body.

This inexperience was clear in the daft manner in which the United States dealt with the EFS early in its tenure. Ominously, in 1941, the US government demanded that each EFS staffer at the IAS fill out a rigorous "Alien Registration Form" with detailed information on his or her past. Soon after, the Selective Service turned its gaze to the Princeton group. Hungry for manpower, the local draft board inquired about the status of its members. Fearing these valuable imports might be called away, Aydelotte was forced to petition the State Department, and he even dragged Cordell Hull into the issue before it was made clear that American draft rules did not apply to his displaced international civil servants. The US government also attempted to tax the EFS. Officials at the IAS were reduced to pleading with the Rockefeller Foundation to go to the State Department and clarify the issue on their behalf. After the foundation's intervention, the EFS was eventually excused from tax obligations, although a sour Sweetser noted, "The more I study this question of proper courtesies to international officials in this country, the worse the situation seems to me to be."[80]

These bureaucratic escapades drive home the fact that the League had become a de facto ward of the United States. However, in its efforts to establish a liberal world order in its own image, the US government had to learn how to host international organizations without treating them like foreign bodies.

Responding to this need, in August 1942 the Carnegie Endowment for International Peace began a program to explore the "administrative problems of international organization."[81] It was an acknowledgment that the United States needed tutelage on a complex subject. However, the US did have a repository of information on that very subject. The best—and essentially only—example was the League Secretariat, parts of which were conveniently harbored in the United States itself. There was also an archive of individuals. As they began to plan a conference on the subject, they reached out to those they knew well who knew the ropes. Condliffe, who was working with the CEIP on economic issues, was asked for guidance, and Sweetser, another obvious choice, was also recruited.[82]

With the variety of technical demands seen to feed into a particular sort of international administration, the Secretariat remained "the Thing." The Endowment's inquiry eventually grew into a series of conferences, books, and other publications drawing on the operations of the League.[83] These publications, covering a wide selection of the activities and organization of the League and its programs, remain a fascinating trove. At the time, they were an extremely valuable resource for those grappling with the complications surrounding the construction a new and viable international body.

The scope that was sought was provided by *Pioneers in World Order*, which appeared in 1944. It pulled together the figures available to write on largely technical issues in a volume that was headlined by Sweetser and Fosdick. Such publications are markers of interest, but the overall effort reached deeper. It was emblematic of a variety of studies and discussions of how the experience of the League provided the analysis on which to base new structures.[84]

Other exiles tutored Americans on the technical aspects of liberal internationalism. Martin Hill, who had helped construct the Bruce report, was contracted to produce a book on the economic work of the League. This was of considerable value, as the experience of the economic organs had long been held up as an example for designing new bodies to govern the international economy.[85] Another League veteran recruited by the CEIP project, Egon F. Ranshofen-Wertheimer, produced *The International Secretariat*, a thick description of the structure and culture of a body he had served; a boon for planners, it remains one for scholars.

Ranshofen-Wertheimer was no uncritical booster of the institution, but he did represent a selection of internationalists who understood that efforts to shape and channel social and economic life were part of a larger historical trend. The urge to govern aspects of swaths of human life had meant "the range of public power, whether Fascist, Communist, or democratic, has been extended over an ever-increasing sector of life." These national efforts reflected transnational concerns in economic, health, and communications spheres that reached beyond the grasp of individual nation-states. Global war had only intensified these trends: a "sudden and overwhelming need for concerted international action of a nonpolitical nature will be felt," meaning that "world of tomorrow will witness an extraordinary development of such technical bodies, exerting governmental functions in clearly defined fields and covering, in some cases, the whole civilized world." But even such a flowering of technical agencies demanded structures to provide command and control, which emphasizes a sober understanding that there was no way that "technical bodies, however numerous and important, can safeguard peace. They are not substitutes for political organizations."[86]

These basic views guided Ranshofen-Wertheimer as he literally schooled Americans on international organization, teaching the subject at American University in downtown Washington. Although it might not have been the boot camp for "basic training" on postwar requirements that Riefler sought, these were the kind of classes that harried government officials could easily attend.[87]

These various programs all illustrate how US civil society institutions, in this case advocacy bodies, foundations, and universities, turned to the activities of the Geneva organizations as a repository of examples for postwar ambitions. These activities also signal the disintegration of the League—its reduction from an active center in world affairs into information and analysis needed to feed liberal international relations. The League and its affiliated bodies still mattered, but increasingly they were valued for what they could teach their successors.

BLUEPRINTS

Given all the discussions of postwar ideas swirling around the government, the CFR, and American society at large in the 1940s, there is a danger of reading what FDR might have called "talky-talk" as a reflection of reality. But putting ideas into action required individuals who could do the hard tasks of implementing a program and securing a commitment by the US government. Here again, international society played a role.

Among the competing visions of the postwar world in wartime Washington was a study in the State Department initiated by Sumner Welles. Called FDR's "strategist," Welles took over considerable bureaucratic turf that related to what was to happen after the struggle.[88] It was Welles, allied with Pasvolsky, who did much to shape early US blueprints for a "World Organization." In July 1942 he convened in the State Department's Division of Special Research a subcommittee on international organization.[89]

In the early phases of the US involvement in the conflict, the subcommittee's discussions were infused with the League's example. Indeed, Welles stocked his committee with longtime League collaborators like the LNA's Clark Eichelberger and the CEIP's James Shotwell. The group was also directly tied to other postwar schemes, Welles having recruited Isaiah Bowman and Walter Sharp, both members of the CFR's War and Peace Studies.

A less heralded but enduring figure in implementation was Gerig, who joined the committee a few months after its formation. After closing the League Pavilion and transferring office equipment to Princeton, Gerig had been offered a position as associate professor of political economy at Haverford College by its new president, League booster Felix Morley. But Gerig soon heeded Welles's call to arms. Gerig's own belief in international cooperation undoubtedly structured his views, as did his long service in the League Secretariat, and he channeled his experiences into the subcommittee's discussions. He was one of those who commit themselves to ideas and undertake the unremarked toil of implementation. He also knew the key figures who could add operational perspective on the rapidly evolving institutions of the new "World Organization" that many were discussing and provided necessary continuity as these ideas were transferred and actualized in new circumstances. His presence is one reason technical subjects retained their prominence from the earliest phases of US planning. Welles would fall from grace in 1943, his ambition succumbing to rivals who capitalized on a sex scandal to drive him from office. But the groundwork was in place, and Gerig remained at his station and steered considerable thinking about the new international institutions.

Like Welles himself, the committee acknowledged the legacies and examples of the League and even earnestly discussed the realities of reviving the body and its covenant in early meetings.[90] However, these were downplayed as plans moved closer to reality. What remained constant from the Geneva example was the commitment to an expansive technical body within a larger organization. This was articulated in some of the very first and speculative scaffolding for a new organization. "Economic and Social Cooperation" became an assumed core of a World Organization. This might be fulfilled by a "Bureau of Technical Services." It would cover enormous ground including "general economics and finance," labor, trade, relief, health, trusteeship, migration, and cultural relations. But this wide mandate was necessary if the cooperation were to dedicate itself to ensuring "effective use of the world's human and material resources, to increasing the wealth and improving the standards of living of all nations, and to promoting social security, economic stability," and with it "well-being and peace."[91]

As consideration of this course of global uplift grew more important, the preceding experiment in international order became more instructive. The League itself was being reduced to a database. More importantly, League veterans and precedents were given pride of place while being heavily mined for guidance by those considering the world to come. As a result, future discussions about the world economy would be inflected by debates about international efforts at governance that reframed and redirected discussions that had emerged during the interwar years. The commanding questions of governance, instrumental to liberal order, required international cooperation—that in turn required a set of agencies to provide the information and expertise to make it all function.

DINNER AND A MOVIE

While Welles's committee met and sketches of an "International Development Authority" and similar concepts were floating around Washington, related ideas were rushing toward institutionalization. Increasingly, the idea that an international organization would not only secure the peace but also provide the operational sinew to maintain a world economy became a standard appeal.

McDougall, again, slipped himself into high-level discussions as he came to know Washington well. As he spent more time in the city, he found it could be "extraordinarily unpleasant climatically."[92] Despite the heat, long days, and hard work, he found his counterparts agreeable. He enthused that "it's all extraordinarily interesting. I like these Americans." At the same time, sharing many concepts about world order did not erase national or imperial interests. McDougall complained to Bruce, "There is a tendency here to desire to work out American solutions of world problems and expect other countries to accept these without much demur. A good number of highly placed people however see that such a course involves the danger of the schemes being regarded either as American interference or even American imperialism."[93] McDougall saw that there were other points of divergence among political leaders and those implementing policy. The seam of distaste for the British ruling elite that ran through US officialdom was hard to miss and was reflected in US openness to Indian independence.[94] Other tensions crept into McDougall's own relationships. In 1944, as Wallace lay increasingly isolated from centers of power, McDougall suggested to that he should have been "a little more careful putting my name on poorly considered statements." Wallace took this to refer to a pamphlet he had authored calling for the "emancipation of . . . colonial subjects."[95]

Still, the Americans and their Allied interlocutors spoke a lingua franca about internationalism that grew from a patois of the interwar years. Crucial terms and topics that had been created or evolved through interactions with the League were translated into instrumental war aims. By 1942, McDougall, drawing from others in the Allied camp, was sketching for Bruce visions of a "World Authority" that was deeply invested in the sorts of issues that had animated discussions in the 1930s. These discussions increasingly threaded nutrition ideas—portrayed as uncontroversial—into larger issues of reform, such as the concept of standard of living, that were connected to international development.

One crucial service that an international body would perform was to integrate the multiplicity of technical activities that were seen as vital to maintaining a working world order after the war. For this reason many drafts pointedly included an "Economic and Social" side of the organization as a catchall for these services. Newly generated flowcharts displayed continuities with interwar experience, the Bruce report, and concepts that had since emerged. Rubrics tentatively assigned to technical bodies began to reflect the specific missions they might undertake. Different sketches of these proposals referred to a bureau for the "Economic Development of Backward Areas" in one variant and in another as an organ for the "Development of Backward Races."[96]

The war of ideas connected many of the thoughts that had animated Bruce and McDougall in the interwar period. Ideas about reformed world trade on liberal principles had to be leavened by an increase in the overall standard of living. Throughout, the Australian duo remained empire men. They saw crucial parts of their war aims centered on maintenance of a healthy British imperium, even if they did not always agree with Whitehall's prescriptions.

The economics of food was unsurprisingly central to the agenda McDougall pushed into Allied war aims. Armies are said to march on their stomachs, and the same is true for whole societies staggering through total war. The variety of work on nutrition done in the interwar period had a decisive relevance to contemporary events, as total war turned seemingly prosaic concerns regarding food stocks and agricultural production into deeply strategic and deadly serious issues. This was not merely a matter of nutrition or social justice—although those issues earnestly animated McDougall. Guaranteeing equitable food distribution was a critically important answer to the larger strategic, political, and propaganda questions of how to reestablish an expansive world economy.

Early in the conflict, McDougall, using an idea Sweetser had articulated some years before, called for a "UN Economic General Staff" that could process the tough questions brought by war and recovery. Around the Allied encampment figures like Orr and Frank Boudreau (then head of the US Food and Nutrition Board) had gained positions of influence. For McDougall and those around him, food and agriculture were core economic issues that underlay questions of global trade and stability. He was comfortable suggesting that Loveday and others from the League brotherhood could illuminate the economic impact of these questions. In fact, while they were never formally given the title, Loveday and others served as a back office providing advice and details for the effort to establish a UN agricultural and food condominium. There had been earlier efforts, and the International Institute of Agriculture in Rome had pioneered some of these elements. However, as these discussions began to influence Allied strategy the institute was largely moribund at the southern terminus of the Rome–Berlin axis.

As much as these ideas drew directly on emerging nutrition science and terms and analysis developed in the interwar years, they came to be framed by the rhetoric and imperatives of global war. McDougall remained welded to "Freedom from Want." It became a jumping-off point for his interventions into the issue. Again, American political rhetoric was easily attached to what were internationalist sentiments and proved a perfect vessel for McDougall's ideas.[97] His ideas blended seamlessly with a focus on food, which fulfilled the promise of freedom from want. Furthermore, this link underlined how propaganda was a means to aggressively wage the "war of ideas." As McDougall noted, focus on food offered an answer from the Allies to the quotidian question of peoples around the world: "What will I have for breakfast?" It also clarified the sometimes fuzzy issue of the standard of living for the world public. By making food and agricultural production a priority, the United Nations was letting the peoples of the world know that the organization was not thinking solely about relief but also establishing a world order where there would be ongoing, general, and generous improvements in their daily lives. People would not only have something to eat; they would have more and better things to eat. An improved worldwide regime of science, production, trade, and distribution would bring about this new type of "freedom."[98]

McDougall's growing popularity around Washington allowed him to carefully cultivate relationships with the influential and powerful. Wallace's affinity was such that the vice president brought him and his formulations to the attention of Eleanor Roosevelt. After reading some of McDougall's memorandums, the First Lady invited him to lunch. Impressed with ideas that segued with her own, she shaped not only the debate over postwar aims but also the UN itself by extending an invitation to a "family" dinner and a movie at the White House. During the meal, on August 24, 1942, McDougall was seated next FDR, where the two discussed the "war of ideas" with considerable animation. The amiable Australian made an impression, but it was he who fell under a spell, discovering that the president's "immense vivacity is extraordinarily attractive."[99] It was to be an important step on a journey to building a new slate of international institutions.

THE VIRTUES OF A CON MAN

Once again McDougall's fertile mind was offering ideas inspired by the internationalist thinking that Americans had long invested in financially and intellectually, showing that the war was not a point of disjuncture between past and future. His sweeping suggestions, rooted in prewar discussions, presupposed a postwar order that reflected aspects of Washington's own assumptions and ambitions. Nevertheless, McDougall's vision has long been credited as the spur for the Roosevelt administration to call a major meeting on the issue of food and agriculture. It convened at the Homestead Hotel in Hot Springs, Virginia, in May and June 1943.

The United Nations Conference on Food and Agriculture, while a step-child in the history of postwar planning, was quite significant in its moment, even if it perhaps did not live up to FDR's assessment of it as "epoch making."[100] It was the first major UN conference and effort to create entirely new institutional machinery for the postwar world. It was looked upon at the time as a dress rehearsal for what was shaping up to be a longer performance of institution building.

This first phase contained several missteps. The seemingly noncontroversial "technical" conference generated outrage when it was discovered that the Homestead Hotel (not unlike many hotels in the United States) "vigorously enforced" discriminatory policies against various racial and ethnic groups. Its bigotry against Jews was particularly unpalatable against the background of world events. However, the row this caused was secondary to the prolonged drubbing the administration received in the media for keeping reporters away from the conference.

From an international perspective, another problem was that the US government ran the conference purely as an American show. It was this sort of chauvinism that triggered an intervention from Sweetser. From his position as deputy director of the OWI, he urged that temptations to control the conference should be ignored and that other nations should be actively involved. He held to the view that the United States should make its allies feel welcome on the American estate: "This, I feel, would make the conference really United Nations and international, give all the delegates the feeling of being at home, and obviate any chance of criticism that the meetings were unduly influenced or controlled by a single nation."[101]

Sweetser's volley had only a glancing impact. The State Department dominated the organizational work, ensuring that American officials presided over the meeting. As a concession, four vice presidents (chairs of the delegations of Britain, China, Brazil, and the Soviet Union) were conjured into being, but the posts were effectively honorary.

For all their influence on the basic ideas for the conference, the State Department shunned delegates from the League and the ILO. But focusing on the representation of the institutions themselves at the gathering misses how international society operated; individuals associated with the League could introduce liberal international ideas into larger discussions during the conference. It happened that one of the most influential Geneva partisans was there in the form of the indefatigable McDougall. Having done so much to prepare the ground on the question of nutrition, standard of living, and war aims, he was asked for by name and placed front and center in the Australian delegation. McDougall used this status to employ the Princeton office to help steer proceedings. Even if Geneva refugees could not officially participate, the information they generated was present. They served as a back office providing statistical and analytical heft for the project. Loveday was recruited to produce a report explicating the League's labors on issues in play at the conference, which the Australians distributed to the assembled delegates.[102]

Herbert Coombs, chief of the Australian delegation, fathomed the depth of McDougall's influence. He reported to Canberra that McDougall was working "quite closely in collaboration with the Americans. . . . They appear to be seeking his advice and criticism on the preparation of material and the working out of plans for the conference. This is proving quite valuable to us." Indeed, McDougall's access put Coombs face to face with key US officials. At the same time, McDougall's intellectual agility revealed to his colleague a "very interesting bloke, a bit of a charlatan, but a very appealing one with an element of good sense in the line that he was taking . . . a kind of virtuous con-man."[103]

If McDougall was working a scam, one that reached back into the interwar years for its tricks, the grift was a success. An interim commission, the seed of the Food and Agriculture Organization (FAO), was planted. This body was not exclusively aimed at improving cultivation. It was seen from the start as the first among many institutional components of a larger international organization. The birth of the FAO shows that McDougall and the views that he and various internationalists had tended were being planted in the wider postwar order, which readily absorbed the economic and developmentalist ideas that had been germinating inside and outside the League in the 1930s and in bureaus in Princeton and Washington in the 1940s.

Roosevelt would make the connections clear in a speech broadcast to congratulate the delegates on their accomplishments at Hot Springs. The institutional machinery they had constructed was not just for recovery but also for "long run" problems of food production and access and how these would have an impact on issues of human nutrition and health worldwide. Roosevelt and his advisers, plugged into the standing discussions of these issues, knew they were threaded into the knotty economic and social problems of the era. Roosevelt reminded delegates that, although some challenges might seem to "lie outside the scope of the work you have undertaken . . . their solution is none the less essential to its success." Goals regarding food could not be met without "increased industrial production and . . . increased purchasing power." The new organization was merely a first step, as "there must be measures for dealing with trade barriers, international exchange stability and international investment." Finding solutions to these meant that "better use of natural and human resources must be assured to improve living standards." Regardless, the possibility the FAO represented of "orderly international procedures for the solution of international problems" provided the desperately needed means to attain both "freedom from want and freedom from fear." Referencing those much-discussed freedoms was more than a rhetorical gesture. FDR and a slew of figures were well aware that the act of creation in Virginia was bringing speculation regarding the postwar world to life and loosing a weighty salvo in the war of ideas.[104]

To play its role in achieving all this, the FAO was given an institutional mandate to raise "standards of living" and agricultural production worldwide. This mission recognized an essential pillar supporting modern societies and the modern world economy. It united elements of the international dialogue on "Peaceful Change" from the 1930s with the demands of ideological war. It also embraced liberal tropes about how modernity was progressively shrinking the world and breeding interdependence. The FAO would not only spread information but also offer "technical assistance" to member nations. Its mission demanded that "the modern knowledge of nutrition [and] of production . . . must be shared," as "these scientific developments will enable us to achieve many things through cooperation that were thought impossible before, among them [being] freedom of want. . . . No nation can hope to achieve this solely on its own."[105] The FAO represented liberal reform, not revolution, as "changes in the economic and social arrangements of nations will be needed"—"an evolution that has been hastened in our time." Yet "progress will necessarily be gradual."

Knowledge was a critical justification, but it was also a means to put these grand ideas into actual practice. Research to benefit member states was to be a significant mission, and the "regular collection and systematic presentation of relevant statistics . . . will be fundamental." Food and agriculture required work across a variety of areas beyond the fields to fulfill its developmental mission.[106]

At first glance the questions surrounding agriculture seem more diffuse—even woolly—compared to the putatively hardheaded questions of an international financial order or a durable security apparatus that were soon to follow. These have received far more historical attention. But for actors in the midst of a grim global war, there was no escaping the gnawing strategic imperative of food.[107] The creation of the FAO meant that the UN alliance was already pulling together the analytical ability to harness this critical resource for the war itself and the reconstruction that would follow.

At the same time, it provided heavy ordinance for the "war of ideas." It was the Allies who were working to deliver security to the greatest number of people possible regarding a basic human need, food.

More importantly, those invested in reform at the time realized that the Depression had not solely been a financial or industrial crack-up. Agriculture was decisively linked to the economic and social breakdown of the interwar years. Indeed, the chronic crisis of international agriculture markets around the world in the 1920s presaged the larger economic disaster.[108] Taking the step of organizing a body to foster international governance of the foundational commodity of food was a statement that the United Nations Alliance was taking active measures to prevent a recurrence of the troubles that had brought war. Victory would mean no return to the *status quo ante*.

In an enthusiastic letter to Bruce, McDougall joined those pleased by the outcome. He saw the continuity: "I can only tell you that our initiative of 1935 [at the League] looks like [it is] getting fully launched."[109] An interim commission was formed in Washington and McDougall played a foundational role. The exiled League was formally franchised so it might continue to provide invaluable commodities: data and analysis. Loveday and Ansgar Rosenborg were officially attached as "expert advisors."[110]

McDougall's central part in the founding of the FAO has become part of the lore of an organization remarkably sensitive to its history. But his achievement should be qualified. There were numerous other figures who were instrumental not just in bringing the FAO into existence but also in making nutrition an international concern. Sweetser would grouse that many, particularly in the press, willfully overlooked how "the League was . . . parent of the present United Nations Food Conference." Nevertheless, the Australian's role was vital. Wallace, who himself deserves a share of credit, clearly saw the decisive impact of one father figure, calling McDougall the "brains and initiative behind . . . Hot Springs."[111]

AGRICULTURAL MACHINERY

The Americans took pains to keep the brains. Fully employing an internationalist Rolodex, Wallace asked Welles to tell Winant to request that Bruce command McDougall to remain in the United States and stand up to the Interim Commission on Food and Agriculture.[112] The Australian did stay, joining the commission in a grand house on McGill Terrace—a tony quarter of a humid capital that would increasingly become the address for embassies and other legations. This proto-agency demonstrated that Washington was indeed growing into its role as an international and internationalist center.

Proof came from the documents and reports that began to spill from the Interim Commission. These dramatized the scale of the problems facing the world but also the potential of the reforms the Allies were promising. Globally comparable data was mustered, not always for specifically agricultural issues. Indeed, it was used to delve into issues that had justified its founding: to compare how peoples around the world were faring and how policy corrections might improve conditions in specific locations. Differences in standard of living and quality of life could easily be inferred by comparing vital and economic statistics. As one report slyly noted, "The quantity of life that an individual can enjoy is the most basic factor in any conception of welfare and 'living' is the principal component of 'the standard of living.'" Discussions of life span and infant mortality were not only measures of health; they also served to expose limits in consumption and nutrition that were necessarily conditioned by economic issues of trade and production. These initial forays into questions that continue to bedevil the international community were grounded in analysis and data that had been generated by the League and composed by figures who had made their reputations there.[113]

Those who saw the FAO's foundation as a basis for further institution building were right. What McDougall's activities within the Allied war effort expose is the direct transference of ideas and techniques not merely to the institutional sinew of a new liberal world order but also to core US strategy. That Australians and British, thinking about their respective national interests in conjunction with those of their shared empire, were able to influence the conception and even the structure of the building blocks of a new "world organization" is a sign of the extended nature of the discourses on economic reform.

Yet these figures were hardly introducing Americans to the ideas; they were emphasizing themes that Americans had already accepted as valuable and had cultivated themselves. It was the international society of the interwar years that the League had coordinated that provided a seedbed for some of the most desirable fruits. Now, however, key currents of liberal internationalism were subject to American dominance because the United States found these elements vital to their own interests. Like many others, McDougall and Bruce never forgot—despite the ambitions and demands of their country and empire—that it was the Americans who were in the proverbial driver's seat when it came to postwar order.

ROVER BOYS

The discussions around nutrition, living standards, and war aims that would lead to the FAO were connected with other organizational elements that were sprouting up to contend with the massive problem of relief. Contemporaneously efforts were underway to construct the United Nations Relief and Rehabilitation Administration (UNRRA). This alliance project was to have a vast, global mission. Again, the limited capacity of the United States demanded that it draw on the ideas and individuals circulating in international society.

Defining the mission of the UNRRA involved Condliffe and Loveday, and they attracted a devoted member of the ISC and the War and Peace Studies program, Eugene Staley, as well as CFR study leaders Viner and Hansen.[114] Condliffe provided an intellectual framework for the organization. He linked the UNRRA's goals to the example of the League and the EFS, showing how far that historical example could be stretched. Loveday and the Princeton office were part of the discussion at an early stage and provided rafts of reports and studies on post–Great War relief and loan programs, as well as up-to-date statistics on issues around food and commodities, to US bodies engaged in planning relief and reconstruction.[115] The director designate of the UNRRA, Herbert Lehman, recognized the League's contributions and desired to receive "technical assistance" and to "establish the closest possible working relationship" between the UNRRA and the EFS.[116] This cooperation also explains why League observers were invited to the first meeting of the council of the UNRRA just down the road in Atlantic City, New Jersey, in November 1943.[117]

The fact that all these figures were involved in the laying of foundational elements of what was to be a multibillion-dollar relief organization demonstrated how assumptions about the need for international bodies to conduct reform of the international commons, which had been part and parcel of internationalist discussions in the interwar years through the Phony War, did not dissipate in talk but contributed to the actual implementation of relief by liberal powers.[118] This genealogy of ideas also helps explain why the mission of an organization vested in relief readily spilled over into developmental activities.[119]

Staley, like other members of the Geneva circle, had a busy war. His talents were harnessed to the $3 billion undertaking that was the UNRRA. Under its aegis he would travel to China and publicize its needs in the *Far Eastern Survey* (the house organ of the IPR). His prescriptions regarding the sorts of technical aid that China would need for postwar reconstruction were extensive. Yet they mirrored many of the categories the League had long been supporting through its technical assistance to the Nationalist regime—a regime itself vocally supportive of international commitments to development aid.[120] That these components were considered part of a larger package of relief demonstrates just how firmly they were positioned in mainstream dialogue, where development was waxing as a wartime and postwar goal.

Beyond the waging of war, the League's example and its work became a primary means to "reconstruct" the world when peace finally came. In this the League was actually playing the role in postwar reconstruction it had anxiously claimed when the descent into war began in 1939. Equally important, the League was filling the role that Americans like Bucknell had suggested for the organization. What remained of the League—increasingly stripped down to ideas, examples, and information—was indeed a useful tool in waging war. Postwar planning was the key political front of that that effort. A magazine of ideas and information had indeed become a political, even practical weapon, even if it was just one part of a larger arsenal. The variety of liberal ideas and practices that had passed through or germinated within the galleries of Geneva necessarily played an important role in a war for international society and liberal world order.

INTERNATIONAL UNITS

The birth of new technical bodies raised the question of how they might actually be employed in a postwar world. As a result, the information and analysis the Geneva organizations produced became caught up in an ongoing debate over one means to shape the future world economy. The controversy would demonstrate how such organs fit into an international society embracing a concept that would have a profound role in the postwar world—international development.

It was a question with a backstory. Condliffe was among those who had witnessed the growing industrial capacity and potential of Asian economies in the wake of World War I and pondered their effect on the world. Talk of economic appeasement had leaned on developmental components. What is more, there were templates for the international assistance seen as necessary to drive a worldwide process forward. Nationalist Chinese ambitions to promote national development after the conflict built on prewar experience that recognized international assistance melded with economic planning and control as useful tools for China's economic advance.[121]

The calls by China and other less industrialized states for assistance became pronounced as the war ground on. But they raised uncomfortable questions for richer and more industrialized countries. Would recovery plans and hopeful agendas to extend economic capacities in other parts of the world actually work to dilute the prosperity of all? This apprehension reflected an urge to guard established privilege and power, but it was also a predictable anxiety born of the Depression. Would global forces again conspire against elements that could produce prosperity?

There was hardly unanimity on the issue internationally or in the United States itself. For critics, expanding the pale of industrial modernity led to what were often framed as logical questions of who would benefit. There was immediate pushback against the sort of vision Wallace expounded upon. Classically, the vice president's call for milk for everyone as a symbol of raised standards of living (a point McDougall surely seconded) was derided as "milk for every Hottentot" as part of a larger critique of his postwar international visions.[122]

Daily allowances of dairy aside, there were critics who conscientiously questioned assumptions. One was C. Hartley Grattan, a writer well versed on the issue of the standard of living. A fascination with Australia led him to Colin Clark. Embracing concepts emerging from the economist's research, Grattan became one of the first to introduce general US audiences to Clark's globally comparable data and the related concept of the "international unit."[123]

Grattan, however, deployed that expertise as a challenge. Before the US entered the war he was certain that at its conclusion, "the world will be confronted by the problem of development." Aware of various plans being bandied about in early 1942 (he had served the BEW before being dismissed), he noted, "How to reorder world trade after the war, how to plan new international economic relations—these are favorite topics to-day both with the stratospheric politicians, economists, and sociologists, and also with the Rover Boys of Reconstruction who plan for the future with good will in their hearts and memories of the Versailles Treaty in their heads." Grattan's reference to a set of vapidly upstanding heroes, protagonists in a series of juvenile adventure books churned out by the syndicate that also produced the Hardy Boys and the Bobbsey Twins, dismissed reformers as callow. They had not truly considered the impacts as international growth—inspired by historical trends but also the war—advanced industrial production in other parts of the world. Grattan stated that the simple concern was that industrial countries, having endured the Depression and war, were breeding competitors, a development that promised economic competition and dislocation. This seemingly commonsense critique reflected larger skepticism of the postwar agendas being offered by establishment voices.[124] It was also unsurprising that someone who had established himself as a member of a "revisionist" circle of writers on the Great War would remain skeptical of growing global commitments.[125]

Thus, as international institutions aimed at promoting economic reform took form, they did so in the midst of not simply a discussion but an argument. This debate increasingly fleshed out concepts of economic development—and particularly its *international* variant—because the controversy required clear, partisan articulation. The honing of opinions and stances drew on not only the ideas and discourse spooled up around questions of appeasement and postwar planning but also the figures of and institutions of an international society in the process of recasting itself.

The controversy demonstrated how information and analysis emerging from international organizations and other nodes of international society remained relevant even during conflict. The response of the "Rover Boys" was to deploy these tools in the debate. Condliffe's crew in the Bay Area had ready-made rejoinders. Hirschman trained his statistical skills on it, producing a study that was not only another early marker in his career but also an important statement on the issue. His view was drawn from a party line (sketched from a larger research project of Condliffe's that had received input from Staley). As Hirschman phrased it, "Today schemes for the future industrialization of underdeveloped countries, such as China or Southeastern Europe, are proposed and discussed in many quarters; and the future economic mission of the older industrial countries is conceived less as the mechanical workshop of the world than as the initiator and educator in industrial processes. International trade has nothing to fear from these developments." This shift was to be welcomed because the world economy was dynamic and "it is most *improbable* that *any particular pattern* of the international division of labor will last forever." He ended his study with: "To conclude that world trade is doomed because the traditional pattern of the international division of labor seems imperiled is the result of one of those flights of the imagination at the start of which we find a lack of real imagination: the incapacity to conceive of a reality not opposite but different from that with which we have been acquainted."[126]

In 1942, even before Hirschman published his missive, the ILO, angling to influence postwar discussions, recruited Staley to take up the question of the "effect of industrialization of new areas on older established areas." The ILO reflected the international networks intersecting in the United States. It showed that international bodies still had the reach, connections, and background to deal with the sprawling question of what a war based on raising standards of living meant. Between trips to China for UNRRA— and with perspective from Chinese figures such as H. D. Fong (an IPR member)—Staley put together a wide-ranging book. It touched on many issues, from population to planning, that would become part of a discourse of international development in the postwar years.[127]

Staley offered a definition of a concept coming into its own. It was being stripped of its connections to ideas like appeasement and increasingly seen as a means to legitimate and extend liberal order: international development (or "modernization").

What is economic development? It is a combination of methods by which the capacity of a people to produce (and hence to consume) may be increased. It means introduction of better techniques; installing more and better capital equipment; raising the general level of education and the particular skills of labour and management; and expanding internal and external commerce in a manner to take better advantage of opportunities for specialisation. Economic development is a broader term than "industrialisation"—if the latter is understood, as is generally the case, to stress the increase of manufacturing and other "secondary" production as compared with agriculture and other "primary" production. The greatest opportunities for raising productivity and income in many less developed areas will lie in modernisation of their agriculture, their forestry, their fisheries, etc., and not, at least at first, in the increase of manufacturing.[128]

Staley's ILO-backed intervention, based in part on research exploring how societies transitioned from conflict that was funded by Rockefeller, was hardly a singular statement.[129] It was part of a larger debate that was itself a reflection of elements threaded through official and unofficial postwar planning and was part of a transnational discussion.

The question was prominent enough that Loveday's detachment at Princeton also produced a study on it. The book offered an argument similar to Staley's, articulated in a drier, analytical manner. It too made the case that greater economic growth and industrial capacity did not threaten countries that had already industrialized. Although the book was credited to the League, Loveday acknowledged that Folke Hilgerdt, a Swedish veteran of the EFS, was the prime mover.

All the work depended on a spectrum of statistical information, critically the comparable data compiled by the League. Hilgerdt employed the reams of data brought to and generated at the IAS to root his study in a set of statistic-rich appendixes. The close relationship between Staley's and Loveday's inquiries shows not only the importance of the raw material they were using to produce increasingly influential analysis but also the continued role of the networks and concepts fostered by the League as a hub of international society. The interrelationship of not just the League's personnel but also its alumni network along with existing ideas all had ascribed to cannot be overlooked as crucial intellectual scaffolding for "international development" was hoisted into place as part of postwar planning.[130]

This is not to say that everyone got along all the time. The dialogue between Staley and Loveday over his book exposed tensions and rivalries. Although Loveday was apprised of the project from the start, he would complain that his office had not been aware of Staley's efforts. This led to testy exchanges between Loveday and Edward Phelan, then head of the ILO. Loveday's critique was flavored by sour grapes, backhandedly complimenting the competition's "superficially attractive" elements, even as he professed that he did "not feel that this is Staley at his best."[131]

It was Staley's book that reached a larger audience and had clear impacts, although Hilgerdt's study would have its own influential legacy. Both were important early statements on where these issues of development could and would lead. More important than who received credit is how the research and analysis emerging from a Geneva-in-exile was part of a larger discussion ongoing within liberal international society about how to shape the world economy.

TRANSITIONS

The Geneva exiles made numerous other contributions to the postwar debate. Much of the League's influential work centered on its Committee on Depressions, originally convened in 1937. Various wartime reports were issued despite the difficulties of censorship and the dislocation brought by war. Some of this work defined the legacies of the immediate past. There was the thick yet influential work of the Estonian Ragnar Nurkse, who undertook a major study of a crack-up of a significant segment of the international economy in the 1930s. His *International Currency Experience*, which reflected his wartime research, appeared in 1944 and was a persuasive explanation of international financial problems of the era.[132] It retains considerable, if debated (it was paid the compliment of an attack by Milton Friedman), influence on the subject.[133] This and other works by Nurkse gained him respect and attention from American hosts hungry for perspective on the Depression and how to prevent its recurrence.

Similar concerns lay behind a major study, *Transition from War to Peace Economy*. The Depressions committee was stocked with many of the usual suspects, including McDougall and Grady—as well as Riefler, who took a break from economic warfare to again consider the peace. The volume not only showed the lingering anxiety about a return to depression conditions after the war; it was also further proof that the EFS's work from the interwar period had been carried over into the new world of war. More than a plan, it was a commitment to learn from the past in order to show that the Allies had a way to the future. The 1943 report discussed the inadequacies of the post–World War I reconstruction. Drawing from analysis of what went wrong in the interwar years, in seven points it laid out what economic policy should achieve. Production should guarantee stable economies and rising standards of living. But that translated into goods and resources to meet the needs of "all classes of the population" and to protect "the individual" from interruption of "earning power" and the "liberty" to choose an occupation while assuring access to education and opportunity. Countries required the "liberty" to access to raw materials and markets. Removal of trade barriers, as well as "courageous international measures of reconstruction and development, would facilitate the modern methods of production which would allow individual benefit." However, the liberal economics it supported were not rearticulations (or a foreshadowing) of rigidly laissez-faire concepts as it reflected lessons learned from recent economic history. The report called for government activism, intergovernmental coordination, and even planning, as markets could not achieve these goals alone.[134]

Even as the study fluently analyzed the problems of the Depression years, the program it promised was explicitly "no return to the past." Like much discussion across international society, it assumed the need for international coordination to ease the transition to a stable and growing world trade. It pleaded for an "international organ" that would facilitate this goal; first among its several tasks would be to "study and analyze the facts" concerning global exchange.[135]

Emphasis on liberty and the individual betray a decisively liberal stance on the issue of reconstruction and reconversion. The focus on standards of living, prosperity, "quality of life," and national income show how tautly these interwar elements had been laced into discussion of a postwar world to come. However, these elements had been present in the thinking of the EFS and a parade of League boosters well before the war. In the American context, such themes are often seen as attached to the New Deal order. They undoubtedly were, but they were also tied to a community of reformers who wanted to create a viable international liberalism. The *Transition* report again shows the influence of research and analysis sponsored by the League on the United States as it sketched a world after war. The report provided further grist for the various mills churning out their own plans. When the fruits of the committee's work were finally published, the CFR led the way in celebrating a harvest that was well received in academia and the media.[136]

The Depressions committee's research was just one among a long slate of studies compiled by the Princeton office that display the variety of technical subjects that crossed into economic territory. Beyond established serials of statistics, there were studies on interwar relief and reconstruction, currency problems, raw materials issues, population research, and food and nutrition research, as well as numerous others launched amid policy discussions and public debates over the postwar world (and cataloged and presented to pleased patrons at the RF). The researchers were certain to record the systems of data collection that the League had used to gather the raw materials for its analytical mill.[137] This litany of research and analysis took up an important space in a debate that had moved beyond the confines of international society and into policy being hammered out among the governments and publics of the United Nations.

IN THE MOUNTAIN AIR

Bretton Woods, formally the International Monetary and Financial Conference of the United and Associated Nations, years of speculation on mechanisms necessary to promote economic governance would come to a head. An International Bank for Reconstruction and Development, as well as an International Monetary Fund, were conjured into existence to supply capitol and stabilize currencies. These new bodies were based on much thinking about the core problems within the world economic system exposed by depression and war. There were important continuities in terms of foundational ideas as well as some seemingly mundane elements that gave away the persistent importance of data and analysis. For example, to join the International Monetary Fund, member states would have to agree supply a portfolio of statistics and other data to the institution.[138]

Ideas that had circulated for some time were present at the proceedings in the White Mountains, and so were some of the League's itinerants. The role of the League and its exiles was limited but they were involved. Sweetser would attend as assistant to Treasury Secretary Henry Morgenthau, earning praise for easing relations between competing factions—although those were mostly within the American delegation.[139] After producing studies and reports that had shaped discussions priming the meeting, Loveday and Nurkse also made their way to New Hampshire as official representatives of the League. Their status as observers, however, did not allow them officially to serve on or chair the committees that moved the meeting. Various histories omit these nonmembers. Like other delegates, they were overshadowed by wrestling between the great powers and the imposing figures of Harry Dexter White and, above all, John Maynard Keynes. Indeed, the conference has sometimes been reduced to a struggle between those two men.[140]

Of course, the variety of agendas that came together in the New Hampshire mountains had arrived from a diversity of sources. A critical example was the existing international organization. In a radio statement prepared during the meeting, Loveday complimented the proposals hammered out at the Mt. Washington Hotel as embracing lessons learned from the League's economic experience.[141] Such approval aside, those looking at the ideas implemented to secure a postwar liberal capitalist world economy have seen the imprint of the League's economic work on the goals and structure of the International Monetary Fund (IMF) and World Bank.[142]

Scholars have uncovered the fingerprints of the League on these initiatives because of its experience and simply because they were "in the air."[143] But if they were circulating around Mt. Washington, it is because structures of international society had relentlessly fanned them. The League's flora

FIGURE 4.2. *Circulating in the mountains. Sweetser meeting with another member of the American delegation to the Bretton Woods Conference, 1944. (Library of Congress)*

of commissions, studies, sections, and staff in exile had played a crucial role, but a variety of American institutions had provided them with audiences and support. Now at Bretton Woods, as at other meetings, the Allied powers sought to codify aspects of the League's resources in a permanent international bureaucracy. A central issue that would be written into the institutional structure of the postwar settlement was international development, elaborated in wartime discussions fostered by a roving band of experts. But even as ideas surrounding the concept had nested in the most powerful capital of the United Nations alliance, a diverse set of supporters ensured that they were incorporated into the emergent United Nations Organization. While development benefited from advocacy by established members of a liberal international society, a slate of states in the Pacific, Latin America, and Asia were supportive of initiatives that vested new international organs with writs of development.

These states were not simply toeing a line drawn by great powers. They had long articulated their own interests and saw international institutions as means to further them. Latin American states and China saw levers to access and channel resources and expertise. Along with balanced international trade, India advocated for mechanisms to promote development. As much as US demands, it was this broader international support that assured the bodies given life at the 1944 Bretton Woods Conference had developmental missions etched into them (a development role would also find its way into the forthcoming economic and social council via a proliferating set of regional commissions).[144] Almost immediately the Guomindang government sought to utilize parts of the emergent UN system for its own ends, and after that regime was driven to Taiwan, Chinese officials and technicians would continue to work on a variety of international projects in Asia.[145]

THE BACKSTOP

The scattering of agencies given life by the UN alliance compelled attention to the overall structure of a "new international organization" in 1944. As ideas and plans began to solidify with growing Allied success, Gerig (still at his post at State), like many other Americans, turned to what had become a back office at Princeton for insight on this question. Loveday offered sustained commentary on the institutional needs and focus of international organization.[146] Prompted by Gerig, the Englishman offered sketches of a new "International Economic Organization" ("Social" would be added to later drafts) during 1943 and 1944.

A forgotten part of the story of the UN Organization is that the whole emerged after its component parts. As a means to implement some of its war aims, the UN alliance had committed to setting up an extended roster of new international technical bodies with a variety of overlapping responsibilities. Yet by the middle of the war, there was no overarching system to tie them together. The constitution of the FAO itself hinted at something larger, presuming that it would be one part of a "general international organization." With the ILO and FAO extant, and other organizations on health, communication, commercial policy—as well as a "monetary authority" and "international investment authority"—about to take form, coordination became critical.

This paramount need agitated Loveday early on. The willy-nilly creation of an uncoordinated scrum of agencies had the potential to be counterproductive. He saw a tendency in Canada and a "rampant" proclivity in the US to create "independent organizations having specific functions without any over-all controlling body." Economists and those he termed "fonctionnaires [sic] who want to keep nursing their own babies" were particularly guilty. Loveday called on J. V. Wilson, a New Zealander who operated a planning group at Chatham House, to check trends in this regard in the UK. The question was vital, for "if the object of governments after this war is to create ... a world order ... they must have some permanent central organ ... that is ... some instrument ... though which they can perform ... common functions of unification and co-ordination."[147]

With Gerig's invitation, Loveday was able to influence the debate, showing how it was critical that what he termed "A" components be integrated though a larger international organization's deliberative organs (he fell back on established terms like "Assembly" and "Council"). These larger representative bodies were necessary to coordinate the technical work to address world concerns. To contend with distinct and immediate questions, these bodies would be supplemented by a set of committees. Loveday's suggestions replicated one in existence, an "Anti-Depression Committee," and stressed the necessity of a "Statistical Committee." Loveday thus emphasized basic demands for technical work, but to construct the agencies to meet them he took ideas off the shelf. Indeed, in his early drafts he noted that in his ideas there was nothing "in contradiction with the general line of policy sketched in the 'Bruce Committee.'"[148]

The need for a larger body to coordinate technical endeavors helped to drive the formation of a larger world organization. Loveday's ideas were widely disseminated around the UN encampment and the US government. Gerig was effusive with praise for the Englishman, who had "carried the thinking and analysis on this subject further than anyone else," and he was sure that his work would have "great influence." Crucially, Loveday's points also ended up in Pasvolsky's hands and, through direct conversation, ears.[149]

Pasvolsky's receptiveness to Loveday's assertions was due in part to the fact that many of them had already been accepted in outline by Gerig's counterparts in the State Department. Loveday had further legitimated them. American attention to the creation of some sort of economic and social committee for the organizational side of the United Nations alliance had remained steady throughout the war. This foresight reflected a lesson learned during the Depression, namely that world economic and social stability required, in some form, the ability to foster cooperation and generate information on global conditions. It was an integral part of the proposal that the US delegation brought to the UN meeting that sought to create operational blueprints for the new organization—the Washington Conversations on International Peace and Security Organization held at the estate of Dumbarton Oaks.

That the US position on the necessity of technical services was maintained throughout interminable discussions in Washington that stretched from the sultry late summer to midautumn of 1944 is hardly surprising. Gerig and his chief, Harley Notter, formed a literal and figurative backstop for Pasvolsky and the new secretary of state, Edward Stettinius, in the seating at the conference.[150] In contrast to their British and Soviet counterparts, the Americans pushed relentlessly for a technical organ at the heart of the new international organization. The Soviets lost no time asserting that while technical services could be revived and extended, there was no desire to build (or resuscitate) an organization that might expel them as the League had.[151] The Americans displayed their deep investment in the view that a liberal international order needed not only levers for international security and diplomacy to defend it but also the informational and analytical tools necessary to sustain it.[152]

The long-standing US interest in fostering technical services was underlined when the prime mover in the American Delegation, Alger Hiss, made a point of disabusing the British and Soviet delegates of the use of the very term "technical." The Bruce Report echoed again as Hiss insisted that the capacious construction "economic and social questions" be used.[153] This terminology would be etched into the organization with the creation of an Economic and Social Council (ECOSOC) to carry on the necessary coordination, even if in the wake of the conference the United States questioned whether it was broad enough to cover some issues (such as air travel) and cultural questions.[154]

After the conference adjourned, Gerig contacted Loveday. He was sure that the Englishman already had a good idea of what had transpired. Many confidential points discussed in the meeting had been aired by James Reston in the *New York Times*, and many elements adopted were those that Loveday had advocated.[155] In terms of particular items this is true, but it again points to the existence of a feedback loop for all of these critical internationalist elements. Loveday's points reflected the views of an Englishman as well as those of a veteran of the EFS, but they were widely accepted tropes within a mobilized international society.

Dumbarton Oaks marked the end of the major meetings bent on conceiving new agencies. Much discussion of the blueprints drawn up for the new organization has focused on the creation of a security council—a mechanism that suggests a focus on a great power system rather than one of technical cooperation. But considered as a whole, the proposals provided the first overview of the structure of the institution and the variety of missions it would be given tools to accomplish. The conference was followed by campaigns to build public and elite support for the new organization. Gerig expended considerable effort educating Republican figures in Congress, such as Arthur Vandenberg and Warren Austin, on the value of the new, improved international organization in contrast to the League. This strategy of diminution is one reason Geneva was progressively erased from US discourse.[156] For those not walking the corridors of power, Condliffe transmitted the Dumbarton proposals via the Yale Institute of International Studies, where he was visiting professor. The veteran believed that the League offered proof of viability of the proposals even if the fundamental issue remained coordination of a diverse slate of work.[157]

Pasvolsky held his place as an influential voice among the chorus of advocates in the US government. He had long explained the need to understand how economics, particularly international trade, fit into the question of peace. Trade could be a tool for the promotion of "human welfare," but when blocked and manipulated it mutated into "the most potent instrument of economic war, which serves inexorably as a depressant of human welfare." Pasvolsky summarized why the issue preoccupied so many by citing its tremendous impacts: "International economic relations are not an end in themselves. They are rather an integral part of the whole complex of economic activity whereby the material wants of man are satisfied."[158]

Pasvolsky adhered to this principle as he stumped for the Dumbarton proposals and explained why the new mechanisms were necessary.

> One of the great lessons of the recent unhappy past is that it is entirely possible to have, in a period of political and military peace, a condition of violent and destructive economic warfare.... It would obviously be an exaggeration to say that the second world war was caused solely by the condition of international economic strife which prevailed in the twenties and even more virulently in the thirties.... But it is not too much to say that so long as international economic relations remained in the state they were in the recent decades, both peace and prosperity were forlorn hopes, and the fatal drift toward disaster could not be arrested.

If nations could cooperate, such breakdown could be prevented. Demonstrating that Loveday's views had indeed melded with official American thinking, Pasvolsky underlined that a major step at the conference was coordinating these extensive technical activities that could do much to mold and influence world affairs. Again the League's flickering example, particularly the EFS, lit the way. However, it and the system it belonged to ultimately lacked the capacities to meet the vast array of global challenges. Here reforms based on that experience were vital. It was imperative to create an evolving set of agencies and commissions that could meet the shifting demands of a changing world. As Pasvolsky explained, "A system of international relations must grow and develop, and the machinery established for stimulating its growth must be flexible and capable of adaptation to changing conditions. A technique of systematic and centralized investigation and analysis used as a basis of recommendations for action, should be admirably suited to the end in view."[159]

Given the primacy of trade in international relations, Pasvolsky's emphasis on economics within the technical corpus was unsurprising. The need for the leading international institution to have built-in mechanisms for surveillance and analysis of the whole of the global economy was a lesson born of recent history. This would give the organization the ability to respond to global concerns and crises. However, the primacy of such a group in plans for the League's successor was in part a carryover of the reputation and position of the economic and financial activity of the League itself. That it took the particular form it did can in part be credited to the links that had been forged in the interwar years between American institutions and their Geneva counterparts. The information and analysis they provided was solicited and incorporated precisely because they converged with the views that were accepted by a broad spectrum of Americans concerned with shaping international life after the latest world war.

As the new institutions were framed, elements from the old were cannibalized to help in their construction. This was frustrating to Loveday, as there he saw a "tendency of the United Nations to side-step the League" in many matters.[160] Sweetser shared some of this frustration but also recognized that there was much more going on in the background than most appreciated. In 1943 he vented to Loveday: "One of the startling, and even alarming, facts in present-day thinking is not only that many people think the League 'dead,' but that they consider it to have been engulfed 'without leaving a trace.' They do not seem to have the slightest idea not only that it is alive and operating today, but that it is woven deep into the fabric of international life."[161]

This was true in an operational sense. Increasingly components of the League and ILO were being directly incorporated into the Allied war effort. Staff were siphoned off to governments and war work. As early as 1943, Loveday complained that his team was "evaporating" as other professional opportunities beckoned.[162] Nevertheless, in line with the Princeton office's role as a sort of administrative head office for the League, Loveday brokered many of the transfers. The core of the League's Health Unit was handed to UNRRA during the winter of 1944–1945. More prosaic but still important sections were shaved off at roughly the same time. The Statistical Division was handed over to the UN alliance in July 1944 to be incorporated into the UN organization (this is one reason UN data on certain issues stretches back into the 1920s). Plans were made for the EFS to be incorporated as well, even as larger organs based on its example were taking shape.[163] The League did not disappear without a trace. Important features were absorbed, piece by piece and idea by idea, into an international order being brokered in the United States. This was easily done because the new order was constructed to embody basic assumptions embraced by liberal international society.

STREETS OF SAN FRANCISCO

As planning hastened toward the creation of a tangible international organization, the eclipse of the League as a living body became more and more
apparent. So did attempts to distance the new institution from the political
burdens of the past, as seen at the consummation of the United Nations
Organization, the San Francisco Conference. For all the attention lavished
on the meetings at Bretton Woods, Potsdam, and Yalta as moments that
shaped the postwar world, it was the conference at the Golden Gate that
ratified a good number of agreements and plans that were to buttress the
order that would come out of the chaos of global war. The central means
to that end—the final construction of that much-discussed "new international organization"—was the reason for the two-monthlong affair.

Yet the conference itself was a mash-up. It was a wartime event, called
on short notice. Thousands of delegates, members of the press, and observers from various organizations jammed into San Francisco from the
end of April to the end of June 1945. For a brief moment there was an international city within a city. Beyond the conference there were cultural
events to celebrate the various nationalities represented at the conference.
There was even a movie theater devoted to films of the member countries
of the United Nations Alliance who were lining up to join a United Nations
Organization—as well as films produced by the colonial possessions of
those members.[164]

From his position at the OWI, Sweetser directly appealed to Pasvolsky
to invite Geneva exiles as well as the new organizations to assist with the
thicket of questions arising from the "liquidation" of the old and the coordination among the new set of agencies.[165] This was duly accomplished,
adding international civil servants to the swirl of national delegates. Mc-
Dougall's shifting loyalties were clear as he made for California as a representative of the Interim Commission on Food and Agriculture. Loveday
and Lester would constitute the whole of the League's formal representation in San Francisco. Of course, they were dwarfed by a massive US delegation traveling on its own special train that wound its way west across
the country on a four-day journey from Washington. But even when compared to some of the missions from smaller states, the League embassy was
a token.

At a diplomatic conference that should have been ruled by protocol, the
dwarf League delegation came in for some decidedly inelegant treatment.
Loveday and Lester were not received formally when they arrived and were
put up in a "second rate hotel." At the last minute the pair was given a single
ticket for the conference's opening session—in an upper tier of seats, in the
next-to-last row.[166]

More troubling was that when substantive meetings began, Soviet delegates began to raise questions about the official participation of Loveday and Lester and other League veterans. What is more, US officials started to politely deflect them from participating. This resistance persisted even as key committees raised substantive issues that the two were well equipped to answer. It was all the more frustrating given that much of what they were there to do was largely to "sign their own death warrant." An incensed Sweetser immediately brought the issue to superiors—and likely the media.[167] That a frustrated Lester departed in the middle of the conference was noted by the press.[168] But neither gesture altered the great powers' behavior.

These affronts should be taken in context. Similar slights were directed at other international agencies. Even within the US government there was confusion and infighting. The OWI was initially left off the list of participating agencies by the State Department. Sweetser, who led its delegation, had to "bluff" to get credentials at the conference.[169] Failings of protocol were less important than the treatment of League alumni by the great powers. Altogether, resistance to official participation by the exiles was emblematic of growing American ambivalence toward and Soviet distaste for a moribund League and signaled an eagerness to distance it from a new organization that was nevertheless based on its example.

The snubs do not detract from the fact that some elements that would give life to the international body being stitched together in San Francisco came from the League. The ECOSOC was a reality. Smaller states fought for greater appreciation of the council and its role.[170] Equally important was the human capital and experience that ECOSOC contained—resources that many had pointed to earlier in the war as instrumental to setting up a new order. In fact, in the substantive discussions it was, again, an experienced cadre of international civil servants who played a role shaping the organization.

Charles Darlington, a veteran of the EFS (not an exile, having left the League in 1931 for the Bank for International Settlements before returning to the United States) was the executive officer of the meeting's Executive Committee, which drafted the UN charter. Pavilion veterans returned for one final pageant. Undisguised as a member of the Netherlands delegation, Adrian Pelt also sat on the Executive Committee, foreshadowing his further work for the UN.[171] Gerig was promoted to secretary-general, but of the US delegation. There he again played a significant role keeping afloat Stettinius, who was out of his depth. There were others, too. Even if Loveday was formally waved away from the Executive Committee, basic ideas of his were already embedded in the structure of the institution and its founding documents. This was a sign that the League's adherents

FIGURE 4.3. *Old-timers in a new world order. Sean Lester, left, and Sweetser at the 1945 San Francisco Conference. (Library of Congress)*

sustained concepts that were instrumental to liberal internationalism. But these concepts, newly recast and absorbed into the UN, were bigger than the League itself.

Sweetser, although pleased that a new international organization had finally emerged, found the conference at the Golden Gate "grim." Familiar faces left him confounded as to "whether I was in Frisco in 1945 or in Geneva in in 1935. . . . The only difference from some viewpoints was that some . . . old friends looked the five years [*sic*] older that they are." The point was telling, as after years of planning and weeks of negotiations it was clear that "we are going to come out to something very much like the old League." In what should have been heady days, the apparent continuity served as a sedative, depressing the enthusiast. To be sure, there would be substantive changes on the "military" and security side along with a dramatically expanded secretariat. Nevertheless, the true believer thought, "It is an indescribable tragedy to me . . . to think that we have had to go through the second World War to come out about where we were in 1919, except for the cooperation of the U.S. and Russia."[172]

DISPOSABLE HEROES

Liquidation of the League was possible because crucial niches it had occupied in an international ecosystem had been filled by new institutions that would perform its tasks in an enhanced manner. This emphasized that with the end of the conflict, liberal international society not only survived but had been revived. A variety of ideas had been carried forward from the interwar years to serve in a new world. In this process the League was cannibalized, providing basic concepts, examples, and past experience of aspects of international society. By the final years of the war, as the UN began to fledge, the League was hardly irrelevant but had increasingly been transformed from an actor in its own right into an archive of internationalist data and experience.

The activities of the Geneva exiles and their interlocutors in international society demonstrate that crucial elements of the postwar order envisioned and then concocted by the United States were not purely a US confection. The new liberal order was linked to many transnational trends that had been defined before and during the war. The League had been a pillar of liberal order in the interwar period, and its ideas reprised that role in a modified form in the American world that was being built. The information and analysis the League generated had a proven track record in making global concerns legible and therefore solvable in ways previously not possible. These achievements buttressed broad contours of global liberalism.

At the same time, the League and the bodies clustered around it in Switzerland were not insulated from the United States. Many individuals, nations, and trends influenced them, but crucial segments were dependent on the United States. Not only were Americans active contributors and participants in their meetings and programs, but their very existence and reach was something that had been carefully cultivated over time by interested parties in the United States. Not only had the Rockefeller Foundation funded large sectors of the research and studies that had burnished the reputation of the EFS, it had also been instrumental to its very survival in the desperate 1940s. The RF also supported US institutions that kept its example and ideas on the postwar docket. These institutions—universities, activist organizations, and think tanks—had been central to the creation of many concepts that were linked to the League. During the war they helped to sustain these concepts and propel them into wider discussion, and eventually institutionalization. Thus, investments American internationalists had paid into international society had come full circle back to them. Exiles had assisted by providing not simply research and concepts but also examples for the actual institutional structures that would serve, albeit inconsistently, the international community for generations to come.

In a crisis, policymakers reflexively turn to ideas that are "on the shelf." The calamity of World War II was no exception. When postwar issues became acute, the shelves perused by internationalists, literally and figuratively, held volumes from the League. Of course, these tomes owed much to US contributors. Regardless, the US needed these elements as part of the new order it was building because they could illuminate the "technical" issues that were perpetual parts of global affairs. The ease, speed, and degree to which individuals such as McDougall, Condliffe, Loveday, and others were franchised into what has often been portrayed as a purely American discussion betrays just how infused US thinking was by internationalist ideas not bounded by national borders.

This internationalist feedback loop was not restricted solely to the Geneva institutions, but it can be readily divined by focusing on them. The League and assorted individuals from an extensive club of Geneva alumni could never have accomplished what they did without American support, acceptance, and patronage. This came from a variety of angles: individuals, advocacy groups, universities, and foundations. While the US government was equivocal, the back channel and informal support offered in the waning years of the 1930s and early 1940s was vital. This assistance not only provided a point of hope in a period of potential dissolution, but it also provided a spur to reforms that would shape the League's successor. Above all, there was the crucial financial and political support of US civil society organizations that not only assisted in the construction of League research programs but also worked in light and shadow to secure the last functional components of the League for the Allies in 1940. Altogether these efforts were part of larger and longer streams of internationalism that are neither wholly American nor simply a filament of the League. Critically, these strands amplified voices from smaller states, modulating various agendas. Overall, campaigns to institutionalize knowledge and analysis to particular ends were an interconnected, collective effort as well as a further reminder that internationalism was international.

Americans did not simply crib knowledge from the League or retread its ideas. There was much new in what the superpower and the UN would attempt and would face in the world after 1945. Despite omissions and innovations, when the structure of the new organization and the larger settlement surrounding it are considered, the League was present at the creation of a new liberal world order, as much as for what it had been and what it represented. The League was relevant because it participated in something larger. The United States could not have created the institutions and relationships it did without the contributions of a body it supported but never officially joined. Yet the League had the resonance it did because it reflected and engaged the broad imperatives of building and maintaining liberal international society. The League was always a means to the end of a larger project of liberal order.

CODA:
GREAT LEAPS FORWARD

We cannot cure our troubles unless we know in the first place what those troubles are. . . . There is no substitute for facts, for clear and systematically organized facts. They alone can be relied upon to measure resources and potentialities for progress and to direct policies and actions designed to achieve the objectives of all civilized peoples.

TRYGVE LIE, 1947

Much has already been done.

JOHN BELL CONDLIFFE, 1950

His history reflects this association. . . . It tells the story of a great and daring design—the first effective move in the history of mankind toward the organization of a world-wide political and social order.

RAYMOND FOSDICK, 1952

LOST WORLDS OF INTERNATIONALISM

New York City hides some secrets in plain sight. Those who travel to the former 1939 fairgrounds will find nothing commemorating the League's only international pavilion. There is a solitary survivor of the 1939 (and 1964) World's Fair, the New York Building, housing the Queens Museum of Art. Visitors find both events commemorated by exhibits within, but little that references the League and its desperate appeal. Indeed, this past might seem to have been swept away, like so much, by the rush of urban life. Of course, legacies are sustained by ideas and individuals as much as by institutions and physical structures. The latter elements are hard to discern on a landscape that has been built and rebuilt over the years, most recently into the Billie Jean King National Tennis Center and a broad, open public park. But there are hints. Look closely and traces left by international society emerge. Beyond the 1964 World's Fair—which, like its 1939 predecessor, celebrated commerce as much as global interconnections—that corner of Queens would again offer liberal internationalism a refuge.

EXILES RETURN

As World War II lurched to its brutal conclusion, various US investigators cast their eyes across Europe, Asia, and North and South America for a city to host a new United Nations Organization. Switzerland, where Lester was still holding down a nearly vacant Palace of Nations, was considered. Influential voices (including Gerig) realized many would see "Geneva as Failure" and advocated passing.[1]

After the San Francisco Conference, the search took on a new intensity. New York was among those cities that vied for the honor, albeit haphazardly. But the bid did have powerful patrons. Robert Moses, the empire-building parks commissioner of New York City, hoped to lure the body to the site of that previous festival of internationalism, the 1939 fair, grandly retitled Corona Park but commonly called Flushing Meadows. The UN offered a fresh opportunity to scheme for the redevelopment of the site. Moses would advertise the former dump as the "natural and proper home for the U.N." and thus the "capital of the world."[2]

Consigning a new world organization to the ash heap of Queens would remain among Moses's dreams, but it did eventually have its moment. After deliberation by a commission in London, New York City was handed the honor of host. Grover Whalen managed once again to be the master of ceremonies as chair of the city's UN Committee, assisting with the mad scramble to find space for an already expanding organization in an overcrowded city.

The critical Security Council held its first meetings in the gymnasium at Hunter College's campus in the Bronx. The space was immediately deemed inadequate. The council, along with a nascent "Thing," the UN Secretariat, would quickly decamp for a surplus Sperry Corporation factory in a Long Island town seemingly named to goad the organs to fulfill their promise: Lake Success.[3]

Corona Park did get a chance to shine, for the General Assembly required a long-term sublet while a permanent headquarters was constructed. Tethered to the bustle of Manhattan by a subway line, it seemed a good compromise. But in the intervening years the former fairground had become a "lost world." It lay largely deserted, dotted by ruins and remnants belonging to what had become another era. Most regular visitors were possums. The only significant edifice that remained was the charmed New

York State Building, then a skating rink, which abruptly became a world headquarters.[4]

Hurriedly slapped into shape, on October 23, 1946, the building welcomed the four-hundred-odd delegates dropped off after a motorcade shuttled them across the city and through sedate crowds. With sparse recognition of the past, the UN General Assembly convened on the internationalist outcropping in Queens. It would meet there, through some of the UN's defining moments, until 1951.[5]

Both Whalen and Moses agitated to keep the UN or parts of it in Flushing Meadows, but to no avail. The eventual decision on a permanent site again owed much to Rockefeller resources. The family shelled out $8.5 million in 1947 to underwrite the UN's purchase of a chunk of land in Turtle Bay on Manhattan. A place hitherto known for slaughterhouses and a pencil factory would be transformed into a campus for international understanding.[6]

While they waited for the soaring new headquarters to be scratched out across the East River, the delegates in Queens might have recalled that they were sharing a site where internationalist shibboleths of interdependence and peace now chanted at the UN had earlier been given physical form. Some might have noted the irony that they were just a short walk (once a brief tram ride) from where the League pleaded for American attention and staked a commitment to a brand of internationalism. It had been a strange and circuitous trip, but integral elements of liberal international society had finally set permanent footings in a new world.

A DEATH IN GENEVA

As life was breathed into an international body in New York, one in Geneva took its final breaths. The dismembered League had been on borrowed time longer than many would admit, but the San Francisco Conference and the end of the war made its existence redundant. A final session was held in Geneva in April 1946, closing the book on the organization to the cry of "The League is dead, long live the United Nations." One of the last official acts of the assembly was to pass a resolution formally thanking the IAS, Princeton University, and the Rockefeller Foundation for supporting its sections while at large.[7] A South African delegate astutely summarized the war years, noting that the early days of the war "did represent a grave defeat, or perhaps a Dunkirk, for the League idea." However, what was euphemistically referred to as the "decentralization" of technical and administrative services allowed crucial aspects to survive for reintegration into international society.[8] The triumph of the United Nations alliance, supported by refugees from Geneva, promised a "fresh chance for what remains of the League."[9]

At what was an institutional wake, Hambro took his final bow as president of the League Assembly (a title held since 1939 and never renounced), his remarks making explicit the link between the League's ideas and organizations and the UN cause and the new international order its success had ensured. The task was to "assist with the great work of reconstructing and remolding." As he lionized the leaders of the Allied powers, Hambro surrendered the remainder of the institution to a process that sought to "add bricks and straw to the building of the wall of security which rests on their vision and victory."[10]

BRICKS WITH MORTAR

Much figurative masonry was being done to complete the goal of cementing a new world order into place. The more mundane elements of the final meeting were the League's completion of the transfer of its infrastructure and its example to a new order. Even as the last bits of the League were figuratively and literally disassembled to be handed over to the UN or consigned to oblivion, there were moves to assure that the accomplishments of the League were preserved and broadcast beyond like-thinking delegates in Geneva.

Even with the add-ons to the United Nations Organization and its specialized agencies that were devoted to technical work (specifically economic subjects), the legacies—particularly through institutional continuities—were hard to miss. Some are obvious. In one of the biggest, the deserted Palace of Nations was eventually repopulated with UN agencies. In the early twenty-first century, as the grand building cradles parts of its successor, visitors find they are walking through gates or eating off service branded with "SDN" (Société des Nations). Some of those agencies are the heirs, whether they acknowledge it or not, of the efforts attempted when Geneva was the center of the internationalist universe.

That edifices and serving vessels survive is perhaps testament to the quality of their construction than that of the League itself. Why some of its activities burrowed into the marrow of its successor is less about the League than the perceived requirements of liberal order. The need for a stable stream of information had been confirmed by the League along with ranks of collaborators across international society. Demands had not changed, even if the actors had.

The postwar period would see remarkable growth in the infrastructure of internationalism. This expansion made the flowering of international society in the decades after World War I look like a forest of dwarf seedlings and began a move away from a transnational community toward a more explicitly global one.[11]

This transformation was not immediately apparent as World War II ended. For the Rockefeller Foundation, the closing days of the conflict brought into view the end of the EFS "mission" to Princeton. This was cause for anxiety, something broadcast by Willits. Its fate occupied a prominent place in a broad review of international relations the foundation undertook before the end of the war. With a raft of fresh global commitments, the US government needed to be "aided in a very legitimate way" to construct a "mature and integrated foreign policy." Foreign economic policy in the interwar period had been a "failure"; wise policy in the face of inward pressures was "crucial, and the task is difficult." One of the best assets was fading away: "When Loveday's venture at Princeton passes out of existence there will be no major center in this country devoted primarily to studies of world trade and economic relations outside of official agencies where much of the work is secret and the total picture is confused. Our scholarly effort reflects the domestic emphasis that is traditional with us. This 'cultural lag' should not continue. There is need of one (or more) independent centers where efforts to study international trade and economic policy generally can be established and continued over the long run."[12]

Willits need not have worried, the reconstruction of liberal order continued. The technical activities for which the League had served as the hub continued to evolve without it because they had already been seen as necessities by postwar planners. Among the myriad meetings held to define and detail the new institutional arrangements of the now definitely postwar world was a 1947 conference meeting of the International Statistical Institute. The Washington meeting was one among many in the postwar years, but at the same time it belonged to a longer tradition of congresses on the issue. It was just one part of a revival and reformation of liberal international society. It mirrored earlier meetings on statistics, only now there were new actors. This meeting was part of the emergence of a new internationalist capital on the Potomac. But it also acknowledged the importance of a central international body while at the same time showing that such organizations were means to ends and, ultimately, expendable. The League, which had played a coordinating role in earlier international meetings on statistics, had readily been replaced.

Much of the meeting coalesced around the new Bretton Woods institutions—themselves heirs to the Bruce report—which were busily setting footings in a provincial city struggling to become an international capital. In fact, International Statistics Institute organizers worried that UN bodies would dominate the meeting. They came to dominate more than meetings. The Bretton Woods twins quickly asserted themselves, along with the UN Statistical Organization, as major sources of policy-relevant data on international and global issues. This was the point. The UN occupied a central role in the liberal international society revived by Allied victory. The International Bank for Reconstruction and Development and the IMF were enhanced versions of the international Secretariat that so many had valorized and seen as necessary for a functioning postwar world. They were to be "the Thing" and they would assume and usurp vital roles in international affairs.[13]

Joining the United Nations Organization and the International Statistical Institute in Washington were a cast of characters drawn from the ranks of international society: universities, research institutes, and a swelling rank of state institutions. Human continuity with interwar discussions was apparent. Riefler took time from his directorship of the NBER to serve as the official US delegate (before consulting on US foreign aid and then ensconcing himself in the US Federal Reserve system). Kuznets and Tinbergen were also in attendance, among numerous others.[14]

The latest secretary-general, only now of a United Nations Organization, the Norwegian Trygve Lie, opened the session with a reminder that international organizations had an important place in this system. The presence of Lie emphasized how Norway's commitment to international organization transcended distinct periods. Recognizing this also highlights the importance of the commitment of smaller states to fundamental aspects of international order, whether there was a League or not. They had their own interests in making the system work. In Norway, Lie was a political rival of Hambro, but on the international scene the two shared assumptions about global governance.

Welcoming the delegates, Lie pointed to the continued need for statistics to support not merely renewed international cooperation but a new international reality:

> We cannot cure our troubles unless we know in the first place what those troubles are. Likewise we cannot achieve international understanding, which is the basis of advancement, unless the peoples of the world are given the facts about each other. Nations are now too large, economic affairs too complicated and too highly interrelated to rely upon the accounts of returned travelers for our information on economic and social progress. . . . There is no substitute for facts, for clear and systematically organized facts. They alone can be relied upon to measure resources and potentialities for progress and to direct policies and actions designed to achieve the objectives of all civilized peoples. . . . Secondly, the statistics must be carefully organized. By this I mean that they must be comparable from time to time and from place to place. This problem of comparability is especially acute when we deal with the interrelated problems of many countries of vastly different characteristics. . . . Unless it is solved, we shall

be seriously handicapped in studying and dealing with problems on an international scale. It is shocking to realize that no statistics worthy of the name exist for probably half of the world's peoples.[15]

Averell Harriman, then US commerce secretary, spoke for the United States when he confidently noted that the nation "is the largest producer of statistics in the world" and that an innate grasp of their importance meant, "no American, I believe needs to be convinced of the importance of statistics" gathered by government and nongovernmental bodies. Still, there "were enormous blanks" on the "factual map of the world." If "an intelligently functioning world community" was to be built, there needed to be more information, "for not only do we need more facts, but we need them collected and presented in such a manner . . . comparable from country to country and . . . add[ing] up to a world view."[16] A mission continued in a new world.

Both figures were correct to highlight shortcomings. For all the prewar accomplishments, there had been decisive limitations. Much of the world was not effectively measured or had been subsumed in imperial structures. These were glaring omissions, particularly as the new imperative of economic development began to take on an international role. This demanded new categories and analytical tools, themselves requiring rafts of fresh information for what had been marked as a global mission. The plea for data to support the analysis and policy demands of international life had traversed the chasm of war, even as Harriman suggested a revised mission in poorer areas of the globe.

The 1947 statistics conference was only one meeting among many. But it serves to demonstrate that the role of information in the service of international order was on the agenda. The conference might have lacked the glamour or gravity of other meetings but it once again demonstrates how order can be best discerned at an operational level. Washington had become a center of activity not only because of its growing power but because two key institutions of the postwar settlement, the IMF and the World Bank, had settled there. Coupled with other parts of the UN Secretariat (which would grow over the postwar period), their existence underlined that technical issues would no longer depend on voluntary associations or grand international conferences. They were vested in permanent, imposing bureaucracies. The perpetual desire for reliable information and the urge for new capabilities were still linked together by the sinew of international society.

The proliferation of new international organs and reconnections between various networks in international society showed the continued appreciation of information as grease for the wheels of global interaction.

Loveday's exile outpost in Princeton could disappear and rapidly be forgotten because partisans of liberal order had already moved to establish a host of replacements. Crucially, the new organs were part of a larger change whereby US government participation was complemented by a growing contribution from US civil society. All were part of an emergent "Pax America" that had been prescribed for the world's ills by members of international society in what now seemed a remote past.

The figure of the economist gained considerable policy and cultural cachet in the postwar years. Particularly, the realm of international economics would get considerable play, with its subset of development economics gaining remarkable influence in the early Cold War. In the US, a rapid expansion of national capabilities, particularly in the economic field, supplanted elements that had once been external. Partly as a reflection of the construction of an information regime outside the pale of international organizations and within the bounds of the US itself, economists and economics gained an authority in politics and in the culture at large that they had not held before. This national focus has often obscured longer continuities and international links and origins. Nevertheless, an American economics built on statistical growth measurement came to define not only the growth reshaping the country but the United States' own self-concept as a wealthy, powerful nation with enormous power to shape the globe.[17]

LIVES IN ORDER

The "Pax Americana" was hardly placid; it was defined by the Cold War and decolonization, which were only parts of ongoing and dramatic global change.[18] Nevertheless, there was continuity in some of the characters playing roles in the international society it leaned upon. There are continuities in analysis and approach between the interwar years and the Cold War in part because of the lives and careers of some key individuals. The flow of people and ideas between what are commonly treated as distinct eras demonstrates the primacy of international society over a single international organization.

For Sweetser, the international dream he had begun to walk through after the nightmare of World War I did not end. Like other components of the League, he was scooped up by the new United Nations Organization, where he remained faithful to "the highest secular cause on earth."[19] A man who served Eric Drummond, Joseph Avenol, and Sean Lester in Geneva toggled his loyalties to Lie in New York City, becoming a member of the unique club of those who worked for the first four individuals titled "secretary-general." Holding a public affairs post throughout, Sweetser continued to cultivate an extensive portfolio of connections until his retirement.

Sweetser's promiscuous loyalties illuminate the transformation of the United States into the international estate that he had forecast in 1942. They also show how quickly liberal internationalism transferred its devotions. His move tracked the shift of liberal internationalism's center of gravity from Europe to North America. The initial site may have been New York, but Washington would soon see the arrival of international organizations and their servants in the form of the World Bank and IMF (whose familial links to the UN are politely obscured, rather like those of the UN to the League) and a slew of ancillary bodies. An international secretariat of the sort Sweetser and others extolled became part of everyday life in a global liberal regime guarded by the power of the United States. His long and influential career assured that his passing in 1968 was marked by prominent obituaries, including a tribute by Fosdick (who revealed that Sweetser's fondness for golf masked his true passion, networking) that recounted a life framed by his experience as head of the unofficial "American Section" in Geneva.[20]

Appropriately, the EFS section in Princeton outlived the League in Geneva. It persisted until August 1946, when it wrapped up operations and transferred its resources and talents to the new UN. New Jersey remained a haven for Loveday for a bit longer. Immediately after his band of exiles disbanded, he spent a term at the IAS, funded by the RF. He drifted back to his roots as a political theorist in a lively correspondence with Willits. In a conversation that began before the war ended and stretched for several years into the cold peace, the two fretted about the appeal of communism, particularly in France.[21] Echoing views that had evolved during the crisis years of the 1930s, both saw how the pressures, particularly economic ones, driving individuals fostered temptations to offload the complexities of modern life onto the State. For Loveday, this was how totalitarians generated support. Fascism, Nazism, and communism were respectively "ethical," "mystical," and "materialistic." That "all three philosophies require the dominance of the state over the individual" could lead to simple equivalence, but they were "three distinct . . . scarcely reconcilable philosophies." Nevertheless, they had their appeal and generated faith in those attracted to them. Yet liberalism after prolonged crises brought the hollow question, "Behind democracy remains—what?"

Part of the exchange between Loveday and Willits centered on whether analysis in the West was prepared to understand the challenge that the Depression era continued to present. This question directly related to Willits's bailiwick at Rockefeller, the social sciences. Loveday mused, "What might the social sciences require, therefore? I think it requires to be dethroned." Rather than provide answers in an "a-literary jargon about social motivation," the science of the social needed a philosophy—a social credo—

comprehensible to "people and to peoples" that would inspire those who "now see their old liberties set about."[22]

For Loveday, these concerns would persist and develop into an early Cold War warning. The varieties of economic and social uncertainty that generated personal insecurity among populations and drove them into the arms of statist (i.e., totalitarian) movements meant that during the years after the Depression and war, "the threats to democracy are real and immediate." Like other elements, this view was a carryover from the 1930s demonstrating how liberal anxieties of the interwar years were grafted onto the Cold War.[23]

After doing his own stint with the UN, serving its Nuclear, Economic, and Employment Commission, in 1950 Loveday went to Nuffield College, Oxford, where he had been elected a fellow. After serving as Nuffield's warden, he retired in 1954. He would continue the trend of turning League experience into information to support a new international society, publishing a treatise on international administration.[24] When he passed in 1962, he was eulogized for cultivating a wide selection of human talent which by then had salted international institutions around the world. The "universal respect" Loveday curried was remembered, but his great legacy was seen as the construction of a "remarkable system of economic intelligence."[25]

Others who epitomized liberal internationalist ends feathered nests in a new order. McDougall relocated to Rome, finding a seat at the very table he crafted, the FAO. Absorbing and replacing the International Institute of Agriculture, the new organ of the UN took on the issue many had sketched in the 1930s and transmitted into the 1940s: a regime of international development. In 1947 McDougall himself saw this mission as a means of squaring the needs of European and world reconstruction with the circle of demands of what were now commonly classified as "underdeveloped" areas. Once again, he linked a set of imperatives. Committing to a revised global agenda would serve to buck up Western states emerging victorious from World War II, but "with diminished prestige and with a rival system challenging our whole concept of a civilization based on the liberty of the individual." World development posed the question of whether by solving "our own political and economic problems can we help Asia, Africa, and South America solve theirs?"[26] Ideas about growth and the standard of living were no longer appeasement. They were now part of a perpetual cold "war of ideas." Grouped under the banner of international development and, increasingly, "modernization," they were deployed on a battlefield of a postwar, postcolonial world. McDougall was embracing an idea that had already become a means in US foreign policy to secure a world economy and extend a liberal order. "Modernization" would consume a great deal

FIGURE C.1. *Shared histories. Frank Lidgett McDougall presenting a copy of* The Story of FAO, *a history of the organization, to Eleanor Roosevelt in 1955. Roosevelt's support of McDougall's wartime initiatives led directly to the FAO's founding and was one of the various ways each played significant roles during and after World War II in shaping the League's successor.*

of bandwidth in thinking about international economics and international affairs generally in the Cold War.[27]

By the war's end McDougall's reputation was well established, and he quickly became a fixture at the UN. Others, particularly the FAO's first director and sometime collaborator with McDougall and Bruce, John Boyd Orr, deserve a healthy serving of the credit for accomplishments around food and agriculture (recognition was granted to Orr through a 1949 Nobel Peace Prize). But the UN body McDougall helped conceive never forgot his importance. The FAO offered a fitting tribute to a prime example of the species of international civil servant that now had a secure niche in postwar international society. It published a collection of McDougall's

prolix yet incisive interventions, going back to 1935. These linked his thinking on nutrition and standard of living through international organizations
and the international development efforts aimed at a revived liberal international society. The title memorialized not just the man but the form that
he had masterfully wielded: *The McDougall Memoranda.*[28]

Condliffe managed to escape the pull of international organizations
but was already gripped by the very Pax Americana he advocated. He too
grew to "like these Americans," or at least their real estate. Seduced by the
Bay Area, Condliffe would stay at Berkeley (with a later appointment at the
Stanford Research Institute) but would submit to the lure of the new imperative of international development that he had helped frame.

Condliffe engaged popular audiences on the issue in collaboration with
established advocacy groups. For the Foreign Policy Association, Condliffe
analyzed the "bold new" venture to catalyze a regime of worldwide economic development: President Truman's 1949 "Point Four" program. Such
initiatives underlined that the world had fundamentally changed. People
in underdeveloped areas were "moving rapidly" toward the goal of independence, indicating that "empire has become an anachronism." Such new
global conditions dramatized the link between "economic development
and freedom." Freedom was essential to assure economic improvement,
central to any people's national ambitions, because "without freedom they
cannot organize their economic activity to support their own ends." At the
same time, economic stability protected freedom, for "economic compe-
tence is the essential complement of political liberty." Condliffe stirred
echoes from the interwar years, asserting that such capacity kept newly
established freedoms from being lost to "some form of despotism, native or
foreign." Fostering improved living standards also had a mission in a new
cold war. It would help foster "allegiance" in a divided world. Crucially, the
US aid program and a larger international commitment to development
promised to tie together these urgent issues with the requirements of industrialized states in an interdependent, modern world economy.

Even if there had been dramatic change, there was remarkable continuity. The development being attempted was more than just investment,
indeed an all-encompassing effort. Even before the war many shared Condliffe's view that "economic development entails modernization rather
than industrialization. It constitutes a social rather than an industrial revolution." The agenda's scope meant private enterprise and capital markets
were no longer adequate. Economic issues rooted in global interdependence continued to demand international cooperation. Achieving this
was beyond the reach of one state, even the leviathan of the United States.
Condliffe approvingly noted how the portfolio of technical assistance and
capital activities vested in the ECOSOC and the Bretton Woods institutions

were already primed to support this agenda. In what could be an epigram for the postwar vogue of development, he noted that the new programs "did not launch the idea of economic development but gave it a new impetus" because "much has already been done."[29]

Condliffe would follow many academic figures into what became a major industry in a rapidly changing postwar international society. Like many peers he found a market for his services abroad: organizations fostering what had become known as "modernization," as well as the variety of "new nations" seeking their own versions of development. It suited his itinerant career. He undertook missions to Indonesia and southwestern Asia. Such travels exposed a widening international circuit of expertise in a more plural international society. Not only were more counterparts drawn from areas outside the West that had dominated international society, but postcolonial states increasingly changed the dynamics of certain interactions.

Condliffe would follow a path to South Asia that Henry Grady had traveled as the first ambassador of the United States to an independent India. Starting in 1959, Condliffe spent two years in India working for the National Council of Applied Economic Research under Palamadai Lokanathan (former chief of one of ECOSOC's bouquet of regional commissions, ECAFE). These tours of duty demonstrate how liberal internationalist ideas were actively threaded into the emerging postcolonial order. Condliffe was among a wider stream of economists and other advisers who offered advice to an Indian establishment that had Cold War leverage to pick and choose what advice it took.[30]

Condliffe's foundational work with the IPR, the League, the BEW, the UNRRA, Berkeley, and other organizations epitomizes how liberal international society and the concepts supporting it traversed chasms of depression, global war, and cold war. It was never dependent on one center but rested on a cluster of overlapping conversations, institutions, and networks. These developed and extended ideas that provided them with legitimacy and projected them into discourse, then policy, and thence into the world. The paths might be crooked, but that itself was a significant reason why concepts and approaches endured—they did not depend on a single patron.

Condliffe's personal influence has sometimes fallen off the map (a fate shared with his homeland, New Zealand).[31] His importance in extending the reach of the League's economic work, particularly the impact of the *WES*, is part of this oversight. Ironically, his use of that very data to elucidate the defining element of the interwar period is widely recognized, even if his contribution is overlooked. The "spider's web" that he helped popularize, which illustrated for global audiences how world trade collapsed, remains a staple of the economic history of the period. It demonstrates how defining the visual display of information and analysis can be for grasping international topics. However, the Kiwi has been denied credit along with those who inspired him. The web has become famous as the "Kindleberger spiral" following that scholar's use of it in an influential 1973 study of the Great Depression.[32]

Despite this, the hive of economically minded thinkers Condliffe cultivated at Berkeley would play an ongoing roles in the postwar world. Bay Area alumni, some of whom had cut their teeth at the ISC, focused on the pressing issue of international economics in the 1930s and would have real and theoretical impacts on critical aspects of global economics, development, and governance.

Condliffe's eye for talent was clear from those he sent forth from Berkeley. Henry Tasca would move to the State Department. In the early 1950s he would be given a decisive role in shaping what was the up to that time, the largest single development program in the world, the massive US and UN aid program for war-ravaged South Korea. His 1953 analysis, which became the "Tasca Report," would set a benchmark for that massive, complicated, and uneven effort.[33] Alexander Gerschenkron would leave the fold to go to Harvard and put "Economic Backwardness in Historical Perspective" through his work in international economics while maintaining a personal life self-enriched by his career as a fabulist.[34]

Standing above the others was Hirschman, whose early work on international economics channeled through the ISC would translate into a portfolio of economic development work around the world in the 1950s and 1960s. Carrying forward aspects of the pragmatism that defined his Kiwi mentor, he would become an incisive critic of doctrinaire approaches to development. Capping an accomplished career, he was invited to join the faculty of that haven for refugees, the IAS. In the twenty-first century, Hirschman's life itself became a data set, a means to explore the history of the social sciences and international development as well as an archetype of the cosmopolitan, émigré scholars who influenced the course of the twentieth century.[35]

The trajectories of others chart a broadcasting of expertise in the postwar years. Loveday's exiles would be sprinkled around a growing roster of international institutions. Tinbergen would also ride the circuit of development experts. Like others, he made an important stop in India. As part of his professional journey he would become a leading proponent of econometrics. Nurkse's analysis of currency would provide a platform for his own interventions in the global discourse on international development. His analysis would meld with that of Rosenstein-Rodan with the theory that a "big push" of development aid and capital investment might carry developing states forward. Rosenstein-Rodan's acolyte H. W. Arndt would emigrate to Australia, where he found a career in international development and provided a useful genealogy of its origins, crediting Staley's wartime work for the ILO with popularizing the concept in US circles.[36]

As much as established figures rode the new institutions into new phases of their careers, some of that infrastructure would turn toward different agendas. ECOSOC failed to live up to hopes that it would serve as a "primary organ" of the UN. Nevertheless, its proliferating regional committees very quickly became platforms for remarkable research and propagators of human talent, some of whom challenged the received wisdom about an expanding global economy and whom it benefited. Indeed, some of the early eruptions in the intellectual history of the United Nations were dependent on the information and data bequeathed by the defunct League and the wartime debate on economic development. Hilgerdt was part of the handover of League assets to the UN. When he became chief of its new Statistical Office, one Hans Singer was assigned to him. Singer pivoted from the rich wartime tables in *Industrialization and Foreign Trade* (which owed much to the data and talent smuggled out of Geneva in 1940) to the ideas that eventually led to the Prebisch-Singer hypothesis, which posited that prices of raw materials and other primary products tend to deteriorate. This suggested that the existing terms of international trade disadvantaged those countries that depended on the production of raw materials and primary commodities. Reflecting aspects of the wartime debate, in his early work Singer proposed that policies that supported industrialization could be the response.[37]

The enduring effects of the hypothesis provide a lesson. They illustrate the authority that statistical analysis had established as well as the integration of institutions into an evolving international society. Singer's collaborator, the Argentine Raúl Prebisch, found a mechanism within ECOSOC, namely the Economic Commission for Latin America. This body became a fulcrum to shift prevailing assumptions about the international economy during the Cold War. Prebisch would prime much discussion in the UN Conference on Trade and Development of 1964, which has been seen as an outrider for the campaign by developing nations for a "New International Economic Order" in the 1970s.

Changes in the structure and dialogue of international society that came with a rush in the postwar years nevertheless betray links to issues and institutions from the interwar years. Aspects of the raw materials and standard-of-living inquiries still echoed, as did some League studies on the Depression and even double taxation.[38] More importantly, even if the line is not straight and the consequences unintended or contrary, liberal world order had demanded institutions that cultivated and promulgated analysis of international interactions. Ironically, these often served as mechanisms to further critiques of some of the very relationships and systems that earlier members of international society had sought to advance.[39]

The trajectory of these careers and the ideas that journeyed with them not only show continuity but also depict how internationalist concepts were recast to meet the new conditions of the postwar era. The emphasis on providing the information and analysis that could be deployed to solve international issues had indeed become second nature to the liberal international society as it reset its foundations after World War II. But as that system dug in, some of its pillars became so firmly embedded that they slid beneath the surface.

Even as the international arms of the liberal body became more critical—or more correctly, reflective of a more plural international society—these international technical bodies became less singular as states evolved some of the capacities once focused on spots like Geneva. In many quarters, elements pioneered by a wide-ranging set of figures in the 1930s to understand global collapse became the tools to understand and implement the global vogue of economic growth and "development." Globally comparable measures such as National Income and the "international unit" were absorbed into gross national product and gross domestic product, which themselves became omnipresent. They fed a focus on growth that often privileged the advancement of such economic indicators. The influence of these measures extended beyond development and economic debates. They worked their way into policymaking and public discussion, even if their effectiveness would increasingly be questioned and their impacts seen as invidious.[40]

International development is merely one venue that shows how the inputs of international society, focused by the League but supported by an array of other actors, evolved and were integrated into world affairs. There are numerous other illustrative issues in health, security, communication, and the environment that remain foundational with respect to the twenty-first-century global interactions that demonstrate the value of information and analysis to governing the world.

HISTORIES OF THE PRESENT

History itself is an instrumental but underappreciated form of information and analysis wielded to sustain (or distain) systems and ideologies, including liberal order. Perhaps the final sign of the transformation of the League into agencies of information and analysis in service to international society is that it became history. In 1946 Frank Walters, another long-serving member of the League, a former under-secretary-general of political activities, embarked upon a massive history of the institution under the aegis of Chatham House. However, so vast a topic would take time and required sustained financial support. As with so many League technical projects, the usual suspect stood in the wings to offer assistance.

The Rockefeller Foundation seized this opportunity to sustain its agenda in the postwar world with a usable history—while having someone else do the writing. This was not simply a measure to safeguard the legacy of its own investments in the League with a "definitive" volume on the subject but also a chance to offer new efforts in international organization and governance some lessons from the very recent past. Rockefeller was assuring that the right kind of history was made. Once again, it was less the institution than the perspective and lessons surrounding it that mattered. Walter's analysis was one node of a writing (and rewriting) of the history of a newly christened "interwar" period. Indeed, the League history was to stand among a set of studies commissioned to take a hard look at the "present period" so that "a record of successes and failures may be available for the guidance of the future," as a way of providing footings for the global commitments the United States had embraced.[41]

To this end RF provided £5,000 (£223,000 or $292,000 in 2022) to Chatham House to offer hearth and home to Walters and those assisting him. When Walters's chosen publisher of Allen and Unwin balked at the massive, two-volume tome that emerged, the foundation intervened again. Rockefeller enticed a leery Oxford University Press with a generous subvention, assuring publication and wide distribution.[42] Willits took a further step to assure that the League's legacy was burnished in the public eye. A direct appeal to Arthur Sulzberger, publisher of the *New York Times*, coaxed the paper's Sunday book-review section into surrendering the most prominent of its precious pages. Willits even suggested a reviewer who happened to have been a "prime mover getting this study under way."[43]

Accordingly, the piece commissioned was laden with praise, calling the plump volumes a "concise well-told story." But the real compliments were saved for an organization that offered a "Great ... Leap Forward," leading to the best parts of its successor, the United Nations. This effusive, hopeful tribute came from another League under-secretary-general. Admittedly he was an abortive one. He also happened to be a former president of the Rockefeller Foundation, Raymond Fosdick.[44]

Incestuousness in the publishing and literary worlds is hardly unknown. Nevertheless, it should not be surprising, considering how intertwined the League was with the foundation, that a Rockefeller-funded project describing another Rockefeller grantee was reviewed by a former Rockefeller Foundation president. Still, the history was perhaps the last technical enterprise centered on the League that Rockefeller sponsored. The League had finished its own journey from living institution to exemplary information, in this case becoming a historical data set for analyzing the possibilities of liberal governance in the Cold War world. Like all the technical work sponsored in the decades before, it had a political end. The Rockefeller

Foundation had again spoken, generating a history of a particular present that would shape histories that followed. The League's example could
frame the emergent Pax Americana and the international society that lay
within it.

Fosdick made a point others agreed with at the time and since, that "the
League had laid the groundwork for its successor." That foundation was
most apparent in the technical structures. Fosdick made the linkages explicit:

> The "sections" of the League have become the great specialized agencies
> of today. The League's Health Section . . . has expanded into the World
> Health Organization . . . ; the Economic Section has been continued in
> vastly larger form in the International Bank, the International Monetary
> Fund and the Economic and Social Council. The League's Nutritional
> Committee has become the Food and Agriculture Organization; the Com-
> mittee on Intellectual Cooperation has been magnified into UNESCO. . . .
> Even President Truman's "bold, new plan" known as Point IV [to further
> international development] . . . had its counterpart in the League's "tech-
> nical assistance to China."[45]

Such praise was part of Fosdick's own program. On other fronts he was
laboring to create a usable internationalist past to provide further mortar
for the bricks in the structure of liberal order. He etched interwar technical
accomplishments into his own history of the Rockefeller Foundation and
foisted continuity on the leadership of international organizations with a
retrospective on the first six secretaries-general of both the League and the
UN.[46] It was these efforts in support of global governance that were valued
and would endure. What had changed was that these elements were no
longer officially external, they were formal, constituent parts of the liberal
global order that had been internalized by the United States and which that
superpower sought to maintain, defend, and extend.

As the Cold War wore on, the League's memory was overlaid with the
frustrations and disappointments surrounding its successor, as well as the
limitations of postwar liberal internationalism and variants of global cooperation. Later histories would be critical, even dismissive, of the League.
In part, this was a reaction to laudatory, or at least utilitarian, views of the
League that had been pushed immediately following the war. New views
focused on the political, emphasizing "tragicomic" failures to keep the
peace while leaving the technical story by the wayside.[47]

After the Cold War and the glossy focus on "globalization" that came
with an emphasis on interconnection and interdependence, such dismissive interpretations have been superseded by those who have come back to

the League of Nations. The League, particularly its Secretariat, has again become "the Thing." Such attention is most revealing not when it tells the story of a single organization but when it is part of a larger historical inquiry. In other words, the League is a way to investigate the means and not an end in itself. The purpose of the exploration of the importance of information and analysis to a transnational community is less to reify or deify liberal internationalism than to interrogate it. A thorough grilling shows the important place of the League *within* an international society that pivoted on it but also granted the organization reach and legitimacy and, when it had served its purpose, stripped it for parts and discarded it.

Geneva and the liberal international society that employed it have long provided a mirror for scholars. They now offer a means to consider a "globalization" that has lost much of its luster, as well as a way of asking hard questions of the present—by revisiting transnational and international issues in the years between two great wars—as liberal order again sags in the twenty-first century. This attention is hardly a surprise, as liberal ideas were the exposed core of an era where an international system was stretched beyond the breaking point. Continuities from that earlier time lie within the system in which historians scribble about the League at the start of the twenty-first century. The distillation of the League during the crisis years of the twentieth century from a living organization trafficking in data and analysis down to raw information to feed liberal agendas is part of the reason it has become an irresistible historical example for another present. It is still grist for transnational dialogue. That conversation is mostly reserved for scholars who remain, as denizens of academic institutions and professions, franchises in liberal international society. Even so, not all are cognizant of the imperatives that reduced the League to the usable data now harvested for ongoing inquiry. Nevertheless, it remains a means to an end. What has been left continues to be molded into analysis to divine the continuities, complexities, contractions, and possibilities up to and beyond liberal order.

ACKNOWLEDGMENTS

This book is a happy accident. Immersed in my research on how the Great Depression refocused US views of the world it became clear, contrary to some scholarly conventional wisdom, that many key American figures and institutions interacted with the League of Nations. Many of these individuals even spent time in the international hub that was interwar Geneva. Curiosity was one thing, but more importantly I was fortunate to secure some travel funds, so I unwittingly found myself caught in an earlier migratory pattern and made for Switzerland.

As is the case when one looks closely, I discovered there was a much more complicated relationship between the United States and the institutions clustered around Geneva. Digging deeper, I realized a book had set itself to simmering among other ingredients I had collected. Aspects of the American relationship to the League were indeed part of the global story of the US in the 1930s, as well as a window on some larger international themes.

The true surprise was the variety of scholarship that was emerging on the League, which not only broadened an understanding of the institution and its activities but also its links to vital elements of international affairs and transnational questions. Engaging this literature was an unexpected pleasure of this project.

I was fortunate to receive the support necessary to turn my efforts toward this book. At Tufts, the tireless Faculty Research Awards Committee showed willingness to entertain funding requests for parts of this project. The offer of a Senior Semester Leave to put various parts together was particularly appreciated. Early on, the Center for the Humanities at Tufts provided a faculty fellowship that fostered the realization that I really did have a book on my hands. Dean Bárbara Brizuela offered a skosh more funding when unexpected proximity made research in Australia and New Zealand possible. I was supremely lucky to be chosen as a scholar-in-residence at Tufts's European Center in Talloires, France. This appointment again put me in striking distance of the International Labour Organization and

League archives and in the footsteps of some of the characters in this tale. It also immersed me in the delightful reservoir of educational comradery that Gabriella Goldstein maintains by Lake Annecy.

Beyond the Hill, Truman-Kaufman Fellowship enriched this project, as did a series of grants from the Earhart Foundation. Just down the Red Line, John Tirman and the Center for International Studies at Massachusetts Institute of Technology were superbly generous with space and collegiality in letting me visit for periods while putting this project together.

Research spanning three continents, seven countries, and dozens of repositories and collections brought the pleasure of exploring new archives and libraries as well as the chance to reacquaint myself with ones I thought I knew. A slew of archivists and librarians around the world have been patient and helpful—indeed indispensable—to the project.

The Rockefeller Archive Center funded time for me to return to its rich collections and superb staff. I ran deeper into debt to the late Tom Rosenbaum, whose passing is a loss to scholarly inquiry. His colleagues Michele Hiltzik and James Allen Smith are a reminder that an archive's best resources can be its people. Erica Mosner proved this truism by guiding me through the collections of the Institute of Advanced Studies. The professionalism of the staff at the Australian and US National Archives, as well those countries'—and New Zealand's—national libraries, was such that it was almost invisible but hugely appreciated. However, one clear distinction among these venerable institutions must be made. The Australian National Library is unrivaled in the gastronomic delights it offers to complement its revealing collections.

The League of Nations lives on in its archives on an upper floor of the "Rockefeller Wing" of the Palace of Nations—soon to be available online to all. This legacy of raw information recently moved to a room with a view of Mont Blanc, where the cries of the peacocks that have long haunted the grounds can still be heard. Chief among all these unique treats for the researcher are the contents of a remarkable collection that has been fortunate to have had stewards in Bernhardine Pejovic, Lee Robertson, and Jacques Oberson, who have made it accessible to an international society of researchers.

I am forever impressed with the librarians of the Tisch and Ginn Libraries at Tufts, who tirelessly hunt down all sorts of materials that I might request. In particular, Pamela Hopkins at Tufts' Digital Collections and Archives showed a pitch of efficiency that is matched by her boundless good humor and patience with requests.

It is a depressing reality of scholarly work that research projects, competing with other demands and commitments, develop slowly. I have been lucky to have an international succession of research assistants who have had a hand in the project. Some of the students in various places and countries who assisted with early phases of the project have moved through the system, and some now even hold academic posts of their own. I am grateful to Isabel Loyola Barrera, Eric Vanden Bussche, Isabell Creed, Bård Drange, Grace Goudiss, James Lee, Neeraj Prasad, Uella Rodriguez, Josh Savala, Lindsay Schakenbach, Juhi Shahin, Laura Tavolacci, and Wescott Yeaw for all their efforts.

My trespass into another realm of inquiry was enriching beyond the topic itself. It put me in touch with an international set of scholars. I am grateful to Martin Bemmann, Brooke Blower, Patricia Clavin, Thomas David, Simon Reed-Henry, Akira Iriye, Julia Irwin, David Lowe, Mark Mazower, Susan Pedersen, Andrew Preston, Katharina Reitzler, Agnieszka Sobocinska, Iselin Theien, Trigvy Thronviet, Ludovic Tournès, and Tom Zeiler for their input, feedback, and perspective on aspects of the project in various forms and forums. Above all, I have valued (and shamelessly exploited) the tireless comradery and hospitality of Davide Rodogno, who not only gave encouragement but, on occasion, a place to sleep.

International work forges networks, and I have been lucky to have enjoyed several overlapping webs on this accidental journey. Travel for this project has been an unexpected and fortunate pleasure. A fellowship at the Norwegian Nobel Institute brought focus. Asle Toje and Geir Lundestad, as well as the institute's generous staff of remarkable taste, sustained a stimulating environment that was palpable, particularly at the lunch table. I also found one of the most challenging games of darts I have encountered, as well as an indulgent audience for a recitation of Longfellow.

An unexpected year and a half in Fiji provided time and a fascinating backdrop to begin writing up this project. Taraivosa Baikeirewa, James Johnson, Jacob Mati, Keri Mills, Ryota Nishino, Tuinawi Rakuita, and Morgan Tuimalealiifano all extended the generosities of the School of Social Science at the University of the South Pacific to a visiting scholar who abruptly appeared at their door.

In the South Seas I ended up being close (in a Pacific Basin sense) to collections that otherwise might have been out of reach. Research in Australia was facilitated by an all-too-brief fellowship at the US Studies Centre at the University of Sydney. Simon Jackman and Aaron Nyerges were superb hosts, while Ian Bickerton, Sarah Graham, Michael McDonnell, Glenda Sluga, and Ian Tyrrell all made an impossibly sunny winter in Sydney even brighter. Philip Fountain and Valerie Wallace lured me to Victoria University in New Zealand, which not only made archives in Wellington accessible but also exposed me to a lively intellectual environment under the Southern Cross.

This project was fortunate to find a place at the University of Chicago Press. I learned that editor Tim Mennel lives up to the reputation that circulates among my colleagues of being "one of the best." He, Susannah Engstrom, and other staff at the press have been superb partners. As the gears of production began, Gene McGarry again showed himself to be a peerless copy editor. I am also grateful to the Meijer Foundation Fund for an award that assisted in bringing this book into print.

Friends and family were indispensable. Work and Life are now joined as professional buzzwords, but too often institutions—for all the bureaucratic chanting of these terms—actively fail to connect them in practice. This failure only highlighted how much I leaned on a collective of friends who assisted with kids and provided other means to sustain sanity particularly as a pandemic stretched across years: Alisha Rankin and John Kuczwara; Dan and Shira Rosan; Scott Benjamin and Carmina Erdei; Anna and Leiran Biton; Wayne and Amanda Weiss; Rachel and Bernie Del Vecchio; Meg and Jim Bride; and Aviva and Jeremy Rothman-Shore. To all of them, since they regularly and kindly asked, yes, the book is done.

Outside the pale of parenting, Patricia Rosenfield has been an indefatigable mentor and a booster—as well as a spur to action. In DC my mother and father-in-law Bertha and Marc Levin shared some of their boundless hospitality and Louise and Rich Wild generously offered a sober retreat during repeated visits. Ian and Liz Ferguson offered space to make rounds from London. Grant Milthorp and Christina Munzer and their impressive sons showed me Australian hospitality leavened with Yankee charm and gave me an appreciation of the Geneva of the Southern Hemisphere, Canberra. Manjiri and Jay Bhalwakar and their daughters patiently put me up on two occasions, showing me the pleasures of going native in a part of France that was, at least I can claim, close to archives.

Doreen Cutonilli visited our household in Fiji and stayed to become part of the family. Her assistance with the administration of daily life allowed me to work at a time when professional demands were secondary.

My parents again deserve much for providing foundations on which I stand. Their pride and support means as much as it always has.

None of this would have been possible without Leah, who is so much more than a partner. We share so much but she has undoubtedly earned more than a simple share of the credit. At low points when institutions showed aggressive disregard, she kept me focused on the big picture. Belief is a priceless commodity, and I owe her forever for believing in me. She also has a smile that is historic in its radiance.

There remain two wonderful, amazing people who deserve more than a book dedication. My daughters, Lillis and Caton, appeared and grew as this project was conceived and evolved. They have been so much, but one thing they have indisputably proved is that life is multifaceted and lives beyond text. The things I do, I do for them.

ARCHIVAL COLLECTIONS AND ABBREVIATIONS

All collections here were drawn on in the course of research for this book. Those with abbreviations listed are cited directly in the notes.

Alexander Turnbull Library, National Library of New Zealand (Te Puna Mātauranga o Aotearoa), Wellington, New Zealand
    John Bell Condliffe Papers: JC-ATLNZ
Archives and Special Collections, Mount Holyoke College, South Hadley, MA
    Mary Emma Woolley Papers: MW-ASCMC
Bancroft Library, University of California, Berkeley, CA
    John Bell Condliffe Papers: JC-BLUC
Bodleian Library, Oxford University, United Kingdom
    Lionel Curtis Papers
    Gilbert Murray Papers
    Arnold Toynbee Papers
    Alfred Zimmern Papers
British Documents on Foreign Affairs: BDFA
Digital Collections and Archives, Tufts University, Medford, MA
    Eugene Staley Faculty File
    Fletcher School of Law and Diplomacy Records
    World Peace Foundation Archives: WPF-DCAT
Documents on Canadian External Relations: DCER
Foreign Relations of the United States: FRUS
Franklin Delano Roosevelt Presidential Library, Hyde Park, NY
    Adolf Berle Diary: ABD-FDRL
    Adolf Berle Papers: AB-FDRL
    Henry Morgenthau Diary: HMD-FDRL
    Official File: OF-FDRL
    Presidents Personal File: PPF-FDRL
    White House Stenographer's Diary: WHSD-FDRL
    White House Usher's Log: WHUL-FDRL
    Henry Wallace Papers: HW-FDRL

Sumner Welles Papers: SW-FDRL

John Winant Papers

Fryer Library, University of Queensland, Brisbane, Australia.

Colin Clark Papers: CC-FLUQ

Geneva Research Centre *Information Bulletin*: IB-GRS

Harry S. Truman Presidential Library, Independence, MO

Charles Darlington Papers: CD-HTL

Henry Grady Papers: HG-HTL

Charles Kindleberger Papers: CK-HTL

Harvard Law School Archives, Harvard University, Cambridge, MA

Manley Hudson Papers: MH-HLA

Harvard University Archives, Pusey Library, Harvard University, Cambridge, MA

Gottfried Haberler Papers: GH-HUA

Simon Kuznets Papers: SK-HUA

Arthur Sweetser Papers: AS-HUA

Hoover Institution on War, Revolution, and Peace Archives, Stanford University, Stanford, CA

Edward Eyre Hunt Papers: EH-HIA

Houghton Library, Harvard University, Cambridge, MA

Jay Pierrepont Moffat Papers: JM-HLHU

International Labour Office Archives, International Labour Organization, Geneva

Adrien Tixier Papers: AT-ILOA

International Labour Office Administrative Files: AF-ILOA

Postwar Reconstruction Files: PR-ILOA

International Monetary Fund Archives, Washington, DC

Bretton Woods Collection: BW-IMFA

League of Nations Archives, United Nations Office, Geneva

Joseph Avenol Papers: JA-LNA

Economic and Financial Section Records: EFS-LNA

Financial Section and Economic Intelligence Service, Office of the Director: OD-LNA

Martin Hill Papers: MH-LNA

Sean Lester Diary: SLD-LNA

Sean Lester Papers: SL-LNA

Alexander Loveday Papers: AL-LNA

Registry Files: R-LNA

Arthur Salter Papers

Library of Congress, Manuscripts Division, Washington, DC

Edward Bernays Papers

Raymond Leslie Buell Papers: RB-LCMD

Herbert Feis Papers: HF-LCMD

Henry Prather Fletcher Papers: HPF-LCMD

Benjamin Gerig Papers: BG-LCMD

Cordell Hull Papers: CH-LCMD

Leo Pasvolsky Papers: LP-LCMD
Arthur Sweetser Papers: AS-LCMD
Henry Wallace Papers: HW-LCMD
Library of Congress, Photos Division, Washington, DC
New York World Collection: WF-LCPD
Manuscripts and Archives, Yale University, New Haven, CT
Institute of International Studies Records
Manuscripts Division, New York Public Library, New York
Clark M. Eichelberger Papers: CE-NYPL
World's Fair Records: WF-NYPL
McGill University Archives, Montreal, Canada
RG 4 Subject Files
RG 40 Gerhard R. Lomer Files: GL-MAMU
National Archives of Australia, Canberra, Australia
Stanley Bruce Papers: SB-NAA
Department of External Affairs Records: DEX-NAA
Commonwealth Council for Scientific and Industrial Research Records:
CSIR-NAA
National Archives and Records Administration, College Park, MD
RG 43 Records of International Conferences, Commissions, and Exhibitions
RG 59 General Records of the US Department of State: RG59-NAMD
RG 84 Foreign Service Posts of the Department of State, American Legation,
Bern, General Records: RG84-NAMD
RG 169 Records of the Foreign Economic Administration
RG 200 National Archives Gift Collection, Winfield Riefler Papers, 1929–1971:
WR-NAMD
RG 208 Records of the Office of War Information: RG208-NAMD
National Library of Australia, Canberra, Australia
Heinz William Arndt Papers: HA-NLA
Frank Lidgett McDougall Papers: FM-NLA
Nuffield College Archives, Oxford University, Oxford, United Kingdom
Alexander Loveday Papers: AL-NCA
Rare Book and Manuscript Library, Columbia University, New York,
Carnegie Endowment for International Peace Records: CEIP-RBML
Institute of Pacific Relations Archives
James G. McDonald Papers
James Shotwell Papers
Riksarkivet, Oslo, Norway
Carl Hambro Papers: CH-RN
Rockefeller Archive Center, Sleepy Hollow, New York
RG 1 Rockefeller Foundation Records, Projects (Grants): RG1-RAC
RG 2 Rockefeller Foundation Records, General Correspondence: RG2-RAC
RG 3 Rockefeller Foundation Records, Administration Program and Policy: RG3-
RAC

Raymond Fosdick Diary
John Marshall Diary
Trustee's Minutes
Royal Institute of International Affairs Library, London
Royal Institute of International Affairs Records: RI-RIL
Schlesinger Library, Radcliffe Institute, Harvard University, Cambridge, MA
Vera Dean Papers
Seely G. Mudd Manuscript Library, Princeton University, Princeton, NJ
Hamilton Fish Armstrong Papers: HFA-MLPU
Council on Foreign Relations Archives
Derso and Kelen Collection
Harold Dodds Papers: HD-MLPU
Edward Meade Earle Papers: EE-MLPU
Raymond B. Fosdick Papers: RF-MLPU
Ragnar Nurkse Papers: RN-MLPU
Princeton University Archives
Jacob Viner Papers
Shelby White and Leon Levy Archives Center, Institute of Advanced Study,
Princeton, NJ
Frank Aydelotte File
General File: GF-IASA
Special Collections, Milton S. Eisenhower Library, Johns Hopkins University,
Baltimore
Isaiah Bowman Papers
RG 8.010 Walter Hines Page School Relations Records: WHPS-SCJHU
Studies of American Interests in the War and the Peace Political Series: WPS
Wisconsin State Historical Society, Madison, WI
Foreign Policy Association Archives: FPA-WSHS

NOTES

INTRODUCTION

1. See Jenifer Van Vleck, *Empire of the Air: Aviation and the American Ascendancy* (Cambridge, MA: Harvard University Press 2013).

2. "Yankee Clipper Delayed by Winds," *New York Times*, August 22, 1940.

3. See Ludovic Tournès, "American Membership of the League of Nations: US Philanthropy and the Transformation of an Intergovernmental Organisation into a Think Tank," *International Politics* 55, no. 6 (2018): 852–69; Ludovic Tournès, *Les États-Unis et la Société des Nations (1914–1946): Le système international face à l'émergence d'une superpuissance* (Bern: Peter Lang, 2016).

4. Susan Pedersen, "Back to the League of Nations," *American Historical Review* 112, no. 4 (2007): 1091–1117.

5. Daniel Gorman, *The Emergence of International Society in the 1920s* (New York: Cambridge University Press, 2012).

6. Frank Moorhouse, *Dark Palace: The Companion Novel to "Grand Days"* (Milsons Point: Random House Australia, 2000).

7. The literature on internationalism has flowered in recent years, moving far beyond the liberal. See Philippa Hetherington and Glenda Sluga, "Liberal and Illiberal Internationalisms," *Journal of World History* 31, no. 1 (2020): 1–9; Arnd Bauerkämper and Grzegorz Rossolinski-Liebe, eds., *Fascism without Borders: Transnational Connections and Cooperation between Movements and Regimes in Europe from 1918 to 1945* (New York: Berghahn Books, 2017); Jens Steffek, "Fascist Internationalism," *Millennium* 44, no. 1 (2015): 3–22; Patricia Clavin and Glenda Sluga, eds., *Internationalisms: A Twentieth-Century History* (Cambridge: Cambridge University Press, 2017); Minkah Makalani, *In the Cause of Freedom: Radical Black Internationalism from Harlem to London, 1917–1939* (Chapel Hill: University of North Carolina Press, 2011); Abigail Green, "Liberals, Socialists, Internationalists, Jews." *Journal of World History* 31, no. 1 (2020): 11–41; Abigail Green and Vincent Viaene, eds., *Religious Internationals in the Modern World* (Basingstoke, UK: Palgrave Macmillan, 2012).

8. Daniel T. Rodgers, "In Search of Progressivism," *Reviews in American History* 10, no. 4 (1982): 113–32.

9. Randolph S. Bourne, "Trans-National America," *Atlantic*, July 1, 1916.

10. Alan Dawley, *Changing the World: American Progressives in War and Revolution* (Princeton, NJ: Princeton University Press, 2003), 27; Lucian M. Ashworth, "Progres-

sivism Triumphant? Isaiah Bowman's New Diplomacy in a New World," in *Progressivism and US Foreign Policy between the World Wars*, ed. Molly Cochran and Cornelia Navari (New York: Palgrave Macmillan, 2017), 73–74.

11. Defining work on transnational progressivism is Daniel T. Rodgers, *Atlantic Crossings: Social Politics in a Progressive Age* (Cambridge, MA: Belknap Press of Harvard University Press, 1998).

12. See Ashworth, "Progressivism Triumphant."

13. Alan Ryan, *The Making of Modern Liberalism* (Princeton, NJ: Princeton University Press, 2012), 456–72.

14. Ryan, *Liberalism*, 21–44.

15. Defining scholarship on the concept is Hedley Bull, *The Anarchical Society: A Study of Order in World Politics*, 2nd ed. (New York: Columbia University Press, 1995).

16. See Frank A. Ninkovich, *The Global Republic: America's Inadvertent Rise to World Power* (Chicago: University of Chicago Press, 2014).

17. On international society, see Gorman, *International Society*; Glenda Sluga, *Internationalism in the Age of Nationalism* (Philadelphia: University of Pennsylvania Press, 2013); Erez Manela, "International Society as a Historical Subject," *Diplomatic History* 44, no. 2 (2020): 184–209.

18. Lila J. Rupp, *Worlds of Women: The Making of an International Women's Movement* (Princeton, NJ: Princeton University Press, 1997); Glenda Sluga and Carolyn James, eds., *Women, Diplomacy and International Politics since 1500* (Abingdon, UK: Routledge, 2015).

19. See Mark Mazower, *Governing the World: The History of an Idea* (New York: Penguin, 2012).

20. An example of this genre is James Palmer, "Nobody Knows Anything about China," *Foreign Policy*, March 21, 2018, http://foreignpolicy.com/2018/03/21/nobody-knows-anything-about-china/.

21. Credit for linking power and knowledge is often given to Michel Foucault. For an overview of his later thinking on the issue, see Michel Foucault, *Power/Knowledge: Selected Interviews and Other Writings, 1972–1977* (New York: Pantheon, 1980). The general statement that knowledge is power is sometimes credited to Francis Bacon or William Shakespeare, but attestations to the interrelation of these concepts can be found in the Old Testament as well as in Sanskrit texts.

22. Erez Manela, *The Wilsonian Moment: Self-Determination and the International Origins of Anticolonial Nationalism* (New York: Oxford University Press, 2007), 35–53. See also John Maxwell Hamilton, *Manipulating the Masses: Woodrow Wilson and the Birth of American Propaganda* (Baton Rouge: Louisiana State University Press, 2020).

23. C. A. Bayly, *Empire and Information: Intelligence Gathering and Social Communication in India, 1780–1870* (New York: Cambridge University Press, 1996), 1–9.

24. See Canadian Institute of International Affairs, *The Canadian Economy and Its Problems: Papers and Proceedings of Study Groups of Members of the Canadian Institute of International Affairs, 1933–1934* (Toronto: Canadian Institute of International Affairs, 1934); Harold A. Innis, "The Canadian Economy and the Depression," in *Essays in Canadian Economic History*, ed. Mary Q. Innis (Toronto: University of Toronto Press, 2017), 123–40; H. A. Innis, "The Penetrative Powers of the Price System," *Canadian Journal of Economics and Political Science / Revue Canadienne d'Economique et de Science Politique* 4, no. 3 (1938): 299–319; Harold Innis, *Empire and Communications* (1950; repr.,

Lanham, MD: Rowman & Littlefield, 2007); Harold A. Innis, *The Bias of Communication* (Toronto: University of Toronto Press, 1951); Edward L. Bernays, *Propaganda* (New York: Liveright, 1928); Walter Lippmann, *Public Opinion* (New York: Harcourt, Brace, 1922); Walter Lippmann, *Liberty and the News* (New York: Harcourt, Brace and Howe, 1920); Walter Lippmann, *An Inquiry into the Principles of the Good Society* (Boston: Little, Brown, 1937).

25. Adam J. Tooze, "Imagining National Economies: National and International Economic Statistics, 1900–1950," in *Imagining Nations*, ed. Geoffrey Cubitt (Manchester, UK: Manchester University Press, 1998), 212–28.

26. Theodore M. Porter, *The Rise of Statistical Thinking, 1820–1900* (Princeton, NJ: Princeton University Press, 2020).

27. See Timothy Mitchell, *Rule of Experts: Egypt, Techno-Politics, Modernity* (Berkeley: University of California Press, 2002).

28. For accounts that reflect a rather dismissive, later-twentieth-century view of the League, see George Scott, *The Rise and Fall of the League of Nations* (London: Hutchinson, 1973); Elmer Bendiner, *A Time for Angels: The Tragicomic History of the League of Nations* (New York: Knopf, 1975). A more balanced but still critical take is F. S. Northedge, *The League of Nations: Its Life and Times, 1920–1946* (New York: Holmes & Meier, 1986).

29. Thomas Andrew Bailey, *Woodrow Wilson and the Great Betrayal* (New York: Macmillan, 1945); John Milton Cooper, *Breaking the Heart of the World: Woodrow Wilson and the Fight for the League of Nations* (New York: Cambridge University Press, 2001); Thomas J. Knock, *To End All Wars: Woodrow Wilson and the Quest for a New World Order*, new ed. (Princeton, NJ: Princeton University Press, 2019).

30. See Mark Mazower, *No Enchanted Palace: The End of Empire and the Ideological Origins of the United Nations* (Princeton, NJ: Princeton University Press, 2009).

31. See Warren F. Kuehl, *Keeping the Covenant: American Internationalists and the League of Nations, 1920–1939* (Kent, OH: Kent State University Press, 1997).

32. This sort of monographic exploration of particular bureaus has been evolving elsewhere. See, e.g., Patricia Clavin, *Securing the World Economy: The Reinvention of the League of Nations, 1920–1946* (Oxford: Oxford University Press, 2013); Iris Borowy, *Coming to Terms with World Health: The League of Nations Health Organisation, 1921–1946* (Frankfurt: Peter Lang, 2009).

33. See Ian Tyrrell, *Transnational Nation: United States History in Global Perspective since 1789* (London: Palgrave Macmillan, 2015).

34. Sluga, *Internationalism.*

35. David Engerman, "American Knowledge and Global Power," *Diplomatic History* 31, no. 4 (2007): 599–622.

CHAPTER 1: THE LEAGUE IS THE THING

1. Zara Steiner, *The Triumph of the Dark: European International History, 1933–1939* (New York: Oxford University Press, 2011), 100–161.

2. James Barros, *Betrayal from Within: Joseph Avenol, Secretary-General of the League of Nations* (New Haven, CT: Yale University Press, 1969), 146–205; Martin Dubin, "Toward the Bruce Report: The Economic and Social Program of the League in the Avenol Era," in *The League of Nations in Retrospect / La Société des Nations: Rétrospective*, by

United Nations Library and Graduate Institute of International Studies (Berlin: Walter de Gruyter, 1983), 43–45.

3. Oral history interview with Joseph Avenol, August 3, 1951, box P16, JA-LNA.

4. See Adam Tooze, *Wages of Destruction: The Making and Breaking of the Nazi Economy* (New York: Penguin Books, 2008).

5. Amelia M. Kiddle, "Separating the Political from the Technical: The 1938 League of Nations Mission to Latin America," in *Beyond Geopolitics: New Histories of Latin America at the League of Nations*, ed. Alan L. McPherson and Yannick Wehrli (Albuquerque: University of New Mexico Press, 2015), 239–57.

6. "Reaction of Opinion to International Political Developments in the Past Two Years," n.d. [1939], box P84, MH-LNA.

7. Gorman, *International Society*.

8. See, for example, Charles S. Maier, Niall Ferguson, Daniel J. Sargent, and Erez Manela, eds., *The Shock of the Global: The 1970s in Perspective* (Cambridge, MA: Harvard University Press, 2010); Thomas L. Friedman, *The Lexus and the Olive Tree* (New York: Farrar, Straus & Giroux, 1999).

9. Jürgen Osterhammel, *The Transformation of the World: A Global History of the Nineteenth Century* (Princeton, NJ: Princeton University Press, 2014); Philipp Blom, *The Vertigo Years: Europe, 1900–1914* (New York: Basic Books, 2008); Stephen Kern, *The Culture of Time and Space, 1880–1918* (Cambridge, MA: Harvard University Press, 1983).

10. See Clavin and Sluga, *Internationalisms*; Makalani, *In the Cause of Freedom*.

11. See Tyrrell, *Transnational Nation*.

12. Katharina Rietzler, "From Peace Advocacy to International Relations Research: The Transformation of Transatlantic Philanthropic Networks, 1900–1930," in *Shaping the Transnational Sphere: Experts, Networks, and Issues from the 1840s to the 1930s*, ed. Davide Rodogno, Bernhard Struck, and Jakob Vogel (New York: Berghahn, 2015), 173–93; Glenda Sluga, *The Nation, Psychology, and International Politics, 1870–1919* (New York: Palgrave Macmillan, 2006), 36; Katharina Rietzler, "Before the Cultural Cold Wars: American Philanthropy and Cultural Diplomacy in the Inter-War Years," *Historical Research* 84, no. 223 (2011): 148–64.

13. Frank G. Boudreau, *Ancient Diseases—Modern Defences: The Work of the Health Organization of the League of Nations* (New York: Columbia University Press, 1939).

14. Borowy, *World Health*, 160.

15. Randall M. Packard, *A History of Global Health: Interventions into the Lives of Other Peoples* (Baltimore: Johns Hopkins University Press, 2016), 54.

16. David Lincove, "Data for Peace: The League of Nations and Disarmament 1920–40," *Peace & Change* 43, no. 4 (2018): 498–529.

17. David Petruccelli, "The Crisis of Liberal Internationalism: The Legacies of the League of Nations Reconsidered." *Journal of World History* 31, no. 1 (2020): 111–36.

18. Gorman, *International Society*, 51–81; George Wilton Field, "Memorandum on Oil Pollution Presented Before the Economic Committee of the League of Nations," October 1931, box 2533, Decimal File 1930–39, 500.C1199/95, RG59-NAMD.

19. Akira Iriye, *Cultural Internationalism and World Order* (Baltimore: Johns Hopkins University Press, 1997), 57–66; David Long, "Who Killed the International Studies Conference?," *Review of International Studies* 32, no. 4 (2006): 603–22.

20. See James McAllister, *Wilsonian Visions: The Williamstown Institute of Politics and American Internationalism after World War I* (Ithaca, NY: Cornell University Press, 2021).

21. Robert D. Schulzinger, *The Wise Men of Foreign Affairs: The History of the Council on Foreign Relations* (New York: Columbia University Press, 1984).

22. Donald Philips Dennis, *Foreign Policy in a Democracy: The Role of the Foreign Policy Association* (New York: Foreign Policy Association, 2003).

23. John B. Condliffe, *Reminiscences of the Institute of Pacific Relations* (Vancouver: Institute of Asian Research, University of British Columbia, 1981), 1.

24. Notes on a Visit to the World Peace Foundation Office, Boston, July 19 and 20, 1932, box R4752, R-LNA.

25. Report of the American Committee of the League of Nations Association, September 15, 1933, box 1, subject files, WPF-DCAT.

26. Benjamin Gerig, Arthur Sweetser, Felix Morley, Pittman Potter, and T. G. Spates, "Research Data From Geneva," March 12, 1930, box 1, subject files, WPF-DCAT.

27. Raymond B. Fosdick, *Chronicle of a Generation: An Autobiography* (New York: Harper, 1958), 142–213.

28. Raymond B. Fosdick, *The Old Savage in the New Civilization* (Garden City, NY: Doubleday, Doran, 1931).

29. Fosdick to Tumulty, January 19, 1920, in Raymond B. Fosdick, *Letters on the League of Nations: From the Files of Raymond B. Fosdick* (Princeton, NJ: Princeton University Press, 2015), 104–5.

30. Rockefeller to Fosdick, May 21, 1928; Fosdick to Richardson, May 18, 1928, box 9, RF-MLPU. The sum John D. Rockefeller gave to FDR was a not inconsiderable $20,000 (over $320,000 in 2022).

31. Fosdick, *Chronicle*, 243–49, 251–95.

32. Susan Sweetser Clifford, *One Shining Hour: A Memoir* (privately printed, 1990), 68; "Mrs. Fosdick Kills Two Children, Self," *New York Times*, April 5, 1932. Clifford states that Winifred Fosdick suffered from manic depression.

33. Arthur Sweetser, "Harvard 1911: Summary of 25 Years since College Days Prepared for 25th Class Anniversary," June 1936, box 1, AS-HUA. Sweetser may have borrowed his colorful phrase directly from an African American spiritual or the title of Eugene O'Neill's 1924 play *All God's Chillun Got Wings*.

34. Arthur Sweetser, *Roadside Glimpses of the Great War* (New York: MacMillan, 1916).

35. Sweetser, "Summary of 25 Years since College Days"; Arthur Sweetser, *The American Air Service: A Record of Its Problems, Its Difficulties, Its Failures, and Its Final Achievements* (New York: D. Appleton and Co., 1919).

36. Letter from Sweetser, August 3, 1933, box 16, AS-LCMD.

37. Memo for the Secretary of State, February 11, 1937, PPF 506, PPF-FDRL.

38. See Frank Moorhouse, *Grand Days* (Sydney: Macmillan Australia, 1993).

39. Henshaw to Huss, June 15, 1942, reel 46, HW-FDRL.

40. The ur-text that frames interwar "idealists" was itself a plea for the policy of appeasement from the period: Edward Hallett Carr, *The Twenty Years' Crisis, 1919–1939: An Introduction to the Study of International Relations* (London: Macmillan, 1940). See also Lucian M. Ashworth, "Where Are the Idealists in Interwar International Relations?," *Review of International* Studies 32, no. 2 (April 2006): 291–308.

41. Sluga, *Internationalism*; Vanessa Ogle, *The Global Transformation of Time: 1870–1950* (Cambridge, MA: Harvard University Press, 2015).

42. "Verbatim Record of Mr. Young's Address in Cincinnati," n.d. [1931], box 1, series 1, 2, 3, WHPS-SCJHU, 5–6.

43. Franklin D. Roosevelt, "Our Foreign Policy: A Democratic View," *Foreign Affairs* 6, no. 4 (1928): 581.

44. Melvyn P. Leffler, *Safeguarding Democratic Capitalism: U.S. Foreign Policy and National Security, 1920-2015* (Princeton, NJ: Princeton University Press, 2017), 50-56.

45. Sweetser to Fosdick, January 27, 1938, box 18, series 100, RG1-RAC.

46. "Secretary Hoover's Statement to the Republican National Convention," June 14, 1928, in *The New Day: Campaign Speeches of Herbert Hoover* (Stanford, CA: Stanford University Press: 1928), 39; "League Expects Aid in Work from Hoover," *New York Times*, November 8, 1928.

47. United States President's Research Committee on Social Trends, *Recent Social Trends in the United States: Report of the President's Research Committee on Social Trends* (New York: McGraw-Hill, 1933); David Kennedy, *Freedom from Fear: The American People in Depression and War, 1929-1945* (New York: Oxford University Press, 1999), 10-13.

48. See, for example, Abraham Flexner, *The American College: A Criticism* (1908; repr., New York: Arno Press, 1969).

49. Flexner to Fosdick, April 25, 1927, box 21, RF-MLPU. Emphasis in original.

50. Flexner to Fosdick, August 13, 1926, box 21, RF-MLPU.

51. See Gorman, *International Society*.

52. Abraham Flexner, "A Memorandum Suggesting Possible Activities in the Field of International Relations," n.d. [1927], box 22, RF-MLPU.

53. Note by Fosdick, October 10, 1964, box 21; Fosdick to Drummond, February 18, 1927; Loveday to Rose, December 2, 1930, box 22, RF-MLPU.

54. Thomas Neville Bonner, *Iconoclast: Abraham Flexner and a Life in Learning* (Baltimore: Johns Hopkins University Press, 2002), 236-63.

55. Herbert Feis, *Research Activities of the League of Nations: A Report Made to the Committee on International Relations of the Social Science Research Council on the Methods and Progress of Research in the League of Nations and International Labour Organization, June, 1929* (Old Lyme, CT: Old Lyme Press, 1929), 2-5.

56. "Memorandum on the History and Progress of the Study of National Income for 1929-1933," September 7, 1933, box 1, SK-HUA; Stephen J. Macekura, *The Mismeasure of Progress: Economic Growth and Its Critics* (Chicago: University of Chicago Press, 2020), 25-28.

57. Simon Kuznets, "Data for the Science of Economics," 1930, box 1, SK-HUA, 3, 20.

58. Simon Kuznets, "Factors Determining the Supply of Economic Statistics," 1930, box 1, SK-HUA, 1-2.

59. Simon Kuznets, "Data for the Science of Economics," 1930, box 1, SK-HUA, 15.

60. Simon Kuznets, "Factors Determining the Supply of Economic Statistics," 1930, box 1, SK-HUA, 12.

61. Kuznets to Clark, February 10, 1937; Clark to Kuznets, June 20, 1938, box 11, CC-FLUQ.

62. Colin Clark, *The Conditions of Economic Progress* (London: Macmillan, 1940).

63. Jan Tinbergen, *Statistical Testing of Business-Cycle Theories. I. A Method and Its Application to Investment Activity* (Geneva: League of Nations, Economic Intelligence Service, 1939).

64. Tinbergen to Clark, October 21, 1936; Clark to Tinbergen, November 5, 1936, box 11, CC-FLUQ.

65. J. Steven Landefeld, Eugene P. Seskin, and Barbara M. Fraumeni, "Taking the Pulse of the Economy: Measuring GDP," *Journal of Economic Perspectives* 22, no. 2 (2008), 194. See also Richard Froyen, *Macroeconomics: Theories and Policies*, 4th ed. (New York: Macmillan, 1993).

66. Berle to Roosevelt, "Memorandum for President Roosevelt," n.d. [1938], box 47, AB-FDRL.

67. Proceedings of the International Conference Relating to Economic Statistics, Geneva, November 26–December 14, 1928, League of Nations Publications II. Economic and Financial 1929, II 21; Roser Cussó, "Building a Global Representation of Trade through International Quantification: The League of Nations' Unification of Methods in Economic Statistics," *International History Review* 42, no. 4 (2020): 714–36.

68. Kuznets to Willits, "Memorandum on the Development of Work in the National Income Field," September 25, 1939; Willits to Kuznets, July 14, 1939; Kuznets to Willits, August 1, 1939, box 1, SK-HUA.

69. Memo from Willits, October 25, 1940, box 10, series 910, RG3-RAC.

70. Maxwell S. Stewart, *Your Money and Mine: An Analysis of Our National Income* (New York: Foreign Policy Association, 1935), 20.

71. "Geneva Institutions Concerned with International Relations," February 15, 1935, box 7, series 910, RG3-RAC.

72. Inderjeet Parmar, *Foundations of the American Century: The Ford, Carnegie, and Rockefeller Foundations in the Rise of American Power* (New York: Columbia University Press, 2012).

73. Corrado Gini, *Report on the Problem of Raw Materials and Foodstuffs* (Geneva, 1921).

74. Corrado Gini, "The Scientific Basis of Fascism," *Political Science Quarterly* 42 (1927): 99–115; Jean-Guy Prévost, *Total Science: Statistics in Liberal and Fascist Italy* (Montreal: McGill-Queen's University Press, 2009).

75. Alison Adcock Kaufman, "In Pursuit of Equality and Respect: China's Diplomacy and the League of Nations," *Modern China* 40, no. 6 (2014): 605–38; Y. C. Hoe, *The Programme of Technical Cooperation between China and the League of Nations* (N.p.: Institute of Pacific Relations, 1933); Margherita Zanasi, "Exporting Development: The League of Nations and Republican China," *Comparative Studies in Society and History* 49, no. 1 (2007): 143–69.

76. Xianting Fang, *Toward Economic Control in China: Papers Presented at the Sixth Conference of the Institute of Pacific Relations, Yosemite National Park, California, August 15 to 29, 1936* . . . [no. 3] (Shanghai: China Institute of Pacific Relations, 1936), 4:83.

77. See Kiran Klaus Patel, *The New Deal: A Global History* (Princeton, NJ: Princeton University Press, 2016).

78. See Martin Bemmann, "Comparing Economic Activities on a Global Level in the 1920s and 1930s: Motives and Consequences," in *The Force of Comparison: A New Perspective on Modern European History and the Contemporary World*, ed. Willibald Steinmetz (New York: Berghahn, 2019), 242–65.

79. Macekura, *Mismeasure*, 18–31.

80. Edward Eyre Hunt, "Memorandum of Meetings of Representatives of Economic Councils and Research Institutes, Geneva, March 2–4, 1931," March 4, 1931, box 17, EH-HIA; Edward Eyre Hunt, "The Business Depression: Memo of Meeting in Geneva, March 2–4, 1931," box 18, series 100, RG1-RAC.

81. Hunt to Mitchell, August 1, 1931, box 17, EH-HIA.

82. Alexander Loveday, "Problems of Economic Insecurity," in *The World's Economic Future*, by A. Loveday et al. (London: Allen & Unwin, 1938), 17–21.

83. Loveday, Memo to Secretary General, December 14, 1933, box 41, AL-NCA.

84. Loveday to Riefler, April 12, 1938, box 50, AL-NCA.

85. Loveday, "Mr. Loveday's Report on Mission to Canada and the USA," 1934, box P150, AL-NCA.

86. J. B. Condliffe, Draft Autobiography, "Growing Up," John Bell Condliffe Papers, JC-ATLNZ 24.

87. Interview of J. B. Condliffe, New Zealand Broadcasting Corporation, April 29, 1973, JC-ATLNZ.

88. Cullather, "Development."

89. John Bell Condliffe, "The Industrial Revolution in the Far East" (pt. 1), *Economic Record* 2, no. 3 (1926): 180–209; John Bell Condliffe, "The Industrial Revolution in the Far East" (pt. 2), *Economic Record* 3, no. 4 (1927): 82–101.

90. John Bell Condliffe, "The Distribution of Power and Leadership," in *The World's Economic Future*, by A. Loveday et al. (London: Allen & Unwin, 1938), 43–64.

91. Institute of Pacific Relations, *Problems of the Pacific* (Chicago: University of Chicago Press, 1927), 513–54. On the League mandates section, see Susan Pedersen, *The Guardians: The League of Nations and the Crisis of Empire* (Oxford: Oxford University Press, 2015).

92. Interview with Condliffe, 1973, ATLNZ.

93. Elisabetta Tollardo, "International Experts or Fascist Envoys? Alberto Theodoli and Pietro Stoppani at the League of Nations," *New Global Studies* 10, no. 3 (2016): 283–306.

94. Condliffe to Day, November 16, 1931, box 18, series 100, RG1-RAC.

95. Gunn to Day, December 31, 1931; Grant, April 12, 1933; box 18, series 100, RG1-RAC.

96. Condliffe, draft autobiography, "The Twilight of the League," Condliffe Papers, ATLNZ, 3.

97. Condliffe, "Twilight," 41–43.

98. Condliffe, "Twilight," 41.

99. Condliffe, "Twilight," 4.

100. Condliffe, "Twilight," 6.

101. H. D. Henderson, "Review of *World Economic Survey*: Third Year, 1933–34." *Economic Journal* 45, no. 177 (1935): 147–49; D. C. MacGregor, "Review of *World Economic Survey*, Fourth Year, 1934–35; *Review of World Trade*, 1934; *World Production and Prices*, 1925–1934; *Statistical Year-Book of the League of Nations*, 1934–5," *Canadian Journal of Economics and Political Science* 1, no. 4 (1935): 639–40.

102. Neary to Feis, March 2, 1934, box 26, HF-LCMD.

103. "Studies Home Life of $7 Day Ford Men to Fix Pay Abroad," *New York Times*, June 16, 1930.

104. "World Decline in Joblessness Noted," *New York Times*, July 10, 1933; "Out of the Depression," *Chicago Daily News*, April 22, 1934.

105. "The Staff of Nations," *New York Times*, September 4, 1937; League of Nations Mixed Committee of Experts on Nutrition, *Nutrition: Final Report of the Mixed Committee of the League of Nations on the Relation of Nutrition to Health, Agriculture and Economic Policy* (Geneva, 1937).

106. Condliffe, "Twilight," 43–45.

107. World Peace Foundation, World Economic Survey Advertisement, 1935, box 4518, EFS-LNA.

108. Rich to Schnabel, October 1, 1935; Rich to Schnabel, September 6, 1935, box 4518, EFS-LNA.

109. League of Nations Secretariat, *World Economic Survey, 1932–33* (Geneva: League of Nations, 1933), 8.

110. Loveday, "Condliffe: World Economic Survey, 1932–33, General Observations," n.d. [mid-1933], box 50, AL-NCA; Monatsberichte des Österreichischen Institutes für Konjunkturforshung, 4, 1933, 63; Quinn Slobodian, *Globalists: The End of Empire and the Birth of Neoliberalism* (Cambridge, MA: Harvard University Press, 2018), 59. A variant of this spiral also appeared in a newspaper notice in 1933 for the London Economic Conference.

111. J. B. Condliffe, *War and Depression* (Boston: World Peace Foundation, 1935), 24.

112. Who actually drew the "spider's web" for Condliffe's publications is unclear. The issue of the WES that included it was published in August 1933 and has a citation that compares its global representation to the Austrian/German view of Morgenstern's institute, printed earlier that year. It is not credited either in the WES or in *War and Depression*, nor are sources for it cited, which might suggest Condliffe's own hand, even though it was based on others' examples. The volume WES he compiled was the first to publish it to wide distribution, and the FPA publication dramatically enhanced its visibility in the US. Many later works that reproduce it or variants of it merely reference League of Nations data or publications, but not the graphic depiction in the WES or Condliffe's book.

113. A. M. Endres, *International Organizations and the Analysis of Economic Policy, 1919–1950* (Cambridge: Cambridge University Press, 2002).

114. "Agenda for Conference Called by the Rockefeller Foundation to Consider the Desirability and Feasibility for Encouraging Coordination of Fundamental Economic Research upon Problems of Economic Change," July 1936, box 18, JC-BLCU.

115. "Proceedings of the Conference Called by the Rockefeller Foundation to Consider the Desirability and Feasibility of Encouraging Coordination of Fundamental Economic Research on the Problem of Economic Change," July 3–5, 1936, box 18, JC-BLCU.

116. Gottfried Haberler, *Prosperity and Depression: A Theoretical Analysis of Cyclical Movements* (Geneva: League of Nations, 1937); Loveday to Haberler, February 12, 1936, box 50, AL-NCA; Loveday to Haberler, November 6, 1959, box 1, GH-HUA.

117. Tinbergen, *Statistical Testing*.

118. Slobodian, *Globalists*, 55–90.

119. John Maynard Keynes, "Professor Tinbergen's Method," *Economic Journal* 49 (1939): 568.

120. Memorandum, Pasvolsky to Welles, November 10, 1937, box 1, LP-LCMD. The Economic Committee was distinct from the EFS. Committee members were often figures from outside the institution. Nevertheless, it and other similar committees, like the Financial Committee and Depression Committee, remained part of the League's Economic Organization and a means by which parts of international society could directly engage the League.

121. See, for example, Ben S. Bernanke, *Essays on the Great Depression* (Princeton, NJ: Princeton University Press, 2009).

122. "F.D.'s Expert Is Identified," *Washington Daily News*, November 2, 1933; Riefler, "A National Program for Modernized Housing," March 19, 1934; Riefler to Bruere, April 29, 1940, box 1, WR-NAMD.

123. Keynes to Riefler, May 20, 1934, box 1, WR-NAMD.

124. Riefler to Flexner, July 14, 1938, box 1, WR-NAMD.

125. Flexner to Riefler, July 18, 1938, box 1, WR-NAMD.

126. Flexner, "Geneva," May 30, 1938, box 32, GF-IASA.

127. Flexner, "Geneva," 2–3.

128. Ibid.

129. Loveday to Flexner, October 17, 1938, box 32, GF-IASA.

130. Flexner, "Geneva," 3.

131. Varian Fry, *Bricks without Mortar: The Story of International Cooperation* (New York: Foreign Policy Association, 1938), 61.

132. Fry, *Bricks*, 66.

133. Report to the Rockefeller Foundation on the Program of Popular Education of the Foreign Policy Association, November 7, 1940, box 336, series 200, RG1.1-RAC. It would become a reasonably popular title and was reprinted due to institutional and public interest. Summary of Office Reports, May 23, 1941, reel 1, FPA-WSHS.

134. Martin Hill, *Economic and Financial Organization of the League of Nations: A Survey of Twenty-Five Years' Experience* (Washington, DC: Carnegie Endowment for International Peace, Division of International Law, 1946), 3–4.

135. Scott, *Rise*, 395. Neither the British, French, nor Czechoslovaks brought the issues that inspired the Munich crisis to the League. The Soviet Union did raise the issue in Geneva during the crisis, but the institution did not take it up.

136. Sweetser to Fosdick, October 4, 1938, box 154, series 100, RG2-RAC.

137. Sweetser to Fosdick, October 4, 1938, box 154, series 100, RG2-RAC. Emphasis in original.

CHAPTER 2: PLOWSHARES INTO SWORDS

1. File, Expositions—Worlds Fair—NY—League of Nations Exhibit, WF-LCPD.

2. Letter from Benjamin Gerig, August 8, 1939, box 1497, WF-NYPL; See also Gerlof D. Homan, "Orie Benjamin Gerig: Mennonite Rebel, Peace Activist, International Civil Servant, and American Diplomat, 1894-1976," *Mennonite Quarterly Review* 73, no. 4 (1999): 751–82.

3. See David Allen, "International Exhibitionism: The League of Nations at the New York World's Fair, 1939-1940," in *International Organizations and the Media in the Nineteenth and Twentieth Centuries: Exorbitant Expectations*, ed. Jonas Brendebach, Martin Herzer, and Heidi Tworek (New York: Routledge, 2018), 90–116.

4. Radio talk by Robert D. Kohn, December 17, 1936, box 918, WF-NYPL.

5. "War, Peace, and Propaganda," *The March of Time*, vol. 5, episode 11, 1939, http://video.alexanderstreet.com/watch/war-peace-and-propaganda.

6. Robert H. Kargon, "Whose Modernity? Utopia and Commerce at the 1939 New York World's Fair," in *World's Fairs on the Eve of War: Science, Technology, and Modernity, 1937-1942*, ed. Robert H. Kargon (Pittsburgh: University of Pittsburgh Press, 2015), 57–82.

7. Emily S. Rosenberg, "Transnational Currents in a Shrinking World," in *A World*

Connecting, 1870–1945, ed. Emily S. Rosenberg (Cambridge, MA: Belknap Press of Harvard University Press, 2012), 887–901; Osterhammel, *Transformation of the World*, 14–15.

8. See Helen McCarthy, *The British People and the League of Nations: Democracy, Citizenship, and Internationalism, c. 1918–45* (New York: Palgrave Macmillan, 2011).

9. The League of Nations and Modern Methods of Spreading Information Utilized in the Cause of Peace, September 1, 1937, A.18.1937; Means of Spreading Information at the Secretariat's Disposal, Report Submitted by the Sixth Committee to the Assembly, October 1, 1937, A.7.1937; on media and the League, see also Carolyn N. Biltoft, *A Violent Peace: Media, Truth, and Power at the League of Nations* (Chicago: University of Chicago Press, 2021).

10. "The League at Work," 1937.

11. Hersley to Avenol, December 1, 1936, box R5764, R-LNA.

12. Whalen to Avenol, June 28, 1937, box R5764, R-LNA.

13. Report by the Supervisory Commission, Participation of the League of Nations in the New York World's Fair, n.d. [1938], box R5764, R-LNA.

14. "Experts' Suggestions on League Exhibit at the New York World's Fair," March 3, 1938, box 16, AS-LCMD.

15. "Experts' Suggestions."

16. Pelt to Sweetser, March 15, 1938, box 16, AS-LCMD.

17. "A Preliminary Plan for the Organization of the League Pavilion," n.d. [1938], box 16, AS-LCMD.

18. "Tentative Suggestions for the Presentation of the League Pavilion," January 25, 1938, box R5765, R-LNA.

19. "League of Nations Pavilion," March 20, 1939, box 16, AS-LCMD.

20. Franklin Roosevelt, "Fireside Chat," October 12, 1937, American Presidency Project, https://www.presidency.ucsb.edu/documents/fireside-chat-16.

21. "Room IV," box R5768, R-LNA; "League of Nations Pavilion," March 20, 1939, box 16, AS-LCMD.

22. James Mauro, *Twilight at the World of Tomorrow: Genius, Madness, Murder, and the 1939 World's Fair on the Brink of War* (New York: Ballantine Books, 2010), 132; Roosevelt to Wallace, June 23, 1939; Rhodes to Roosevelt, June 21, 1939, *Roosevelt and Foreign Affairs: Second Series, January 1937–August 1939* (New York: Clearwater, 1979), 15:308–10.

23. Map, League File, 1938, box 1497, WF-NYPL.

24. Standley to Sweetser, August 30, 1938; Director of Exhibits and Concessions to Vice President, August 12, 1938, box 1497, WF-NYPL.

25. Standley to Sweetser, August 31, 1938; Sweetser to Standley, September 5, 1938; Standley to van Erp, September 29, 1938, box 1497, WF-NYPL.

26. Sweetser to Pelt, March 9, 1938; Whalen to Sweetser, February 28, 1938, box R5766, R-LNA; Mauro, *Twilight*, 183–85.

27. Revised Budget, March 16, 1939, box 5770, R-LNA. In 1940, one Swiss Franc was worth between twenty-two and twenty-three cents.

28. Note to Roosevelt, June 14, 1938, box 16, AS-LCMD.

29. Arthur Sweetser, "Address on the Occasion of the Laying of the Cornerstone of the League of Nations Building," November 10, 1938, box 16, AS-LCMD.

30. Roosevelt to Sweetser, December 9, 1936, PPF 506, PPF-FDRL.

31. Raymond Buell, "Confidential Memorandum, Interview with the President,"

September 15, 1936, box 41, RB-LCMD; Entry, September 15, 1936, WHSD-FDRL; http://www.fdrlibrary.marist.edu/daybyday/daylog/september-15th-1936/. Buell was recounting a meeting FDR had with Sweetser on September 8, 1936; Entry, September 8, 1936, WHSD-FDRL, http://www.fdrlibrary.marist.edu/daybyday/daylog/september-8th-1936/. Buell's own conversation spurred discussions for a conference focused on the international trade in raw materials.

32. "Mr. Sweetser's Report," April 21, 1938, box 5766, R-LNA.

33. Sweetser to Roosevelt, April 9, 1938, PPF 506, PPF-FDRL.

34. Howard Bucknell to Secretary of State, "The Present Status of the League of Nations," August 23, 1938, box 22, RG 84-NAMD.

35. League of Nations Document A.76.1938.VII, Geneva, September 29, 1938.

36. Memorandum from the Secretary of State, February 2, 1939, reel 45, CH-LCMD.

37. "U.S. Note to the League," *The Times (London)*, February 23, 1939.

38. Pelt to Avenol, June 8, 1939, box P84, MH-LNA.

39. "Sweetser's Report."

40. Bucknell to Secretary of State, January 16, 1939, RG 84-NAMD, 3.

41. Sweetser to Lester, March 10, 1940, box 17, AS-LCMD.

42. Howard Bucknell, "Confidential Conversation with the Secretary-General of the League of Nations," April 5, 1939, box 33, RG84-NAMD, 2-3.

43. "Confidential Conversation," 4.

44. Draft Speech of Avenol, "Crisis of the League. Crisis of the World and of Peace," April 1939, box R5769, R-LNA.

45. Image, April 30, 1939, box 16, AS-LCMD.

46. Avenol Speech, "Addresses Delivered on the Occasion of the Official Opening of the League of Nations Pavilion," May 2, 1939, box 5767, R-LNA.

47. Russell B. Porter, "League of Nations Building Opened at Fair," *New York Times*, May 3, 1939.

48. Henry A. Wallace, *America Must Choose: The Advantages and Disadvantages of Nationalism, of World Trade, and of a Planned Middle Course* (Boston: World Peace Foundation, 1934), 2.

49. John C. Culver and John Hyde, *American Dreamer: The Life and Times of Henry A. Wallace* (New York: W. W. Norton, 2001), 51; Norman D. Markowitz, *The Rise and Fall of the People's Century: Henry A. Wallace and American Liberalism, 1941-1948* (New York: Free Press, 1973), 14-15. See, for example, Henry A. Wallace, *Agricultural Prices* (Des Moines, IA: Wallace Publishing, 1920).

50. "Addresses Delivered on the Occasion of the Official Opening of the League of Nations Pavilion," May 2, 1939, box 5767, R-LNA.

51. See Patel, *New Deal*.

52. Sweetser to Avenol, May 11, 1939, box R5769, R-LNA.

53. Report of the American Committee in Geneva, 1939, box 122, MH-HLA, 4-5.

54. Marie Ragonetti, "Guiding the Fair," *New World*, November 1939, 12.

55. Report of the American Committee, 3.

56. Ragonetti, "Guiding the Fair," 12.

57. Stanley Bruce, "President. United States of America," May 4, 1939, M104 7/4, SB-NAA.

58. Pelt to Gerig, April 11, 1940, box R5770, R-LNA.

59. "Agreement between the League of Nations and an American Citizens' Com-

mittee for the Purpose of Operating the League of Nations Pavilion at the New York World's Fair 1940," 1939, box 5770, R-LNA; Pelt to Gerig, March 19, 1940, and Gerig to Pelt, April 2, 1940, box 3, BG-LCMD.

60. "Reactions of Opinion," n.d. [1939], box P84, MH-LNA.

61. Report on the Forty-Ninth Session of the Economic Committee, April 5, 1939, box 2535, Decimal File 1930–39, 500.C119/378, RG59-NAMD.

62. Henry Grady, "Adventures in Diplomacy," box 1, HG-HTL, 108–15; League of Nations Committee for the Study of the Problem of Raw Materials, *Report of the Committee for the Study of the Problem of Raw Materials* (Geneva: League of Nations, 1937); K. William Kapp, *The League of Nations and Raw Materials, 1919–1939*, Geneva Studies 12:3 (Geneva: Geneva Research Centre, 1941).

63. Eugene Staley, *Raw Materials in Peace and War* (New York: Council on Foreign Relations, 1937); Frederick Sherwood Dunn, *Peaceful Change: A Study of International Procedures* (New York: Council on Foreign Relations, 1937).

64. Thomas P. Brockway, *Battles without Bullets: The Story of Economic Warfare* (New York: Foreign Policy Association, 1939).

65. Henry Grady, "Summary of Material Obtained by Commissioner Grady Regarding German Trade Relations with Certain Balkan Countries," July 1939, box 1, HG-HTL.

66. Grady, "Summary," 10; Grady, "Adventures in Diplomacy," 113.

67. George H. Morison, "Germany's Trade Improved in May," June 26, 1939, *New York Times*.

68. Brockway, *Battles*, 51–54, 93–94.

69. Press feature: Grady, Henry Francis, July 1950, box 1, HG-HTL.

70. Grady, "Adventures in Diplomacy," 114–15. "Containment" is a term scholars have applied to British policies in Southeast Europe in the same period; see Richard Overy, *The Origins of the Second World War* (New York: Routledge, 2017), 45.

71. Avenol to Bruce, May 27, 1939, box 5740, R5740, R-LNA; Memo, box P84, MH-LNA.

72. David Lee, *Stanley Melbourne Bruce: Australian Internationalist* (London: Continuum, 2010), 121–35.

73. Frank McDougall, "Notes for Radio Broadcast," October 23, 1933, A10666/4, CSIR-NAA, 1–2.

74. Nick Cullather, "The Foreign Policy of the Calorie," *American Historical Review* 112, no. 2 (2007): 337–364.

75. Frank McDougall, "The Agriculture and Health Problems" [1935], in McDougall and Bruce, *McDougall Memoranda*, 2–17.

76. Right Honorable Stanley Bruce, "Comments to the League Assembly," September 11, 1935, in McDougall and Bruce, *McDougall Memoranda*, 18–24. See also League of Nations Mixed Committee of Experts on Nutrition, *Nutrition*; Gove Hambidge, *The Story of FAO* (New York: Van Nostrand, 1955).

77. Economic Committee, "National and International Measures to be Employed for Raising the Standard of Living," November 30, 1937, box 4448, EFS-LNA.

78. Economic Committee, "Note by the Secretariat: National and International Measures to Be Deployed for Raising the Standard of Living," November 30, 1937, box 4448, EFS-LNA.

79. N. F. Hall, "Preliminary Investigation into Measures of a National or Interna-

tional Character for Raising the Standard of Living," June 13, 1938, League of Nations
Pub. II. Economic and Financial, 1938, II.B.4.

80. Summary of a Lecture on the Difficulties of Agricultural Policy by Professor
Myrdal at the National Economic Association of Stockholm, March 3, 1938, box R4448,
EFS-LNA.

81. Note, March 13, 1938; Note, March 19, 1938, AA1970/559, SB-NAA.

82. Wendy Way, *A New Idea Each Morning: How Food and Agriculture Came Together
in One International Organisation* (Canberra: ANU Press, 2013), 189–92. See also Christopher Waters, *Australia and Appeasement: Imperial Foreign Policy and the Origins of
World War II* (London: I. B. Tauris, 2012).

83. Frank McDougall, "Economic Appeasement," December 21, 1936, A10666/5,
CSIR-NAA.

84. Frank McDougall, "Economic Appeasement," February 23, 1937; Stoppani, "Mr.
McDougall's Memorandum for 'Economic Appeasement,'" March 23, 1937; box R4440,
EFS-LNA.

85. McDougall to Sterling, March 15, 1939, A981, DEX-NAA.

86. Frank McDougall, Report on trip to Washington with Bruce, n.d. [1938], box 3,
FM-NLA.

87. See David Lee, *Australia and the World in the Twentieth Century* (Beaconsfield,
Australia: Circa, 2006).

88. Stanley Bruce, "Mr. Cordell Hull," May 2, 1939, M104 7/4, SB-NAA.

89. McDougall to Bruce, April 14, 1939, box 3, MS 6890 3/2, FM-NLA.

90. Secretary General's Note for Bruce Committee, June 30, 1939, AL-NCA.

91. "League and Non-Members," n.d. [1939], box P84, MH-LNA.

92. "Notes on Objectives," n.d. [1939], box P84, MH-LNA.

93. "Notes on Objectives."

94. Notes on Fourth Meeting, Bruce Committee, n.d. [1939], box P84, MH-LNA.

95. Report of the Special Committee [Bruce Report], "The Development of International Co-operation in Economic and Social Affairs," Special Supplement to the
Monthly Summary of the League of Nations, August 1939.

96. Notes on Fourth Meeting.

97. Sweetser to Shotwell, August 31, 1939, box 17, AS-LCMD.

98. Moffat to Messersmith, August 30, 1938, box 2478, Decimal File, 1930–39,
RG59-NAMD.

99. Willits to McDougall, February 1, 1940, box 18, series 100, RG1-RAC.

100. Sweetser to Grady, December 18, 1939, box 17, AS-LCMD.

101. See Johan Hambro, *C. J. Hambro: Liv og drøm* (Oslo: Aschehoug, 1984).

102. C. J. Hambro, *Glimt fra Amerika* (Oslo: Aschehoug, 1925), 1–40.

103. Hambro, *C. J. Hambro*, 160.

104. H. B. Elliston, "Back to The Hague Plan in World Co-operation," *Christian
Science Monitor*, February 13, 1940.

105. "Meeting of the Organizing Committee for the Central Committee of
the League of Nations on Economic and Social Affairs," February 20, 1940, A981,
DEX-NAA, 2.

106. "The Bruce Report," *Economist*, February 3, 1940, 199–200.

107. "All-Nation Talk at the Hague," *Sunday Times*, February 4, 1940.

108. "Parlay at the Hague Under Police Guard," *New York Times*, February 8, 1940;
"A Non-Political League," *Economist*, February 10, 1940, 246.

109. William Percy Maddox, *European Plans for World Order* (Philadelphia: American Academy of Political and Social Science, 1940), 21–23.

110. J. B. Condliffe, Draft autobiography, "Life in London," JC-ATLNZ, 27.

111. Condliffe, Draft autobiography, "Life in London," JC-ATLNZ, 13–19.

112. Henry J. Tasca, *World Trading Systems: A Study of American and British Commercial Policies* (Paris: International Institute of Intellectual Co-operation, League of Nations, 1939).

113. Jeremy Adelman, *Worldly Philosopher: The Odyssey of Albert O. Hirschman* (Princeton, NJ: Princeton University Press, 2013), 161–63.

114. Akira Iriye, *The Globalizing of America, 1913–1945*, vol. 3 of *The New Cambridge History of American Foreign Relations*, rev. ed. (Cambridge: Cambridge University Press, 2013), 134–51.

115. Eugene Staley, "Power Economy versus Welfare Economy," *Annals of the American Academy of Political and Social Science* 198, no. 1 (1938): 9–14.

116. Eugene Staley, *World Economy in Transition: Technology vs. Politics, Laissez Faire vs. Planning, Power vs. Welfare* (New York: Council on Foreign Relations, 1939), 279–86.

117. Entry, August 26, 1939, HMD-FDRL, http://www.fdrlibrary.marist.edu /_resources/images/morg/md0270.pdf.

118. Condliffe, Draft Autobiography, "Life in London," Condliffe Papers, ATLNZ, 27–28.

119. International Studies Conference, *Economic Policies in Relation to World Peace: A Record of the Study Meetings Held in Bergen, from August 26th to August 29th, 1939* (Paris: International Institute of Intellectual Co-operation, League of Nations, 1940), 219, 232–33.

120. J. E. Meade, *The Economic Basis of a Durable Peace* (London: Allen & Unwin, 1940).

121. A concept of core economic zones was fundamental to the thinking of figures like George Kennan, who saw five "centers" structuring the global economy and the application of containment. George Kennan, "Contemporary Problems of Foreign Policy," September 17, 1948, box 299, GK-MLP. See also John Lewis Gaddis, *George F. Kennan: An American Life* (New York: Penguin, 2011).

122. J. B. Condliffe, *The Reconstruction of World Trade: A Survey of International Economic Relations* (New York: Norton, 1940), 356–58.

123. Condliffe, *Reconstruction*, 394.

124. Memo from Viple, October 11, 1939, Series Z 8/1/3, AF-ILOA.

125. "Distribution of the League Exhibits of the New York World's Fair," November 13, 1940, box R5770, R-LNA; Gerig to Hambro, November 13, 1940, box 3, BG-LCMD; *Haverford News*, March 18, 1941; *The Institute News*, December 1941, Franklin Institute, Philadelphia. Among the universities, only Haverford College was able to confirm receipt of some "tapestries" and "mural wood carvings," which at one point were mounted in its library.

CHAPTER 3: INTERNATIONALIST DUNKIRK

1. Sweetser to Shotwell, August 31, 1939, box 17, AS-LCMD.

2. Robert A. Divine, *Second Chance: The Triumph of Internationalism in America during World War II* (New York: Atheneum, 1967), 29; Loveday diary, September 1, 1939, box 20, AL-NCA.

3. Luke Fletcher, "Confusion and Convergence: The Nazi Challenge to World Order and the CFR Response, 1940–1941," *International Politics* 55, no. 6 (November 2018): 888–903.

4. J. B. Condliffe, Draft autobiography, "Life in London," 29–33; "The War Years," 21, JC-ATNZ. The Condliffes (traveling with Tasca) were able to sell their film for $100 upon arrival in New York, meaning that the sinking of the tanker *Emile Miquet* and the family's rough passage on the liner SS *President Harding* were immortalized in a British Pathé newsreel.

5. "Memorandum on a Proposal to Initiate a Chatham House Study on the Problems of a European Settlement," September 9, 1939, Study Groups, 9/18e, RI-RIL; Kittredge to Willits, October 30, 1939, box 4, series 401, RG1.1-RAC. See also James Cotton, "On the Chatham House Project: Interwar Actors, Networks, Knowledge," *International Politics* 55, no. 6 (2018): 820–35.

6. McDougall to Bruce, April 14, 1939, box 3, MS 6890 3/2, FM-NLA.

7. Kittredge, "European Investigations of Peace Settlement," January 31, 1940, box 4, EE-MLPU.

8. Note of Interview with Mr. Kittredge, September 12, 1939, box 36, AL-NCA.

9. Stanley Bruce, "The League and Economic Reconstruction," n.d. [1940], box 37, AL-NCA.

10. Hugh Wilson, "Memorandum on World Order," January 22, 1940, http://www.gutenberg-e.org/osc01/images/osc03ba.html; David Reynolds, *From Munich to Pearl Harbor: Roosevelt's America and the Origins of the Second World War* (Chicago: Ivan R. Dee, 2001), 74.

11. Loveday, "Postwar Planning Plan of Work," 1939; "The Peace Settlement," November 29, 1939, box 36, AL-NCA; Riefler to Loveday, October 28, 1939; Loveday to Riefler, November 27, 1939, box R4468, EFS-LNA.

12. "Note Given the Foreign Office," February 27, 1940, SLD-LNA.

13. "Emergency Measures," September 20, 1939, box 130, SL-LNA; Budget Memo, 1939, box 37, AL-NCA; Ernest S. Hediger, "Geneva Institutions in Wartime," *Foreign Policy Reports* 19, no. 4, May 1, 1943.

14. Statement by the Secretary General, January 15, 1939; Budget Breakdown, n.d. [1939], box 52, AL-NCA. The sum in this proposed budget appears to have been more than the League spent in 1940.

15. "Mr. Loveday's Observations," n.d. [1939], box 52, AL-NCA.

16. McDougall to Willits, January 30, 1940, box 36, AL-NCA.

17. Peace and Disarmament Committee of the Women's International Organizations, "The League and the I.L.O. in Time of War," October 1939, box 17, AS-LCMD; American Interorganizational Council in Geneva, "The Social and Economic Work of the League Needs Help," October 1, 1939, box 17, RF-MLPU.

18. Mark Mazower, *Hitler's Empire: How the Nazis Ruled Europe* (New York: Penguin, 2008), 43–45, 556–57.

19. Geoffrey Roberts, "A League of Their Own: The Soviet Origins of the United Nations," *Journal of Contemporary History* 54, no. 2 (2019): 303–27; Northedge, *League*, 273–74.

20. Tittmann to Secretary of State, "The League Wireless Station, 'Radio-Nations,'" October 16, 1939, box 2477, 500.C01/95, Decimal File, 1930–39, RG59-NAMD.

21. Woolley to Roosevelt, February 17, 1936; Woolley to Roosevelt, December 4, 1939; Watson to Woolley, December 9, 1939; PPF 537, PPF-FDRL.

22. Memo, "Safeguarding the League's Technical Work," 1940, box 18, CE-NYPL.

23. Watson to Woolley, March 4, 1940, box 14, MW-ASCMC; Entry, March 8, 1940, WHSD-FDRL, http://www.fdrlibrary.marist.edu/daybyday/daylog/march-8th-1940/.

24. Gerig to Pelt, April 4, 1940, box 3, BG-LCMD. It is interesting that Gerig's letters to Geneva were addressed from 4 West Fortieth Street, the shared New York City offices of the FPA, WPF, and LNA.

25. Grady to McDougall, March 6, 1940, box 36, AL-NCA.

26. McDougall to Willits, January 30, 1940, box 36, AL-NCA.

27. Loveday Diary, March 12, 1940, box 20; Notes of Interview with Mr. Kittredge, March 12, 1940, box 45, AL-NCA.

28. TBK [Kittredge] to JHW [Willits], March 16, 1940, box 203, Series 700, RG2-RAC.

29. Memo, "Proposed Grant to the Central Committee of the League of Nations," April 6, 1940, box 18, series 100, RG1-RAC.30. Grant, League of Nations Central Committee, April 3, 1940, box 18, series 100, RG1-RAC.

31. Grant, April 3, 1940, box 18, series 100, RG1-RAC.

32. See Justus D. Doenecke, *Storm on the Horizon: The Challenge to American Intervention, 1939–1941* (Lanham, MD: Rowman & Littlefield, 2000).

33. See Kuehl, *Keeping the Covenant*.

34. "League of Nations Drops Plans for Move to France," *Chicago Daily Tribune*, August 27, 1939.

35. Gerig to Pelt, April 4, 1940, box 3, BG-LCMD; "Safeguarding the League's Technical Work," 1940, box 18, CE-NYPL.

36. Sweetser to Gerig, May 4, 1940, box 3, BG-LCMD.

37. Berle, Memo for the President, March 22, 1940, box 67, AB-FDRL.

38. Roosevelt to Woolley, April 4, 1940, OF 184, OF-FDRL.

39. Berle, Memo for the President, April 2, 1940, box 67, AB-FDRL.

40. Gerig to Pelt, April 4, 1940, box 3, BG-LCMD.

41. "America Likely to Be Haven for Part of League," *Chicago Daily Tribune*, May 19, 1940.

42. Loveday Diary, May 10, 1940, box 20, AL-NCA.

43. Loveday to Willits, July 2, 1940, box 18, RG1-RAC.

44. Confidential Memorandum, May 30, 1940, file 140, AT-ILOA.

45. Personal Notes of Loveday, n.d. [1940], box 52, AL-NCA.

46. "Text of Chancellor Hitler's Speech before the Reichstag, October 6, 1939," *International Conciliation* 354 (1939): 495; Laura Puffer Morgan, "Geneva Carries On," October 25, 1939, IB-GRS, 1.

47. Adam LeBor, *Tower of Basel: The Shadowy History of the Secret Bank That Runs the World* (New York: Public Affairs, 2013), 41–71; Mazower, *Governing*, 191–192.

48. Memorandum of Conversation with E. J. Phelan, October 23, 1940, vol. 46, JM-HLHU.

49. See Benjamin Martin, *The Nazi-Fascist New Order for European Culture* (Cambridge, MA: Harvard University Press, 2016).

50. Funk speech, July 25, 1940, *Official Statements of War and Peace Aims* (Geneva: Geneva Research Centre, December 1940), 30–31; Stephen G. Gross, "Gold, Debt and the Quest for Monetary Order: The Nazi Campaign to Integrate Europe in 1940," *Contemporary European History* 26, no. 2 (2017): 287–309.

51. Arthur Sweetser, "Exit Geneva . . ." May 1940, box 17, AS-LCMD.

52. Sweetser to Loveday, June 6, 1940, box R5770, R-LNA.

53. Sweetser to Loveday, June 4, 1940, box 39, GF-IASA. Emphasis in original.

54. Sweetser to Loveday, June 4, 1940, SLD-LNA, 450–51.

55. Memo from Willits, "If Hitler Wins," June 3, 1940, box 46, series 200, RG1.1-RAC.

56. Sweetser to Loveday, July 27, 1940, SLD-LNA, 589–91.

57. See Iselin Theien, *Fra krig til krig: En biografi om C. J. Hambro* (Oslo: Spartacus, 2015); Hambro, *C. J. Hambro*. See also Carl Joachim Hambro, *I Saw It Happen in Norway* (New York: D. Appleton-Century, 1940). I am particularly grateful to Theien for her insights on Hambro as an international figure, his views on the US, and his relationship with FDR.

58. Hambro would employ Princeton as his pivot for travel around the US during the war; see Princeton File, box L0008, CH-RN.

59. Dexter Fergie, "Geopolitics Turned Inwards: The Princeton Military Studies Group and the National Security Imagination," *Diplomatic History* 43, no. 4 (2019): 644–70; David Ekbladh, "Present at the Creation: Edward Mead Earle and the Depression-Era Origins of Security Studies," *International Security* 36, no. 3 (2011): 107–41.

60. Press release, Mary E. Woolley Committee, "Committee formed to Aid Non-Political Work of League of Nations," June 1, 1940, box 18, CE-NYPL

61. Winant to Bowman, August 9, 1940, Series Z, 8/1/8, ILOA.

62. Tittmann to Secretary of State, June 14, 1940, Series Z, 8/1/8, ILOA

63. Hull to Consul, Geneva, June 18, 1940; Green to Hull, June 24, 1940, Series Z, 8/1/8, AR-ILOA.

64. Message from Winant to Secretary of State, June 23, 1940, box 33, RG 84-NAMD.

65. Message from Winant to Secretary of State, June 23, 1940, box 33, RG84-NAMD.

66. Hull to Winant, July 1, 1940, box 33, RG 84-NAMD.

67. Aydelotte Memo, August 1940, box 39, GF-IASA

68. Sweetser to Avenol, June 10, 1940, box 16, AS-LCMD.

69. Dodd, Ten Broeck, and Aydelotte to Hull, June 11, 1940, box 120, HD-MLPU; Aydelotte Memo, August 1940, box 39, GF-IASA

70. Dodds to Avenol, June 11, 1940, box 120, HD-MLPU.

71. Aydelotte Memo, August 1940, box 39, GF-IASA.

72. Draft Avenol to Dodds, June 15, 1940, box P16, JA-LNA; Avenol to Dodds, June 15, 1940, box 120, HD-MLPU.

73. Avenol Interview, 1951, box P16, JA-LNA.

74. Barros, *Betrayal*, 212–22.

75. Letter to Sweetser, June 19, 1940, SLD-LNA.

76. Entry, June 25, 1940, SLD-LNA, 458.

77. Frank Boudreau Memo, June 1940; Woolley to Roosevelt, June 15, 1940, OF 184, OF-FDRL.

78. Memo to the President, June 15, 1940; Draft Memo to the President, June 15, 1940, box 67, AB-FDRL.

79. Letter to Woolley, June 25, 1940, box 1, OF 184, OF-FDRL.

80. Brakeley to Aydelotte, June 17, 1940, box 38, GF-IASA.

81. Cable, Willits to Loveday, June 18, 1940; Loveday to Willits, June 21, 1940, box 18, RG1-RAC.

82. "Tomorrow's Books," December 1937, TB-RAC, 5–9.

83. Aydelotte to Willits, June 18, 1940, box 38, GF-IASA; Grant, June 24, 1940, box 18, RG1-RAC.

84. Entries, June 20 and 22, 1940, SLD-LNA, 467.

85. Memo from Willits, July 2, 1940, box 18, RG1-RAC.

86. Loveday to Willits, July 2, 1940, box 18, RG1-RAC.

87. Marvin R. Zahniser, "Rethinking the Significance of Disaster: The United States and the Fall of France in 1940," *International History Review* 14, no. 2 (1992): 252–76; David Reynolds, "1940: Fulcrum of the Twentieth Century?," *International Affairs* 66, no. 2 (1990): 325–50.

88. Cable from White, May 17, 1940, box 15, MW-ASCMC.

89. National Policy Committee, "Memorandum of the Special Committee on Implications to the United States of a German Victory," 1940, 14–18; Aydelotte to Jones, August 5, 1940, box 38, GF-IASA; Condliffe, *Reconstruction*, 356.

90. Lothian to Aydelotte, June 24, 1940, box 2, Riefler Papers, WR-NAMD.

91. Kelly to Halifax, June 20, 1940, *BDFA*, series J, vol. 8, 199.

92. Halifax to Kelly, June 23, 1940, *BDFA*, series J, vol. 8, 200.

93. Halifax to Kelly, June 25, 1940, *BDFA*, series J, vol. 8, 200; Memorandum received, June 27, 1940, box C1624, OD-LNA.

94. League record of conversation, June 28, 1940, box P16, JA-LNA.

95. Consul Geneva to Halifax, June 27, 1940, *BDFA*, series J, vol. 8, 201.

96. Consul Geneva to Halifax, June 27, 1940, *BDFA*, series J, vol. 8, 201; Record of conversation, June 27, 1940, SLD-LNA, 459–65. Lester noted in his diary next to this entry: "The Official Record."

97. Record of conversation, June 27, 1940, SLD-LNA, 465.

98. Record of conversation with Mr. Tittman [*sic*], June 28, 1940, box P16, JA-LNA; Memo, Tittmann to Secretary of State, "Transfer Proposed by Avenol of Technical Services of the Secretariat of the L of N," June 27, 1940, box, 46, RG 84, NAMD.

99. Hull to Consul General at Geneva, June 29, 1940, *FRUS*, 1940, 2:320–21.

100. Memo from JHW [Willits] to SHW and RBF, July 2, 1940, box 187, RG2-RAC.

101. "Sinking League of Nations Gets Ready for Death," *Chicago Daily Tribune*, June 26, 1940.

102. Loveday letter, July 2, box 18, RG1-RAC.

103. Memo from Willits, July 2, 1940; Memo from Willits, July 3, 1940, box 18, RG1-RAC.

104. Way, *New Idea*, 223; McDougall to Loveday, June 5, 1940; McDougall to Willits, May 22, 1940, SLD-LNA, 428–31.

105. Memo from JHW [Willits] to SHW, RBF and TBK, July 2, 1940, box 187, RG2-RAC.

106. Diary entry, July 17, 1940, SLD-LNA.

107. Aydelotte to Lothian, July 11, 1940, box 38, GF-IASA.

108. Dodds, Aydelotte, and Ten Broeck to Avenol, July 12, 1940, box 120, HD-MLPU.

109. Hambro to Avenol, July 19, 1940, box 39, GF-IASA.

110. Felix Morley, "League Sanctuary," *Washington Post*, July 20, 1940.

111. "Princeton and the League," *New York Times*, July 17, 1940.

112. Entry, July 8, 1940, box 212, ABD-FDRL.

113. Tittmann to Secretary of State, July 6, 1940, box, 46, RG84-NAMD.

114. Tittmann to Secretary of State, July 11, 1940, box 46, RG84-NAMD.

115. Tittmann to Secretary of State, July 17, 1940, box 46, RG84-NAMD.

116. Entry, July 17, 1940, SLD-LNA, 495–96.

117. Entry, July 18, 1940, SLD-LNA, 491; Barros, *Betrayal*, 246.

118. Tittmann to Secretary of State, July 18, 1940, box 46, RG84-NAMD; Entry, July 18, 1940, SLD-LNA, 491.

119. Letter dated July 19, 1940, SLD-LNA, 494; Avenol to Dodds, July 23, 1940, box 120, HD-MLPU; Memo from Jacklin, July 24, 1940, box C1620, OD-LNA.

120. Avenol Letter of Resignation, July 25, 1940, box P16, JA-LNA.

121. Poem, Lester diary, July 25, 1940, SLD-LNA, 499. The poem is Arthur Hugh Clough's "Say Not the Struggle Naught Availeth"; the final two stanzas are quoted here.

122. Avenol to Loveday, July 26, 1940, box C1620, OD-LNA; Avenol to Dodds, July 26, 1940; Dodds to Avenol, July 26, 1940, box 120, HD-MLPU.

123. Memo, Director of Personnel and Internal Services, July 25, 1940, box C1620, OD-LNA.

124. Entry, July 26, 1940, WHUL-FDRL, http://www.fdrlibrary.marist.edu/day byday/daylog/july-26th-1940/.

125. Welles to U.S. Representative in Geneva, July 27, 1940, box 46, RG84-NAMD.

126. Christie to Winant, July 26, 1940, Series Z, 8/1/8, AF-ILOA; Memo from Under Secretary of State for External Affairs to Prime Minister, July 25, 1940, "Transfer of ILO to Canada"; Secretary of State for External Affairs to Minister in the United States, July 26, 1940, *DCER* (Ottawa: Queen's Printer, 1974), 7:1098–99.

127. "League Technical Services to Move Offices to U.S.," *Christian Science Monitor*, August 6, 1940; "I.L.O. Aides Leave Geneva," *New York Times*, August 7, 1940.

128. "23 League Officials Injured in Bus Crash," *New York Times*, August 7, 1940; Aydelotte Memo, August 1940, box 39, GF-IASA.

129. "Travel Notes: Geneva to Lisbon," August 1, 1940, series Z, 8/1/7, AF-ILOA.

130. John G. Winant, *A Letter from Grosvenor Square: An Account of a Stewardship* (London: Hodder & Stoughton, 1947), 17.

131. Letter, July 27, 1940, series Z, 8/1/8, AF-ILOA.

132. Letter, July 27, 1940; Evan's Journey to Lisbon, July 3–8, series Z, 8/1/8, AF-ILOA.

133. Jacklin to Loveday, July 31, 1940, box C1620, OD-LNA; Bill, Avenida Palace Hotel, August 20, 1940, box P150, AL-LNA.

134. Cable, Rosenborg to Riefler, August 20, 1940, box 2, WR-NAMD.

135. Everett to Secretary of State, "Departure of Mr. Loveday for New York," August 21, 1940, box 46, RG84-NAMD.

136. "League Offices on Move," *Christian Science Monitor*, August 17, 1940; "League Unit Sets Up Branch in Princeton," *New York Times*, August 23, 1940.

137. Report of the Director (Aydelotte), October 14, 1940, box 58, GF-IASA, 11–12; Telegram from Montesstoril, September 6, 1940, box 46, RG84-NAMD; "Nazis Strip France," *New York Times*, September 14, 1940.

138. Lester to Loveday, December 5, 1940, box 130, SL-LNA.

139. Douglas Gageby, *The Last Secretary General: Sean Lester and the League of Nations* (Dublin: Town House and Country House, 1999), 213.

140. Notes, October 3, 1940, box 130, SL-LNA.

141. Sweetser to Loveday, July 29, 1940, box C1620, OD-LNA.

142. Donald Fleming and Bernard Bailyn, *The Intellectual Migration: Europe and*

America, 1930–1960 (Cambridge, MA: Belknap Press of Harvard University Press, 1969).

143. Fry to Condliffe, November 20, 1940; Fry to Condliffe, February 10, 1941, box 16, JC-BLUC; Adelman, *Worldly Philosopher*, 181–84.

144. Aydelotte Memo, August 1940, box 39, GF-IASA.

145. Gerig to Bieler, September 18, 1940, box 3, BG-LCMD.

146. McDougall to Loveday, August 29, 1940, box P150, AL-LNA.

147. McDougall to Loveday, August 29, 1940, box P150, AL-LNA.

148. "Record of Discussion Held September 18, 1940," box C1755, OD-LNA.

149. Sweetser to Aydelotte, October 29, 1940, box 39, GF-IASA.

150. Aydelotte memo, August 1940, box 39, GF-IASA.

CHAPTER 4: THE ROVER BOYS OF RECONSTRUCTION

1. Tyler to Bowman, September 27, 1944, box 8, LP-LCMD.

2. This roughly translates as "Do not give the animals paper or other harmful material."

3. Royall Tyler, "The Secretariat of an International Organization," September 27, 1944, box 8, LP-LCMD.

4. Address delivered by Mr. Leo Pasvolsky at the American Labor Conference on International Affairs, December 16, 1944, box 8, LP-LCMD.

5. Wilson to Pasvolsky, December 29, 1944, box 8, LP-LCMD.

6. Stephen C. Schlesinger, *Act of Creation: The Founding of the United Nations* (Boulder, CO: Westview Press, 2003).

7. Andrew Williams, "Leo Pasvolsky and an Open World Economy," in *Progressivism and US Foreign Policy between the World Wars*, ed. Molly Cochran and Cornelia Navari (New York: Palgrave Macmillan, 2017), 91–113.

8. Paul Samuelson, "Unemployment Ahead," *New Republic*, September 11, 1944, 298; Jim Lacey, *Keep from All Thoughtful Men: How U.S. Economists Won World War II* (Annapolis, MD: Naval Institute Press, 2011), 32.

9. Frank A. Ninkovich, *The Global Republic: America's Inadvertent Rise to World Power* (Chicago: University of Chicago Press, 2014), 144–70.

10. See Mazower, *No Enchanted Palace*.

11. Address given by Harold Dodds, April 19, 1941; "Reunion of Americans Who Have Participated in the Technical and Non-Political Activities Associated with the League of Nations," April 19 and 20, 1941, box 38, GF-IASA.

12. "World Organization," Princeton, April 1941, box 18, AS-LCMD.

13. Damien Keane, "An Ear toward Security: The Princeton Listening Center," *Princeton University Library Chronicle* 71, no. 1 (2009): 45–62.

14. Eleanor Kittredge, "Seeking Eternal Truths in a World of Chaos," *New York Times*, January 5, 1941.

15. Grants to Support League of Nations Office in Princeton, 1940–1942, series 100, box 18, RG 1, RAC.

16. Memo from Kittredge, "Notes on the League of Nations, Economic and Financial Section, November 14, 1940; Interviews by Kittredge, December 9, 1940, series 100, box 18, RG1-RAC; Kuznets to Loveday, March 30, 1942, Pasvolsky to Loveday, March 25, 1942, box C1622; Pasvolsky to Loveday, February 3, 1941, C1756, OD-LNA.

17. Arthur Sweetser, "The Non-Political Achievements of the League," *Foreign Affairs* 19 (1940): 190.

18. Sweetser, "Non-Political," 183–84.

19. Frank McDougall, "Notes on the Restatement of Our Aims," October 22, 1940, box 4, FM-NLA.

20. McDougall, "Economic Aspects of a General Settlement," March 15, 1939; McDougall to Bruce, April 14, 1939, box 3, FM-NLA.

21. McDougall, "Our Aims."

22. McDougall to Pasvolsky, July 24, 1940; McDougall and Bruce, "War Aims," n.d. [July 1940], box 7, LP-LCMD.

23. Carl Bridge, "Allies of a Kind: Three Wartime Australian Ministers to the United States, 1940–46," in *Australia Goes to Washington: 75 Years of Australian Representation in the United States, 1940–2015*, ed. David Lowe, David Lee, and Carl Bridge (Canberra, Australia: ANU Press, 2016), 23–38.

24. "'Freedom from Want,' the Food Problem, List of Principal People Seen," September 11, 1941, M104 9/1, SB-NAA.

25. J. V. Wilson to Arndt, September 30, 1941, box 5, HA-NLA.

26. J. V. Wilson to Arndt, October 6, 1941, box 5, HA-NLA.

27. "Contributions of Science to World Order," *The Times*, September 27, 1941.

28. F. L. McDougall, "Freedom from Want: The Food Problem," August 25, 1941, M104 9/1, SB-NAA.

29. F. L. McDougall, "Freedom from Want: A Beginning," n.d. [1941], MS 6890 4/6, FM-NLA.

30. See Mazower, *Hitler's Empire*.

31. Franklin Roosevelt, "The Four Freedoms," January 6, 1941, https://www.fdrlibrary.org/documents/356632/390886/readingcopy.pdf/42234a77-8127-4015-95af-bcf831db311d, FDRL.

32. Atlantic Charter, August 14, 1941, https://avalon.law.yale.edu/wwii/atlantic.asp. See also Elizabeth Borgwardt, *A New Deal for the World: America's Vision for Human Rights* (Cambridge, MA: Belknap Press of Harvard University Press, 2005).

33. Sumner Welles, "Address at the Norwegian Legation, July 22, 1941," in *The World of the Four Freedoms* (New York: Columbia University Press, 1943), 11–15.

34. "Text of Secretary Welles's Address at the World Trade Dinner Here," *New York Times*, October 8, 1941.

35. "Post-War Food Program Urged By Morgenthau: Grange Told a Minimum Health Standard Is Vital for World of Tomorrow," *New York Herald Tribune*, November 16, 1941.

36. Executive Order 8839 Establishing Economic Defense Board, July 30, 1941, https://www.presidency.ucsb.edu/documents/executive-order-8839-establishing-the-economic-defense-board.

37. Ritchie Calder, "Supplementary Report on United States Visit: Informal Discussions on Post War Reconstruction in Terms of Political Warfare Needs," June 5, 1942, M104/10, SB-NAA.

38. John C. Culver and John Hyde, *American Dreamer: The Life and Times of Henry A. Wallace* (New York: Norton, 2000), 257–309.

39. Franklin Roosevelt, "The Four Freedoms," January 6, 1941, https://www.fdrlibrary.org/documents/356632/390886/readingcopy.pdf/42234a77-8127-4015-95

af-bcf831db311d, FDRL; "The Atlantic Charter," August 14, 1941, https://avalon.law
.yale.edu/wwii/atlantic.asp; Henry Wallace, *The Price of Free World Victory* (New York:
L. B. Fischer, 1942); Henry Wallace, "Foundations of the Peace," *Atlantic Monthly*, January 1942, 34–41. The ideas in the "Price of Free World Victory" were so popular that
William H. Pine, a producer who worked with Paramount Pictures, distributed a 1942
film version for propaganda purposes.

40. See Tore C. Olsson, *Agrarian Crossings: Reformers and the Remaking of the US and
Mexican Countryside* (Princeton, NJ: University Press, 2017).

41. Huss to Riefler, July 23, 1941, reel 40, HW-FDRL; Alfred Friendly, "Economic
Defense Council Named with Wallace as Head," *Washington Post*, August 1, 1941.

42. Winfield Riefler, "Government and the Statistician," *Journal of the American Statistical Association* 37, no. 217 (1942), 1–11.

43. Brooke L. Blower, "New York City's Spanish Shipping Agents and the Practice
of State Power in the Atlantic Borderlands of World War II," *American Historical Review*
119, no. 1 (2014): 111–41.

44. See, for example, Charles Kindleberger, "Lord Zuckerman on Bombing for
Overlord," n.d., box 2, CK-HTL.

45. A sign of the importance of economic warfare was the British feature film *The
Big Blockade* (1942), which dramatized effort for the public at large. Riefler to Stone,
March 20, 1942, box 2, WR-NAMD.

46. Winfield Riefler, "A Program to Stimulate International Investment," October 4, 1941, WR-NAMD.

47. Riefler to Wallace, September 9, 1942, reel 40, HW-FDRL. Emphasis in original.
No program of this specific sort was established.

48. Gerschenkron to Condliffe, May 25, 1940, box 21, JC-BLUC.

49. Condliffe, Autobiography, "The War Years," JC-ATLNZ, 10–11.

50. J. B. Condliffe, *Agenda for a Postwar World* (New York: Norton 1942), 167, 180–
83, 227–28.

51. Condliffe, Autobiography, "The War Years," JC-ATLNZ, 10–11.

52. G. John Ikenberry, "A World Economy Restored: Expert Consensus and the
Anglo-American Postwar Settlement," *International Organization* 46, no. 1 (1992): 289–
321.

53. McDougall to Bruce, August 20, 1942; McDougall to Bruce, September 6, 1942,
M104/10, SB-NAA.

54. "Meeting at Columbia University to Discuss Programme of Reconstruction of
the ILO," December 28, 1941, box 01/19, PR-ILOA.

55. International Labour Office, "Economic and Social Reconstruction: Work Arising out of Conference in New York, October-November 1941," January 31, 1942, box
1/19; "The International Labor Organization: Program," December 1941, box 1/04,
PR-ILOA.

56. "The I.L.O. and Reconstruction," February 2, 1942, M104/10, SB-NAA.

57. Xianting Fang, *The Post-War Industrialization of China* (Washington, DC: National Planning Association, 1942); H. D. Fong, "The Prospect for China's Industrialization," *Pacific Affairs* 15, no. 1 (1942): 44–60.

58. Raymond Leslie Buell, *Isolated America* (New York: Alfred A. Knopf, 1940), 398–
400; Vera Micheles Dean, *The Struggle for World Order* (New York: Foreign Policy Association, 1941). Buell had proposed a regime of development aid for Poland before the

outbreak of the war as a means to stabilize and strengthen that country, see Raymond Leslie Buell, *Poland: Key to Europe* (New York: Alfred A. Knopf, 1939).

59. Welles to Bruce, October 14, 1942, M104/10, SB-NAA.

60. Sweetser to Roosevelt, May 16, 1942, PPF 506, PPF-FDRL.

61. See Stephen Wertheim, *Tomorrow, the World: The Birth of U.S. Global Supremacy* (Cambridge, MA: Belknap Press of Harvard University Press, 2020).

62. See Schulzinger, *Wise Men.*

63. George S. Messersmith, Memorandum of Conversation: Proposed Activities of the Council on Foreign Relations in the Field of Research and Collaboration with the Department of State, September 12, 1939, box 44, HFA-MLPU.

64. Council on Foreign Relations, War and Peace Studies Progress Report, June 1940, box 100, series 100S, RG1-RAC.

65. War and Peace Studies Project, Attendance Record, Political Group, 1941–1942, box 100, series 100S, RG1-RAC.

66. Arthur Sweetser, "American Interests Abroad," May 20, 1941, box 74, AS-LCMD.

67. Walter R. Sharp, "Basic American Interests," July 10, 1941, WPS, P-B23.

68. Sharp, "Basic," 3.

69. "Alternative Bases for the Development of Future World Organization," draft, September 28, 1942, box 39, AS-LCMD.

70. Arthur Sweetser, "The League Experience and the Social Objectives of the Atlantic Charter," April 27, 1942, WPS, P-B38.

71. Arthur Sweetser, "Washington International Center," 1942, box 38, AS-LCMD; See also Madeleine Herren and Isabella Löhr, "Being International in Times of War: Arthur Sweetser and the Shifting of the League of Nations to the United Nations," *European Review of History / Revue Européenne d'Histoire* 25, nos. 3–4 (2018): 535–52.

72. Arthur Sweetser, "Washington: United Nations Center," April 27, 1942, WPS, P-B39.

73. Arthur Sweetser, "Our Future International Society," 1941, Proceedings of the Institute of World Affairs, Eighteenth Session; Arthur Sweetser, "Problems Involved in Organizing International Society," box 39, AS-LCMD.

74. Roberts, "League of Their Own."

75. "The League and Postwar International Organization," box 39, AS-LCMD. Emphasis in original.

76. Mallory to Loveday, December 29, 1941, box C1617, OD-LNA.

77. Alexander Loveday, "Note on Post-War Foreign Capital Needs," January 24, 1942, WPS, E-C7.

78. Samuel Zipp, *The Idealist: Wendell Willkie's Wartime Quest to Build One World* (Cambridge, MA: Belknap Press of Harvard University Press, 2020), 282–84; Andrew Preston, "Franklin D. Roosevelt and America's Empire of Anti-Imperialism," in *Rhetorics of Empire: Languages of Colonial Conflict after 1900*, ed. Martin Thomas and Richard Toye (Manchester: Manchester University Press, 2017), 75–90; David B. Woolner, Warren F. Kimball, and David Reynolds, *FDR's World: War, Peace, and Legacies* (New York: Palgrave Macmillan, 2008), 91–121.

79. Arthur Sweetser, "Notes on Meeting with FDR on World Organization," May 29, 1942, box 38, AS-LCMD.

80. Hambro to Aydelotte, August 5, 1941; Reber to Loveday, March 18, 1941; Sweetser to Aydelotte, February 26, 1943, box 38, GF-IASA.

81. There were similar efforts in the UK. See Benjamin Auberer, "Digesting the League of Nations: Planning the International Secretariat of the Future, 1941–1944," *New Global Studies* 10, no. 3 (2016): 393–426.

82. Finch to Condliffe, July 29, 1943, box 15, JC-BLUC; Jessup to Sweetser, August 17, 1942, box 211, CEIP-RBML.

83. Conference on Training for International Administration, August 21–22, 1943, box 15, JC-BLUC.

84. Harriet Eager Davis, *Pioneers in World Order: An American Appraisal of the League of Nations* (New York: Columbia University Press, 1944).

85. Hill, *Economic and Financial Organization*.

86. Egon Ferdinand Ranshofen-Wertheimer, *The International Secretariat, a Great Experiment in International Administration* (Washington, DC: Carnegie Endowment for International Peace, 1945); Egon Ferdinand Ranshofen-Wertheimer, *Victory Is Not Enough: The Strategy for a Lasting Peace* (New York: W. W. Norton, 1942), 298–307.

87. Syllabus, "International Public Administration of the United Nations," American University, 1944, box 1/06, PR-ILOA. The main campus of the university was in the city's Northwest quadrant, however, there was a downtown campus on 1901 F Street for evening classes, just a few blocks from the future site of the World Bank.

88. See Benjamin Welles, *Sumner Welles: FDR's Global Strategist* (New York: St. Martin's Press, 1997).

89. Christopher D. O'Sullivan, *Sumner Welles, Postwar Planning, and the Quest for a New World Order, 1937–1943* (New York: Columbia University Press, 2003); Organization Meeting Minutes, July 17, 1942, box 189, SW-FDRL.

90. Subcommittee on International Organization, Minutes, July 31, 1942; August 14, 1942, box 189, SW-FDRL.

91. "Draft Constitution of the International Organization," April 12, 1943, box 189, SW-FDRL, 19.

92. McDougall to Bruce, September 20, 1942, M104/10, SB-NAA.

93. McDougall to Bruce, September 6, 1942, M104/10, SB-NAA.

94. McDougall to Bruce, September 6, 1942, M104/10, SB-NAA.

95. Henry A. Wallace, *The Price of Vision: The Diary of Henry A. Wallace, 1942–1946* (Boston: Houghton Mifflin, 1973), 384–85. The pamphlet McDougall mentioned was the IPR-published *Our Job in the Pacific* (New York: Institute of Pacific Relations, 1944).

96. Diagram, "World Council," n.d. [1943], M104 11/1, SB-NAA.

97. McDougall, "Freedom from Want: A Beginning," August 1941, M104/10, SB-NAA.

98. McDougall, "Progress in the War of Ideas," September 1, 1942, box 4, FM-NLA.

99. McDougall to Bruce, August 13, 1942; McDougall to Bruce, August 26, 1942, M104/10, SB-NAA. See also Hambidge, *Story of FAO*, 48–50.

100. Franklin Roosevelt, "Address of the President: United Nations Conference on Food and Agriculture," June 7, 1943, http://www.fdrlibrary.marist.edu/_resources/images/msf/msfb0093

101. Craig Alan Wilson, "Rehearsal for a United Nations: The Hot Springs Conference," *Diplomatic History* 4, no. 3 (1980): 263–82.

102. McDougall to Bruce, May 13, 1943, M104, 11/4, SB-NAA.

103. Way, *New Idea*, 278.

104. Franklin Roosevelt, "Address of the President: United Nations Conference

on Food and Agriculture," June 7, 1943, http://www.fdrlibrary.marist.edu/_resources /images/msf/msfb0093 (accessed March 25, 2022).

105. Constitution of the Food and Agriculture Organization of the United Nations, 1943, reel 30, HW-FDRL, 2.

106. First Report to the Governments of the United Nations by the Interim Commission on Food and Agriculture, August 1, 1944, reel 30, HW-FDRL, 10.

107. See Lizzie Collingham, *The Taste of War: World War II and the Battle for* Food (New York: Penguin, 2013).

108. See Robert Boyce, *The Great Interwar Crisis and the Collapse of Globalization* (London: Palgrave Macmillan UK, 2009); Dietmar Rothermund, *The Global Impact of the Great Depression, 1929–1939* (New York: Routledge, 1996).

109. McDougall to Bruce, June 3, 1943, M104, 11/4, SB-NAA.

110. *First Report to the Governments of the United Nations by the Interim Commission on Food and Agriculture*, Washington, DC, August 1, 1944, reel 30, HW-LCMD, 8.

111. Sweetser to Loveday, May 25, 1943, box 38x, Sweetser Papers, LC; Wallace to Tully, November 13, 1944, reel 30, HW-FDRL.

112. Wallace to Welles, June 23, 1943, reel 30, HW-FDRL.

113. United Nations Interim Commission on Food and Agriculture, Draft Report on The Quantity and Physical Quality of Life in Relation to Poverty and Malnutrition, July 1, 1944, reel 30, HW-FDRL.

114. Persons Attending Discussion of Financial and Economic Issues in Regard to the Establishment of a United Nations Relief and Rehabilitation Administration, June 26, 1943; Eugene Staley, "The Role of Economic Rehabilitation," June 14, 1943, box 22, JC-BLUC.

115. Weintraub to Lindberg, March 1, 1943; Weintraub to Loveday, March 1943; Sayre to Loveday, April 30, 1943; box C1755, OD-LNA.

116. Lehman to Loveday, January 18, 1944, box C1755, OD-LNA.

117. Acheson to Loveday, November 13, 1943, box C1757, OD-LNA; US Group at Conference [Atlantic City], June 20, 1944, box 26, BW-IMFA.

118. Lehman to Loveday, June 11, 1943; Persons Attending Discussions of Financial and Economic Issues in Regard to the Establishment of a United Nations Relief and Rehabilitation Administration, June 26, 1943; box C1757, OD-LNA.

119. Memo from Condliffe, "Economic Factors Determining Relief Policy," n.d. [1943], box 22, JC-BLUC.

120. Eugene Staley, "Relief and Rehabilitation in China," *Far Eastern Survey* 13, no. 20 (1944): 183–85.

121. Fang, *Toward Economic Control*.

122. "Full War Support Pledged by N.A.M.," *New York Times*, December 3, 1942.

123. C. Hartley Grattan, "Living Standards of To-Morrow," *Harper's Magazine*, August 1940, 313–14.

124. C. Hartley Grattan, "There'll Be Some Changes Made," *Harper's Magazine*, June 30, 1941, 206; C. Hartley Grattan, "A Warning to the Peace Planners: America's New Industrial Rivals," *Harper's Magazine*, January 1942, 126. While it is unclear if it influenced Grattan, Merrie Melodies of Warner Bros. Studios happened to make a short that was a send up of the Rover Boys in 1942, which is seen by some as a classic of the genre. See "The Dover Boys at Pimento University" or "The Rivals of Roquefort Hall" directed by Chuck Jones, 1942, https://archive.org/details/MERRIEMELODIES TheDoverBoys1942 (accessed July 14, 2021).

125. C. H. Grattan, *The Deadly Parallel* (New York: Stackpole, 1939); C. Hartley Grattan, *Preface to Chaos: War in the Making* (New York: Dodge, 1936); Warren I. Cohen, *The American Revisionists* (Chicago: University of Chicago Press, 1967). Grattan was drummed out of the BEW in 1942 after congressional accusations of sympathy for the enemy when it was discovered he had written the preface for Germany's 1939 "White Paper," justifying its invasion of Poland. See Germany Auswärtiges Amt, *The German White Paper* (New York: Howell, Soskin, 1940).

126. Albert O. Hirschman, "The Commodity Structure of World Trade," *Quarterly Journal of Economics* 57, no. 4 (1943): 565-95. Emphasis in original.

127. Rogers to Staley, July 30, 1942; Staley to Rogers, August 12, 1942; Staley to Rogers, January 9, 1943; box EXE, PR-ILOA; Paul B. Trescott, "H. D. Fong and the Study of Chinese Economic Development," *History of Political Economy* 34 no. 4 (2002): 789-809.

128. Eugene Staley, *World Economic Development: Effects on Advanced Industrial Countries* (Montreal: International Labour Office, 1944), 5.

129. Grant, Fletcher School, Tufts University, "Study of Economics and Transition and Adaptation" June 30, 1941, box 332, series 200, RG1.1-RAC.

130. League of Nations, Economic and Financial Section, *Industrialization and Foreign Trade* (Geneva: League of Nations, 1945).

131. Loveday to Phalen, November 6, 1943; Loveday to Phalen, March 22, 1944, box EXE, PR-ILOA.

132. Ragnar Nurkse, *International Currency Experience: Lessons of the Inter-War Period* (Geneva: League of Nations, 1944); Ragnar Nurkse, "International Currency Problems: Certain Conclusions drawn from a study of international monetary relations during the period 1919-1939," December 1943, box 2; Ragnar Nurkse, "Currency Problems in German-Occupied Europe," June 1943 box 1, RN-MLPU.

133. Barry Eichengreen, *Globalizing Capital: A History of the International Monetary System*, 2nd ed. (Princeton, NJ: Princeton University Press, 2008), 49-50.

134. League of Nations Secretariat, *The Transition from War to Peace Economy* (Geneva: League of Nations, 1943), 14.

135. League of Nations Secretariat, *Transition*, 19, 107.

136. Mallory to Willits, March 24, 1945, box 97, series 100, RFA, RG1-RAC.

137. "League of Nations System of International Reporting," n.d. 1943, box C1747, OD-LNA; Loveday to Willits, February 19, 1945, box 18, series 100, RG1-RAC.

138. Kurt Schuler and Andrew Rosenberg, eds., *The Bretton Woods Transcripts* (New York: Center for Financial Stability, 2013), 15-16.

139. Memorandum, July 19, 1944, box 38, AS-LCMD; Morgenthau to Davis, August 5, 1944, box 2, entry 1, Records of the Director, 1942-1945, RG208-NAMD.

140. See Benn Steil, *The Battle of Bretton Woods: John Maynard Keynes, Harry Dexter White, and the Making of a New World Order* (Princeton, NJ: University Press, 2013). The actions of League figures are partially obscured because Loveday's diary for 1944 is missing from his papers.

141. Prepared Statement from United Nations Monetary and Financial Conference, July 12, 1944, box 75, AS-LCMD. It is uncertain whether this statement was broadcast.

142. Louis W. Pauly, *The League of Nations and the Foreshadowing of the International Monetary Fund* (Princeton, NJ: International Finance Section, Department of Economics, Princeton University, 1996); Clavin, *Securing*, 303-8.

143. Pauly, *League of Nations.*

144. Thomas G. Weiss, David Forsythe, Roger A. Coate, and Kelly-Kate Pease, eds., *The United Nations and Changing World Politics*, 8th ed. (New York: Routledge, 2018), 249–51.

145. Eric Helleiner, *Forgotten Foundations of Bretton Woods: International Development and the Making of the Postwar Order* (Ithaca, NY: Cornell University Press, 2014), 123–30; Srinath Raghavan, *India's War: The Making of Modern South Asia, 1939–1945* (London: Allen Lane, 2016), 440; Schuler and Rosenberg, *Bretton Woods*, 1504–23, 1523–43.

146. Loveday, "Note I," September 14, 1943, box 2, BG-LCMD; A. Loveday, "Note on International Economic and Social Organization," March 6, 1944, box P150, AL-LNA.

147. Loveday to Wilson, November 20, 1942, P150, AL-LNA.

148. A. Loveday, "Note on International Economic Organization," February 9, 1944, box C1755, OD-LNA.

149. Gerig to Loveday, February 22, 1944; Loveday to Pasvolsky, April 13, 1945, box C1755, OD-LNA.

150. Seating Chart, Dumbarton Oaks, box 2, BG-LCMD. Despite repeated FOIA requests, significant portions of Gerig's papers, including portions relating to Dumbarton Oaks, remain classified.

151. Molotov to Gromyko, quoted in David Reynolds and Vladimir Pechatnov, eds., *The Kremlin Letters: Stalin's Wartime Correspondence with Churchill and Roosevelt* (New Haven, CT: Yale University Press, 2018), 467.

152. Robert C. Hilderbrand, *Dumbarton Oaks: The Origins of the United Nations and the Search for Postwar Security* (Chapel Hill: University of North Carolina Press, 1990), 88–90.

153. Memo to the President, "Progress Report on Dumbarton Oaks Conversations—Twenty-First Day," September 13, 1944, Hiss Files, RG59-NAMD.

154. ISO 45, "General Administration and Secretariat Arrangements for Economic and Social Cooperation," July 15, 1944, box 160; ISO 138, "Meaning of the Phrase 'Economic, Social and Other Humanitarian Problems,'" November 24, 1944, box 163, Notter Files, RG59-NAMD.

155. Gerig to Loveday, October 12, 1944, box C1633, OD-LNA.

156. Memo Gerig to Senator Arthur Vandenburg, "Some Points by Which the Dumbarton Oaks Proposals May be Regarded as an Improvement Over the League of Nations Covenant," January 22, 1945, box 2, BG-LCMD.

157. John B. Condliffe, "International Economic Collaboration: Some Administrative Problems of the Proposed United Nations Economic and Social Council," Yale Institute of International Studies, April 15, 1945, box 5, CD-HTL.

158. Leo Pasvolsky, *The Problem of Economic Peace after the War* (Washington: Department of State, 1942). This address was given at Delaware, OH, on March 8, 1942.

159. Address Delivered by Mr. Leo Pasvolsky at the American Labor Conference, New York City, December 16, 1944, box 5, CD-HTL.

160. Extract of letter from Loveday, July 30, 1943, box P130, SL-LNA.

161. Sweetser to Loveday, May 25, 1943, box 38, AS-LCMD.

162. Loveday to Lester, July 26, 1943, box P130, SL-LNA.

163. "The Extent to Which the Liquidation of the League Depends upon the Assumption by the United Nations of Activities Hereto Exercised by the League," UN Doc. A/LA/W/13, January 22, 1945, box C1633, OD-LNA; A. Loveday, "The Question of Transfer of the Economic and Financial Organization of the League to a New United Nations Organization," November 1944, box 67, AS-LCMD.

164. *Guide: The United Nations Conference on International Organization* (Washington, DC: Government Printing Office, 1945); US Motion Picture Industry, United Nations Theatre Program, box 5, CD-HTL.

165. Sweetser to Pasvolsky, February 28, 1945, box 41, AS-LCMD.

166. Sweetser to Davis, May 5, 1945, box 2, entry 1, Records of the Director, 1942–1945, RG208-NAMD.

167. Sweetser, Memorandum, May 12, 1945, box 41, AS-LCMD.

168. "'Old League' Chief Quits Conference," May 27, 1945, *New York Times*.

169. Sweetser to Davis, May 17, 1945; Sweetser to Klauber, April 19, 1945, box 2, entry 1, Records of the Director, 1942–1945, RG208-NAMD.

170. See James Cotton and David Lee, eds. *Australia and the United Nations* (Barton, Australia: Department of Foreign Affairs and Trade, 2012).

171. Charles F. Darlington, Draft Memoirs, 219–30; Meeting of the Executive Committee, May 1, 1945; box 5, CD-HTL.

172. Sweetser to Ward, June 6, 1945, box 41, AS-LCMD.

CODA

1. Final Report of Location Committee, November 1, 1944, box 29, HPF-LCMD.

2. Robert Moses, "'Natural and Proper Home of the U.N.': Moses States the Case for New York, and Flushing Meadow, as Capital of the World," *New York Times*, October 20, 1946.

3. Sam Roberts, *A History of New York in 27 Buildings* (New York: Bloomsbury, 2019), 231–40.

4. Meyer Berger, "City's Lost 'World' Has 10th Birthday," *New York Times*, April 30, 1949.

5. Frank S. Adams, "A Polite 400,000 See Delegates on Tour," *New York Times*, October 24, 1946; Frank S. Adams, "Ticker-Tape War Tests UN Today Here for First Session of General Assembly," *New York Times*, October 23, 1946.

6. Charlene Mires, *Capital of the World: The Race to Host the United Nations* (New York: NYU Press, 2013), 210–18; C. Brooks Peters, "Whalen Urges U.N. to Stay in Queens," *New York Times*, April 14, 1946; William R. Conklin, "Moses Denounces 'Slur' on the City," *New York Times*, June 6, 1948; George Barrett, "Dwyer's Last Bid to U.N. Urges Early Decision on Site," *New York Times*, December 1, 1946.

7. Lester to Aydelotte, April 24, 1946; Report Approved by League of Nations Assembly, April 18, 1946, box 38, Directors Office, GF-IASA.

8. League of Nations, *The League Hands Over* ([Geneva]: League Secretariat, 1946), 11.

9. Remarks of Leif Egeland in League of Nations, *League Hands Over*, 27.

10. Remarks of C. J. Hambro in League of Nations, *League Hands Over*, 26–27.

11. Thomas Davies, *NGOs: A New History of Transnational Civil Society* (New York: Oxford University Press, 2014), 123–24; Akira Iriye, *Global Community: The Role of In-*

ternational Organizations in the Making of the Contemporary World (Berkeley: University of California Press, 2002).

12. J.H.W. [Willits], "Postwar Policy in the Support of International Relations," May 14, 1945, box 88, series 910, RG3-RAC.

13. Michael Ward, *Quantifying the World: UN Ideas and Statistics* (Bloomington: Indiana University Press, 2004), 46–47.

14. Certificate, August 30, 1947; Affidavit, March 14, 1951, box 2, WR-NAMD.

15. Trygve Lie, "Opening Address," International Statistical Conference, September 6–18, 1947, Washington DC, *Proceedings of the International Statistical Conferences* (Calcutta: Eka Press, 1947), 1:151–53; see also Daniel Speich Chassé, "In Search of a Global Centre of Calculation," in *The Force of Comparison: A New Perspective on Modern European History and the Contemporary World*, ed. Willibald Steinmetz (New York: Berghahn Books, 2019), 266–87.

16. W. Averell Harriman, "Welcome on Behalf of the United States Government," International Statistical Conference, September 6–18, 1947, Washington DC, *Proceedings of the International Statistical Conferences* (Calcutta: Eka Press, 1947), 1:159–61.

17. See Andrew L. Yarrow, *Measuring America: How Economic Growth Came to Define American Greatness in the Late Twentieth Century* (Amherst: University of Massachusetts Press, 2010); Binyamin Appelbaum, *The Economists' Hour: False Prophets, Free Markets, and the Fracture of Society* (New York: Little, Brown, 2019).

18. See David Reynolds, *One World Divisible: A Global History since 1945* (New York: Norton, 2000).

19. "Sweetser Retires as U.N. Publicist," *Washington Post*, January 1, 1953.

20. "Arthur Sweetser, 79, is Dead; U.S. Aide at U.N. and League," *New York Times*, January 21, 1968; Raymond B. Fosdick, "Tribute to Sweetser," *New York Times*, February 10, 1968; "Arthur Sweetser, at 79, was Hub-Born U.N. Aide," *Boston Globe*, Jan 21, 1968.

21. Loveday to Willits, December 6, 1946; Willits to Loveday, November 12, 1946, box P150, AL-LNA.

22. Loveday to Willits, February 30, 1945, box P150, AL-LNA.

23. Alexander Loveday, *The Only Way: A Study of Democracy in Danger* (London: W. Hodge, 1950), 208–14.

24. Alexander Loveday, *Reflections on International Administration* (Oxford, UK: Clarendon Press, 1956).

25. "Mr. Alexander Loveday: Economic Reports for the League," *The Times*, January 22, 1962; "Alexander Loveday, a British Economist," *New York Times*, January 21, 1962.

26. Frank McDougall, "The Challenge to Western Civilization," March 24, 1947, box 3, FM-NLA, 1–4.

27. See Sara Lorenzini, *Global Development: A Cold War History* (Princeton, NJ: Princeton University Press, 2019), 22–32.

28. McDougall and Bruce, *McDougall Memoranda*. The FAO also sponsors an annual "McDougall Memorial Lecture" to honor his legacy.

29. J. B. Condliffe, "Point Four: Economic Development," in *Point Four and the World Economy* (New York: Foreign Policy Association, 1950), 8–10, 20–28.

30. John Bell Condliffe, Unpublished Autobiography, "Decline at Berkeley," 17, "Back to India," 1–2; JC-ATLNZ; David C. Engerman, *The Price of Aid: The Economic*

Cold War in India (Cambridge, MA: Harvard University Press, 2018), 89–116. During the war Grady headed a 1942 technical mission to India that offered a report on how to develop the country's industrial resources for the conflict.

31. BBC News, "The Country That Keeps Getting Left off Maps," https://www.bbc .com/news/av/magazine-41905040/the-country-that-keeps-getting-left-off-maps (accessed March 25, 2022).

32. See Charles Poor Kindleberger, *The World in Depression, 1929–1939* (Berkeley: University of California Press, 1973). Kindleberger credits neither Morgenstern's publications, the *WES*, the FPA book, nor Condliffe for the spiral image, but a set of League data, offering the impression that it was compiled from that information.

33. United States National Security Council, *Strengthening the Korean Economy* [Tasca Report], 1953, http://search.proquest.com.ezp-prod1.hul.harvard.edu /docview/1679083562?accountid=11311 (accessed June 5, 2020).

34. See Alexander Gerschenkron, *Economic Backwardness in Historical Perspective: A Book of Essays* (Cambridge, MA: Belknap Press of Harvard University Press, 1962); Nicholas Dawidoff, *The Fly Swatter: Portrait of an Exceptional Character* (New York: Vintage Books, 2003).

35. Adelman, *Worldly Philosopher*, 498.

36. Engerman, *Price*, 111; Ragnar Nurkse, *Problems of Capital Formation in Underdeveloped Countries* (Oxford: Basil Blackwell, 1953). See H. W. Arndt, "Development Economics Before 1945," 1969, box 21, HA-NLA (this was written to honor Rosenstein-Rodan); H. W. Arndt, "Economic Development: A Semantic History," *Economic Development and Cultural Change* 29, no. 3 (1981): 464–65.

37. Louis Emmerij, "Creativity in the United Nations: A History of Ideas," *Development* 50, no. S1 (2007): 39–46; John Toye and Richard Toye, "The Origins and Interpretation of the Prebisch-Singer Thesis," *History of Political Economy* 35, no. 3 (2003): 437–67.

38. José Antonio Sánchez Román, "Discovering Underdevelopment: Argentina and Double Taxation at the League of Nations," in *Beyond Geopolitics: New Histories of Latin America at the League of Nations*, ed. Alan L. McPherson and Yannick Wehrli (Albuquerque: University of New Mexico Press, 2015), 205–22.

39. Edgar J. Dosman, *The Life and Times of Raúl Prebisch, 1901–1986* (Montreal: McGill-Queen's University Press, 2008); Nils Gilman, "The New International Economic Order: A Reintroduction," *Humanity* 6, no. 1 (2015); Vijay Prashad, *The Poorer Nations: A Possible History of the Global South* (New York: Verso, 2012), 2–3.

40. Diane Coyle, *GDP: A Brief but Affectionate History* (Princeton, NJ: Princeton University Press, 2014); Dirk Philipsen, *The Little Big Number: How GDP Came to Rule the World and What to Do about It* (Princeton, NJ: Princeton University Press, 2015). See also Macekura, *Mismeasure*.

41. Rockefeller Foundation, *Annual Report*, 1946, 33.

42. F. P. Walters, *A History of the League of Nations*, 2 vols. (New York: Oxford University Press, 1952); Walters to Willits, February 1, 1950; "Excerpt from Minutes of SS Staff Meeting #78," June 26, 1950; Willits to Macadam, August 4, 1950; box 22, series 100, RG1-RAC.

43. Royal Institute of International Affairs, Rockefeller Grant Accounting, June 12, 1955; Willits to Sulzberger, October 5, 1951; Letter to Buchanan, June 19, 1950; Brown to Willits, October 15, 1951; box 22, series 100, RG1-RAC.

44. Raymond Fosdick, "A Great and Daring Design, a Bold Leap Forward," *New York Times*, March 9, 1952.

45. Fosdick, "A Great and Daring Design."

46. Raymond Fosdick, *The Story of the Rockefeller Foundation* (New York: Harper, 1952); Raymond Fosdick, *The League and the United Nations after Fifty Years: The Six Secretaries-General* (Newtown, CT, 1972).

47. Even the UN Intellectual History Project has remarkably little to say about the technical work of the League laying the foundation for its various research projects and arms. See, for example, Ward, *Quantifying*, 45–50.

BIBLIOGRAPHY

Adelman, Jeremy. *Worldly Philosopher: The Odyssey of Albert O. Hirschman.* Princeton, NJ: Princeton University Press, 2013.

Allen, David. "International Exhibitionism: The League of Nations at the New York World's Fair, 1939–1940." In *International Organizations and the Media in the Nineteenth and Twentieth Centuries: Exorbitant Expectations*, edited by Jonas Brendebach, Martin Herzer, and Heidi Tworek, 90–116. New York: Routledge, 2018.

Amrith, Sunil, and Patricia Clavin. "Feeding the Worlds: Connecting Europe and Asia, 1930." *Past & Present* 219, no. 1 (2013): 29–50.

Appelbaum, Binyamin. *The Economists' Hour: False Prophets, Free Markets, and the Fracture of Society.* New York: Little, Brown, 2019.

Arndt, H. W. "Colin Clark as a Development Economist." *World Development* 18, no. 7 (July 1, 1990): 1045–50.

———. "Economic Development: A Semantic History." *Economic Development and Cultural Change* 29, no. 3 (1981): 457–66.

Ashworth, Lucian M. "Progressivism Triumphant? Isaiah Bowman's New Diplomacy in a New World." In *Progressivism and US Foreign Policy between the World Wars*, edited by Molly Cochran and Cornelia Navari, 73–90. New York: Palgrave Macmillan, 2017.

———. "Where Are the Idealists in Interwar International Relations?" *Review of International Studies* 32, no. 2 (April 2006): 291–308.

Auberer, Benjamin. "Digesting the League of Nations: Planning the International Secretariat of the Future, 1941–1944." *New Global Studies* 10, no. 3 (2016): 393–426.

Bailey, Thomas Andrew. *Woodrow Wilson and the Great Betrayal.* New York: Macmillan, 1945.

Barros, James. *Betrayal from Within: Joseph Avenol, Secretary-General of the League of Nations, 1933–1940.* New Haven, CT: Yale University Press, 1969.

Bauerkämper, Arnd, and Grzegorz Rossolinski-Liebe. *Fascism without Borders: Transnational Connections and Cooperation between Movements and Regimes in Europe from 1918 to 1945.* New York: Berghahn Books, 2017.

Bayly, C. A. *Empire and Information: Intelligence Gathering and Social Communication in India, 1780–1870.* Cambridge Studies in Indian History and Society 1. Cambridge: Cambridge University Press, 1996.

Bemman, Martin. *The Force of Comparison: A New Perspective on Modern European History and the Contemporary World*. Edited by Willibald Steinmetz. New German Historical Perspectives 11. New York: Berghahn Books, 2019.

Bendiner, Elmer. *A Time for Angels: The Tragicomic History of the League of Nations*. New York: Knopf: 1975.

Bernanke, Ben S. *Essays on the Great Depression*. Princeton, NJ: Princeton University Press, 2009.

Bernays, Edward L. *Propaganda*. New York: Liveright, 1928.

Biltoft, Carolyn N. *A Violent Peace: Media, Truth, and Power at the League of Nations*. Chicago: University of Chicago Press, 2021.

Blom, Philipp. *The Vertigo Years: Europe, 1900-1914*. New York: Basic Books, 2008.

Blower, Brooke L. "New York City's Spanish Shipping Agents and the Practice of State Power in the Atlantic Borderlands of World War II." *American Historical Review* 119, no. 1 (2014): 111-41.

Bonner, Thomas Neville. *Iconoclast: Abraham Flexner and a Life in Learning*. Baltimore: Johns Hopkins University Press, 2002.

Borgwardt, Elizabeth. *A New Deal for the World: America's Vision for Human Rights*. Cambridge, MA: Belknap Press of Harvard University Press, 2005.

Borowy, Iris. *Coming to Terms with World Health: The League of Nations Health Organisation, 1921-1946*. Frankfurt: Peter Lang, 2009.

Boudreau, Frank G. *Ancient Diseases—Modern Defences: The Work of the Health Organization of the League of Nations*. New York: Columbia University Press, 1939.

Bourne, Randolph S. "Trans-National America." *Atlantic*, July 1, 1916.

Boyce, Robert. *The Great Interwar Crisis and the Collapse of Globalization*. London: Palgrave Macmillan UK, 2009.

Bridge, Carl. "Allies of a Kind: Three Wartime Australian Ministers to the United States, 1940-46." In *Australia Goes to Washington: 75 Years of Australian Representation in the United States, 1940-2015*, edited by David Lowe, David Lee, and Carl Bridge, 23-38. Canberra: ANU Press, 2016.

Brockway, Thomas P. *Battles without Bullets: The Story of Economic Warfare*. Headline Books, no. 18. New York: Foreign Policy Association, 1939.

Buell, Raymond Leslie. *Isolated America*. New York: Alfred A, Knopf, 1940.

———. *Poland: Key to Europe*. New York: Alfred A. Knopf, 1939.

Bull, Hedley. *The Anarchical Society: A Study of Order in World Politics*. 2nd ed. New York: Columbia University Press, 1995.

Canadian Institute of International Affairs. *The Canadian Economy and Its Problems: Papers and Proceedings of Study Groups of Members of the Canadian Institute of International Affairs, 1933-1934*. Toronto: Canadian Institute of International Affairs, 1934.

Carr, Edward Hallett. *The Twenty Years' Crisis, 1919-1939: An Introduction to the Study of International Relations*. London: Macmillan, 1940.

Chassé, Daniel Speich. "In Search of a Global Centre of Calculation." In *The Force of Comparison: A New Perspective on Modern European History and the Contemporary World*, edited by Willibald Steinmetz, 266-87. New York: Berghahn Books, 2019.

Clark, Colin. *The Conditions of Economic Progress*. London: Macmillan, 1940.

Clavin, Patricia. *Securing the World Economy: The Reinvention of the League of Nations, 1920–1946*. Oxford: Oxford University Press, 2013.

Clavin, Patricia, and Glenda Sluga, eds. *Internationalisms: A Twentieth-Century History*. Cambridge: Cambridge University Press, 2017.

Clifford, Susan Sweetser. *One Shining Hour: A Memoir*. Privately printed, 1990.

Cochran, Molly, and Cornelia Navari, eds. *Progressivism and US Foreign Policy between the World Wars*. Palgrave Macmillan Series on the History of International Thought. New York: Palgrave Macmillan, 2017.

Cohen, Warren I. *The American Revisionists*. Chicago: University of Chicago Press, 1967.

Collingham, Lizzie. *The Taste of War: World War II and the Battle for Food*. New York: Penguin, 2013.

Condliffe, J. B. (John Bell). *Agenda for a Postwar World*. New York: Norton, 1942.

———. "The Distribution of Power and Leadership." In *The World's Economic Future*, by A. Loveday, J. B. Condliffe, R. Ohlin, E. F. Heckscher, and S. de Madariaga, and with an introduction by D. H. Robertson, 43–64. Halley Stewart Lectures, 1937. London: Allen & Unwin, 1938.

———. "The Industrial Revolution in the Far East" (pt. 1). *Economic Record* 2, no. 3 (1926): 180–209.

———. "The Industrial Revolution in the Far East" (pt. 2). *Economic Record* 3, no. 4 (1927): 82–101.

———. *Markets and the Problem of Peaceful Change*. Paris: International Institute of Intellectual Cóoperation, League of Nations, 1938.

———. *Point Four: Economic Development*. In *Point Four and the World Economy*. Headline Series, no. 79. New York: Foreign Policy Association, 1950.

———. *The Reconstruction of World Trade: A Survey of International Economic Relations*. New York: Norton, 1940.

———. *Reminiscences of the Institute of Pacific Relations*. Vancouver: Institute of Asian Research, University of British Columbia, 1981.

———. *War and Depression*. Boston: World Peace Foundation, 1935.

Condliffe, J. B., and A. Stevenson. *The Common Interest in International Economic Organisation*. Montreal: International Labour Office, 1944.

Cooper, John Milton. *Breaking the Heart of the World: Woodrow Wilson and the Fight for the League of Nations*. New York: Cambridge University Press, 2001.

Cotton, James. "On the Chatham House Project: Interwar Actors, Networks, Knowledge." *International Politics* 55, no. 6 (2018): 820–35.

Cotton, James, and David Lee, eds. *Australia and the United Nations*. Barton, Australia: Department of Foreign Affairs and Trade, 2012.

Coyle, Diane. *GDP: A Brief but Affectionate History*. Princeton, NJ: Princeton University Press, 2014.

Cullather, Nick. "Development? It's History." *Diplomatic History* 24, no. 4 (2000): 641–53.

———. "The Foreign Policy of the Calorie." *American Historical Review* 112, no. 2 (2007): 337–64.

Culver, John C., and John Hyde. *American Dreamer: The Life and Times of Henry A. Wallace*. New York: W. W. Norton & Co., 2000.

Cussó, Roser. "Building a Global Representation of Trade through International Quantification: The League of Nations' Unification of Methods in Economic Statistics." *International History Review* 42, no. 4 (2020): 714–36.

Davies, Thomas. *NGOs: A New History of Transnational Civil Society*. New York: Oxford University Press, 2014.

Davis, Harriet Eager. *Pioneers in World Order: An American Appraisal of the League of Nations*. New York: Columbia University Press, 1944.

Dawidoff, Nicholas. *The Fly Swatter: Portrait of an Exceptional Character*. New York: Vintage Books, 2003.

Dawley, Alan. *Changing the World: American Progressives in War and Revolution*. Politics and Society in Twentieth-Century America. Princeton, NJ: Princeton University Press, 2003.

Dean, Vera Micheles. *The Struggle for World Order*. Headline Books, no. 32. New York: Foreign Policy Association, 1941.

Dennis, Donald Philips. *Foreign Policy in a Democracy: The Role of the Foreign Policy Association*. New York: Foreign Policy Association, 2003.

Divine, Robert A. *Second Chance: The Triumph of Internationalism in America during World War II*. New York: Atheneum, 1967.

Doenecke, Justus D. *Storm on the Horizon: The Challenge to American Intervention, 1939–1941*. Lanham, MD: Rowman & Littlefield, 2000.

Dosman, Edgar J. *The Life and Times of Raúl Prebisch, 1901–1986*. Montreal: McGill-Queen's University Press, 2008.

Dubin, Martin. "Toward the Bruce Report: The Economic and Social Program of the League in the Avenol Era." In *The League of Nations in Retrospect / La Société des Nations: Rétrospective*, 42–72. New York: Walter de Gruyter, 1983.

Dunn, Frederick Sherwood. *Peaceful Change: A Study of International Procedures*. Publications of the Council on Foreign Relations. New York: Council on Foreign Relations, 1937.

Eichengreen, Barry J. *Globalizing Capital: A History of the International Monetary System*. 2nd ed. Princeton, NJ: Princeton University Press, 2008.

Ekbladh, David. "American Asylum: The United States and the Campaign to Transplant the Technical League, 1939–1940." *Diplomatic History* 39, no. 4 (September 1, 2015): 629–60.

———. "Development as . . . Appeasement? From Peaceful Change to Ideological Combat." *History Australia* 17, no. 4 (2020): 611–27.

———. "Present at the Creation: Edward Mead Earle and the Depression-Era Origins of Security Studies." *International Security* 36, no. 3 (2011): 107–41.

Emmerij, Louis. "Creativity in the United Nations: A History of Ideas." *Development (Society for International Development)* 50, no. S1 (2007): 39–46.

Endres, A. M. *International Organizations and the Analysis of Economic Policy, 1919–1950*. Historical Perspectives on Modern Economics. Cambridge: Cambridge University Press, 2002.

Engerman, David C. "American Knowledge and Global Power." *Diplomatic History* 31, no. 4 (2007): 599–622.

——. *The Price of Aid: The Economic Cold War in India*. Cambridge, MA: Harvard University Press, 2018.

Fang, Xianting. *The Post-War Industrialization of China*. Washington, DC: National Planning Association, 1942.

——. *Toward Economic Control in China. Papers Presented at the Sixth Conference of the Institute of Pacific Relations, Yosemite National Park, California, August 15 to 29, 1936*. Vol. 4 [no. 3]. Shanghai: China Institute of Pacific Relations, 1936.

Feis, Herbert. *Research Activities of the League of Nations: A Report Made to the Committee on International Relations of the Social Science Research Council on the Methods and Progress of Research in the League of Nations and International Labour Organization, June, 1929*. Old Lyme, CT: Old Lyme Press, 1929.

Fergie, Dexter. "Geopolitics Turned Inwards: The Princeton Military Studies Group and the National Security Imagination." *Diplomatic History* 43, no. 4 (2019): 644–70.

Fleming, Donald, and Bernard Bailyn. *The Intellectual Migration: Europe and America, 1930–1960*. Cambridge, MA: Belknap Press of Harvard University Press, 1969.

Fletcher, Luke. "Confusion and Convergence: The Nazi Challenge to World Order and the CFR Response, 1940–1941." *International Politics* 55, no. 6 (2018): 888–903.

Flexner, Abraham. *The American College: A Criticism*. 1908. Reprint, New York: Arno Press, 1969.

——. *Do Americans Really Value Education?* Cambridge, MA: Harvard University Press, 1927.

Fong, H. D. "The Prospect for China's Industrialization." *Pacific Affairs* 15, no. 1 (1942): 44–60.

Fosdick, Raymond B. *Adventure in Giving: The Story of the General Education Board, a Foundation Established by John D. Rockefeller*. New York: Harper & Row, 1962.

——. *Chronicle of a Generation: An Autobiography*. New York: Harper, 1958.

——. *The League and the United Nations after Fifty Years: The Six Secretaries-General*. Newtown, CT, 1972.

——. *Letters on the League of Nations: From the Files of Raymond B. Fosdick*. Supplementary volume to *The Papers of Woodrow Wilson*. Princeton, NJ: Princeton University Press, 2015.

——. *The Old Savage in the New Civilization*. Garden City, NY: Doubleday, Doran, 1931.

——. *The Story of the Rockefeller Foundation*. New York: Harper, 1952.

Foucault, Michel. *Power/Knowledge: Selected Interviews and Other Writings, 1972–1977*. New York: Pantheon, 1980.

Friedman, Thomas L. *The Lexus and the Olive Tree*. New York: Farrar, Straus & Giroux, 1999.

Froyen, Richard T. *Macroeconomics: Theories and Policies*. 4th ed. New York: Macmillan, 1993.

Fry, Varian. *Bricks without Mortar: The Story of International Cooperation*. New York: Foreign Policy Association, 1938.

Gaddis, John Lewis. *George F. Kennan: An American Life*. New York: Penguin, 2011.

Gageby, Douglas. *The Last Secretary General: Sean Lester and the League of Nations*. Dublin: Town House and Country House, 1999.

Germany Auswärtiges Amt (Foreign Office). *The German White Paper*. New York: Howell, Soskin, 1940.

Gerschenkron, Alexander. *Economic Backwardness in Historical Perspective: A Book of Essays*. Cambridge, MA: Belknap Press of Harvard University Press, 1962.

Gilman, Nils. "The New International Economic Order: A Reintroduction." *Humanity* (Philadelphia) 6, no. 1 (2015): 1–16.

Gini, Corrado. *Report on the Problem of Raw Materials and Foodstuffs, by Professor Gini, with Annexes Prepared under His Direction*. Geneva, 1921.

——. "The Scientific Basis of Fascism." *Political Science Quarterly* 42 (1927): 99–115.

Gorman, Daniel. *The Emergence of International Society in the 1920s*. New York: Cambridge University Press, 2012.

——. *International Cooperation in the Early Twentieth Century*. New Approaches to International History. New York: Bloomsbury, 2017.

Grattan, C. Hartley. *The Deadly Parallel*. New York: Stackpole, 1939.

——. *In Quest of Knowledge: A Historical Perspective on Adult Education*. American Education: Its Men, Ideas, and Institutions. Series II. New York: Arno Press, 1971.

——. *Introducing Australia*. New York: John Day, 1942.

——. *Preface to Chaos: War in the Making*. New York: Dodge, 1936.

——. *The Three Jameses: A Family of Minds: Henry James Sr., William James, Henry James*. London: Longmans, Green, 1932.

——. *The United States and the Southwest Pacific*. American Foreign Policy Library. Cambridge, MA: Harvard University Press, 1961.

Green, Abigail. "Liberals, Socialists, Internationalists, Jews." *Journal of World History* 31, no. 1 (2020): 11–41.

Green, Abigail, and Vincent Viaene. *Religious Internationals in the Modern World: Globalization and Faith Communities since 1750*. London: Palgrave Macmillan, 2012.

Gross, Stephen G. "Gold, Debt and the Quest for Monetary Order: The Nazi Campaign to Integrate Europe in 1940." *Contemporary European History* 26, no. 2 (2017): 287–309.

Haberler, Gottfried. *Prosperity and Depression: A Theoretical Analysis of Cyclical Movements*. Series of League of Nations Publications. II, Economic and Financial 1936, II, A.24. Geneva: League of Nations, 1937.

Hambidge, Gove. *The Story of FAO*. New York: Van Nostrand, 1955.

Hambro, Carl Joachim. *Glimt fra Amerika*. Oslo: Aschehoug, 1925.

——. *I Saw It Happen in Norway*. New York: D. Appleton-Century, 1940.

Hambro, Johan. *C. J. Hambro, liv og drøm*. 2nd ed. Oslo: Aschehoug, 1984.

Hamilton, John Maxwell. *Manipulating the Masses: Woodrow Wilson and the Birth of American Propaganda*. Baton Rouge: Louisiana State University Press, 2020.

Harriman, W. Averell. "Welcome on Behalf of the United States Government." International Statistical Conference, September 6-18, 1947, Washington, DC. In *Proceedings of the International Statistical Conference*, 1:151-53. Calcutta: Eka, 1947.

Heald, Stephen Alfred. *Action collective et neutralité: Deux études*. Bulletin nos. 3-4. Paris: Publications de la Conciliation internationale, Centre européen de la Dotation Carnegie, Division des relations internationales et de l'éducation, 1936.

Hediger, Ernest S. "Geneva Institutions in Wartime." *Foreign Policy Reports* 19, no. 4 (May 1, 1943).

Helleiner, Eric. *Forgotten Foundations of Bretton Woods: International Development and the Making of the Postwar Order*. Ithaca, NY: Cornell University Press, 2014.

Henderson, H. D. "Review of *World Economic Survey*: Third Year, 1933-34." *Economic Journal* 45, no. 177 (1935): 147-49.

Herren, Madeleine, and Isabella Löhr. "Being International in Times of War: Arthur Sweetser and the Shifting of the League of Nations to the United Nations." *European Review of History / Revue Européenne d'Histoire* 25, no. 3-4 (2018): 535-52.

Hetherington, Philippa, and Glenda Sluga. "Liberal and Illiberal Internationalisms." *Journal of World History* 31, no. 1 (2020): 1-9.

Hilderbrand, Robert C. *Dumbarton Oaks: The Origins of the United Nations and the Search for Postwar Security*. Chapel Hill: University of North Carolina Press, 1990.

Hill, Martin. *The Economic and Financial Organization of the League of Nations: A Survey of Twenty-Five Years' Experience*. Studies in the Administration of International Law and Organization. Washington, DC: Carnegie Endowment for International Peace, Division of International Law, 1946.

Hirschman, Albert O. "The Commodity Structure of World Trade." *Quarterly Journal of Economics* 57, no. 4 (1943): 565-95.

Hoe, Y.-C. (Yung-chi). *The Programme of Technical Cooperation between China and the League of Nations*. N.p.: Institute of Pacific Relations, 1933.

Homan, Gerlof D. "Orie Benjamin Gerig: Mennonite Rebel, Peace Activist, International Civil Servant, and American Diplomat, 1894-1976." *Mennonite Quarterly Review* 73, no. 4 (1999): 751-82.

Hoover, Herbert. *The New Day: Campaign Speeches of Herbert Hoover, 1928*. Stanford, CA: Stanford University Press, 1929.

Hubbard, G. E. *Eastern Industrialization and Its Effect on the West*. London: Oxford University Press, 1938.

Ikenberry, G. John. "A World Economy Restored: Expert Consensus and the Anglo-American Postwar Settlement." *International Organization* 46, no. 1 (1992): 289-321.

Innis, Harold A. *The Bias of Communication*. Toronto: University of Toronto Press, 1951.

———. "The Canadian Economy and the Depression." In *Essays in Canadian Economic History*, edited by Mary Q. Innis, 123-40. Toronto: University of Toronto Press, 2017.

———. *Empire and Communications*. Critical Media Studies. 1950. Reprint, Lanham, MD: Rowman & Littlefield, 2007.

———. "The Penetrative Powers of the Price System." *Canadian Journal of Economics and Political Science / Revue Canadienne d'Economique et de Science Politique* 4, no. 3 (1938): 299–319.

Institute of Pacific Relations. *Problems of the Pacific: Proceedings of the Second Conference of the Institute of Pacific Relations, Honolulu, Hawaii, July 15 to 29, 1927.* Chicago: University of Chicago Press, 1928.

International Studies Conference. *Economic Policies in Relation to World Peace: A Record of the Study Meetings Held in Bergen, from August 26th to August 29th, 1939.* Paris: International Institute of Intellectual Co-operation, League of Nations, 1940.

———. *Peaceful Change: Procedures, Population, Raw Materials, Colonies. Proceedings of the Tenth International Studies Conference, Paris, June 28–July 3, 1937.* Vol. 1. Paris: International Institute of Intellectual Co-operation, League of Nations, 1938.

Iriye, Akira. *Cultural Internationalism and World Order.* Albert Shaw Memorial Lectures. Baltimore: Johns Hopkins University Press, 1997.

———. *Global and Transnational History: The Past, Present, and Future.* Basingstoke, UK: Palgrave Pivot, 2013.

———. *Global Community: The Role of International Organizations in the Making of the Contemporary World.* Berkeley: University of California Press, 2002.

———. *The Globalizing of America, 1913–1945.* Vol. 3 of *The New Cambridge History of American Foreign Relations.* Cambridge: Cambridge University Press, 2013.

Kapp, K. William. *The League of Nations and Raw Materials, 1919–1939.* Geneva Studies 12:3. Geneva: Geneva Research Centre, 1941.

Kargon, Robert H. "Whose Modernity? Utopia and Commerce at the 1939 New York World's Fair." In *World's Fairs on the Eve of War: Science, Technology, & Modernity, 1937–1942,* edited by Robert H. Kargon, 57–82. Pittsburgh: University of Pittsburgh Press, 2015.

Kaufman, Alison Adcock. "In Pursuit of Equality and Respect: China's Diplomacy and the League of Nations." *Modern China* 40, no. 6 (2014): 605–38.

Keane, Damien. "An Ear toward Security: The Princeton Listening Center." *Princeton University Library Chronicle* 71, no. 1 (2009): 45–62.

Kennan, George F. "Memorandum for the Minister." *New York Review of Books,* April 26, 2001.

Kennedy, David M. *Freedom from Fear: The American People in Depression and War, 1929–1945.* Vol. 9 of *The Oxford History of the United States.* New York: Oxford University Press, 2001.

Kern, Stephen. *The Culture of Time and Space, 1880–1918.* Cambridge, MA: Harvard University Press, 1983.

Keynes, John Maynard. "Professor Tinbergen's Method." *Economic Journal* 49 (1939): 558–68.

Kiddle, Amelia M. "Separating the Political from the Technical: The 1938 League of Nations Mission to Latin America." In *Beyond Geopolitics: New Histories of Latin America at the League of Nations,* edited by Alan L. McPherson and Yannick Wehrli, 239–57. Albuquerque: University of New Mexico Press, 2015.

Kindleberger, Charles Poor. *The World in Depression, 1929-1939*. Berkeley: University of California Press, 1973.

Knock, Thomas J. *To End All Wars: Woodrow Wilson and the Quest for a New World Order*. New ed. Princeton, NJ: Princeton University Press, 2019.

Kuehl, Warren F. *Keeping the Covenant: American Internationalists and the League of Nations, 1920-1939*. American Diplomatic History. Kent, OH: Kent State University Press, 1997.

Lacey, Jim. *Keep from All Thoughtful Men: How U.S. Economists Won World War II*. Annapolis, MD: Naval Institute Press, 2011.

Landefeld, J. Steven, Eugene P. Seskin, and Barbara M. Fraumeni. "Taking the Pulse of the Economy: Measuring GDP." *Journal of Economic Perspectives* 22, no. 2 (2008): 193-216.

League of Nations. *The League Hands Over*. League of Nations, Series of Publications, General, 1946, no. 1. Geneva: League Secretariat, 1946.

League of Nations Committee for the Study of the Problem of Raw Materials. *Report of the Committee for the Study of the Problem of Raw Materials*. League of Nations. Series of Publications, II. Economic and Financial, 1937, II.B.7. Geneva: League of Nations, 1937.

League of Nations, Economic and Financial Section. *Industrialization and Foreign Trade*. Series of League of Nations Publications, II. Economic and Financial, 1945, II.A.10. Geneva: League of Nations, 1945.

League of Nations Mixed Committee of Experts on Nutrition. *Nutrition: Final Report of the Mixed Committee of the League of Nations on the Relation of Nutrition to Health, Agriculture and Economic Policy*. Geneva: League of Nations Publications, 1937.

League of Nations Secretariat. *The Transition from War to Peace Economy*. League of Nations. Series of Publications, II. Economic and Financial, 1943, II.A 3. Geneva: League of Nations, 1943.

———. *World Economic Survey, 1932-33*. Geneva, 1931.

LeBor, Adam. *Tower of Basel: The Shadowy History of the Secret Bank That Runs the World*. New York: PublicAffairs, 2013.

Lee, David. *Australia and the World in the Twentieth Century*. Beaconsfield, Australia: Circa, 2006.

———. *Stanley Melbourne Bruce: Australian Internationalist*. London: Continuum, 2010.

Leffler, Melvyn P. *Safeguarding Democratic Capitalism: U.S. Foreign Policy and National Security, 1920-2015*. Princeton, NJ: Princeton University Press, 2017.

Lie, Trygve. "Opening Address." International Statistical Conference, September 6-18, 1947, Washington, DC. In *Proceedings of the International Statistical Conferences*, 1:151-53. Calcutta: Eka, 1947.

Lincove, David. "Data for Peace: The League of Nations and Disarmament 1920-40." *Peace & Change* 43, no. 4 (2018): 498-529.

Lippmann, Walter. *An Inquiry into the Principles of the Good Society*. Boston: Little, Brown, 1937.

———. *Liberty and the News*. New York: Harcourt, Brace and Howe, 1920.

———. *Public Opinion*. New York: Harcourt, Brace, 1922.

Long, David. "Who Killed the International Studies Conference?" *Review of International Studies* 32, no. 4 (2006): 603–22.

Lorenzini, Sara. *Global Development: A Cold War History*. America in the World. Princeton, NJ: Princeton University Press, 2019.

Loveday, A. (Alexander). *Britain & World Trade, Quo Vadimus and Other Economic Essays*. London: Longmans, Green, 1931.

———. *The History & Economics of Indian Famines*. New Delhi: Usha, 1985.

———. *The Only Way: A Study of Democracy in Danger*. London: W. Hodge, 1950.

———. "Problems of Economic Insecurity." In *The World's Economic Future*, by A. Loveday, J. B. Condliffe, R. Ohlin, E. F. Heckscher, and S. de Madariaga, and with an introduction by D. H. Robertson, 17–42. Halley Stewart Lectures, 1937. London: Allen & Unwin, 1938.

———. *Reflections on International Administration*. Oxford, UK: Clarendon Press, 1956.

Lowe, David, David Lee, and Carl Bridge. *Australia Goes to Washington: 75 Years of Australian Representation in the United States, 1940–2015*. Canberra: ANU Press, 2016.

Luce, Henry Robinson. *Dumbarton Oaks and San Francisco: An Analysis of the Proposals Together with Suggestions for Improvements to Be Made in the Drafting of the Charter of a World Security Organization*. New York: Time, 1945.

Macekura, Stephen J. *The Mismeasure of Progress: Economic Growth and Its Critics*. Chicago: University of Chicago Press, 2020.

MacGregor, D. C. "Review of *World Economic Survey*, Fourth Year, 1934–35; *Review of World Trade*, 1934; *World Production and Prices*, 1925–1934; *Statistical Year-Book of the League of Nations*, 1934–5." *Canadian Journal of Economics and Political Science / Revue Canadienne d'Economique et de Science Politique* 1, no. 4 (1935): 639–40.

Maddox, William Percy. *European Plans for World Order*. James-Patten-Rowe Pamphlet Series, no. 8. Philadelphia: American Academy of Political and Social Science, 1940.

Maier, Charles S., Niall Ferguson, Daniel J Sargent, and Erez Manela, eds. *The Shock of the Global: The 1970s in Perspective*. Cambridge, MA: Harvard University Press, 2010.

Makalani, Minkah. *In the Cause of Freedom: Radical Black Internationalism from Harlem to London, 1917–1939*. Chapel Hill: University of North Carolina Press, 2011.

Manela, Erez. "International Society as a Historical Subject." *Diplomatic History* 44, no. 2 (April 1, 2020): 184–209.

———. *The Wilsonian Moment: Self-Determination and the International Origins of Anticolonial Nationalism*. Oxford: Oxford University Press, 2007.

Markowitz, Norman D. *The Rise and Fall of the People's Century: Henry A. Wallace and American Liberalism, 1941–1948*. New York: Free Press, 1973.

Martin, Benjamin George. *The Nazi-Fascist New Order for European Culture*. Cambridge, MA: Harvard University Press, 2016.

Mauro, James. *Twilight at the World of Tomorrow: Genius, Madness, Murder, and the 1939 World's Fair on the Brink of War*. New York: Ballantine Books, 2010.

Mazower, Mark. *Dark Continent: Europe's Twentieth Century*. New York: Vintage Books, 2000.

———. *Governing the World: The History of an Idea*. New York: Penguin, 2012.

———. *Hitler's Empire: How the Nazis Ruled Europe*. New York: Penguin, 2008.

———. *No Enchanted Palace: The End of Empire and the Ideological Origins of the United Nations*. Lawrence Stone Lectures. Princeton, NJ: Princeton University Press, 2009.

McAllister, James. *Wilsonian Visions: The Williamstown Institute of Politics and American Internationalism after World War I*. Ithaca, NY: Cornell University Press, 2021.

McCarthy, Helen. *The British People and the League of Nations: Democracy, Citizenship, and Internationalism, c. 1918-45*. New York: Palgrave Macmillan, 2011.

McDougall, Frank, and S. M. Bruce. *The McDougall Memoranda*. Rome: Food and Agricultural Organization of the United Nations, 1956.

Meade, J. E. *The Economic Basis of a Durable Peace*. London: Allen & Unwin, 1940.

Mires, Charlene. *Capital of the World: The Race to Host the United Nations*. New York: New York University Press, 2013.

Mitchell, Timothy. *Rule of Experts: Egypt, Techno-Politics, Modernity*. Berkeley: University of California Press, 2002.

Moorhouse, Frank. *Dark Palace: The Companion Novel to "Grand Days."* Milsons Point: Random House Australia, 2000.

———. *Grand Days*. Sydney: Macmillan Australia, 1993.

Ninkovich, Frank A. *The Global Republic: America's Inadvertent Rise to World Power*. Chicago: University of Chicago Press, 2014.

Northedge, F. S. *The League of Nations: Its Life and Times, 1920-1946*. New York: Holmes & Meier, 1986.

Nurkse, Ragnar. *International Currency Experience: Lessons of the Inter-War Period*. Vol. Series of League of Nations Publications: II. Economic and Financial, 1944, 1944. II.A.4. Geneva: League of Nations, 1944.

———. *Problems of Capital Formation in Underdeveloped Countries*. Oxford, UK: Basil Blackwell, 1953.

Ogle, Vanessa. *The Global Transformation of Time: 1870-1950*. Cambridge, MA: Harvard University Press, 2015.

Olsson, Tore C. *Agrarian Crossings: Reformers and the Remaking of the US and Mexican Countryside*. America in the World. Princeton, NJ: Princeton University Press, 2017.

Osterhammel, Jürgen. *The Transformation of the World: A Global History of the Nineteenth Century*. America in the World. Princeton, NJ: Princeton University Press, 2014.

O'Sullivan, Christopher D. *Sumner Welles, Postwar Planning, and the Quest for a New World Order, 1937-1943*. New York: Columbia University Press, 2003.

Overy, Richard. *The Origins of the Second World War*. New York: Routledge, 2017.

Packard, Randall M. *A History of Global Health: Interventions into the Lives of Other Peoples*. Baltimore: Johns Hopkins University Press, 2016.

Palmer, James. "Nobody Knows Anything about China." *Foreign Policy*. March 21,

2018. http://foreignpolicy.com/2018/03/21/nobody-knows-anything-about
-china/.

Parmar, Inderjeet. *Foundations of the American Century: The Ford, Carnegie, and Rocke-feller Foundations in the Rise of American Power*. New York: Columbia University Press, 2012.

Pasvolsky, Leo. *The Problem of Economic Peace after the War*. Washington, DC: Department of State, 1942.

Patel, Kiran Klaus. *The New Deal: A Global History*. America in the World. Princeton, NJ: Princeton University Press, 2016.

Pauly, Louis W. *The League of Nations and the Foreshadowing of the International Monetary Fund*. Essays in International Finance, no. 201. Princeton, NJ: International Finance Section, Department of Economics, Princeton University, 1996.

Pedersen, Susan. "Back to the League of Nations." *American Historical Review* 112, no. 4 (2007): 1091–1117.

———. *The Guardians: The League of Nations and the Crisis of Empire*. Oxford: Oxford University Press, 2015.

Petruccelli, David. "The Crisis of Liberal Internationalism: The Legacies of the League of Nations Reconsidered." *Journal of World History* 31, no. 1 (2020): 111–36.

Philipsen, Dirk. *The Little Big Number: How GDP Came to Rule the World and What to Do about It*. Princeton, NJ: Princeton University Press, 2015.

Porter, Theodore M. *The Rise of Statistical Thinking, 1820–1900*. Princeton, NJ: Princeton University Press, 2020.

Prashad, Vijay. *The Poorer Nations: A Possible History of the Global South*. London: Verso, 2012.

Preston, Andrew. "Franklin D. Roosevelt and America's Empire of Anti-Imperialism." In *Rhetorics of Empire: Languages of Colonial Conflict after 1900*, edited by Martin Thomas and Richard Toye, 75–90. Manchester, UK: Manchester University Press, 2017.

Prévost, Jean-Guy. *Total Science: Statistics in Liberal and Fascist Italy*. Montreal, QC: McGill-Queen's University Press, 2009.

Raghavan, Srinath. *India's War: The Making of Modern South Asia, 1939–1945*. London: Allen Lane, 2016.

Ranshofen-Wertheimer, Egon Ferdinand. *The International Secretariat, a Great Experiment in International Administration*. Washington, DC: Carnegie Endowment for International Peace, 1945.

———. *Victory Is Not Enough: The Strategy for a Lasting Peace*. New York: W. W. Norton, 1942.

Reynolds, David. "1940: Fulcrum of the Twentieth Century?" *International Affairs* 66, no. 2 (1990): 325–50.

———. *From Munich to Pearl Harbor: Roosevelt's America and the Origins of the Second World War*. Chicago: Ivan R. Dee, 2001.

———. *One World Divisible: A Global History since 1945*. Global Century Series. New York: Norton, 2000.

Reynolds, David, and V. O. Pechatnov, eds. *The Kremlin Letters: Stalin's Wartime Cor-*

respondence with Churchill and Roosevelt. New Haven, CT: Yale University Press, 2018.

Riefler, Winfield W. "Government and the Statistician." *Journal of the American Statistical Association* 37, no. 217 (1942): 1–11.

Rietzler, Katharina. "Before the Cultural Cold Wars: American Philanthropy and Cultural Diplomacy in the Inter-War Years." *Historical Research: The Bulletin of the Institute of Historical Research* 84, no. 223 (2011): 148–64.

———. "From Peace Advocacy to International Relations Research: The Transformation of Transatlantic Philanthropic Networks, 1900–1930." In *Shaping the Transnational Sphere: Experts, Networks, and Issues from the 1840s to the 1930s*, edited by Davide Rodogno, Bernhard Struck, and Jakob Vogel, 173–93. New York: Berghahn Books, 2015.

Roberts, Geoffrey. "A *League of Their Own*: The Soviet Origins of the United Nations." *Journal of Contemporary History* 54, no. 2 (2019): 303–27.

Roberts, Sam. *A History of New York in 27 Buildings: The 400-Year Untold Story of an American Metropolis*. New York: Bloomsbury Publishing, 2019.

Rodgers, Daniel T. *Atlantic Crossings: Social Politics in a Progressive Age*. Cambridge, MA: Belknap Press of Harvard University Press, 1998.

———. "In Search of Progressivism." *Reviews in American History* 10, no. 4 (1982): 113–32.

Roosevelt, Franklin D. *Franklin D. Roosevelt and Foreign Affairs: Second Series, January 1937–August 1939*. Vol. 15. New York: Clearwater, 1979.

———. "Our Foreign Policy: A Democratic View." *Foreign Affairs* 6, no. 4 (1928): 573–86.

Rosenberg, Emily S. "Transnational Currents in a Shrinking World." In *A World Connecting, 1870–1945*, edited by Emily S. Rosenberg, 815–996. A History of the World. Cambridge, MA: Belknap Press of Harvard University Press, 2012.

Rothermund, Dietmar. *The Global Impact of the Great Depression, 1929–1939*. London: Routledge, 1996.

Rupp, Leila J. *Worlds of Women: The Making of an International Women's Movement*. Princeton, NJ: Princeton University Press, 1997.

Ryan, Alan. *The Making of Modern Liberalism*. Princeton, NJ: Princeton University Press, 2012.

Sánchez Román, José Antonio. "Discovering Underdevelopment: Argentina and Double Taxation at the League of Nations." In *Beyond Geopolitics: New Histories of Latin America at the League of Nations*, edited by Alan L. McPherson and Yannick Wehrli, 205–22. Albuquerque: University of New Mexico Press, 2015.

Schlesinger, Stephen C. *Act of Creation: The Founding of the United Nations*. Boulder, CO: Westview Press, 2003.

Schuler, Kurt, and Andrew Rosenberg, eds. *The Bretton Woods Transcripts*. New York: Center for Financial Stability, 2013.

Schulzinger, Robert D. *The Wise Men of Foreign Affairs: The History of the Council on Foreign Relations*. New York: Columbia University Press, 1984.

Scott, George. *The Rise and Fall of the League of Nations*. London: Hutchinson, 1973.

Slobodian, Quinn. *Globalists: The End of Empire and the Birth of Neoliberalism*. Cambridge, MA: Harvard University Press, 2018.

Sluga, Glenda. *Internationalism in the Age of Nationalism*. Philadelphia: University of Pennsylvania Press, 2013.

———. *The Nation, Psychology, and International Politics, 1870-1919*. Palgrave Macmillan Transnational History Series. Basingstoke, UK: Palgrave Macmillan, 2006.

Sluga, Glenda, and Carolyn James. *Women, Diplomacy and International Politics since 1500*. Women's and Gender History. Abingdon, UK: Routledge, 2015.

Staley, Eugene. "Power Economy versus Welfare Economy." *Annals of the American Academy of Political and Social Science* 198, no. 1 (1938): 9-14.

———. *Raw Materials in Peace and War*. Publications of the Council on Foreign Relations. New York: Council on Foreign Relations, 1937.

———. "Relief and Rehabilitation in China." *Far Eastern Survey* 13, no. 20 (1944): 183-85.

———. *World Economic Development: Effects on Advanced Industrial Countries*. Montreal, QC: International Labour Office, 1944.

———. *World Economy in Transition: Technology vs. Politics, Laissez Faire vs. Planning, Power vs. Welfare*. Publications of the Council on Foreign Relations. New York: Council on Foreign Relations, 1939.

Steffek, Jens. "Fascist Internationalism." *Millennium* 44, no. 1 (2015): 3-22.

Steil, Benn. *The Battle of Bretton Woods: John Maynard Keynes, Harry Dexter White, and the Making of a New World Order*. Princeton, NJ: University Press, 2013.

Steiner, Zara. *The Lights That Failed: European International History, 1919-1933*. Oxford History of Modern Europe. Oxford: Oxford University Press, 2005.

———. *The Triumph of the Dark: European International History, 1933-1939*. Oxford History of Modern Europe. Oxford: Oxford University Press, 2011.

Stewart, Maxwell S. (Maxwell Slutz). *Your Money and Mine: An Analysis of Our National Income*. New York: Foreign Policy Association, 1935.

Stone, William Treadwell. *Peaceful Change, the Alternative to War: A Survey Prepared for the National Peace Conference Campaign for World Economic Cooperation*. New York: Foreign Policy Association, 1937.

Sweetser, Arthur. *The American Air Service: A Record of Its Problems, Its Difficulties, Its Failures, and Its Final Achievements*. New York: D. Appleton, 1919.

———. *The First Ten Years of the League of Nations*. International Conciliation, no. 256. Worcester, MA: Carnegie Endowment for International Peace, Division of Intercourse and Education, 1930.

———. *The First Year and a Half of the League of Nations*. American Academy of Political and Social Science. Publication no. 1534. Philadelphia, 1921.

———. *The League of Nations at Work*. New York: Macmillan, 1920.

———. "The *Non-Political* Achievements of the League." *Foreign Affairs* 19 (1940): 179-192.

———. *The Practical Working of the League of Nations: A Concrete Example*. International Conciliation, no. 249. Worcester, MA: Carnegie Endowment for International Peace, Division of Intercourse and Education, 1929.

——. *Roadside Glimpses of the Great War*. New York: Macmillan, 1916.

——. *The United States and the League, the Labour Organisation, and the World Court during 1940*. Geneva Studies, vol. 11, no. 8, December 1940. Geneva: Geneva Research Centre, 1940.

Tasca, Henry J. *World Trading Systems: A Study of American and British Commercial Policies*. Paris: International Institute of Intellectual Co-operation, League of Nations, 1939.

Theien, Iselin. *Fra krig til krig: En biografi om C. J. Hambro*. Oslo: Spartacus, 2015.

Tinbergen, Jan. *Statistical Testing of Business-Cycle Theories: Vol. I. A Method and Its Application to Investment Activity*. Geneva: League of Nations, Economic Intelligence Service, 1939.

Tollardo, Elisabetta. "International Experts or Fascist Envoys? Alberto Theodoli and Pietro Stoppani at the League of Nations." *New Global Studies* 10, no. 3 (2016): 283–306.

Tooze, Adam. *The Deluge: The Great War and the Remaking of Global Order 1916–1931*. London: Allen Lane, an imprint of Penguin, 2014.

——. "Imagining National Economies: National and International Economics Statistics 1900–1950." In *Imagining Nations*, edited by Geoffrey Cubitt, 90–125. York Studies in Cultural History. Manchester, UK: Manchester University Press, 1998.

——. *The Wages of Destruction: The Making and Breaking of the Nazi Economy*. New York: Penguin, 2008.

Tournès, Ludovic. "American Membership of the League of Nations: US Philanthropy and the Transformation of an Intergovernmental Organisation into a Think Tank." *International Politics* 55, no. 6 (2018): 852–69.

——. *Les États-Unis et la Société des Nations (1914–1946): Le système international face à l'émergence d'une superpuissance*. Bern: Peter Lang, 2016.

Toye, John, and Richard Toye. "The Origins and Interpretation of the Prebisch-Singer Thesis." *History of Political Economy* 35, no. 3 (2003): 437–67.

Trescott, Paul B. "H. D. Fong and the Study of Chinese Economic Development." *History of Political Economy* 34, no. 4 (2002): 789–809.

Tyrrell, Ian. *Transnational Nation: United States History in Global Perspective since 1789*. London: Palgrave Macmillan, 2015.

United Nations Library and Graduate Institute of International Studies. *The League of Nations in Retrospect / La Société des Nations: Rétrospective: Proceedings of the Symposium*. Serial Publications (United Nations Library, Geneva, Switzerland), Series E, Guides and Studies 3. Berlin: Walter de Gruyter, 1983.

United States President's Research Committee on Social Trends. *Recent Social Trends in the United States: Report of the President's Research Committee on Social Trends*. New York: McGraw-Hill, 1933.

Van Vleck, Jenifer. *Empire of the Air: Aviation and the American Ascendancy*. Cambridge, MA: Harvard University Press, 2013.

Walker, J. Samuel. *Henry A. Wallace and American Foreign Policy*. Westport, CT: Greenwood, 1976.

Wallace, Henry A. *Agricultural Prices*. Des Moines, IA: Wallace Publishing Co., 1920.

———. *America Must Choose: The Advantages and Disadvantages of Nationalism, of World Trade, and of a Planned Middle Course*. Boston: World Peace Foundation, 1934.,

———. *Our Job in the Pacific*. New York: American Council, Institute of Pacific Relations, 1944.

———. *The Price of Free World Victory*. New York: L. B. Fischer, 1942.

———. *The Price of Vision: The Diary of Henry A. Wallace, 1942–1946*. Boston: Houghton Mifflin, 1973.

Walters, F. P. *A History of the League of Nations*. 2 vols. New York: Oxford University Press, 1952.

Ward, Michael. *Quantifying the World: UN Ideas and Statistics*. United Nations Intellectual History Project. Bloomington: Indiana University Press, 2004.

Waters, Christopher. *Australia and Appeasement: Imperial Foreign Policy and the Origins of World War II*. London: I. B. Tauris, 2012.

Way, Wendy. *A New Idea Each Morning: How Food and Agriculture Came Together in One International Organisation*. Canberra: ANU Press, 2013.

Weiss, Thomas G., David Forsythe, Roger A. Coate, and Kelly-Kate Pease, eds. *The United Nations and Changing World Politics*. 8th ed. New York: Routledge, 2018.

Welles, Benjamin. *Sumner Welles: FDR's Global Strategist: A Biography*. New York: St. Martin's Press, 1997.

Welles, Sumner. *The World of the Four Freedoms*. New York: Columbia University Press, 1943.

Wertheim, Stephen. *Tomorrow, the World: The Birth of U.S. Global Supremacy*. Cambridge, MA: Belknap Press of Harvard University Press, 2020.

Williams, Andrew. "Leo Pasvolsky and an Open World Economy." In *Progressivism and US Foreign Policy between the World Wars*, edited by Molly Cochran and Cornelia Navari, 91–113. New York: Palgrave Macmillan, 2017.

Wilson, Craig Alan. "Rehearsal for a United Nations: The Hot Springs Conference." *Diplomatic History* 4, no. 3 (1980): 263–82.

Winant, John G. "The I.L.O. in Wartime and After." *Foreign Affairs* 19, no. 3 (1941): 633–40.

———. *A Letter from Grosvenor Square: An Account of a Stewardship*. London: Hodder & Stoughton, 1947.

Woolner, David B., Warren F. Kimball, and David Reynolds. *FDR's World: War, Peace, and Legacies*. World of the Roosevelts. New York: Palgrave Macmillan, 2008.

World Statistical Congress (Washington, DC). *World Statistical Congress, September 6–18, 1947, Washington, D.C.* Edited by William J. Bruce. Proceedings of the International Statistical Conferences, vol. 2. Calcutta: Eka Press, 1948.

Yarrow, Andrew L. *Measuring America: How Economic Growth Came to Define American Greatness in the Late Twentieth Century*. Amherst: University of Massachusetts Press, 2010.

Zahniser, Marvin R. "Rethinking the Significance of Disaster: The United States and the Fall of France in 1940." *International History Review* 14, no. 2 (1992): 252–76.

Zanasi, Margherita. "Exporting Development: The League of Nations and Republican China." *Comparative Studies in Society and History* 49, no. 1 (January 2007): 143–69.

Zeiler, Thomas W., David Ekbladh, and Benjamin C. Montoya, eds. *Beyond 1917: The United States and the Global Legacies of the Great War*. New York: Oxford University Press, 2017.

Zipp, Samuel. *The Idealist: Wendell Willkie's Wartime Quest to Build One World*. Cambridge, MA: Belknap Press of Harvard University Press, 2020.

INDEX

Gerig, Benjamin: Berle, 139; decline of League, 139–40; League Pavilion, 71, 88, 136; Loveday, 218–20, 224; United Nations, 218, 229; Welles, 200; Woolley, 136, 139

Germany: Britain declares war on, 123, 128; Cold War with, 93–95, 101–4, 123; decline of League, 128, 130, 134, 142, 144–50; economic issues, 56, 64; free trade, 103–4; invades Poland, 128; Nazi, 73, 103, 118, 130, 134, 141–44, 151, 153, 157, 159, 167, 177, 181, 236; Phony War, 94, 100; reconstruction, 177, 180; weaponized knowledge, 73, 94, 100–104, 109, 123; withdrawal from League, 12, 24, 48

Gerschenkron, Alexander, 241

"Gini coefficient," 44

Ginn, Harold, 29

global economy, 3, 8, 43, 72, 103, 180, 184, 221, 242

globalization, 6, 25, 128, 245–46

Gödel, Kurt, 175

governance: constructing equipment of, 8; control, 7, 17, 71, 190; conventional wisdom, 66; economic, 8, 17, 46, 66, 83, 106–7, 110, 123, 184, 200, 207, 216, 241; good, 12–16; Great Depression, 46; League tools for, 7–8, 27, 83, 171; liberal, 7, 12, 19–22, 27, 66, 71, 86, 93, 110, 123, 171, 184, 190–91, 201, 244–45; reconstruction, 170–71, 184, 190–91, 200, 207, 216; stability, 21, 34, 47, 191; United Nations, 233, 241, 244–45; weaponized knowledge, 71, 79, 83, 86, 93, 106–7, 110, 123

Grady, Henry: decline of League, 129, 136–37, 142; postwar planning, 214; super-university concept, 30; weaponized knowledge, 101–4, 110, 116

Grattan, C. Hartley, 170, 211, 281n125

Great Depression: Committee on Depressions, 107, 176, 184, 214–15, 219; effects on postwar planning, 171–72, 176, 180, 183–84, 207, 210–11, 214–16, 219; as failure, 171; food, 54, 107, 109, 207, 215; internationalism, 6–7, 10, 17–18, 22; Kuznets, 39; problems revealed

by, 130, 172, 176, 180, 183–84, 207, 210–11, 215–16, 219; remaining challenges of, 236–37, 240–42; Riefler on, 61; super-university concept, 24, 38–41, 44–61, 66; Tariff Commission, 101; weaponized knowledge, 71–74, 83, 87, 99, 101, 106–9, 113–21, 120

Great War. *See* World War I

Greece, 103–4

Green, William, 146

"Green Revolution," 182

Guomindang, 45, 190, 218

Haberler, Gottfried, 58–60

Hague, The, 31, 79, 84, 117–19

Halifax, Lord, 154, 179

Hall, N. F., 108–9

Hambro, Carl, 272n58; Avenol, *111*, 158; background of, 117; final bow of, 231; growing portfolio of, 117; Lie, 233; as "northern friend," 165; as refugee, 145; Roosevelt, 162; technical resources, 117–18, 158

Hansen, Alvin, 58, 187, 209

Harriman, Averell, 234

Harvard University, 31–32, 59, 99, 241

Hayek, F. A., 120

Hayek, Friedrich von, 60

health issues: decline of League, 139, 148–50, 157, 159; *International Health Yearbook*, 5, 26, 32, 98, 206; internationalism, 8, 13; League of Nations Health Organization (LNHO), 26–27, 76, 100, 149, 245; nutrition, 43, 53–54, 67, 81–82, 88, 105–10, 171, 180–82, 187–90, 193, 201–8, 215, 239, 245; postwar planning, 17–21, 177, 180, 193, 196–202, 205, 208, 218, 222; Rockefeller Foundation, 26–27, 50, 114, 148; super-university concept, 25–28, 34, 40–41, 45, 50, 54, 66; United Nations, 243, 245; weaponized knowledge, 76, 80, 88, 90, 92, 100, 107–8, 113–14, 122

Health Section, 122, 157, 245

Hilgerdt, Folke, 213, 242

Hill, Martin, 198

Hirschman, Albert, 120, 166–67, 185, 212, 241